The Silent Revolution

RONALD INGLEHART

The Silent Revolution

Changing Values and Political Styles
Among Western Publics

Princeton University Press, Princeton, New Jersey

Published by Princeton University Press,
Princeton, New Jersey
In the United Kingdom: Princeton University Press,
Guildford, Surrey

Parts of Chapter 2 of this book previously appeared as a chapter in Leon Lindberg (ed.),
Politics and the Future of Industrial Society (New
York: McKay, 1976); part of Chapter 5 appeared
in *Comparative Political Studies* 9, 4 (January,
1977); and an abridgement of Chapter 12 appeared in *Government and Opposition* 12, 2
(Spring, 1977).

Library of Congress Cataloging in Publication Data
will be found on the last printed page of this book

Publication of this book has been aided by a grant
from The Andrew W. Mellon Foundation

Printed in the United States of America
by Princeton University Press,
Princeton, New Jersey

This book is affectionately dedicated to my wife Margaret *and my daughters,* Elizabeth *and* Rachel

Contents

List of Figures and Tables

x — List of Figures and Tables

PREFACE

This book could not have been written without the help and encouragement of Jacques-René Rabier, special advisor to the Commission of the European Community. It is a pleasure to thank him for the many suggestions he has contributed, and the Commission, for generously making the European Community survey data available to me and other social scientists. I am also greatly indebted to a group of colleagues who have discussed these topics with me, in the process of developing an ongoing investigation of political change among mass publics that has led to a forthcoming volume edited by Samuel Barnes and Max Kaase. This investigation has done much to stimulate and clarify the analysis in this book. Besides Barnes and Kaase, my colleagues in this broader project are Mark Abrams, Klaus Allerbeck, Anselm Eder, Cees de Graaf, David Handley, Felix Heunks, M. Kent Jennings, Henry Kerr, Hans-Dieter Klingemann, Alberto Marradi, Alan Marsh, David Matheson, Warren Miller, Pertti Pesonen, Leopold Rosenmayr, Giacomo Sani, Risto Sankiaho, Dusan Sidjanski, and Philip Stouthard. A number of other friends and colleagues have contributed valuable suggestions and criticism, in particular Paul Abramson, Gabriel Almond, Frank Andrews, David Appel, Philip Converse, Karl Deutsch, Richard Hofferbert, Leon Lindberg, Seymour Martin Lipset, A.F.K. Organski, Robert Putnam, Helène Riffault, David Segal, Donald Stokes, Burkhard Strumpel, and Steven Withey.

The University of Michigan provided a grant from the Horace H. Rackham School of Graduate Studies and a sabbatical leave during which most of the chapters were written; both are greatly appreciated.

PART I

Introduction

CHAPTER 1

Changing Values and Skills Among
Western Publics: An Overview

I. INTRODUCTION

T HE values of Western publics have been shifting from an over-whelming emphasis on material well-being and physical security toward greater emphasis on the quality of life. The causes and implications of this shift are complex, but the basic principle might be stated very simply: people tend to be more concerned with immediate needs or threats than with things that seem remote or non-threatening. Thus, a desire for beauty may be more or less universal, but hungry people are more likely to seek food than aesthetic satisfaction. Today, an unprecedentedly large portion of Western populations have been raised under conditions of exceptional economic security. Economic and physical security continue to be valued positively, but their relative priority is lower than in the past.

We hypothesize that a significant shift is also taking place in the distribution of political skills. An increasingly large proportion of the public is coming to have sufficient interest and understanding of national and international politics to participate in decision-making at this level. Mass publics have played a role in national politics for a long time, of course, through the ballot and in other ways. Current changes enable them to play an increasingly active role in formulating policy, and to engage in what might be called "elite-challenging" as opposed to "elite-directed" activities. Elite-directed political participation is largely a matter of elites mobilizing mass support through established organizations such as political parties, labor unions, religious institutions, and so on. The newer "elite-challenging" style of politics gives the public an increasingly important role in making specific *decisions*, not just a choice between two or more sets of decision-makers. One of the most important elements contributing to this change is the fact that potential counter-elites are distributed more widely among the public than ever before.

The two processes of change reinforce each other. One aspect of the change in values, we believe, is a decline in the legitimacy of hierarchical authority, patriotism, religion, and so on, which leads to declining confidence in institutions. At the same time, the political expression of new values is facilitated by a shift in the balance of political skills between elites and mass. Certain basic values and skills seem to be changing in a gradual but deeply rooted fashion. Undoubtedly there will be counter-trends that will slow the process of change and even reverse it for given periods of time. But the principal evolutionary drift is the result of structural changes taking place in advanced industrial societies and is unlikely to be changed unless there are major alterations in the very nature of those societies.

This book will focus on these two changes, moving both backward and forward from them: backward along the causal chain to seek the *sources* of these changes; and forward in an attempt to analyze their likely *consequences*. How we will do this is suggested by Figure 1–1, which provides an overview of the book. The remaining sections of this chapter will briefly discuss each of the variables shown in the diagram and in doing so, lay out the argument more explicitly. Our analysis moves from the system level to the individual level and back again. It starts with events in given societies, turns to their impact on what people think, and finally examines the consequences these intrapersonal events may have on a society. The values and skills of individuals are at the center of the diagram, and they will be the central concern—for relatively little is known about them. Yet we must never lose sight of the setting in which an individual lives. If we devote less attention to the economic, social, and political structures of given countries, it is not because we consider them unimportant: their role is crucial. But a number of excellent studies of these aspects of given societies are already available. The present work is intended to supplement them, providing insight into a relatively unexplored set of influences on Western politics. The central focus is on things that exist within individuals, and these things can best be measured with survey data. But we trace their causes to changes in a society as a whole; and we are interested in their eventual impact on the political system. The linkages between the individual and the system are complex. We cannot take it for granted that if increasing

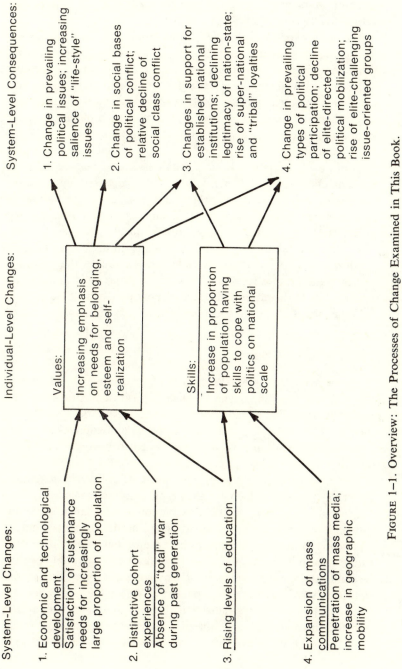

System-Level Changes:

1. Economic and technological development
   Satisfaction of sustenance needs for increasingly large proportion of population

2. Distinctive cohort experiences
   Absence of "total" war during past generation

3. Rising levels of education

4. Expansion of mass communications
   Penetration of mass media; increase in geographic mobility

Individual-Level Changes:

Values:
Increasing emphasis on needs for belonging, esteem and self-realization

Skills:
Increase in proportion of population having skills to cope with politics on national scale

System-Level Consequences:

1. Change in prevailing political issues; increasing salience of "life-style" issues

2. Change in social bases of political conflict; relative decline of social class conflict

3. Changes in support for established national institutions; declining legitimacy of nation-state; rise of super-national and "tribal" loyalties

4. Change in prevailing types of political participation; decline of elite-directed political mobilization; rise of elite-challenging issue-oriented groups

FIGURE 1–1. Overview: The Processes of Change Examined in This Book.

numbers of people hold given values, their political system will automatically adopt policies which reflect those values. It depends partly on how politically skilled those people are. And it depends at least equally on the political institutions of the given country. What the people get is conditioned not only by what the people want, but by whether they have one dominant party or several competitive political parties; a Presidential system or a Parliamentary system; a free press or a controlled press; and numerous other institutional factors. It depends, in short, on their country's political structure.

While certain changes in values and skills seem to be more or less universal among advanced industrial societies, political institutions are not. They differ profoundly from nation to nation. A country's political structure must be kept in mind at every stage of our analysis, and we will refer to it frequently, for it can facilitate or hinder values and skills from having an impact on politics.

Thus, not two but three variables are crucial to the analysis: values, skills, and structure. These three types of variables, we believe, largely determine the pace of political change. Now let us turn our attention to the socio-economic roots of change.

II. Sources of Change

Before undertaking an exploration of social change, we need to ask a simple but fundamental question: *is* change, in fact, taking place? A prevailing stereotype in comparative politics used to depict the Third World as being in the process of rapid change and development, while the West was assumed to have reached some sort of end state.

It seems that in many ways, the industrialized world is actually undergoing change which is more rapid and more genuinely new than what is occurring in the New Nations. But change in the industrialized world is far harder to grasp, harder to conceptualize. One tends to use familiar images because we have no model of the future. The notion that the Third World countries would come to resemble the contemporary West may have been an illusion, but it at least provided a concrete picture of where they were headed. Change in highly industrialized nations is even more of a leap into the unknown. In a confused way, one senses change in all directions—in sex roles, morals, life-styles, fashions, in the ecology, the economy, and politics. Finally, one is tempted to fall back on the past, in search of solid ground.

Is change taking place? On one level, we can give an unequivocal yes. Reliable time series data demonstrate clearly that massive change *is* taking place in the infrastructure of advanced industrial society. These system-level changes might well alter individual-level values, beliefs, and behavior. Among the many forces for change are economic development, expansion of secondary and higher education, the growing size and diversity of the mass media, and discontinuities in the life experiences of large numbers of people.

Statistics on income, education, mass communications, and foreign travel all tell a similar story. In the United States the rate of access to higher education doubled from 1950 to 1965. It more than doubled in West Germany during that period, and more than tripled in France. In the electorate that participated in the 1952 American Presidential election, people whose education was limited to grade school outnumbered people with any college education by nearly three to one. In 1972, people who had been to college outnumbered the grade school educated by more than two to one.[1] Secondary and university-level education are now far more widely distributed among Western populations than ever before, and this change has had a particularly heavy impact on the younger age-cohorts.

Television and foreign travel have become a part of the common man's experience in the post-war era. In 1963, only a third of the households in France and Italy had television sets; by 1970, TV was present in more than 70 percent of the households of those countries. Foreign travel is no longer limited to the very top and bottom of the economic scale. Before World War II, only a tiny minority of native-born Americans had ever visited Europe; in the last twenty years, higher incomes and charter flights have enabled millions of Americans to cross the Atlantic. Similarly, by 1970 most Western Europeans had visited at least one foreign country; indeed proportionately more Germans visited Italy than Americans visited Florida that year.

---

[1] Philip Converse points out this striking shift in "Change in the American Electorate," in Angus E. Campbell and Philip Converse (eds.), *The Human Meaning of Social Change* (New York: Russell Sage, 1972), 263–337. We have updated his figures, using data from the 1972 election survey carried out by the University of Michigan's Center for Political Studies.

Technological Innovation—The thread of technological innovation ties these changes together. Technology has made possible the unprecedented productivity that underpins advanced industrial society; it renders expanded educational opportunities both necessary and possible; it has created the contemporary mass media; and it involves men and women in drastic shifts in personal environment that uproot them from previous patterns.

Changes in Occupational Structure—Daniel Bell has emphasized the importance of changes in occupational structure probably more than any other recent writer. Indeed, they are the basis of his definition of "Post-Industrial Society."[2] Bell foresees a society in which the creation and utilization of knowledge provides the axis along which a new stratification system is emerging. He anticipates a continuing displacement of industrial employment into the tertiary sector, especially into what is often called the knowledge industry. This emerging society values most highly those elites who possess theoretical knowledge, followed by technicians and administrators of knowledge industries. In addition, Bell emphasizes the importance of new industries that exploit technological innovation. He predicts a growing divergence of outlook between the new elites oriented toward scientific and professional goals and older elites attached to profits, economic growth, and their own particular firms or bureaucracies. The dynamics of organizations in Post-Industrial societies reinforce these tendencies, Bell argues. As professionalization increases in an organization, members become more and more oriented toward external points of reference such as their own professional group's norms of behavior and universalistic rather than particularistic concerns.

Technology is creating the Post-Industrial society just as it created the Industrial society. Innovations in agricultural production already have enabled a very few people to feed the rest. Now industrial innovation is reducing the proportion of the population needed to produce an increasing quantity of manufactured goods. In the United States only a minority of the labor force is engaged in the agricultural and industrial sectors, and other Western countries are approaching or are already at the point of having 50 percent of the work force in the tertiary or service sector.[3] In France,

---

[2] See Daniel Bell, *The Coming of Post-Industrial Society* (New York: Basic Books, 1973).

[3] See Robert L. Kahn, "The Meaning of Work: Interpretation and Proposals for Measurement," in Campbell and Converse, *Human Meaning,*

for example, 37 percent of the population was still employed in the primary sector as recently as 1946; this had declined to a mere 12 percent in 1970. Within a few years, a majority of the French work force will be employed in the tertiary sector. The United States passed this milestone in 1956, becoming the world's first "Post-Industrial" society. But by 1980, most Western European countries will also be "Post-Industrial."

In a sense, Bell's analysis may give an exaggerated impression of the growth of the middle class. His figures are accurate, but much of the growth of the tertiary sector reflects the increasing employment of women, most of whom have non-manual jobs. In 1972, 58 percent of non-agriculturally employed American males still had manual jobs. In many households the principal wage earner was a manually employed male, with a secondary income from a female having a clerical or sales occupation. At the risk of being sexist, one might argue that such households remained primarily oriented toward the industrial sector. Still, there is no question that the trend Bell describes does exist: there has been a substantial decline in the share of the work force having manual occupations, even if we consider males exclusively. Thus, it seems more than likely that this change has important implications for the outlook and behavior of Western populations.

Economic Growth—Income levels have shown equally impressive change: real income per capita is now at least double the highest level attained before World War II in virtually all Western countries, and in many it has tripled or even quadrupled economic and physical security, as higher incomes and welfare programs reduce the economic deprivations previously felt by most of the population. Never before have the sustenance needs been secure for such a large share of the population. Although economic growth came to a halt with the Recession of 1973–1975, real income remained at unprecedentedly high levels.

Expansion of Education—Changes in income and occupation are closely tied in with the expansion of higher education. Numerous studies have demonstrated the impact that higher education has on the development of political consciousness and the development of cognitive skills. Indeed, education turns out to be one of the most important variables in almost any cross-national analy-

---

159–203. Cf. Matilda Riley *et al.* (eds.), *Aging and Society III* (New York: Russell Sage, 1972), 160–197.

sis. Summarizing studies of the impact of college, Feldman and Newcomb conclude that college makes students more liberal, less authoritarian, less dogmatic, less ethnocentric, and more interested in political matters.[4] But it is equally true that students enter college already well ahead of the general population on these dimensions.[5]

The fact that the better-educated emphasize certain kinds of values may seem intuitively understandable. But education is an extremely complex variable. We must distinguish between education as an indicator of affluence, education as an indicator of cognitive development, and education as an indicator of integration into a specific communications network. Differences in values and behavior *could* simply reflect differential exposure to given communications networks.

In the recent past, students have been particularly active exponents of new values and political styles: one wonders to what extent this simply reflects the influence of their own particular milieu. The period of maximum isolation of the youth culture, from late high school through college, corresponds with the development of higher cognitive skills and, in Mannheim's words, "political cultural consciousness."[6] At this stage youth has passed the stage of maximum family influence and is groping toward an intellectual justification of beliefs and behavioral predispositions. It seems significant that today this stage tends to be spent in a milieu that minimizes the impact of the larger society.

Development of Mass Communications—The mass media are undoubtedly among the major sources of change, but it is not easy to specify how the influence process works. Information from communications media is filtered through numerous mediating factors and influences and is processed in ways that are not yet thoroughly understood.[7] The expansion of the communications networks of advanced societies has been made possible by technological inno-

---

[4] See Kenneth A. Feldman and Theodore M. Newcomb, *The Impact of College on Students* (San Francisco: Jossey-Bass, 1969), vol. 1, 20–31.

[5] See Stephen Withey, *A Degree and What Else?* (New York: McGraw-Hill, 1971).

[6] Karl Mannheim, "The Problem of Generations," in Philip G. Altbach and Robert S. Laufer (eds.), *The New Pilgrims: Youth Protest in Transition* (New York: McKay, 1972), 25–72.

[7] See J. T. Klapper, *The Effects of Mass Communications* (Glencoe: Free Press, 1960); and Walter Weiss, "Mass Media and Social Change," in Bert T. King and Elliott McGinnies (eds.), *Attitudes, Conflict and Social Change* (New York: Academic Press, 1972), 175–225.

vation. The result has been to make information networks national and even international, and to communicate information very rapidly from anywhere in the world or even from outer space. But such innovation has also made possible a growing diversity of mass communications networks, extending across great distances but reaching specialized audiences.

The pockets of traditionalism within industrialized nations continue to shrink. Even if the adults are not greatly affected in their belief systems by what they see and hear, it undoubtedly will be more difficult than in the past for traditionally oriented adults to pass on their values to the young in an unaltered form. For even when the media are controlled and consciously programmed to reflect the dominant values of a society, their coverage of news leads them to transmit information that is often threatening to existing values. This fact is clearly grasped by protestors, who plan their activities so as to maximize their publicity value.[8] The mass media consequently are a force for change, since they communicate dissatisfaction, alternative life-styles, and dissonant signals, even when they are directly controlled by the "Establishment."

Thus, the role of the mass media is mixed. On the one hand, they serve to incorporate more and more people into larger communication networks. They undoubtedly have increased the knowledge and sophistication of the population, especially through their impact on the young. They probably have a stereotyping and conventionalizing effect in many areas of life. Yet, at the same time, they communicate a great deal of opposition to conventional values, particularly when they are tailored to specialized audiences.

Distinctive Cohort Experiences—Practically all of the factors just mentioned have contributed to the fact that the younger generation in Western countries has been brought up in a quite different world from the one which shaped their parents or grandparents. They have grown up in relatively affluent, communications-rich societies. Numerous other factors make their experience distinctive, but one is of such importance that it will be singled out for special mention: although the older generations have experienced total war in one form or another, the younger generation in these countries has never experienced invasion of their homeland by hostile forces. For them, war has been something that happens in other countries.

[8] See Michael Lipsky, "Protest as a Political Resource," *American Political Science Review*, 62, 4 (December, 1968), 1144–1158.

III. Change in the Individual

We have sketched out some of the factors which may contribute to changing values and skills among Western publics. These changes themselves are less apparent than the forces giving rise to them, for they occur within individuals. To demonstrate their existence and understand their nature will be the central task of this book. It is not an easy one.

While statistics are available showing Gross National Product per capita or the number of students enrolled in secondary schools or the number of hospital beds or foreign tourists or television sets in a given country in a given year, "subjective" changes have barely begun to be measured. Yet we believe that such developments are every bit as real and as important to understanding society as the more familiar "objective" indicators. If two million Italians vote for Fascist candidates, or if half the American public no longer trusts its government, they do so for causes which may not be externally visible, but may be even more significant than the number of tons of steel produced that year in that country.

To follow any process of change, one needs readings at a series of points in time: if one wishes to determine whether employment is rising or falling, one needs information not only about the current rate but also about what it was last year and the year before. And it is here that we are particularly handicapped. We have data that seem to provide a measure, though a rough one, of the value priorities of Western publics covering a period of several years. We can examine short-term changes. But basic values seem to change slowly, and consequently the long-term patterns are likely to be the most significant. Very little evidence is available covering a long span of years. We can estimate the probable shape of long-term patterns only indirectly. Nevertheless, the indirect evidence of change seems strong. And if it *is* taking place, it is too important to ignore.

IV. Some Consequences of Change Among Western Publics

If change is occurring, what impact is it likely to have on the politics of Western nations? Moving from the left-hand side of Figure 1–1 to the right, several topics are outlined.

Political Issues—Change in individual values affects one's orientation toward political issues. If material concerns lessen in relative importance, there may be a decline in the importance of issues that reflect the stratification system of industrial society; ideology, ethnicity, life-style, and so on may assume greater importance. Class politics may decline in favor of status or cultural or "ideal" politics.[9]

We see the outlines of some consequences of change in current demands for participation in decisions that affect one's life, whether it is in schools, universities, welfare agencies, offices, factories, or church. If these demands are successful, they will bring great changes in a wide variety of institutions.

Along with demands for participation, other types of issues are brought into the political arena—issues that derive more from differences in life-style than from economic needs. For example, one can point to such things as protection of the environment, the quality of life, the role of women, the redefinition of morality, drug usage, and broader public participation in both political and non-political decision-making. Few of these issues are completely new. What is changing is their quantitative importance. Conservation of natural resources has been a subject of political controversy for many decades; and students have been politically active for almost as long as there have been students. But it is difficult to find a previous instance of the triumph of environmental interests over major economic interests that is comparable in magnitude to the rejection of the proposed American supersonic transport; or the persisting opposition to off-shore oil drilling and strip-mined coal, in face of an energy shortage. Likewise, it is difficult to find a precedent for the fact that students now make up a larger proportion of the American population than does organized labor.

Changes in Social Bases of Politics—The emergence of these new issues presents the existing political parties with a dilemma. If they realign themselves to appeal to the new groups, they risk losing their existing constituencies. The "new politics" often clash with strongly held traditional values and norms. This has resulted in pressures toward the formation of new political parties and attempts by spokesmen for the new values to influence and capture existing parties.

In the early phases of industrial society, the population tended to be divided between a large mass of poorly paid workers and a

---

[9] See Ann Foner, "The Polity," in Riley *et al.* (eds.), *Aging*, 115–159. Cf. Seymour M. Lipset, "The Changing Class Structure and Contemporary European Politics," *Daedalus* 93 (Winter, 1964), 271–303.

relatively small number of owners and managers having much higher incomes and a radically different life-style. In advanced industrial societies, the ranks of the middle class are greatly increased by growth in the number of people in managerial, technical, clerical and sales occupations; the relative number of manual workers diminishes but their income levels rise and the amount of leisure time at their disposal increases, with the result that many of them are able to adopt a life-style relatively close to conventional middle class standards. A number of analysts, representing various perspectives, have argued that we are likely to witness a shift in social conflict, with a portion of the middle class becoming radical while most of the working class and lower-middle class become increasingly conservative.[10] Data on the relationship between party preference and occupation, income, education, and labor union membership make it clear that the industrial pattern of political cleavage has by no means disappeared. Nevertheless, the evidence indicates that a gradual decline in class voting has been occurring. In the future, new support for parties of the Left may be increasingly recruited from middle-class sources, while status quo parties may draw their support more and more from an embourgeoisified working class.

Support for National Institutions—Apparently, nationalistic sentiments are not being transmitted to the young with the same fidelity as in the past.[11] Governments traditionally have exploited patriotic symbols as sources of legitimacy for their actions. As popular support of these symbols declines, governments can no longer draw so easily on this resource.

Changes in individual value priorities may partially account for the decline in satisfaction with governmental outputs and national institutions that has been documented in surveys of American politics over the past decade.[12] The political and economic systems continue to produce outputs that respond relatively well to traditional demands, but they do not seem to provide adequate satisfaction for other needs and demands that are increasingly important among certain segments of the population. Changing values com-

[10] For example, see David Apter, *Choice and the Politics of Allocation* (New Haven: Yale University Press, 1971).

[11] See Ronald Inglehart, "An End to European Integration?" *American Political Science Review*, 61, 1 (March, 1967), 91–105.

[12] See Arthur H. Miller, "Political Issues and Trust in Government, 1964–1970," *American Political Science Review*, 68, 3 (September, 1974), 951–972.

bine with a growing sense of the inadequacy of existing institutions to encourage the use of new and different political inputs, including protest activity and the formation of new political movements and organizations. These innovations are facilitated by the shift in the distribution of education: political skills are no longer concentrated largely among the holders of official and corporate roles, and formerly peripheral groups are able to act as participants with an unprecedented degree of organizational skill.

At the same time, other groups oppose changing what they see as the rules of the game in which they have come to believe. They are unhappy with existing institutions, but unhappy because they do not function as they used to rather than because they need to be changed. Hence the stage is set for a new polarization.

As expectations of mass publics change, their perceptions of the adequacy of institutional arrangements also change. Key American institutions from the business corporation to the government itself seem to be undergoing a crisis of legitimacy. Many short-run factors undoubtedly intervene to affect confidence, such as progress or lack of it in ending war and racism and specific political scandals, and we certainly do not anticipate a permanent decline in trust. But with changing values and political skills and, consequently, a more involved and critical public, the downward trend in support for national institutions seems to be one symptom of a long-range transformation of Western publics.

One result of this transformation can be an increased openness to international integration. But the search for social identity can also move in the opposite direction. There has been a resurgence of interest in ethnic ties in the United States and demands for autonomy based on language and culture in Belgium and Great Britain. These trends do not simply reflect a reawakened parochialism. Surprisingly enough, a relative emphasis on *both* supranational and subnational ties often exists in the same individuals.

Changing Styles of Political Participation—The politics of classical industrial society were based on mass parties and associated movements such as trade unions and church-related organizations that were generally bureaucratic and oligarchical in structure. Emerging cultural values emphasize spontaneity and individual self-expression. Furthermore, the expansion of education means that increasing numbers of people are available with political skills that enable them to play roles previously limited to a small political elite. For both objective and subjective reasons the old parties are being challenged by new forces that seem less and less amenable to an elite-directed type of organization.

Insofar as these demands of newly articulate groups cannot be accommodated within existing structures, support for governmental institutions may erode. Governments face the same dilemma as the parties: to the extent that governing elites reorient themselves along the new lines they risk suffering a backlash from groups imbued with traditional values. Governments can no longer rely on appeals to nationalism and patriotism as much as in the past. Rising skill levels have been accompanied by a declining emphasis on such values as national security, which traditionally justified the existence of a strong nation-state.

There may be no more dissatisfaction among mass publics today than at various times in the past. But there is reason to believe that the *types* of dissatisfaction now most likely lead to political action have different roots from those of the past. If this is true, it poses difficult problems for the policy-makers of these societies.

A decade ago, it could still be taken for granted that the fundamental test of a society's leadership was the extent to which it achieved economic growth regardless of long-term consequences. And it could still be assumed that leadership which passed this test had gone a long way toward establishing its legitimacy among the general public. These comfortable assumptions are no longer tenable. The public's goals seem to be shifting. Insofar as policymakers seek to promote the general welfare, they will need to take subjective aspects of well-being more and more into account. An increasingly articulate and politically sophisticated public may leave them little choice.

The late 1960's and early 1970's were a period of ferment for advanced industrial societies. In the United States, the combination of the civil rights movement and widespread opposition to the war in Vietnam aroused segments of the population that previously had only sporadically been involved in public affairs. Political action took new and more militant forms with widespread challenges to existing institutions such as schools, parties, churches, and the military. The violent phase seems to have passed. Ghetto riots and university disruptions came to a halt, and with the end of the war in Vietnam there was a decline in the ability of militants to attract active support from broader segments of the population.

Despite the decline in dramatic forms of protest, surveys indicate a continuing withdrawal of support from key institutions. The

American public's feelings of trust for the national government have been measured repeatedly for a number of years. In 1958, a representative sample of the American public gave overwhelmingly positive responses; only 28 percent showed predominantly distrustful attitudes. By the mid-1970's, a clear majority of the public gave distrustful responses.[13] A similar pattern of decline can be seen in public attitudes toward political parties. This decline obviously reflects the impact of short-term events such as the Watergate scandals, but it may also be a symptom of a long-term transformation which is rooted in the formative experiences of given generations and progressively revealed as one generation replaces another. For these changes are not merely American. Decline in patriotism and support for key national institutions can be found among the young of virtually all advanced industrial countries.

The spectacular events of the late 1960's turned theoretical writings like Herbert Marcuse's and lyric writing like Charles Reich's into grist for the mass media. The message, more or less, was: America is on the brink of its own Great Cultural Revolution.

By 1973, Revolution was Out. In the aftermath of the 1972 Nixon landslide, the Sunday supplements were proclaiming that the counter-culture was dead and probably never amounted to much more than a campus fad, like swallowing goldfish or stuffing people into telephone booths.

The mass media seem to be wrong—and for the same reasons that led them to overemphasize Revolution earlier: they tend to focus on dramatic or sensational national events without much reference to underlying processes. Quantitative analysis of the attitudes and values of mass publics seems like tame reading in comparison with accounts of political crises; but it provides a badly-needed complement, for it may help us understand the long-term processes contributing to them.

In this book we will use public opinion survey data to obtain a more realistic assessment of political change. Cross-national survey data in 1970 pointed to a much more temperate assessment of the pace of cultural change than that often presented in the mass media

[13] See *The CPS 1974 American National Election Study* (Ann Arbor: ICPR, 1975) Post-Election Codebook, p. 131. The question was: "How much of the time do you think you can trust the government in Washington to do what is right—just about always, most of the time, or only some of the time?" In the Fall of 1974, 63 percent of the American public said "only some of the time" or "none of the time."

at the time.[14] But these same data suggest that a gradual yet fundamental change *is* taking place in the political role of publics throughout the Western world.

The political equation is changing in ways that leave no immediately apparent traces; but the changes may be so basic as to constitute a Silent Revolution.

[14] See Ronald Inglehart, "The Silent Revolution in Europe: Intergenerational Change in Post-Industrial Societies," *American Political Science Review*, 65, 4 (December, 1971), 991–1017.

PART II

Value Change

CHAPTER 2

The Nature of Value Change

T HE basic value priorities of Western publics seem to be changing as their societies move into a Post-Industrial phase of development. This process of value change is likely to bring new issues
to the fore. It may influence the public's choice of candidates and
political parties. Ultimately, it will help shape the policies adopted
by Western elites.

In this chapter we will examine some of the evidence that value
priorities *are* changing and explore the *kinds* of change taking place.
We will try to answer the question, "What goals are likely to be
given greater emphasis in the post-industrial era?"

The process of change is not as ephemeral as the flow of events
might suggest. Instead it appears to reflect a transformation of
basic world views. It seems to be taking place quite gradually but
steadily, being rooted in the formative experiences of whole gen-
eration-units. Its symptoms manifest themselves in a variety of
ways; sometimes they are explosive, as was the case with the
unexpected student rebellions of the late 1960's. But if, as we
believe, the change is a basic, long-term process, we cannot rely
solely on the more blatant manifestations such as these to give an
accurate picture of the scope and character of value change among
Western publics. Mass survey data offers a more systematic, if less
sensational indication of what is happening. The evidence is still
fragmentary, but a detailed examination of available data suggests
that some profoundly important changes are occurring.

I. Sources of Value Change: Some Hypotheses

Why is value change taking place? It seems to be linked with a
cluster of socio-economic changes including rising levels of education, shifts in the occupational structure, and the development of
increasingly broad and effective mass communications networks.
But two phenomena seem particularly significant:

1. The unprecedented prosperity experienced by Western nations during the decades following World War II. Recent eco-

nomic stagnation does not seem to have undone the effects of the twenty fat years from 1950 to 1970.

2. The absence of total war. The simple fact that no Western nation has been invaded for thirty years may have extremely significant consequences.

In short, people are safe and they have enough to eat. These two basic facts have far-reaching implications.

Our expectation that the value priorities of Western publics are changing is derived from two key hypotheses. The first is that people tend to place a high priority on whatever needs are in short supply. As a result of the two phenomena just mentioned, Western publics have for a number of years experienced exceptionally high levels of economic and physical security. Consequently, they have begun to give increasing emphasis to *other* types of needs.

If we wish to go beyond this simple explanatory scheme, the work of Abraham Maslow is particularly interesting, for it suggests a specific *direction* in which value change will move under given conditions. Maslow argues that people act to fulfill a number of different needs, which are pursued in hierarchical order, according to their relative urgency for survival.[1] Top priority is given to the satisfaction of physiological needs as long as they are in short supply. The need for physical safety comes next; its priority is almost as high as that of the sustenance needs, but a hungry man will risk his life to get food. Once an individual has attained physical and economic security he may begin to pursue other, nonmaterial goals. These other goals reflect genuine and normal needs —although people may fail to give them attention when deprived of the sustenance or safety needs. But when at least minimal economic and physical security are present, the needs for love, belonging, and esteem become increasingly important; and later, a set of goals related to intellectual and aesthetic satisfaction looms large. There does not seem to be any clear hierarchy within the last set of needs, which Maslow called "self-actualization needs." But there

[1] See Abraham H. Maslow, *Motivation and Personality* (New York: Harper, 1954); important efforts to apply Maslow's theory to political analysis include James C. Davies, *Human Nature and Politics* (New York: Wiley, 1963); Davies, "The Priority of Human Needs and the Stages of Political Development," unpublished paper; Amitai Etzioni, *The Active Society* (New York: Free Press, 1968), Chapter 21; and Robert E. Lane, *Political Thinking and Consciousness* (Chicago: Markham, 1970), Chapter 2. A somewhat different analysis of human behavior as goal-seeking activity following a regular hierarchy of needs is presented in Karl W. Deutsch, *The Nerves of Government* (New York: Free Press, 1963).

is evidence that they became most salient only after an individual has satisfied the material needs and belonging needs.[2]

People have a variety of needs and tend to give a high priority to those which are in short supply. This concept is similar to that of marginal utility of the consumer in economic theory. But it is complemented by another equally important hypothesis: that people tend to retain a given set of value priorities throughout adult life, once it has been established in their formative years.

If the latter hypothesis is correct, we should find substantial differences in the values held by various age groups. One of the most pervasive concepts in social science is the idea that people tend to retain a certain basic character throughout adult life once it has been formed in childhood and youth. If there is any truth in this notion, older individuals should show value priorities which reflect the relatively insecure material conditions which prevailed during their formative years. On the other hand, during the thirty years that have passed since World War II, Western countries have experienced an unprecedented period of economic growth and they have all been free from invasion. Consequently, we might expect that younger groups, particularly those brought up since World War II, would place less emphasis on economic and physical security.

It would be ridiculous to argue that no change in basic values occurs during adult life, of course. Our point is simply that the probability of such change diminishes substantially after one reaches adulthood. To the extent that adult relearning does take place, it would tend to erase the differences between age groups. Furthermore, we would not expect to find Post-Materialist values totally absent even among the oldest cohorts. Throughout history there probably has been at least a small stratum of economically and physically secure individuals who give top priority to non-material values. But this stratum should be smallest among the oldest cohorts if, indeed, values tend to reflect the conditions prevailing within a society during a given cohort's pre-adult years.

[2] See Jeanne M. Knutson, *The Human Basis of the Polity: A Psychological Study of Political Men* (Chicago: Aldine, 1972). Allardt, however, questions whether there is any hierarchy among needs. He finds no relationship between income level and scores on subjective indices of Loving and Being; on the other hand, his data indicate that a sense of social support tends to be a prerequisite to emphasis on self-development. See Erik Allardt, *About Dimensions of Welfare: An Exploratory Analysis of a Comparative Scandinavian Survey* (Helsinki: Research Group for Comparative Sociology, 1973).

By the same token, the distribution of these values preferences should vary cross-nationally in a predictable fashion. We would expect the differences in values across a given nation's age groups to reflect that nation's history during the lifetime of the people in the sample. Germany, for example, has undergone particularly extreme changes in the conditions prevailing during the pre-adult years of her respective age cohorts: the older Germans experienced famine and slaughter during World War I, followed by severe inflation, the Great Depression and devastation, invasion, and massive loss of life during World War II. Her youngest cohorts have been brought up in relatively peaceful conditions in what is now one of the richest countries in the world. If value types reflect one's formative experiences, we might expect to find relatively large differences between the older and younger German age cohorts.

Great Britain represents the opposite extreme from Germany: the wealthiest country in Europe prior to World War II, she alone escaped invasion during the war, but has had a relatively stagnant economy ever since. For the last twenty-five years, her European neighbors have had economic growth rates about twice as large as Britain's. One after another, they have moved ahead of Britain in Gross National Product per capita, with the result that by 1970 Britain ranked far behind Germany (and most of the other European Community countries) in per capita wealth. We would expect to find a relatively small amount of value change in Britain.

II. Can Values Be Measured by Mass Surveys?

We will test each of these predictions in this chapter. But in order to do so, we must be able to measure the value priorities of mass publics. Is this a feasible undertaking? We should not underestimate the difficulties involved. We hypothesize that the value priorities of Western publics are changing. This presupposes that these publics *have* meaningful systems of value priorities. But empirical analysis suggests that the political and social views expressed by the general public often represent superficial, virtually random responses.

In the classic study of this subject, Converse found that the belief systems of mass publics show surprisingly little coherent structure or "constraint." The absence of constraint manifests itself in both cross-sectional and cross-temporal analysis: in low correlations between responses to logically related items in a given survey; and in low correlations between responses to a given item asked at

Time 1, and the same item asked at Time 2 in a panel survey.[3] Converse concludes that a substantial portion of the general public does not *have* any real attitudes concerning almost any given topic. When asked their opinion, they may provide one (perhaps from a desire to not seem ill-informed), but it is given literally at random.[4]

This lack of attitudinal constraint is not particularly surprising when it applies to topics of marginal public interest; but it can be found in connection with even the most burning political questions. Opinion toward the war in Vietnam provides an interesting example. Logically, one might expect that those Americans who favored de-escalating American involvement in the war would, unanimously, *not* favor escalation. Yet Verba *et al.* found a surprisingly modest negative correlation between an escalation scale and a de-escalation scale derived from a survey of the American public.[5]

[3] See Philip E. Converse, "The Nature of Belief Systems in Mass Publics," in David Apter (ed.), *Ideology and Discontent* (New York: Free Press, 1964), 202–261; cf. Philip E. Converse, "Attitudes and Non-Attitudes: Continuation of a Dialogue," in Edward R. Tufte (ed.), *The Quantitative Analysis of Social Problems* (Reading, Mass.: Addison-Wesley, 1970).

[4] Pierce and Rose have argued that Converse's technique greatly overestimates the proportion of respondents having non-attitudes: low cross-temporal correlations in responses to a given item may reflect, in large part, an inherent crudeness of survey measurement. Consequently, the assumption that one would *ever* find cross-temporal correlations approaching 1.00 in attitudinal research is unrealistic. Nevertheless, if individual sampling error is randomly distributed, the marginal distribution of responses may be accurate, even if individual scores are not. Thus, the overall distribution of political party identification never varied by more than a few percentage points in the Survey Research Center surveys from 1952 to 1962. Yet in a panel survey included in this series, 39 percent of the respondents actually changed their responses from 1956 to 1958 (this figure includes only those who expressed an identification in both years; other computations yield even higher turnover figures). Converse has written a forceful rejoinder to Pierce and Rose. But both sides seem to agree that the "random" response pattern attributed to as much as 80 percent of those interviewed (in one instance) must not be interpreted to mean "equiprobable": the "random" respondent remains a biased coin—whether because of unmeasured attitudinal predispositions or simply because of response set. See John C. Pierce and Douglas D. Rose, "Nonattitudes and American Public Opinion: the Examination of a Thesis," *American Political Science Review*, 68, 2 (June, 1974), 626–649; cf. Converse, "Comment," *ibid.*, 650–660; and Pierce and Rose, "Rejoinder," *ibid.*, 661–666.

[5] The correlation between these supposedly mirror-image attitudes was —.37; none of the correlations reported among other attitudinal variables are above .30. See Sidney Verba *et al.*, "Public Opinion and the War in Vietnam," *American Political Science Review*, 62, 2 (June, 1967), 317–334. Similar findings are reported in Robert Axelrod, "The Structure of Public Opinion on Policy Issues," *Public Opinion Quarterly*, 31, 1 (Spring, 1967), 51–60.

An even more striking example can be drawn from a recent Quality of Life survey. A carefully designed and validated question about satisfaction with one's own life was asked twice in the same survey, with a time interval of about ten minutes. The correlation between responses was .61.[6] In the context of survey data, this is a very high correlation: it reflects the fact that fully 92 percent of the respondents gave answers at the two time points that were in either identical or adjacent categories on a seven-point scale. Yet statistically speaking, the responses at Time 1 "explain" only 37 percent of the variance in responses at Time 2—a mere 10 minutes later. If this were a question about diplomatic relations with mainland China, one might argue that the failure to explain something close to 100 percent of the variance was due to the fact that many of the informants were too poorly informed or uninterested to have any real opinion. But this was a very clear and simple question concerning a subject about which everyone knows and cares; the man in the street may not have any real preference about China policy but surely he is able to judge whether the shoe pinches him or not.

The imperfect correlation seems to be inherent in research on mass attitudes—*not* necessarily because people do not have real attitudes, but partly because of error in measurement. Some people find it difficult to indicate exactly how they feel. The fact that attitudinal constraint tends to be substantially higher among those who are more educated and those who discuss politics relatively often may be an indication that the rest of the population has not thought enough about a given problem to have any real opinion. But it may also reflect the fact that the less educated are less adept at expressing their feelings. In survey research, we may sometimes only observe the tip of the iceberg.

Consequently, any attempt to survey the value priorities of representative cross-sections of Western publics must be approached with modest expectations. We are unlikely to observe a well articulated ideological structure among mass publics, but we should bear in mind the possibility that this may be partly due to the crudeness of our measuring instrument. A series of depth interviews carried out during a period of several months might well bring forth a more coherent statement of one's world view than can be attained in a one-hour survey interview. Lane has demonstrated the extent to which the average citizen *does* seem capable

[6] See Frank M. Andrews and Stephen B. Withey, "Developing Measures of Perceived Life Quality," *Social Indicators Research*, I (1974), 1–26.

of articulating a coherent political outlook under these conditions.[7] Unfortunately, the cost of depth interviews seems prohibitive for present purposes.

The public opinion survey is not the ideal instrument with which to study basic attitudes and values. Yet it has certain advantages. It can provide a vastly larger number of cases than that normally obtained with depth interviews, and a large N is essential if we hope to make reliable intergenerational comparisons or control for social background factors. Furthermore, the mass survey can provide representative national samples—something extremely useful if one wishes to know what is happening to a society as a whole, or to analyze phenomena in cross-national perspective. Finally, the public opinion survey has proven to be quite accurate for many purposes. There may be a dismaying amount of fluctuation at the individual level, but the overall distribution of responses is often remarkably reliable. Surveys of voting intentions *do* predict the actual election results; data on consumer attitudes *do* predict how the economy is going to behave. The random error inherent in survey research tends to cancel itself out. It is not a perfect instrument, but used skillfully it can be one of the most powerful tools available to social science.

III. RESULTS FROM 1970 AND 1971: A FOUR-ITEM VALUES INDEX

Let us see what light public opinion survey evidence sheds on the problem of value change. A rather exceptional data base is available for our investigation. In 1970 and again in 1971, the European Community carried out public opinion surveys in France, West Germany, Belgium, The Netherlands, and Italy; data for 1970 are also available from Great Britain.[8] These surveys in-

[7] See Robert Lane, *Political Ideology* (New York: Free Press, 1962); cf. Lane, "Patterns of Political Belief" in Jeanne M. Knutson (ed.), *Handbook of Political Psychology* (San Francisco: Jossey-Bass, 1973), 83–116.

[8] These surveys were a part of an ongoing program of public opinion research carried out under the direction of Jacques-René Rabier, special advisor to the European Community. I am indebted to him for sharing these data, and for encouragement and openness to suggestions over a period of several years during which the surveys analyzed here were planned, tested, executed and analyzed. The earlier wave of fieldwork was carried out in February and March, 1970, by Louis Harris Research, Ltd. (London), Institut für Demoskopie (Allensbach), International Research Associates (Brussels), Nederlands Instituut voor de Publieke Opinie (Amsterdam), Institut français d'opinion publique (Paris), and Instituto per le Ricerche Statische e l'Analisi del' opinione Pubblica (Milan). The respective samples had

cluded a series of questions designed to indicate which values an individual would rank highest when forced to choose between security or "Materialist" values such as economic and political stability; and expressive or "Post-Materialist" values.[9] We hypothesized that those who had been socialized under conditions of peace and relative prosperity would be likeliest to have Post-Materialist values.

Representative national samples of the population over fifteen years of age were asked:

If you had to choose among the followings things, which are the *two* that seem most desirable to you?

—Maintaining order in the nation.
—Giving the people more say in important political decisions.
—Fighting rising prices.
—Protecting freedom of speech.

Two choices were permitted; thus it was possible for a respondent to select any of six possible pairs of items.

Choice of the first of these four items ("order") presumably reflects a concern with physical safety; choice of the third item ("prices") presumably reflects a high priority for economic stability. We expected that people who chose one of these items would be relatively likely to choose the other item also: economic insecurity and physical insecurity tend to go together. If a country is invaded, for example, there is likely to be both economic dislocation and loss of life. Conversely, economic decline is often

---

N's of: 1,975 (Britain); 2,021 (Germany); 1,298 (Belgium); 1,230 (Netherlands); 2,046 (France); and 1,822 (Italy). The surveys in the European Community countries were sponsored by the European Community Information Service; a much shorter questionnaire used in Great Britain was sponsored by funds from the University of Michigan. The brevity of the latter questionnaire was due to the fact that quite limited funds were available for this purpose. The 1971 fieldwork was carried out in July by: Gesellschaft für Marktforschung (Hamburg); International Research Associates (Brussels); Institut français d'opinion publique (Paris); Demoskopea (Milan); and Nederlandse Stichting voor Statistiek (The Hague). The respective numbers of respondents were: 1,997; 1,459; 2,095; 2,017; and 1,673.

[9] In earlier publications, we used the terms "Acquisitive" and "Post-Bourgeois" to describe the two polar types on this value priorities dimension. These terms tend to overemphasize the purely economic basis of value change. Both our analytic framework and the way we have operationalized our measurement of value priorities gives an equally important role to the importance of the safety needs. The term "Materialist" should be understood to denote relative emphasis on *both* economic and physical security.

associated with severe domestic disorder, as was the case in Weimar Germany.

Emphasis on order and economic stability might be termed a Materialist set of value priorities. By contrast, choice of the items concerning free speech or political participation reflects emphasis on two Post-Materialist values that, we expected, would also tend to go together. On the basis of the choices made among these four items, therefore, we can classify our respondents into six value-priority types, ranging from a pure Materialist type to a pure Post-Materialist type, with four mixed categories in between.

This set of items was administered to national samples in the six European countries in 1970, and again in five of these countries in 1971. Among those interviewed, those whose first choice was "Fighting rising prices" were at least twice as likely to make "Maintaining order" their second choice as other respondents. Conversely, those whose first choice was "Protecting freedom of speech" were about twice as likely to choose "More say in government" in second place as other respondents. The four "Mixed" pairs, conversely, were relatively *unlikely* to be chosen together. Consequently, about half of each national sample fell into the two polar types, with the other half distributed among the four "Mixed" types.

Various other sets of four items, in similar forced-choice format, were included in the 1970 and 1971 surveys. In no case did the internal structure of the other sets of items compare with that found among these four. The degree of constraint among these items is relatively strong for survey data; it is all the more remarkable in that this pattern persists across eleven surveys carried out at two points in time, in six different countries.[10]

It seems justifiable to group our respondents into Materialist, Post-Materialist, and Mixed types for further analysis. We hypothesize that these categories reflect the value priorities of given individuals. But do they? By one definition, "values differ *operationally* from attitudes only in being fewer in number, more general, central and pervasive, less situation-bound, more resistant to modification and perhaps tied to developmentally more primitive or dramatic experiences."[11] If these items do indeed tap *values*,

[10] The correlation matrices for these items in eleven different surveys appear in Ronald Inglehart, "The Nature of Value Change in Post-Industrial Societies," in Leon Lindberg (ed.), *Politics and the Future of Industrial Society* (New York: McKay, 1976), 57–99 , Table 1.

[11] John P. Robinson and Phillip R. Shaver, *Measures of Social Psychologi-*

they should enable us to predict a much larger number of more specific attitudes. And, as we have already argued, the value types of given age cohorts should tend to persist over time, reflecting the fact that they are tied to important early experiences.

Let us examine the former question first: do the Materialist/ Post-Materialist value categories reflect a central aspect of the individual's outlook on life, with pervasive ramifications among his political attitudes? Yes, quite impressively. Our value typology proves to be a sensitive indicator of a broad range of political preferences.

For example, on the basis of an individual's value type, one can make a pretty accurate prediction of his response to the following item from our 1970 surveys:

> Within the last couple of years, there have been large-scale student demonstrations in (respondent's country) and other countries. In general, how do you view these? Are you:
>
> —very favorable
> —rather favorable
> —rather unfavorable
> —very unfavorable?

In every country, those who choose the Post-Materialist pair are the most favorable to student demonstrations. Overall, they are more than four times as likely to favor the demonstrations as are the Materialist respondents. Those choosing the various mixtures of Materialist and Post-Materialist items fall between these two extremes in their attitudes toward student demonstrations.

Our value types also show significant relationships with numerous other attitudes. For example, in each country surveyed in 1971, the Post-Materialists were far more likely to give a high priority to economic aid to less-developed countries than were the Materialists; and the Materialists consistently gave a higher priority to national prestige. For each of these items across the five countries, there was a mean difference of about 25 percentage points between the Materialist and Post-Materialist types—with the mixed groups falling between the two polar types. The Post-Materialists in each country also showed more concern for women's rights than did the Materialists: in the five 1971 surveys taken

cal Attitudes (Ann Arbor, Michigan: Institute for Social Research, 1969), 410.

together, 49 percent of the Post-Materialists chose this goal, as compared with 29 percent of the Materialists.

There are differences in the amount of constraint among responses of the various nationalities, but the basic configuration of the items is strikingly similar in all six countries.[12] In dimensional analysis, various attitudes fall into two distinct clusters, one linked with Materialist goals and the other with Post-Materialists goals. Moreover, the value types also show striking relationships with social structure and political party preference. This highly structured pattern would scarcely emerge from random or superficial responses. The Materialist/Post-Materialist index seems to tap a central and pervasive aspect of the individual's outlook on life. We believe it provides an indicator of certain basic value priorities.

But it is only a rough indicator. Based on an extremely parsimonious ranking of four basic goals, it can only be viewed as a first step toward developing more broadly based multi-item indicators of relevant values. The four items provide a better measure than one. And a large battery of properly designed questions should provide a more accurate measure than our present simple tool. Imperfect though it may be, we have an indicator that taps a wide range of preferences related to the Materialist/Post-Materialist theme. Accordingly, we are in a position to test our hypotheses concerning value change.

Our first prediction was that the old would be likelier to have Materialist value priorities than the young; conversely, the Post-Materialist type should be more prevalent among the young. In both our 1970 and 1971 surveys, the relationship between age and value type clearly bears out our expectations. In France, for example, there is an immense preponderance of Materialists over Post-Materialists among those who are more than 65 years of age: 52 percent are Materialists and a bare 3 percent are Post-Materialists in our combined 1970 and 1971 data. As we move from older to younger age cohorts, the percentage of Post-Materialist types increases. When we reach the youngest cohort (those who were sixteen to twenty-four years old in 1971), the two types are

---

[12] The responses of the German public show relatively high constraint and this public also reports relatively high levels of political interest in each of our surveys. But constraint is lowest among the British public, which does not report particularly low levels of political interest. This is consistent with the view that value change has not yet become very salient in Britain. It can hardly be attributed to faulty translation: the items were originally written in English. Yet they seem to work least effectively among the English-speaking public.

TABLE 2-1. Value Types by Age Cohort: Combined 1970 and 1971 Data
(Percent of Materialists [Mats.] and Post-Materialists [P.-Mats.])

Age Range of Cohort in 1971	Germany			Belgium			Italy			France			Netherlands			Britain [a]		
	Mats.	P.-Mats.	N	Mats.	P.-Mats.	N	Mats.	P.-Mats.	N	Mats.	P.-Mats.	N	Mats.	P.-Mats.	N	Mats.	P.-Mats.	N
16–25	22%	22%	(544)	20%	26%	(487)	28%	21%	(757)	25%	20%	(754)	26%	20%	(770)	29%	13%	(508)
26–35	36	14	(895)	29	16	(429)	37	13	(650)	38	13	(726)	25	14	(696)	28	10	(680)
36–45	47	9	(768)	29	16	(473)	39	9	(735)	40	12	(697)	38	11	(717)	31	8	(556)
46–55	47	7	(663)	30	11	(378)	46	6	(710)	43	10	(649)	34	12	(547)	35	6	(796)
56–65	58	4	(593)	36	9	(409)	48	6	(571)	50	5	(533)	39	7	(455)	41	6	(662)
66+	55	4	(474)	46	5	(474)	55	3	(400)	52	3	(700)	52	5	(324)	47	4	(748)
Difference between youngest and oldest groups	−33	+19		−26	+21		−27	+18		−27	+17		−19	+15		−18	+9	
Total difference	52 points			47 points			45 points			44 points			34 points			27 points		

[a] Results from a survey carried out in 1971 by the British Social Science Research Council are combined with those from our own British sample in this table.

almost equally numerous: 25 percent are Materialist and 20 percent Post-Materialist.

The same general pattern appears in each of the other five countries. In every case, the Materialists greatly outnumber the Post-Materialist type among the older age-cohorts, but the balance shifts in favor of the Post-Materialists as we move to the younger cohorts.

This pattern raises an important question. It could reflect historical change, as we hypothesized, or it could reflect a life-cycle effect. Conceivably, the young might tend to be relatively Post-Materialist simply *because* they are young, free from responsibilities, rebellious, idealistic, and so on; one might argue that when they become older, they will have the same preferences as the older groups. We must not ignore this possibility. The only way to be absolutely certain that long-term value change is taking place would be to measure a population's values, wait ten or twenty years and then measure them again. Such data are rare. Fortunately, however, certain indirect tests can give us a clearer sense of whether these striking age group differences reflect inter-generational change or life-cycle effects.

The hypothesis that links expected age-group patterns with the historical experience of a given country points to a test that could be very revealing. There is no particular reason why one would expect the life-cycle of Englishmen to differ fundamentally from that of Germans or Frenchmen. But the economic and political history of these countries *does* differ in important respects. If the age-group differences in a given country correspond to the rate of change in the conditions prevailing during a given generation's formative years, we would seem to be on relatively firm ground in attributing these differences to historical change rather than life-cycle effects.

Our expectation was that the British public should show a relatively small amount of value change: she alone escaped invasion in World War II; and she was comparatively wealthy prior to World War II but subsequently has had a relatively low economic growth rate. In respect to both physical and economic security, change has been less pronounced in Britain than elsewhere. The differences between the formative conditions of younger and older groups has been greater in *all* of the Continental countries, but one might expect Germany to show a particularly large amount of value change.

In our 1970 and 1971 data, Britain stands out quite clearly as the country in which the smallest amount of value change seems to have taken place. The difference between the youngest British cohort and the oldest totals 27 percentage points across the two value types. The amount of apparent change across the German age cohorts is nearly twice as great: a total of 52 percentage points. The other four countries fall between these two extremes, most of them being closer to the German pattern than to the British.

The amount of change in value types across a given country's age cohorts *does* seem to correspond to the amount of economic and political change that country has experienced. If this is true, our value types must be highly resistant to modification during the lifetime of an individual: the responses of a given age cohort show traces of experiences that took place a generation or more ago.

IV. FURTHER TESTING IN 1972 AND 1973

In 1972 and 1973, a number of additional surveys were carried out. As a result, data are available from the countries discussed above plus several others. The new cases include Denmark, Ireland, Switzerland, and the United States.[13] The modern history of the latter countries has distinctive features that give rise to certain expectations about the relative amount of value change which we might find across age cohorts.

In the analyses just described, Germany, Belgium, Italy, and France showed relatively large amounts of value change across age groups; Britain showed relatively little. We now have four countries that logically should make up an intermediate group: Switzerland, Denmark, The Netherlands, and Ireland. We would expect them to occupy an intermediate position for two reasons:

1. The oldest cohort in each of these four countries has experienced less of the devastation of World Wars I and II than the corresponding cohort among the German, French, Belgian, and Italian publics. Switzerland was neutral in both world wars; Denmark, The Netherlands, and Ireland were neutral in one of these wars. This should tend to place them near the British end of the spectrum.

---

[13] We also have 1973 data from Luxembourg. But the small size of the sample (N = 330) makes any conclusions based on age-group analysis less reliable than for the other countries. For comparative purposes, findings for Luxembourg are included in Table 2–2, but they are to be interpreted with caution.

2. In the period following World War II, these four countries have had "intermediate" rates of economic growth—below the German, French and Italian rates, but appreciably above the British rate. This, too, would tend to place them above the British but below the Germans, Italians and French.

Recent American history is similar to that of Great Britain in a number of respects. Like Britain (only more so) the United States has had the advantages of geographic isolation, and escaped invasion and devastation during the World Wars. But more recently, she has experienced relatively great foreign and domestic conflict. Until 1973, she was at war in Vietnam. The war, together with racial problems and a high crime rate, have contributed to domestic turbulence. During the formative years of the older cohorts, America was a haven of relative tranquillity by comparison with most of Europe; today the positions seem to be reversed. In regard to physical security, there has been less difference between the formative experiences of America's older and younger cohorts, which should be reflected in a relatively small amount of value change across age groups.

The United States resembles Britain in another way: she already was relatively wealthy at the turn of the century, ranking far ahead of the other countries with which we are dealing. Like Britain (only less so) her post-war economic progress has been slower than that of other Western nations. For more than two generations, the United States had the highest per capita income of any nation in the world. But her growth rate has become relatively slow in recent decades. In 1975 she dropped to third place.[14] In sum, one might expect the older American cohorts to be relatively Post-Materialist, but the population as a whole should show less *change* across age groups than any of the various European nationalities except perhaps for the British.

The data confirm these expectations. Table 2–2 shows the distribution of the two "pure" value types in each of the eleven countries surveyed in 1972 and 1973.[15] To simplify a complex table,

[14] Agency for International Development figures indicate that both Sweden and Switzerland moved ahead of the United States in 1975. The above comments leave certain mini-states such as Kuwait or Qatar out of consideration; if they were included, the United States would rank lower.

[15] The Swiss survey was carried out by the Universities of Geneva and Zürich, supported by a joint grant from the Swiss National Fund. Fieldwork was performed by KONSO (Basel) in January-June, 1972, with a total of 1,917 interviews. I am grateful to Dusan Sidjanski and Gerhard Schmidtchen for making these data available. Ten other surveys were carried out in 1973,

TABLE 2–2. Value Type by Age Cohort
(Original four-item index, tabulated

	Germany		France		Italy		Belgium		Ireland	
Ages:	Mats.	P.-Mats.	Mats.	P.-Mats.	Mats.	P.-Mats.	Mats.	P.-Mats.	Mats.	P-Mats.
19–28	24%	19%	22%	20%	26%	16%	18%	23%	24%	13%
29–38	39	8	28	17	41	8	20	17	31	9
39–48	46	5	39	9	42	7	22	10	41	6
49–58	50	5	39	8	48	6	25	10	37	6
59–68	52	7	50	3	49	4	39	3	45	2
69+	62	1	55	2	57	5	39	5	51	4
Total spread across cohorts	56 points		51		42		39		36	

[a] Swiss data are from 1972; U.S. data are combined results of surveys in May, 1972; November-December, 1972; and March-April, 1973.

only the two polar types are shown: the column headed "Mats." gives the percentage of Materialists and the column headed "P.-Mats." gives the percentage of Post-Materialists within each group (if one wishes to know the percentage falling into the mixed types, one can simply add up the figures for the two polar types and subtract from 100). All eleven countries show the same basic pattern that was found in 1970 and in 1971: the younger cohorts have a much higher proportion of Post-Materialists and a lower proportion of Materialists than the older cohorts. Again and again, in country after country, we find this same indication of change. But the *rate* of change varies from country to country in a striking yet consistent and predictable fashion. The American sample shows less value change than any other country except Britain. The *oldest* American cohort has a higher proportion of Post-Materialists than their peers in any European nation—reflecting the greatly

all sponsored by the European Communities Information Service. The first was executed in March-April by the Gallup Organization (Princeton) with an N of 1,030. The publics of the nine member-countries of the European Community were all surveyed in September-October; the survey organizations and number of interviews for the respective countries were as follows: France, Institut français d'opinion publique (IFOP), N = 2,227; Belgium, International Research Associates (INRA), N = 1,266; The Netherlands, Nederlandse Stichting voor Statistiek, N = 1,464; Germany, Gesellschaft für Marktforschung, N = 1,957; Italy, Instituto per le Ricerche Statistiche e l'Analisi del' opinione Pubblica (DOXA), N = 1,909; Luxembourg, INRA, N = 330; Denmark, Gallup Markedsanalyse, N = 1,200; Ireland, Irish Marketing Surveys, N = 1,199; Great Britain, Social Surveys, Ltd., N = 1,933. Here, again, I wish to thank Jacques-René Rabier for enlisting my participation in the design of these surveys and making the data available. Interested scholars can obtain data from all of the European Community surveys from the Inter-university Consortium for Political Research.

in Eleven Countries, 1972–1973 [a]
by age cohorts used in 1970 survey)

Netherlands		Denmark		Switzerland		Luxembourg[b]		United States		Britain	
Mats.	P.-Mats.	Mats.	P.-Mats.	Mats.	P.-Mats.	Mats.	P.-Mats.	Mats.	P.-Mats.	Mats.	P.-Mats.
27%	14%	33%	11%	27%	15%	26%	19%	24%	17%	27%	11%
22	17	34	9	26	17			27	13	33	7
28	9	47	4	30	15	40	7	34	13	29	6
40	10	44	5	35	9			32	10	30	7
41	12	48	4	34	6	44	8	37	6	36	5
51	5	58	2	50	6			40	7	37	4
35		34		32		29		26		17	

[b] Because of the small size of the Luxembourg sample, it is broken down into only three age groups (ages 19–38; 39–58 and 59+).

privileged position this country once had—but the *youngest* American cohort has not moved toward Post-Materialism as rapidly as many of their European peers.

The Irish, Dutch, Danish, and Swiss cases form an intermediate group, as we anticipated: their rates of value change seem to fall in the middle range of the scale. And the Germans are at the high end of the scale, with the British at the opposite pole, precisely where they were in 1970–1971. There is a remarkable stability in the relative position of given countries. The amount of value change seems to reflect a given nation's recent history.

We believe that our translations do a good job of providing functional equivalents for the various goals, across the eleven countries from which we have data. But cross-national comparisons are always somewhat hazardous: the cutting points may not be the same from one language or culture to another. Consequently, we will generally compare the patterns found *within* given countries, rather than make direct comparisons of raw scores. Thus, we have not emphasized the fact that only 31 percent of the American public falls into the Materialist category, whereas 42 percent of the German public does so. Instead we have focused on the fact that there is a great deal more *change* across age groups within the German sample than in the American one. The former comparison might be distorted by a variety of linguistic and cultural factors. The latter comparison, while not completely fool-proof, at least does not assume that the German and American questionnaires impose identical cutting points within their respective cultures: it is possible that a German Materialist may be somewhat more (or less) materialistic than an American Materialist.

Nevertheless, even if this were true, it is clear that young Germans differ from old Germans more than young Americans differ from old ones. In short, second-order comparisons *within* given samples may be accurate, even if the absolute levels are not comparable from one country to another.

Having made this disclaimer about the direct comparability of survey data from different countries, let us nevertheless take a brief glance at the proportion of Materialists and Post-Materialists in each of the national samples. We will want to have at least a general idea of how the respective types are distributed. Moreover, we have an hypothesis to test: subject to the limitations of linguistic and cultural equivalence, we would expect the richer countries to show relatively high proportions of Post-Materialists although, as we have noted, there would be a time lag between attaining affluence and the emergence of Post-Materialist values. A country such as Germany, that has become wealthy only recently, would need some time before her public's values reflected the nation's economic level. Table 2–3 shows the relevant data.

TABLE 2–3. Distribution of Value Types by Nation, 1972–73[a]

	Materialist	Post-Materialist	Post-Materialists as Percentage of Materialists
1. Belgium	25%	14%	56%
2. Netherlands	31	13	42
3. United States	31	12	39
4. Switzerland	31	12	39
5. Luxembourg	35	13	37
6. France	35	12	34
7. Britain	32	8	25
8. Italy	40	9	23
9. Germany	42	8	19
10. Ireland	36	7	19
11. Denmark	41	7	17

[a] A 1976 survey finds 37% materialists and 10% post-materialists in Denmark, which would move that country up several places in this table.

One important fact is immediately evident from the table: the Post-Materialists are heavily outnumbered by the Materialists in each of the eleven countries. The Materialist preponderance ranges from a ratio of about two to one to better than five to one. Western society remains predominately Materialist. It is only among the youngest age-cohorts that the Post-Materialists are almost as numerous as the Materialists.

The expectation that the wealthier countries would have relatively high proportions of Post-Materialists is borne out reasonably well. The two nations ranking highest in per capita income at the time of these surveys, the United States and Switzerland, rank second and third highest in their proportion of Post-Materialists to Materialists. Belgium ranks highest. Though not as affluent as the United States or Switzerland, Belgium does rank among the wealthier countries, and has been relatively well-off for a long time—a fact that should be important in view of the hypothesized time-lag between economic change and value change. Italy and Ireland are the two poorest nations and they rank relatively low. Until recently Japan was poorer than any of these countries; if included here, she would rank last (see page 110). Denmark ranks lowest of all, and provides an unexplained anomaly: ranking fifth in per capita income, her public seems decidedly more Materialistic than it should be. Nevertheless, apart from this deviant case, the cross-national pattern is roughly what one would expect: a less Materialist outlook tends to be found among those publics that have been relatively prosperous for a long time.

V. DEVELOPMENT OF A MORE BROADLY BASED VALUES INDICATOR

Our four-item index seems to provide a measure of something pervasive and enduring in one's outlook. But we must not overlook this index's shortcomings. Its most serious weakness is the simple fact that it is based on only four items. Consequently, it may be excessively sensitive to short-term forces. For example, one of the items in the index concerns rising prices. Western countries have experienced extraordinary inflation in recent years. It seems more than likely that the proportion of respondents giving high priority to "Fighting rising prices" would increase not as the result of fundamental value change, but simply because this is a very serious current problem. This type of instability probably would be much greater if we simply asked the respondents to rate the importance of rising prices *by itself*; but in our index, one's choice of this item is constrained by the fact that it must be ranked against *other* desired goals. Almost everyone was aware that rising prices were a more important problem in 1973 than in 1970; but by no means all of those who ranked "Freedom of speech" above "Rising prices" in 1970 would be willing to change this ranking in 1973. The four items provide a better measure than one, but a more broadly based index would spread the risk over a still larger number of items, making it less likely that an individual's score would be unduly distorted by any particular recent event. Furthermore, a broader-based index might help reduce the amount of error in measurement, something that is always a major problem in survey research. In reply to survey questions, a substantial number of respondents give superficial answers, more or less "off the top of their heads." With a single item, it is difficult to distinguish between those whose answers reflect a genuine attitude, and those whose response is essentially meaningless. But a set of consistent responses to a large series of related questions probably *does* reflect a genuine underlying preference.

In our 1973 surveys, we attempted to develop a broader indicator of an individual's value priorities. Analysis of the results should give us a more reliable measure of whether value change is taking place. It may also provide a more detailed picture of the respective world-views of the Materialist and Post-Materialist types.

The 1973 surveys included the four items from the original value priorities index, but this time they were supplemented with eight additional goals. The following questions were asked:

There is a lot of talk these days about what the aims of this country should be for the next ten years. (HAND RESPONDENT CARD A.) On this card are listed some of the goals which different people would give top priority. Would you please say which *one* of these you, yourself, consider most important?

CARD A

A. Maintaining a high rate of economic growth.
B. Making sure that this country has strong defense forces.
C. Seeing that the people have more say in how things get decided at work and in their communities.
D. Trying to make our cities and countryside more beautiful.

And which would be the next most important?

(HAND RESPONDENT CARD B.) If you had to choose, which one of the things on this card would you say is most desirable?

CARD B

E. Maintaining order in the nation.
F. Giving the people more say in important government decisions.

G. Fighting rising prices.

H. Protecting freedom of speech.

And what would be your second choice?

Here is another list. (HAND RESPONDENT CARD C.) In your opinion, which one of these is most important?

CARD C

I. Maintain a stable economy.

J. Progress toward a less impersonal, more humane society.

K. The fight against crime.

L. Progress toward a society where ideas are more important than money.

What comes next?

Now would you look again at all of the goals listed on these three cards together and tell me which one you consider the *most* desirable of all? Just read off the one you choose.

And which is the next most desirable?

And which one of all the aims on these cards is *least* important from your point of view?

This series of questions enabled us to obtain relative rankings for twelve important goals. The introductory sentences placed the questions in a long-term time framework, and the choices deal with broad societal goals rather than the immediate needs of the respondent: we wanted to tap long-term preoccupations, not one's response to the immediate situation. The twelve options themselves were designed to permit a fuller exploration of Maslow's need hierarchy. Figure 2–1 indicates the basic need that each item was intended to elicit (with the four items from the original index appearing in capital letters). Six items were intended to emphasize the physiological or Materialist needs: "Rising prices," "Economic growth" and "Stable economy" being aimed at the sustenance needs; and "Maintain order," "Fight crime" and "Strong defense forces" being aimed at the safety needs. The remaining six items were designed to tap various Post-Materialist needs.[16] We view the latter needs as potentially universal: every human being has a need for esteem, an inherent intellectual curiosity, and aesthetic satis-

[16] In the American survey, the item "Protect nature from being spoiled and polluted" was used instead of "Trying to make our cities and countryside more beautiful." As we shall see, neither of these items was particularly effective in tapping the intended dimension.

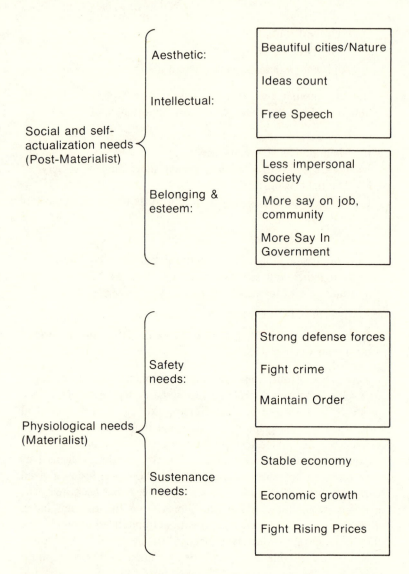

Figure 2–1. Items Used in 1973 Surveys and Needs They Were Intended To Tap.

faction; he or she will act on these needs unless circumstances force one to stifle them. Put another way, "Man does not live by bread alone," particularly when he has plenty of bread. Our expectation, therefore, is that emphasis on the six Materialist items will tend to form one cluster, with the Post-Materialist items in another distinct cluster.

In order to test this hypothesis, we performed conventional factor analyses of the rankings of these goals in each of the ten countries.[17] The loadings on the first factor in each country are shown in Table 2–4.

The results show a cross-national consistency that is almost breath-taking. In each case, five items—the *same* five items in every country—cluster near the positive end of the continuum. Six items—again, the same six in every country—are grouped near the negative pole. The remaining item falls near the midpoint.

The items that cluster toward the negative pole are the six Materialist items. And five of the six Post-Materialist items fall into the opposite group. A single item—the one concerning "More beautiful cities" (or "Protect nature from pollution," in the American data)—does not fit into either category. This item clearly does not behave according to our expectations, a fact that we must explore in more detail. But the other eleven items live up to expec-

[17] For this analysis, each item was recorded as a separate variable with codes ranging from "1" to "6." If the given item was chosen as the "most desirable" among the entire set of twelve items, it was coded as "1"; if it ranked second overall, it was coded as "2"; if it ranked last overall, it was coded as "6." If chosen first among its set of four items (but not first or second overall) it was coded "3"; if ranked second in its set of four, it was coded "4." Items not singled out for either high or low rankings were coded as "5." Our use of factor analysis in this case is somewhat unconventional. Our variables are based on relative rankings, not absolute scores. This is crucial to operationalizing our hypothesis, but it means that the items are not independent. And this would make factor analysis quite inapplicable with a small pool of items. With only two items, for example, the rank of the first item determines the rank of the second, automatically generating a -1.0 correlation between them. With three items, one would expect negative correlations of about .5. With a pool of four items, this effect is still important: the rank of the first item leaves only three possibilities, and random answering would generate negative correlations of about .3 between *all four* items, so that only two of them could load on the first factor. With a pool of twelve items, the degree to which one item's rank determines that of another becomes minor. There is still some tendency for all of the items to be negatively correlated; thus, the non-independence of our rankings tends to spread the items over several dimensions, diminishing the amount of variance that can be explained by the first factor. But, as our empirical results show, this effect is dominated by a much stronger tendency for Materialist items to be chosen together, on one hand, and Post-Materialist items to be chosen together, on the other.

TABLE 2-4. The Materialist/Post-Materialist Factor in Ten Countries
(Loadings of value priorities items on first factor)

	Country									
Goal:	France (23%)[a]	Germany (22%)	United States (20%)	Belgium (20%)	Luxembourg (20%)	Denmark (20%)	Italy (20%)	Netherlands (19%)	Britain (18%)	Ireland (17%)
More say on job	.636	.562	.451	.472	.659	.604	.599	.568	.611	.636
Less impersonal society	.592	.675	.627	.532	.558	.566	.553	.451	.498	.393
Ideas count	.499	.498	.508	.562	.476	.577	.577	.539	.482	.453
More say in government	.400	.483	.423	.478	.434	.464	.566	.514	.506	.572
Freedom of speech	.486	.575	.409	.564	.527	.330	.499	.338	.210	.401
More beautiful cities	.087	.092	.278	.040	-.089	.181	-.100	.141	.197	-.073
Fight rising prices	-.305	-.440	-.334	-.511	-.342	-.154	-.386	-.306	-.238	-.395
Strong defense forces	-.498	-.359	-.464	-.324	-.322	-.366	-.326	-.414	-.295	-.375
Economic growth	-.412	-.398	-.397	-.297	-.497	-.517	-.245	-.442	-.536	-.152
Fight crime	-.457	-.418	-.484	-.417	-.347	-.387	-.490	-.405	-.233	-.465
Stable economy	-.441	-.451	-.435	-.407	-.345	-.523	-.322	-.410	-.574	-.202
Maintain order	-.558	-.376	-.491	-.497	-.488	-.440	-.462	-.549	-.346	-.459

[a] Percent of total variance explained by first factor for each national sample appears in parentheses.

tations to an almost uncanny degree. The consistency of responses to these items cannot be attributed to such common sources of spurious correlation as response set: the items were asked in a "cafeteria-style" format, which gives no cues to the "right" answer.

Figure 2–2 maps the relative position of each item on the Materialist/Post-Materialist dimension in the ten countries as a whole. The configuration of responses gives additional support to the hypothesis that these items tap a set of hierarchically ordered needs. Given respondents tend to be preoccupied with a consistent set of needs located at either the Materialist or Post-Materialist range of the continuum. Eleven of the twelve items fall into two separate clusters, reflecting Materialist and Post-Materialist priorities, respectively (as we see when we compare these results with Figure 2–1). The item designed to tap aesthetic needs fits into neither cluster; with the same consistency by which the eleven other items *did* fit into their expected places, this one fails to show a loading above the .300 level in any of the ten countries. Why?

The answer, apparently, is that this item does *not* simply evoke aesthetic needs, as it was intended to do. Instead, it seems to tap an Industrial/anti-Industrial dimension on which collective economic development is seen as conflicting with one's personal security, and it shows a surprisingly strong relationship with the safety needs. An examination of the second factor that emerged from our analysis illustrates this point. As Table 2–5 shows, there is considerable cross-national variation in the make-up of the second factor by contrast with the remarkable uniformity of the first factor. This cross-national variation seems to reflect the developmental level of the respective countries. Our countries fall into three distinct groups: the first composed of Germany, France, and the Benelux nations; the second of Great Britain, the United States, and Denmark; and the third of Ireland and Italy. This third group is particularly interesting. In the first two groups, "More beautiful cities" has strong negative loadings; overall, it is the highest-loading item on the second factor. In Ireland and Italy, "More beautiful cities" is only very weakly related to this factor.

Ireland and Italy happen to be the two poorest countries among the ten analyzed here. They are also the only two countries in which more than half of the population still lives in rural areas.[18]

The theme of this second dimension varies from group to group,

---

[18] For the European countries, these figures are from *A Survey of Europe Today* (London: Reader's Digest Association, 1970), 14; for the United States, from *Reader's Digest Almanac*, 1973, 121.

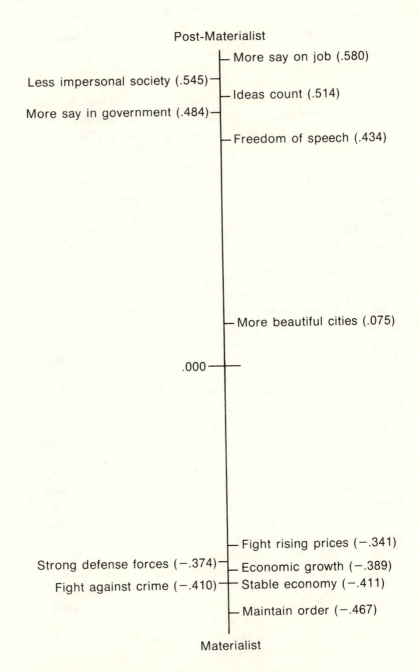

FIGURE 2–2. The Materialist/Post-Materialist Factor.
Mean loadings on first factor in analyses of surveys from ten countries, 1973.

Country (Type 1)

Goal:	Belgium (14%)	France (13%)	Luxembourg (13%)	Germany (12%)	Netherlands (12%)
More beautiful cities	-.621	-.587	-.416	-.606	-.516
Fight crime	-.479	-.485	-.501	-.534	-.504
Fight rising prices	-.312	-.467	-.494	-.450	-.279
Ideas count	-.056	-.029	-.153	-.133	-.116
Maintain order	-.046	.061	.055	.089	.193
Less impersonal society	-.029	.054	.238	.059	-.121
More say on job	.038	-.011	-.165	-.043	.150
Freedom of speech	-.047	.079	.062	.055	.208
Strong defense forces	.083	.128	.112	.102	.047
More say in government	.329	.377	.287	.287	.293
Stable economy	.564	.466	.418	.448	.597
Economic growth	.685	.583	.563	.535	.560

Country (Type 2)

Goal:	Britain (13%)	Denmark (12%)	United States (13%)
More beautiful cities	-.508	-.491	-.551"
Maintain order	-.574	-.498	-.375
Freedom of speech	-.395	-.407	-.378
Strong defense forces	-.139	-.215	-.215
Less impersonal society	-.259	-.209	-.089
Ideas count	-.176	-.055	-.292
Fight crime	-.138	-.138	.022
Economic growth	.109	.306	.202
Stable economy	.314	.320	.239
Fight rising prices	.456	.446	.215
More say on job	.398	.284	.574
More say in government	.453	.456	.559

Country (Type 3)

Goal:	Italy (12%)	Ireland (14%)
Fight crime	-.567	-.500
Fight rising prices	-.429	-.385
Strong defense forces	-.023	-.446
More say on job	-.229	-.217
Ideas count	-.107	-.167
More beautiful cities	-.127	-.108
Less impersonal society	-.002	-.025
Freedom of speech	-.052	.039
More say in government	.261	-.013
Maintain order	.044	.225
Stable economy	.576	.627
Economic growth	.669	.756

" This loading is based on the item "Protect nature from being spoiled and polluted" in the American sample.

but broadly speaking it seems to involve a reaction against the problems of urban industrial society. In the countries of Type 1, it pits a concern with "More beautiful cities" and crime against emphasis on political activism and economic stability; in Ireland and Italy, the pattern is similar to that of Type 1, except that concern for "More beautiful cities and countryside" is not present among the key items. If this factor reflects different responses to urban-industrial problems, it seems significant that a concern for "beauty" is intimately involved only in those countries where economic development and urbanization are relatively far advanced— sufficiently advanced that the public is relatively sensitive to the *lack* of beauty in the environment. In such countries, ugliness may be seen as an integral part of the urban problem—linked with the crime and disorder that seem to be economic development's seamy side.

In poorer, less urbanized societies such as Ireland and Italy, economic growth is prized relatively highly, and there is only a weak tendency to feel that it may be detrimental to the beauty of the environment, which is given relatively low priority in any case. The Irish and Italians accord "Economic growth" a higher priority than any other public except that of Luxembourg; and they rank "Beautiful cities" lower than any public except the Germans (see Table 2–6, below). In Ireland and Italy an anti-Industrial dimension is present, but a concern with environmental beauty does not play a significant part. In the other eight countries, a concern with beauty forms part of the anti-industrial syndrome; but while it is negatively correlated with emphasis on economic growth and stability, as we would expect, it tends to be *positively* linked with a concern for the safety needs. Its position is ambiguous: examination of the correlation matrices shows that emphasis on "More beautiful cities" is positively correlated with a high priority for "A less impersonal, more humane society" and "A society where ideas count more than money." But it is *also* linked with a high priority for the "Fight against crime." The net result is that "Beautiful cities" shows only a weak overall association with the Post-Materialist cluster.

There are two versions of the anti-Industrial dimension among the wealthier, more urbanized countries. Both of them pit the defense of physical security and beauty against economic gains: the cities are seen as unbeautiful because they are unsafe. But in Type 1, which prevails in France, Germany, and the Benelux countries, the anti-Industrial reaction emphasizes *personal* security against

TABLE 2–6. Goals of Western Publics, 1973

(Percentage choosing given goal as 1st and 2nd most important out of twelve)

Goal:	Country									Mean Nine European Countries	United States
	Belgium	France	Luxem-bourg	Ger-many	Nether-lands	Den-mark	Britain	Ireland	Italy		
Fight rising prices (E)[a]	52%	43%	29%	44%	26%	24%	50%	44%	41%	39%	25%
Economic growth (E)	19	18	33	24	14	23	29	29	31	24	16
Fight crime (S)	21	20	9	21	26	21	17	25	37	22	22
Stable economy (E)	12	12	22	39	16	28	25	24	16	22	21
Maintain order (S)	10	21	28	18	18	31	11	16	17	19	20
More say on job (B)	18	13	22	12	24	20	15	20	9	17	16
Less impersonal society (B)	17	28	11	11	26	17	12	8	14	16	12
More say in government (B)	11	9	19	9	14	8	15	15	11	12	16
Protect free speech (A)	17	14	7	11	13	11	11	6	9	11	10
More beautiful cities (A)	15	9	7	4	10	7	6	5	3	7	18[b]
Ideas count (A)	7	11	9	3	10	7	4	3	5	7	8
Strong defense forces (S)	2	3	3	5	4	2	6	6	7	4	16

[a] Letters in parentheses indicate category of the given goal: (E) = Economic, (S) = Safety, (B) = Belonging, (A) = Self-Actualization.

[b] In the United States, the item was: "Protect nature from being spoiled and polluted."

collective economic goals: the fight against crime is salient, together with "beauty" at the anti-Industrial end of the continuum. Type 2, which prevails in Britain, Denmark, and the United States, has more of a political tone: the still pervasive polarization between environment and economy is reinforced by a concern for the defense of public order and free speech, on the former side, and an emphasis on political and social activism, on the latter side. In both versions, "beauty" shows an unsuspected linkage with law and order.

Overall, the item concerning "More beautiful cities and countryside" seems to take on a nostalgic tone, evoking not only aesthetic gains, but the idea of a safer, slower-moving society. And, unlike the five other items that were intended to tap Post-Materialist needs, this item tends to be given relatively high priority by *older* respondents.[19] On balance, this item leans toward the Post-Materialist pole in the more developed countries, at any rate. But its linkages with Post-Materialist items are all but neutralized, among mass publics, by the fact that it can also take on connotations of anti-Industrial reaction.

In retrospect, it seems easier to understand why our indicator of aesthetic concerns did not, in fact, form part of the Post-Materialist cluster. According to our theoretical framework, emphasis on aesthetic needs represents one of the highest levels of need satisfaction. Most of the countries covered in our surveys have not yet reached a level of affluence at which aesthetic needs *per se* are a really salient public concern. As we move from poorer to richer nations, there is a tendency for the loadings of our environmental item to rise, moving it into the Post-Materialist cluster. In the Irish and Italian samples, this item has negative loadings on the first factor.[20] The loadings are positive in the other countries, approaching the .300 level in the wealthiest one, the United States. Whether at some future time of higher affluence and security this item will show strong positive correlations with the five Post-Materialist items is a question that, of course, we cannot answer. But the data hint that this may be the case.

[19] This is not true of the corresponding item used in the United States: "Protecting nature from being spoiled and polluted" is given a significantly higher priority by younger than by older respondents. This item also has a relatively strong tendency to be linked with the Post-Materialist cluster.

[20] Surprisingly enough, the "Beautiful cities" item also has a slightly negative loading on the Materialist/Post-Materialist factor in our analysis of data from Luxembourg, which is considerably wealthier and more urbanized than Ireland or Italy. We should bear in mind the small size of the Luxembourg sample in evaluating this fact, however.

For the present, only a small number of people give a high priority to "More beautiful cities and countryside." This item ranks in a tie for tenth place among the publics of the nine European Community countries. Table 2–6 shows the manner in which the top two choices of Western publics are distributed over the twelve items. This table gives a portrait of the goals most valued by each public. There are some fascinating cross-national differences. For example, the American public places much less emphasis on fighting rising prices and maintaining economic growth than most of the European publics, probably a reflection of the relative economic security that the Americans have enjoyed in past decades. The German public, on the other hand, is distinguished by an exceptionally strong concern for economic stability, an attitude that may reflect lingering traces of the incredible inflation and exceptionally harsh Depression which affected the Germany of the Weimar era. There are numerous other cross-national variations, but certain common features stand out starkly—the most significant, perhaps, being the fact that the items dealing with economic (or "Sustenance") goals comprise three of the four most widely chosen items. They are indicated by an "E" on Table 2–6. Furthermore, among the five top goals, the two remaining ones are both indicators of the safety needs (designated by an "S" on Table 2–6). The next three goals are indicators of the needs for belonging (indicated by a "B"); and they are followed by the three items aimed at expressive and intellectual needs (indicated by an "A").

The distribution of emphasis corresponds to what the need-hierarchy concept might lead us to expect among a predominately Materialistic public. The sustenance and safety needs are most likely to be given top priority, while needs for belonging and self-actualization are given least emphasis. But situational circumstances affect these frequencies: the item concerning "Strong defense forces" provides a clear illustration of this fact. As a "Safety" indicator, one might, *a priori*, expect it to rank in fourth, fifth, or sixth place among a totally Materialist public. In fact, it is given *lowest* priority in most of the European countries. In the United States it gets significantly greater emphasis, ranking sixth among the twelve items. In the three decades since World War II, the European publics have come to de-emphasize safety against *foreign* threats to a very great extent. Only in the United States, which was still at war as recently as 1973, do military priorities retain a moderately high rank.

The foregoing analyses provide additional validation for the four-item index used in 1970 and 1971: all four of those items show a good empirical fit with the dimension they are intended to tap.[21] But these analyses also enable us to go beyond the original measure and construct an index based on the responses to the broader pool of items used in 1973. Scores on this new index range from "0" (those whose choices were overwhelmingly Materialist) to "5" (those who made a maximum number of Post-Materialist choices).[22] We will continue to use the four-item index for certain

[21] These items also form a reasonably good Guttman scale. Using the European data, we scaled the ten items for which both the factor loadings and the percentage distributions correspond to expectations derived from the need-hierarchy model.

The scalability is fairly good. In the combined nine-nation sample, the ten items form a Guttman scale having a coefficient of reproducibility of .88. This is slightly below the .90 level usually considered to be the criterion of a good scale, but rather high considering the fact that, theoretically, one would not *expect* there to be any particular order among the three "Economic" items, for example: insofar as they tap the same need, one's preference order among the three would be unpredictable, tending to inflate the number of "errors" made in ranking the items. We allowed a maximum of two "errors" per respondent; those giving more than two responses which did not fit the scalar pattern were classified as non-scalar types. In our combined European sample, 71 percent were scalar types. And the scalar order of the items conforms to Maslovian expectations, for a predominately Materialist population. Ranked from "easiest" to "most difficult," the Materialist items are:

1. Fight rising prices
2. Economic growth
3. Stable economy

4. Fight against crime
5. Maintain order.

In other words, the three "Sustenance" items are empirically easiest followed by the two "Safety" items. The Post-Materialist items, of course, have opposite polarity from the Materialist items and were reflected in this analysis. Among them, the three "Belonging" items were easiest, followed by the two self-actualization items.

These results tend to support the hypothesis that one responds to these items in hierarchical fashion, but this is not an ideal test of the Maslovian model: the model implies that, as the environment changes, the prevailing ordering will shift. In other words, the items scale only insofar as a Materialist outlook still tends to predominate.

[22] Our index of Materialist/Post-Materialist value priorities was constructed in two stages. In the first stage, each respondent received a score of "+2" if both his first and second choices overall were "Post-Materialist" items, and a score of "+1" if only one was; we then added an additional point if the *lowest* priority overall was given to a Materialist item ("More beautiful cities" or "Protect nature from being polluted" was treated as neutral in this stage). Scores at the end of the first stage, therefore, ranged from "0" to "3." We next added one point to this score for each pair of two Post-Materialist items chosen within the three respective four-item sets; and we deducted one point for each pair of Materialist items chosen among the four-item sets. Negative scores were coded as "0" and scores of "5" and "6" were merged, to avoid an excessive number of categories. Our final index

purposes—comparisons across time, for example. We can do so with some confidence, for the two indices correlate with each other at the .6 or .7 level in each of the countries surveyed in 1973. But whenever possible, we will use the new index, for empirical tests show that it is consistently a stronger predictor of other attitudes than the original four-item index: it taps the same dimension, but seems to do so with greater accuracy.

Finally, let us note that the broader-based value priorities index shows an even stronger correlation with age than did the original index. Figure 2–3 depicts the relationship between age and the respective value types among the combined nine-nation European sample as a whole.[23] As we move from older to younger respondents, the erosion of the Materialist predominance is striking and continuous. Once again, the evidence suggests that a process of change may be at work.

VI. Value Type and Occupational Goals

Before exploring the political implications of value change, we should answer one more question about the nature of value change in Western societies. The items used to measure one's value priorities refer to broad societal goals. This is intentional: we wished

---

thus has scores ranging from "0" (the Materialist extreme) to "5" (at the Post-Materialist pole).

[23] Here, as at various other places in this book, we make use of the pooled samples from the nine European Community countries. The question naturally arises, "What is the appropriate weighting system for a pooled sample?" One possibility would be to weight each country according to its population—in which case the German sample would have about twelve times as much weight as the Danish sample and about twenty times as much weight as the Irish. If we were trying to predict who would win in a Community-wide election, this approach would make sense. But for many other purposes, it does not. The intellectual interest and theoretical significance of a given society does not necessarily depend on its size: why *should* the German results count twelve times as heavily as the Danish? Perhaps one should weight each nation equally—treating each case on a par with the others. Although the latter argument is appealing, we have chosen to modify the "One Country, One Vote" approach slightly. We have weighted each sample according to the number of interviews from that country, on the grounds that the larger the N, the more reliable the results will be; in other words, we have simply pooled the 13,484 interviews *without* further weighting. The result gives somewhat greater weight to the large countries than to the small ones, simply because a larger number of interviews were gathered in each of the four larger countries than in the five smaller ones (the impact on Luxembourg is especially great, since only 300 interviews were collected there—thus, it has only 15 percent as much weight as Germany). Unless otherwise specified, when we refer to results from "Europe as a whole" in this book, it signifies that we are using the pooled nine-nation sample, with each interview given equal weight.

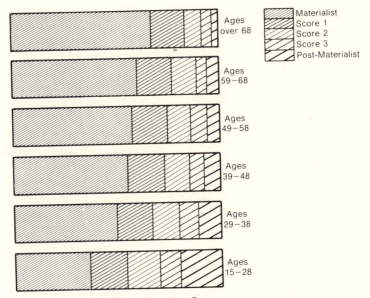

FIGURE 2–3. Value Types by Age Group.

Combined nine-nation European Community sample, 1973. Based on twelve-item values index (N = 13,484).

to tap one's long-term preferences in the widest possible perspective. But our theory implies that these choices also tend to reflect one's *personal* goals. Do they?

In order to test this assumption, our respondents were asked:

> Here are some of the things people usually take into account in relation to their work. Which one would you personally place first? . . . and which next?
>
> —A good salary so that you do not have any worries about money
> —A safe job with no risk of closing down or unemployment
> —Working with people you like
> —Doing an important job which gives you a feeling of accomplishment.

This question refers to much more immediate and personal concern than the societal goals dealt with above. The first and second alternatives were intended to tap Materialist personal goals: income and security. The third and fourth alternatives were designed to tap "higher order" needs in the Maslovian hierarchy. As one might expect, the respective pairs tend to be chosen together.

Are our respondents merely giving lip service to goals which are fashionable in their milieu and age group, but unrelated to their personal preferences? Apparently not. We cross-tabulated one's job goals by our new and broader index of Materialist/Post-Materialist value priorities. Table 2–7 summarizes the results for the nine countries surveyed in 1973. In each country, Materialist respondents are relatively likely to choose "A good salary" and "A safe job," while the Post-Materialists tend to choose "Working with people you like" and "A feeling of accomplishment." In the nine nations as a whole, the Post-Materialists are more than twice as likely to choose the two latter items as are the Materialists. And with few exceptions, there is a monotonic increase in emphasis on needs for "Belonging" and "Self-actualization" as we move from the pure Materialist type, across the four intermediate types, to the pure Post-Materialist type. Figure 2–4 depicts the shift in emphasis on each of the four job goals as we move from Materialist to Post-Materialist: between types "2" and "3," there is a transition point at which a sense of accomplishment begins to outweigh emphasis on salary; and congenial co-workers begin to outweigh emphasis on job security. The first three types might be described as predominately Materialist and the last three as predominately Post-Materialist.

TABLE 2–7. What People Look for in a Job by Value Type and Nationality (Percent choosing "people you like" or "feeling of accomplishment" as first choice)

Value Type	France	Belgium	Netherlands	Germany	Italy
Materialist	34%	33%	51%	26%	29%
Score = 1	38	33	46	31	40
Score = 2	39	44	59	42	46
Score = 3	47	51	63	55	59
Score = 4	56	59	68	70	60
Post-Materialist	70	71	85	89	87

	Luxembourg	Denmark	Ireland	Britain
Materialist	35%	60%	35%	39%
Score = 1	48	59	41	41
Score = 2	32	61	46	43
Score = 3	63	64	57	56
Score = 4	77	82	55	59
Post-Materialist	79	86	90	77

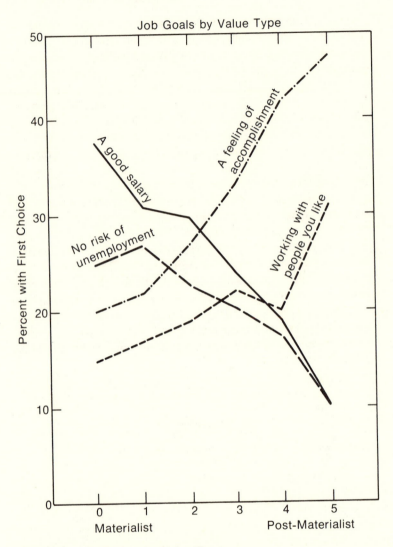

FIGURE 2–4. Job Goals by Value Type.

First choice among "things which are most important in a job."
Based on combined nine-nation European Community sample, 1973
(N = 13,484).

One's choice of long-term societal goals tends to be integrated with one's immediate personal goals. This suggests that if Post-Materialist types are becoming increasingly widespread, changing demands will be made on employers, and there are various indications that this is already occurring to a certain extent. But value change in Western societies has a number of other implications, some of which have an even more direct political relevance.

VII. THE NEED HIERARCHY AND THE SCOPE OF ONE'S HORIZONS

In a theoretical and empirical analysis of the Maslovian need hierarchy, Knutson concludes that the basic needs could be viewed as points along a continuum which runs from "concern with one's self" to "concern with the environment (and self in relation to it)."[24] As long as an individual is preoccupied with needs for sustenance and safety, he or she is likely to have little energy available to deal with more distant concerns. It follows that the Post-Materialist types should have broader horizons than the Materialist types: they should be less parochial, more cosmopolitan in a very basic sense.

In an effort to tap one's sense of political identity, European respondents were asked:

Which *one* of the following geographical units would you say you belong to first of all? . . . and the next?

—The locality or town where you live
—The region or province where you live
—(Your nation) as a whole
—Europe
—The World as a whole.

Cross-tabulation of one's first and second choices revealed that this item has a strong tendency to tap a parochial-cosmopolitan dimension: that is, those whose first choice was the town or locality in which they live were by far the most likely to choose their region or province as second choice; conversely, those who identified first of all with the world as a whole were most likely to name Europe as their second choice. And those who identified with their

[24] Knutson, *Human Basis of Polity*, p. 28. Knutson undertakes an empirical test of the Maslovian need hierarchy and finds evidence which tends to confirm its applicability. Her analysis is insightful and provocative but her data base (like my own) is limited. In her case, the size and composition of the sample leaves much to be desired; in my case, a larger battery of items would be useful.

nation were much more apt to feel they also belonged to Europe than those who identified with their town first of all.

Figure 2–5 shows the percentage among each value type who identify with some geographic unit larger than the nation, in the European Community as a whole. There are large cross-national variations, with the Germans, Italians, and Dutch most likely to have a cosmopolitan sense of identity, and the Danes and Irish seemingly least cosmopolitan.[25] But within any given nation, the Post-Materialists are far likelier than the Materialists to have a sense of identity which transcends national boundaries. In France, for example, only 20 percent of the Materialists identify with a unit beyond the nation-state; 64 percent of the Post-Materialists do so. The political implications are important, particularly for the European countries. If there *is* a gradual but persistent ongoing shift toward Post-Materialist value priorities, this process should enhance the potential support for supranational integration. In the long run, it would constitute a pressure favorable to European integration. In a still longer time perspective, it might be expected to work in favor of even broader forms of integration, such as an Atlantic Community or an eventual world government, for the Post-Materialist types are markedly more likely to feel that they belong to such broader political units.

By the same reasoning, leading us to anticipate that Post-Materialist types would be more likely to have a cosmopolitan sense of identity, we might expect them to be relatively open to innovation in general: responsive to ideas rather than immediate circumstances and to things that are relatively remote in time rather than those which prevail at present. This also proves to be true. European respondents were asked:

> Some people are attracted to new things and new ideas, while others are more cautious about such things. What is your own attitude to what is new?
>
> —Very much attracted
> —Attracted on the whole
> —It depends; varies
> —Cautious on the whole
> —Very cautious.

The Post-Materialist types were a good deal more likely to choose the first two alternatives than were the Materialists. In the nine-

[25] In the Danish case, a sense of Scandinavian identity may be widespread, but is not tapped by our question.

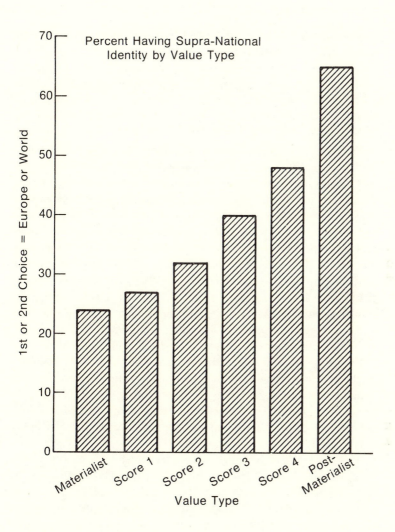

FIGURE 2–5. Geographical Identity by Value Type.

Percent choosing "Europe" or "the world as a whole" as first or second choice for "the geographical unit I belong to first of all." Based on combined nine-nation European Community sample, 1973 (N = 13,484).

nation European sample as a whole, only about one third of the Materialists said they were "attracted" or "very much attracted" to new things. A clear majority (58 percent) of the pure Post-Materialist type expressed an attraction to new things.

VIII. Value Type and Political Preferences

Does this openness to innovation on the part of the Post-Materialists extend into the political sphere? Logically, one might expect them to take a relatively change-oriented position on political issues and to support the more change-oriented political parties. Yet this expectation conflicts with two facts: first, the Post-Materialist types are likely to come from relatively affluent backgrounds. Our theoretical framework implies that this should be the case, and empirically the tendency is quite pronounced, as we will see in the next chapter. But second, those with higher incomes and occupational status tend to support the more *conservative* political parties; this phenomenon has been demonstrated many times in the past, and our present survey data show that it continues to hold true in all ten of the countries surveyed in 1972 and 1973. When we put these two facts together, they suggest that the Post-Materialists might be a conservative rather than change-oriented group: their general openness to innovation might tend to be offset by their social background. Are the personal values of the Post-Materialists strong enough to counter-balance the influence of their predominately midde-class milieu?

The answer is yes, though the extent to which it is true varies from country to country. As one would anticipate, the political traditions and institutions of a given country limit the degree to which an individual's values influence his political position. Nevertheless, the Post-Materialists in each of our ten countries seem to take a less conservative, more change-oriented stand in politics than the Materialist types.

Practical considerations make this a rather difficult point to demonstrate. Any specific issue is likely to have somewhat different connotations from one nation to another. Furthermore, what may be a burning political question in one society may be irrelevant in another. Race relations are of paramount importance in the United States, for example; they are almost negligible in the politics of Denmark or Italy. Because of such situational differences, it would be naïve to expect that any given issue would serve as an equally good indicator of how change-oriented the public is in all countries. What serves as a sensitive indicator of conservatism in one context, may even be linked with a *radical* outlook in another setting. In each of our European countries, most people are able and willing to place themselves on a Left-Right scale, which they use to summarize their overall political stance; similarly, in the United States most people can describe themselves as falling somewhere on a continuum ranging from "very liberal" to "very conservative." One's self-placement on this continuum may help us to classify the political views of the publics of these ten nations in reasonably comparable fashion.[26] European respondents were asked: "In political matters people talk of 'the Left' and 'the Right.' How would you place your views on this scale? (SHOW SCALE 1— DO NOT PROMPT.)" The respondent was handed a horizontal scale divided into ten boxes, with the word "Left" at one end and "Right" at the opposite end. In the United States, respondents were asked a similar question, except that the alternatives were "Very Liberal," "Liberal," "Conservative" and "Very Conservative." Table 2–8 shows the proportion placing themselves on the "Left" or "Liberal" half of the continuum for each of the six value types.[27]

In each of the ten countries, a decline in Materialist values is associated with a rise in support for a "Left" or "Liberal" political position. On the average, about 46 percent of the respondents belonging to the pure Materialist type place themselves on the Left; 80 percent of the pure Post-Materialist type does so. The strength of the relationship varies from a maximum in France and Italy to a minimum in Ireland and Belgium, but in every case the pure Post-Materialist type is located to the Left of any other group.

We will not undertake a detailed country-by-country discussion of these findings here. Let us simply suggest that the cross-national differences reflect the degree to which the politics of the given country have become aligned along the Materialist/Post-Materialist dimension. In some nations, established political loyalties are

[26] For supporting evidence see Ronald Inglehart and Hans D. Klingemann, "Party Identification, Ideological Preference and the Left-Right Dimension Among Western Publics" in Ian Budge *et al.* (eds.), *Party Identification and Beyond* (New York: Wiley, 1976), 225–242.

[27] Those who could not place themselves on the Left-Right scale and those Americans who described themselves as "middle of the road" (although this was not one of the alternatives offered) are excluded from the percentage base in Table 2–8.

strongly institutionalized and persistent; given individuals may be affiliated with the Left or the Right almost regardless of their personal values. In other settings the structure of macro-politics is relatively fluid, allowing an easier translation of individual values into political position. Moreover, the process of value change is not equally advanced in all societies: it has already had great impact in some, relatively little in others. Finally, in some instances it is difficult to say which of two rival political groups is really more change-oriented than the other. Even apart from the Tweedle-dee-Tweedledum situation which often exists in two-party systems, there may be a good deal of ambiguity: are Belgium's ethnic nationalist movements located on the "Left" or the "Right," for instance? Most outsiders would probably assume they are on the Right, but their adherents tend to see themselves in quite another light. For all these reasons, the *strength* of the relationship between value type and Left-Right self-placement varies a good deal from one country to another. This diversity is illustrated by Table 2–8. But the basic pattern is the same in all ten countries: the Post-Materialists fall to the Left of any other group.

Despite their relatively high levels of income and occupation, the Post-Materialist types are significantly more likely to align themselves with the "Left" or "Liberal" position than are the Materialist types. In a broad sense, Post-Materialists tend to take a favorable view of political change. Their preferences among the twelve items used to measure value types give some idea of the specific *kinds* of change that the Post-Materialists are likely to emphasize.

The respective value types display distinctive and coherent worldviews across such diverse fields as attitudes toward innovation, one's work, one's sense of geographical identity and one's political preferences. There is a basic difference in the scope of the respective world-views: the Materialist concentrates on the means to survival; the Post-Materialist is more concerned with ultimate ends.

IX. Some Other Views of Value Change

Emphasis on ultimate ends rather than economic rationality is certainly nothing new. Throughtout history, in a variety of ways, prophets have asked "What shall it profit a man if he gain the whole world and lose his soul?"

In a more academic vein, Max Weber was deeply concerned with the conflict between functional and substantive rationality.

TABLE 2–8. Left-Right Self-Placement by Value Type
(Percent placing selves on left)[a]

					Country					
Value Type:	France	Belgium	Netherlands	Germany	Italy	Luxembourg	Denmark	Ireland	Britain	United States
Materialist	43%	53%	38%	44%	64%	41%	50%	36%	47%	43%
Score = 1	57	49	45	50	73	56	53	39	55	50
Score = 2	68	49	49	55	75	67	53	42	55	55
Score = 3	74	51	48	63	84	59	67	43	62	49
Score = 4	80	57	56	77	89	78	61	53	59	70
Post-Materialist	86	68	72	83	94	80	80	84	76	77

[a] For the American sample, the percent describing themselves as "liberal" or "very liberal."

He saw a basic contradiction between industrial society's emphasis on the values of efficiency and productivity, and some of the most basic values of Western civilization—the importance of individual autonomy and creativity. To Karl Mannheim, writing in 1929, it seemed clear that the dominant secular trend involved a downgrading of ultimate goals, with an increasing emphasis on immediate means—above all, economic means: "Must not the gradual reduction of politics to economics towards which there is at least a discernible tendency, the conscious rejecting of the past and of the notion of historical time, the conscious brushing aside of every 'cultural ideal,' be interpreted as a disappearance of every form of utopianism from the political arena as well?"[28]

But the trend noted by Weber and Mannheim may be reversing itself. Again, the idea is nothing new. In his saga of the Buddenbrooks family, Thomas Mann portrays a process of inter-generational change that might almost be a description of the emergence of a Post-Materialist type within a predominately Materialist milieu. David Riesman provides another parallel with his argument that American elites are shifting from an "Inner Directed" type to an "Other Directed" type.[29] In *The German Ideology* Marx and Engels argue that "Life involves, before anything else, eating and drinking, a habitation and clothing. The first historical act is to satisfy these needs . . . [But] as soon as a need is satisfied, new needs are made."[30] Though they generally assume conditions of scarcity, Marx and Engels clearly were aware that changing circumstances can lead to emphasis on new goals. More recently, Charles Reich argued that Americans are undergoing a transmutation of basic outlook, and his description of "Consciousness III" bears some similarity to the Post-Materialist outlook explored here.[31] There are important differences as well, particularly the fact that Reich sometimes gives the impression that the American public is being transformed almost overnight, while our own data

[28] Karl Mannheim, *Ideology and Utopia* (New York: Harcourt, Brace, 1949), p. 230.

[29] See Thomas Mann, *Buddenbrooks* (New York: Knopf, 1948). Cf. Walt W. Rostow, *The Stages of Economic Growth* (New York: Cambridge University Press, 1958). Cf. David Riesman *et al., The Lonely Crowd* (New Haven: Yale University Press, 1950).

[30] See Lewis Feuer (ed.), *Marx and Engels: Basic Writings* (Garden City: Anchor, 1959), p. 249.

[31] Charles Reich, *The Greening of America* (New York: Random House, 1970).

suggest that we are dealing with a much more gradual process. The work of Marx, Mann, Riesman, Reich, and others seems insightful, but their observations concerning value change are based on personal impressions rather than quantitative evidence.

Bell and Lipset suggest some concrete reasons why the dominance of economic rationality may be declining. Bell argues that Post-Industrial society is characterized by a shift of manpower from industrial (and agrarian) occupations into service occupations and the "knowledge industry." People employed in the latter sector tend to have a distinctive world view: their function is to process information and produce knowledge rather than material products. Experience in the industrial sector leads one to emphasize efficient production and the effort to maximize one's share of the economic pie; while the service occupations are more likely to orient one toward innovation.[32] Furthermore, people employed in the service sector tend to become professionalized: they become more concerned with the values and goals of a profession as a whole than with the viability of one specific business enterprise.

Lipset agrees with the foregoing but emphasizes the importance of formal education. More than any other occupation in the service sector, academics are concerned with the production and dissemination of knowledge. This outlook is communicated to students and, via the elite communications media, to the professionals and technicians who play an increasingly important role in the economy: "The 'adversary culture' of the intellectuals, their opposition to the basic values and institutions of the owners and controllers of industry and politics in capitalist and post-capitalist societies, is inherent in the nature of their work, the emphasis on creativity, originality and 'break-throughs.' "[33]

Thus, as the number of "socially unattached intellectuals" rises, and as the proportion employed in staff rather than line positions grows, a society is apt to place increasing emphasis on ultimate ends.

Curiously enough, while both Bell and and Lipset conclude that the growth of education and the tertiary sector lead to distinctive values, both argue that the radicalism of the young is mainly due to life-cycle effects. Thus, Lipset cites Aristotle's argument that

[32] See Bell, *Coming of Post-Industrial Society, passim.*
[33] See Seymour Martin Lipset and Richard B. Dobson, "The Intellectual as Critic and Rebel," *Daedalus*, 10 (Summer, 1972), 137–198.

youth "have exalted notions because they have not yet been humbled by life or learned its necessary limitations; moreover their hopeful disposition makes them think themselves equal to great things—and that means having exalted notions. They would always rather do noble deeds than useful ones; their lives are regulated more by moral feeling than by reasoning."[34]

This tendency to discount the possibility of intergenerational change is not entirely logical, for higher education and service sector occupations are heavily skewed by generation, with the younger cohorts far more likely to have both. These cohorts are not likely to revert to lower levels of education or secondary sector occupations as they mature. Moreover, the argument that each generation becomes more conservative as it ages has a dubious empirical foundation. The evidence on which both Bell and Lipset rely is a series of American surveys showing that support for the Republican Party was consistently stronger among older groups at each of several points in time. The authors take this as an indication that aging produces conservatism: if generational effects were involved, they reason, some of the younger cohorts ought to be *more* Republican than some of the older ones.[35]

In fact, the pattern they observe is perfectly consistent with a generational interpretation, provided we assume that there has been a *long-term* drift toward the Democratic Party—an assumption which is supported by a now massive body of evidence. Recently, more detailed studies have used cohort analysis to follow given age groups of the American public over recent decades. They provide convincing evidence that these groups did *not* become more Republican, or more conservative, as they aged.[36] On the contrary,

[34] Aristotle, *The Basic Works of Aristotle* (New York: Random House, 1941), p. 1404, cited in Lipset, "Social Structure and Social Change," paper presented at the 1974 annual meeting of the American Sociological Association.

[35] See Seymour M. Lipset and E. C. Ladd, Jr., "College Generations— From the 1930's to the 1970's," *The Public Interest*, 25 (Fall, 1971), 99–113. Bell cites this study twice and refers to no other evidence on the subject; Lipset refers to it in a number of places. The interpretation in this article is based on Mannheim's concept of political generations, which deals with the alternating rise and fall of given tendencies in given generations. But generational change does not *necessarily* follow an alternating pattern of this type. It could, quite conceivably, move in a given direction for several generations.

[36] See Norval Glenn and Ted Hefner, "Further Evidence on Aging and Party Identification," *Public Opinion Quarterly*, 36, 1 (Spring, 1972), 31–47; and Paul R. Abramson, "Generational Change in American Electoral

Miller and Levitin conclude that there has been a Leftward shift in the political values of the American electorate in recent years—partly attributable to the incorporation of new age cohorts, but partly due to the development of more liberal attitudes even among older voters.[37]

Though they may underestimate the importance of pre-adult experiences contributing to inter-generational value change, there seems little doubt that both Bell and Lipset have called attention to major factors in this process. We will try to sort out the relative importance of the various elements in the following chapter.

The existence of the Post-Materialist type is nothing new, qualitatively speaking; in a sense, there is nothing new under the sun. What *does* seem new, however, is the quantitative incidence of the Post-Materialists: among the youngest cohorts they are nearly as numerous as the Materialists. Given their tendency to be more articulate and more interested in politics than other types,[38] they tend to set the tone of political discussion among their contemporaries. This may be the first time in history that Post-Materialists have come so near to numerical predominance among an entire generation.

Another line of investigation also seems relevant and it is based on an impressive body of empirical research. For the emphasis on order and the parochial, inward-looking perspective of the Materialists seems reminiscent of the "Authoritarian Personality" syndrome.[39] Is the Materialist/Post-Materialist phenomenon simply a manifestation of authoritarianism and its opposite?

From the outset of this research, *The Authoritarian Personality* seemed to have intriguing implications. A standardized set of au-

---

Behavior," *American Political Science Review*, 68, 1 (March, 1974), 93–104; and Norval Glenn, "Aging and Conservatism," *Annals of the American Academy of Political and Social Science*, 415 (September, 1974), 176–186. Cf. Angus E. Campbell *et al.*, *The American Voter* (New York: Wiley, 1960), 155–156; and David Butler and Donald Stokes, *Political Change in Britain*, 2d Edition (London: Macmillan, 1974); and Paul R. Abramson, *Generational Change in American Politics* (Lexington, Mass.: Lexington Books, 1975).

[37] See Warren E. Miller and Teresa E. Levitin, *Leadership and Change: New Politics and the American Electorate* (Cambridge, Mass.: Winthrop, 1976).

[38] See Chapter 11 below for evidence bearing on this point.

[39] The literature on this subject is immense; the classic work is Theodor W. Adorno *et al.*, *The Authoritarian Personality* (New York: Harper, 1950). An excellent recent re-examination appears in Fred I. Greenstein, *Personality and Politics* (Chicago: Markham, 1969), pp. 94–119.

thoritarianism items was used in an earlier cross-national exploration of nationalism and internationalism. The results were disap-
pointing: dimensional analysis showed that the authoritarianism
items did not cluster together as they theoretically should.[40]

Subsequent pilot tests gave similar results. Authoritarianism
items showed relatively weak relationships with each other. Some
of them seemed closely related to the Materialist/Post-Materialist
dimension, but others seemed to tap entirely different dimensions.
Authoritarianism, at least as it has been operationalized thus far,
has a poor empirical fit with Materialism/Post-Materialism.

The theoretical basis of authoritarianism is not necessarily incompatible with that of the Materialist/Post-Materialist dimension,
but there are important differences in focus. The initial concept of
authoritarianism emphasizes the psychodynamics of early child-
rearing practices rather than influences from the broader economic
and political environment. On the other hand, Hyman and Sheatsley, in their critique of the original study, argue a cognitive explanation: certain respondents, especially those from a lower
socioeconomic level, may show an "authoritarian"-type response
because this is a more or less accurate reflection of conditions
governing their adult lives.[41] Our own interpretation of the genesis
of Materialist/Post-Materialist values contains elements of both
positions. It emphasizes the importance of relatively early experiences, but links them with environmental factors other than
parental discipline.

The original authoritarianism hypothesis fails to predict either
the age-group differences or the social class differences that are
strikingly evident in the data (as we shall see in Chapter 3). Indeed, studies of authoritarianism have found that children tend to
be *more* authoritarian than adults. Insofar as authoritarianism and
materialism are related, this finding certainly tends to undermine

[40] Half of the authoritarianism items used had reversed polarities, to
minimize response set. This probably tended to break down the intercorrela-
tions. But even the items with similar polarity failed to show a consistent
pattern from country to country. See Ronald Inglehart, "The New Europeans: Inward or Outward Looking?" *International Organization* (Winter,
1970). Much of what authoritarianism measured (in its original incarnation)
was simply response set: see Richard Christie, "Authoritarianism Revisited"
in Richard Christie and Marie Jahoda (eds.), *Studies in the Scope and
Method of "The Authoritarian Personality"* (Glencoe: Free Press, 1954).

[41] See Herbert H. Hyman and Paul B. Sheatsley, " 'The Authoritarian
Personality': A Methodological Critique," in Christie and Jahoda (eds.),
Studies in Authoritarian Personality, pp. 50–122.

any simplistic notion that young people are always and inherently less Materialistic than older ones.

It would not be impossible to interpret the Authoritarian Personality hypothesis in such a way as to explain the age and class differences. One could argue that child-rearing practices vary according to social class, and have changed over time. But in that case, one would need to seek an explanation of *why* they vary and *why* they have changed. Quite probably, one would eventually trace this explanation to the economic and political changes on which we rest our interpretation. Child-rearing practices may be an important intervening variable; at present we lack the necessary information to say whether they are or not. In any case, the need-satisfaction hypothesis seems to provide a useful basis for the analysis of changing value priorities.

X. CONCLUSION

The findings we have just examined suggest a number of ways in which value change might affect the politics of advanced industrial societies. We will briefly summarize some of the implications here.

Our most general conclusion is that the goals of mass publics cannot be taken as a constant: changing formative conditions tend to produce changes in societal goals. But these changes take place gradually.

An individual's goals seem to reflect the needs that were most critical in his or her pre-adult years. Thus, with a revival of prosperity in the West, one would expect certain types of issues to become increasingly prominent in these countries. The belonging needs would begin to take higher priority than the imperatives of economic growth, and demands for social equality would become more salient than demands for sheer economic equality. Somewhat more gradually, there would come an increasing concern for individual self-expression, even at the expense of economic gains. One can already see some evidence of such a shift in emphasis in such things as workers' demands for reorganization of the assembly line into smaller, more autonomous groups in which each member has a voice in how the job is done. Whether or not they are economically more efficient, such groups seem to provide the individual with a greater sense of belonging and of participating in a meaningful way.

Among the more affluent (and more Post-Materialist) sectors of society, dissatisfaction with traditional hierarchically structured bureaucratic forms of organization is already quite evident. Demands for a more egalitarian style of decision-making in schools, local government and business enterprises are widespread. They may reflect an increasing emphasis on the desire to be a full member of whatever unit occupies one's working hours, and to express oneself as a person, not simply a hired hand.

Our data on the relationship between value type and one's sense of belonging to the Left or Right have striking implications concerning possible realignment in the social bases of politics. Traditionally the bulk of support for the parties of the Left has come from the working class, with most of the middle class voting for parties of the Right in nearly all Western countries. And the persistence of established party loyalties is such that this pattern still held true among the populations surveyed in 1973. Yet there is a consistent tendency for the predominately middle-class Post-Materialist types to identify with the Left, while the less affluent Materialists are more likely to place themselves on the Right. In the long term, this could lead to the neutralization or even the reversal of familiar class-voting patterns. The simple fact that the Post-Materialists tend to think of themselves as belonging on the Left does not mean that they will *vote* for the parties of the Left, of course. A number of other factors enter the equation. But there does seem to be an underlying pressure that could weaken social class voting. We will examine this subject in later chapters.

Finally, let us consider the impact which a process of value change might have on system-support in Western countries. Traditionally, the nation-state has based its claims to legitimacy, in large part, on its function in preserving domestic order and protecting its subjects from foreign enemies. Evoking real or imagined threats to national security has been a perennial means to rally public support for the existing regime. The military establishment still retains a positive public image, but the *priority* accorded to national defense seems to have fallen to a remarkably low level among Western publics. One of the key symbols of nationalism may have lost much of its potency, and a further shift toward Post-Materialist values would imply a further weakening of support for the nation-state.

But the problem goes beyond this. In the decades following World War II, most Western nations were able to attain impressive rates of economic growth, and this tended to satisfy another key demand among their publics. Western governments have only begun to learn how to cope with the types of demands which are most salient to the Post-Materialist types, and it is not clear that they will eventually master these problems. The development of an increasingly Post-Materialist public would bring increasing emphasis on things which Western governments are not very well equipped to handle—at least not yet. It seems likely that it would lead to an erosion of public confidence in government—a process which already seems well advanced in some Western countries.

The future looks difficult for Western governments. If they do not solve current economic problems, they risk losing the support of the Materialist majority of their citizens. But renewed prosperity has its own dangers: it seems likely to evoke a new set of challenges and demands.

CHAPTER 3

Sources of Value Change

I. THE MULTI-FACETED EFFECTS OF EDUCATION

W E will not be *certain* whether inter-generational value change is
taking place until we have measured the value preferences of given
individuals over a period of many years. In the meantime, indirect
evidence strongly suggests that inter-generational change is taking
place. As we saw in the previous chapter, there are striking differences in the value priorities expressed by different age groups; and
the age group pattern found in a given country seems to reflect that
country's history.

We can test the question in another way. The need-satisfaction
hypothesis implies that the distribution of value types will show
two basic patterns. The first (just examined) is that younger cohorts tend to be less Materialist than older ones. But if economic
changes are one of the key factors contributing to value change,
we should also find substantial variation in the distribution of
value types *within* each age cohort. The overall economic level in
these countries has risen markedly, but not everyone has shared
equally. If our hypothesis is accurate, the more prosperous members of a given age group should be more Post-Materialist than the
less prosperous ones. More specifically, those who were economically secure during their formative years will be likelier to have
Post-Materialist value priorities.

It is not easy to determine how economically secure someone
was during his formative years; for many of our respondents, the
relevant events took place thirty or forty years ago. It is fairly
easy to get an indication of one's relative economic level *today*,
however. People in non-manual occupations generally earn more
than manual workers; and farmers tend to earn even less than industrial workers. Since people with middle-class jobs tend to come
from middle-class family backgrounds, one's present status is also
a rough indicator of economic standing during one's pre-adult
years. But the relationship is far from perfect: perhaps a third of

our respondents have experienced either upward or downward inter-generational social mobility.[1] Nevertheless, we would expect middle-class respondents to be most Post-Materialist, working-class respondents less so, and respondents from farm families least so.

Table 3–1 tests this prediction, using data from our 1970 and 1971 surveys (and, therefore, our original four-item values index). The prediction is borne out. In each of the seven countries, middle-class respondents show the lowest proportion of Materialists and the highest proportion of Post-Materialists.[2]

The differences are not particularly large; in the British case, they are very small indeed. The British farm population is so small that it is not separately identified in our data; nor is there much difference between the British middle class as a whole and the working class as a whole. Only when we distinguish between skilled and unskilled workers do we find appreciable value differences for Britain. But modest though they are, the differences are in the expected direction even in Britain. And in all of the other countries, our expectations are confirmed in a modest but consistent way.

Our 1973 surveys obtained data on family income. This variable also shows a weak but consistent relationship with value type: those with higher incomes are more likely to be Post-Materialists. There is an average difference of about 10 percentage points between the lowest income group and the highest.

But the variables we have just examined are indicators of one's *present* economic status, and not necessarily of the variable in which we are really interested—which might be called "formative affluence." Do we have a more accurate measure of what we really want to know? Yes. The respondent's level of education almost certainly gives a more accurate indication of how well-off his family was *when he was growing up*. For most people, one's education was completed during youth or even in late childhood. This is particularly true in Europe, where only a minority of the public have attained a secondary or higher education: the great majority of those who have done so were raised in middle-class homes; most

[1] Our 1971 data indicate inter-generational social mobility rates of about 25 percent for Belgium, France and The Netherlands. The rates for the other countries seem to be somewhat higher. Some statistics on social mobility are cited in Chapter 7.

[2] For further evidence concerning the linkage between higher economic level and less materialist attitudes, see Louis Harris, *The Anguish of Change* (New York: Norton, 1973), 36–41.

Table 3–1. Value Type by Occupation, Chief Wage Earner[a]

	Germany			Italy			France			Netherlands			Belgium		
	Mat.	P.-Mats.	N	Mat.	P.-Mats.	N	Mat.	P.-Mats.	N	Mat.	P.-Mats.	N	Mat.	P.-Mats.	N
Middle class	41%	12%	(1,778)	27%	13%	(1,444)	34%	16%	(1,411)	28%	17%	(1,306)	26%	20%	(1,190)
Working class	45	9	(1,397)	36	11	(936)	41	9	(1,209)	36	10	(768)	36	10	(895)
Farm	48	5	(277)	48	6	(473)	45	7	(451)	38	8	(327)	31	11	(213)

	Great Britain			United States		
	Mats.	P.-Mats.	N	Mats.	P.-Mats.	N
Middle class	34%	8%	(551)	18%	17%	(436)
Skilled workers	34	9	(712)	31	12	(450)
Unskilled workers	40	6	(682)	26	5	(42)

[a] Combined 1970 and 1971 data for European countries; data of May, 1972, for United States.

of those who have not, came from working-class or farm backgrounds. The correlation between educational level and social class origin is probably somewhat weaker today than it was a generation ago, but nearly half of our respondents were *raised* a generation or more ago. There are strong grounds for believing that education should be a better indicator of "formative affluence" than is one's present occupation.

Hence, we would expect value type to be more strongly linked with education than with occupation. Our data confirm this expectation in pronounced fashion: the percentage differences associated with education are nearly three times as large as those associated with occupation. In the Continental countries, Materialists are less than half as numerous among the university-educated as among those with a primary school education; while Post-Materialists are about *five* times as numerous among the university-educated. The differences are smaller in Britain and the United States, but they are striking even there. Our 1973 data show, similarly, that the relationship between education and value type is far stronger than the relationship between *income* and value type: for the former, gamma = .297; for the latter, gamma = .080 in the ten nations as a whole.

The association between education and value type is so pronounced that it needs to be examined closely. Education is a good indicator of "formative affluence," no doubt. But it also reflects several other things, in particular:

1. General cognitive development: the more educated have learned skills they wouldn't otherwise possess.

2. Informal communications patterns: the more educated talk with a different sort of people, read different newspapers, and in general are exposed to different messages from those encountered by the less educated.

3. Explicit indoctrination: it is conceivable that Post-Materialist values are deliberately instilled in the schools.

Let us deal with the last of these possibilities first. Dismaying though it may be to educators, the available evidence indicates that formal education seems to have surprisingly little impact on one's basic attitudes.[3] We might qualify this statement: formal indoctri-

[3] For example, see Kenneth Langton and M. Kent Jennings, "Political Socialization and the High School Civics Curriculum in the United States," *American Political Science Review*, 62, 3 (September, 1968), 852–867; cf. Edgar Litt, "Civic Education, Community Norms and Political Indoctrina-

nation seems relatively ineffective when carried out beyond primary school. Less is known about the effectiveness of indoctrination at earlier stages; presumably, it would be greater. But since our data contrast the primary-educated with those who went farther, the differences would necessarily be based on indoctrination that took place at the higher levels if they were due to indoctrination at all. It seems implausible that this is the chief explanation for the remarkably large value differences which we observe.

The first and second factors listed above seem likely to be more important. The more educated do indeed live in a different milieu from the less educated; they live within communications networks that carry different messages from those received by the less educated. One might expect these influences to shape them in a distinctive fashion. Similarly, the more educated have developed certain skills—above all, skills in dealing with abstractions. These skills might enable them to cope more readily with new ideas and remote objects. The new and the distant might seem less threatening, which could contribute to a relatively open and cosmopolitan world-view, such as that which characterizes the Post-Materialists.

Our data indicate that cognitive development and communications variables are significant influences on value type. But they furnish only a partial explanation. In order to understand *why* given communications networks carry a distinctive content, it is necessary to probe more deeply into the causal sequence, and one of the most important factors involved seems to be the formative experiences of a given generation-unit. Let me give some illustrations.

One of the effects of education is that the educated tend to know more. Not at all surprisingly, our data show that the better educated are much better informed than the less educated. For example, in the early 1970's an agricultural program known as the Mansholt Plan was a subject of considerable controversy in the mass media throughout the European Community countries. In our 1971 survey (carried out in Belgium, The Netherlands, Germany, France and Italy) we asked respondents if they had heard of the Mansholt Plan and (if they had) asked them to describe it. It turned out that more than 40 percent of the respondents in these five countries said they had heard about it. As one would expect, the better educated were much more likely to be familiar with it

---

tion," in Roberta S. Sigel (ed.), *Learning About Politics* (New York: Random House, 1970), 328–336.

than the less educated. Let us take this as a rough indicator of an individual's level of information: those who had not heard about the Mansholt Plan show a relatively low information level, and those who had, a relatively high one.

Our communications hypothesis suggests that more educated people are relatively likely to be linked into elite or "cosmopolitan" communications networks which might propagate distinctive value preferences. Insofar as this is true, the better informed might show different value priorities from the less informed. Do they?

Apparently, yes. Those who had heard of the Mansholt Plan were about twice as likely to be Post-Materialists as those who had not: our information indicator is a rather effective predictor of value type.[4] But does the linkage between values and education simply reflect the fact that the more educated are more apt to be exposed to a cosmopolitan communications network? This is probably a contributing factor, but (insofar as our data enable us to test it) it is only part of the story. If formative affluence is important, we would *also* expect education to show an impact on value priorities even among those with a low level of information. The better educated tend to come from more prosperous families. Even if they are *not* in touch with an elite communications network, their family background should make them likelier to have Post-Materialist values than the less educated.

Table 3–2 shows the results of a test of this hypothesis. Since the pattern is practically identical in each of the five countries, the results are combined in one simplified table. And the hypothesis seems to be confirmed. A high information level goes with a tendency to be Post-Materialist. But the more educated group are much more Post-Materialist than the less educated, even when we control for information level. Indeed, even those among the more educated group who have a *low* information level are significantly more Post-Materialist than the better informed but less educated group. This holds true in all five countries regardless of whether the overall information level is relatively low (as in Italy) or high (as in The Netherlands). Overall, the percentage differences associated with education are about twice as large as those linked with information.

[4] Somewhat surprisingly, the response to this one question is a stronger predictor of value type than combined responses to two items in our 1970 surveys concerning knowledge of who is the premier and who is foreign minister of the respondent's country.

TABLE 3–2. Values by Education, Controlling Information Level
(Combined five-nation sample, 1971)

Respondent's Education:	Low Information Level			High Information Level		
	Mats.	P.-Mats.	N	Mats.	P.-Mats.	N
Primary school	52%	5%	(2,522)	43%	7%	(1,699)
Secondary or beyond	36	11	(1,849)	30	18	(2,366)

One might debate whether information level is a cause or an effect of Post-Materialist values. On the one hand, it could be argued that the better informed are more likely to be Post-Materialist because these values are fashionable in relatively well-informed elite circles. Or, on the contrary, one might argue that the Post-Materialists have a less parochial outlook on life and consequently are more attentive to political events: their information level is higher *because* of their values. Whichever is the case (and there probably is a little of both effects), the purely cognitive aspect does not appear to explain the linkage between education and values. One might, of course, devise better measures of information level. Various attempts have been made to do so; the one employed here has the strongest linkage with values among those explored and it explains some, but by no means all, of the linkage between values and education.

But we can make a stronger test of the relationship between formative affluence and value priorities. Our 1971 European surveys obtained information about the educational level and occupation of the respondent's *father*, during the respondent's youth.[5]

[5] Because only the 1971 surveys contained these items, the following analysis is limited to the five countries surveyed in that year. It was felt that for some of the German respondents, it might disrupt the interview—and possibly be an invasion of privacy—to inquire about one's father's occupation during the respondent's youth. Consequently, we did not ask that question in Germany, and have had to estimate the father's socio-economic status on the basis of his educational level alone within the German sample. The 1972 Swiss survey contained a question about whether the respondent's parents had been "very well-off," "managed to get along" or "found it difficult to make ends meet" during the respondent's youth. By contrast with reports of the father's education and occupation, this item proves to be a very weak predictor of value type. There seems to be a fairly obvious explanation for the relatively poor performance of the latter indicator: it refers to something much less specific and concrete than occupation or education. Most people are probably able to report what occupation or education their father had when they were young with at least a fair degree of

These data enable us to estimate the relative economic security experienced during one's pre-adult years. In the countries for which this information is available, one's *father's* occupation in the past turns out to be a stronger predictor of one's values than one's *own* present occupation or that of the head of the household! When we combine both the father's occupation and education to produce an index of socio-economic status, we obtain a still stronger predictor of value type—and one's father's socio-economic status predicts value type every bit as well as one's *own* socio-economic status.[6]

This is an extraordinary finding. For reasons too obvious to discuss, one's *own* social characteristics normally explain one's attitudes far better than someone else's characteristics. One's own political party identification, for example, is a far stronger predictor of how one votes than is one's parents' party preference. And party identification is something which has an exceptionally *high* rate of inter-generational continuity. For other values and attitudes, the parents' characteristics usually provide a much weaker prediction of the child's attitudes. Furthermore, it is almost certain that the father's reported occupation and education are contaminated by a good deal more error in measurement than is the respondent's report of his own occupation and education.[7] Thus the parent's characteristics are laboring under a severe handicap: they contain more error in measurement—which would tend to reduce the amount of variance they explain. Nevertheless, in accounting for the presence of Materialist or Post-Materialist value priorities, it makes little

---

precision. Their perception of whether their parents were "very well-off" or "fairly well-off" seems apt to be rather vague, meaning different things to different people. Insofar as this is true, it would be heavily contaminated with measurement error and provide a weak predictor.

[6] Our index of socio-economic status was constructed in the same fashion for both father and respondent. Those who had a manual occupation and no more than a primary school education were categorized as "low." Those who had a non-manual occupation and a secondary or university education were categorized as "high." Those with either of the other combinations were coded as "medium." In constructing our index of socio-economic status for the respondent, we used the occupation of the head of household, rather than that of the respondent. This should provide the more accurate indication of economic level, and it provides the stronger predictor of value type.

[7] For evidence based on analysis of actual parent-child pairs, see M. Kent Jennings and Richard G. Niemi, *The Political Character of Adolescence: The Influence of Families and Schools* (Princeton: Princeton University Press, 1974); cf. M. Kent Jennings and Richard G. Niemi, "The Transmission of Political Values from Parent to Child," *American Political Science Review*, 62, 1 (March, 1968), 169–184.

difference whether we take the socio-economic status of the parent or the child: one can predict the child's values about equally well with *either* of them!

Table 3–3 compares the two sets of relationships. Once again, essentially the same pattern emerges in each of the five countries, and we have simplified our table by merging the results for all five countries. As the table indicates, the percentage differences and the gamma coefficients associated with the father's socio-economic status are fully as large as those associated with the respondent's own socio-economic status.

TABLE 3–3. Values by Father's Socio-Economic Status and by Respondent's Own Socio-Economic Status[a]

	By Father's S.E.S.			By Respondent's S E.S.		
	Mats.	P.-Mats.	N	Mats.	P.-Mats.	N
Low	45%	8%	(5,196)	47%	6%	(2,265)
Medium	37	12	(1,740)	39	10	(2,207)
High	32	18	(1,487)	33	17	(2,532)
		gamma = .170			gamma = .169	

[a] Data are from five-nation European sample, 1971.

But there is an interesting discrepancy between the strength of various characteristics of parent and child as predictors of the respondent's values. The respondent's educational level *by itself* provides a stronger predictor of value type than does the respondent's socio-economic status—which is based on education plus occupation. This is not true of the respondent's *father's* education: we improve our prediction when we combine education and occupation to construct an index of socio-economic status. Our *strongest* predictor of value type, therefore, is the respondent's educational level.

Why should the two sets of variables behave differently? The answer, we suspect, lies in the fact that the respondent's *father's* education is more exclusively an indicator of formative affluence, while the respondent's *own* education reflects not only his economic position but also various cognitive and communications effects. A higher level of education for the respondent's *father* does not necessarily imply that the respondent himself knows any more, or is exposed to any particular communications channels. A higher level of education for the respondent himself does. Being farther down the causal chain, the respondent's *own* education blends in reinforcing influences from one's current milieu, and thus constitutes a stronger predictor of one's value priorities.

Let us consider the matter from another perspective. If Post-Materialist values are the result of something inherent in education itself rather than a reflection of one's formative experiences, then by controlling for education we should eliminate the age-linked variation in value types. Younger groups might be relatively Post-Materialist simply because they are much better educated than the older groups. Access to higher education has increased enormously during recent decades: across Western nations, our youngest cohort is three or four times as likely to have received a secondary or university education as is our oldest cohort. The differences in values might be due to cognitive changes resulting from having more education.

On the other hand, if the age-group differences reflect changing levels of economic and physical security at different points in history, we should find sizeable age-group differences *within* each level of education. There have been vast changes over the past several decades. Even those with only a primary school education experienced far greater economic and physical security if they went through their formative years in the 1950's and 1960's than if they went through them in the 1930's and 1940's. The more educated should be more Post-Materialist than the less educated, at every age level: their *relative* economic position was better than that of others being raised at the same time. But differences in formative experiences should leave large residual differences in the value types of the respective age groups. Let us see if they do.

A country-by-country breakdown of values by age, controlling for education, produces a large and cumbersome table; it will not be presented here.[8] It reveals essentially the same pattern across all seven nations, a pattern in which large age-group differences

[8] Those interested in examining this breakdown on a country-by-country basis will find it in Ronald Inglehart, "The Silent Revolution in Europe: Intergenerational Change in Post-Industrial Societies," *American Political Science Review*, 65, 4 (December, 1971), 1004. A similar analysis of values by age controlling for socio-economic status in each of the six European countries appears in *ibid.*, 1002–1003. The pattern is similar. These tables do not contain any American data; separate analyses of American data reveal the same basic pattern except that (as we would expect) the age-group differences are weaker than in the Continental European countries.

persist when we hold education constant. Table 3–4 summarizes this pattern, combining data from the seven countries surveyed from 1970 to 1972. As it clearly indicates, value type is not just a reflection of one's educational level. Nor can we regard the emergence of Post-Materialist values as a phenomenon peculiar to the university subculture—a campus fad, to put it more crudely.

TABLE 3–4. Values by Age, Controlling for Education
in Seven Nations[a]

	Respondent's Education								
	Primary			Secondary			University		
Ages:	Mats.	P.-Mats.	N	Mats.	P.-Mats.	N	Mats.	P.-Mats.	N
16–24	31%	13%	(1,139)	23%	22%	(1,995)	13%	39%	(429)
25–34	38	8	(1,839)	30	15	(1,635)	16	37	(362)
35–44	44	7	(2,169)	33	13	(1,325)	19	31	(259)
45–54	44	6	(2,119)	34	14	(1,015)	25	20	(165)
55–64	49	6	(2,175)	37	9	(693)	36	12	(122)
65+	52	4	(2,221)	51	4	(535)	34	12	(123)
Spread between youngest and oldest cohorts	+21	−9		+28	−18		+11	−27	

[a] Based on combined results of the 1970 and 1971 European surveys, plus the American survey of May, 1972.

The Post-Materialist type is much more prevalent among the younger university-educated cohorts than elsewhere. Indeed, this seems to be the only sector of society where the Post-Materialists outnumber the Materialists—a fact that may have great significance. Parsons and Platt have spoken of the phenomenon of "studentry" that arises when a large proportion of the population begins to attend college.[9] In a somewhat similar fashion, Allerbeck has discussed the importance of contextual effects which take place when large numbers of young people are gathered together in university communities, relatively isolated from the larger society and

[9] See Talcott Parsons and Gerald M. Platt, "Higher Education and Changing Socialization," in Matilda W. Riley et al. (eds.), Aging and Society (New York: Russell Sage, 1972), 3, 236–291.

in contact with adults who tend to be relatively sympathetic toward their values.[10] Among the youngest cohort of university-educated respondents, Post-Materialists are not far from constituting a majority. At the elite universities, they probably *do* comprise a majority. This situation may create a critical mass that legitimates "deviant" life-styles. Cultural norms that are distinct from those of society as a whole may be predominant in the student subculture. Intellectuals tend to be relatively articulate, and unconventional behavior emerging from the university milieu has been highly publicized. Moreover, it has been the object of massive commercial exploitation. A flood of books, articles, films, records, and television programs grossly exaggerated the magnitude of the "counter-culture" in the late 1960's. This was followed, almost inevitably, by a tendency to discount the idea that cultural change was taking place at all. Such commercial fads are often fascinating, but they provide an unreliable indicator of underlying changes.

If our data give at least a rough indication of where basic value change is occurring, and how fast, the picture seems to be as follows:

1. Materialists still outnumber Post-Materialists quite heavily in each of the countries surveyed.

2. A process of value change *does* seem to be taking place, but it is incremental and linked with inter-generational replacement. If America is Greening, it is doing so slowly.[11]

3. Post-Materialists may be predominant in one of the major social institutions, and probably only one: the universities.

4. But the process of value change is by no means limited to the campuses. It seems to pervade Western society.

Post-Materialists seem to be fairly numerous among younger professionals and civil servants. They are a good deal less prevalent among the least educated groups, but a great deal of inter-generational change seems evident even there. Post-Materialist values

[10] See Klaus R. Allerbeck, "Some Structural Conditions for Youth and Student Movements," *International Social Science Journal*, 24, 2 (1972), 257–270.

[11] Charles Reich's *The Greening of America* strikes me as insightful. But its non-empirical approach afforded no basis for estimating how far and how fast change was taking place: was it overnight and everywhere, or only at Yale? Reich's excessive euphoria led to an even more excessive cynicism on the part of his critics. Yet he had intuitive glimpses of an extremely important phenomenon. See Reich, *The Greening of America* (New York: Random House, 1970).

have begun to permeate the working class. This phenomenon is less visible and less advanced than in the university milieu, but it is taking place.

For decades, the European Left has sought to give workers more of a voice in how their factories are run. After years of relative oblivion, this demand has recently taken on new vitality. It is one of the hottest issues in current German politics, with one wing of the Social Democratic Party seeking to vastly expand the role of workers' councils. Even parties of the Right, such as the Gaullists, have sought to make the issue their own. And the workers themselves seem more interested in participating in decision-making than ever before.

In the United States, "job-enrichment" programs and experiments with "industrial democracy" have been spreading rapidly. They reflect the fact that many industrial workers, especially the younger ones, are no longer satisfied with economic rewards alone. They demand more interesting, meaningful work.[12] In practice, this seems to mean work where they have a chance to shape their own jobs—to express their own ideas rather than function as tools in a hierarchical system. This outlook seems to characterize only a minority of American workers at present. The existing system of production is providing higher material rewards than in the past, and a majority seems satisfied with their jobs. But indications of change are widespread, and our data suggest that Post-Materialist demands will become increasingly important in industry. Conflict over these demands takes place in the classic arena of labor versus management, but it reflects an important change in the goals workers are seeking.

II. Formative Experiences and Current Economic Level

Across our seven countries, education is a powerful predictor of value type. But the relationship is complex: education seems to influence values in a variety of ways; furthermore, it is correlated with age cohort, which also seems to have an independent effect on values. Let us try to assess the importance of each of the variables we have just discussed, taking the effects of the others into account at the same time.

The causal model shown in Figure 3–1 provides a concise sum-

[12] For some evidence on this score, see Harold L. Sheppard and Neil Q. Herrick, *Where Have All the Robots Gone?* (New York: Free Press, 1972).

mary of the empirical relationships between five variables in our 1971 data; it shows how strongly each variable influences the others and how strongly the four background variables influence value type. The arrows from one variable to another indicate apparent causal relationships with the figure beside each arrow (the beta coefficient) showing the relative strength of the relationship *after* the effects of the other factors have been taken into account. For example, the arrow from "Respondent's education" to "Value type" has a beta coefficient of .122: this indicates the effect of education on value type, controlling for the effects of the other three variables. Table 3–5 shows the correlations between each of the variables *before* controlling for the impact of other variables. It indicates that the zero-order correlation between education and value type is .269—a considerably higher figure than the one shown in Figure 3–1. The fact that education is linked with information levels, which is also associated with value type, helps reduce the strength of the beta coefficient, as does the fact that age is correlated with both education and value type. Part of the relationship between education and values is due to the tendency of the better educated to be younger.

Let us interpret the meaning of each causal arrow. The strongest relationship is that between father's socio-economic status and respondent's education (which has a beta coefficient of .461). This reflects the fact that the better educated are very likely to come from relatively prosperous homes. But even when we control for this fact, a significant linkage remains between father's socio-economic status and value type. Its strength is indicated by a beta coefficient of .120. The arrow from B to E reflects the effect of relative prosperity during youth, *discounting* the fact that those who were prosperous were likely to get more education. Part of the causality flows from B to C to E. The respondent's education is linked with value type by two routes, one direct and the other indirect. The latter path goes from C to D to E; it reflects the fact that the better educated may be more Post-Materialist because they are better informed, or exposed to distinctive kinds of communications influences. The direct path from C to E is unrelated to being better informed. It might be interpreted as reflecting formative affluence, or it might reflect the effects of *current* prosperity. It is probably due to both, but let us make the very conservative assumption that it reflects current prosperity alone. In that case, the model indicates that relative prosperity during youth

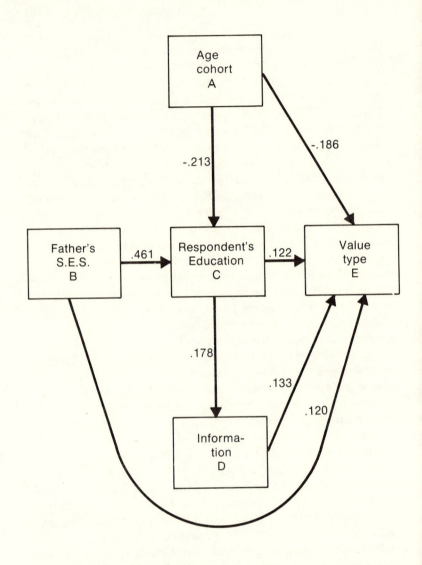

FIGURE 3–1. Influences on Value Type.

Path analysis of data from five European nations, 1971. Includes polar value types only (N = 4,406). Standardaized partial regression coefficients are shown for each path. Multiple R = .358.

TABLE 3–5. Correlation Matrix for Figure 3–1 [a]

	Age	Information	Respondent's Education	Father's S.E.S.
Information	.017			
Respondent's education	−.311	.192		
Father's socio-economic status	−.172	.128	.534	
Value type	−.242	.169	.269	.234

[a] All variables except age have been dichotomized to meet the interval-level assumptions underlying path analysis.

and relative prosperity during adulthood have virtually identical importance, as influences on value type, the respective beta coefficients being .120 and .122. Nevertheless, when we have controlled for all of these effects, a quite sizeable linkage persists between age cohort and value type. The beta coefficient for the path from A to E is negative, reflecting the fact that increasing age goes with a *decreasing* tendency to be Post-Materialist. What does this arrow represent? It could reflect a number of things. For one, it might reflect the different formative experiences of the respective age cohorts, *apart* from differences in educational level. Or it might be the result of life-cycle effects. The results of previous analyses make the latter interpretation somewhat implausible, but we cannot rule it out until we have examined data over the long run. Nevertheless, we may safely conclude that inter-generational value change is almost certainly going on even if the arrow from A to E were *entirely* due to life-cycle effects. A moment's reflection will make it clear why this is true: as the model indicates, education has a strong linkage with value type. Younger cohorts are much more highly educated than the older ones. Clearly, this skewed distribution of education is *not* a life-cycle effect. The young will not become *less* educated as they age; if anything, they may become somewhat more so. Therefore, as younger and more educated groups replace older and less educated ones in the adult population, we may expect to find an increasing proportion of Post-Materialist types in these populations.

Life-cycle effects probably make some contribution to the strength of the arrow from A to E but it seems unlikely that they explain all of it. Two other factors, both of them related to one's formative experiences, are probably important. The first is formative affluence. The arrow from B to E represents the effects of *relative* prosperity during one's youth, but it does not fully take into account the fact that the younger age cohorts as a *whole* have been raised in more prosperous circumstances than older ones. Let us refer back to Table 3–4 to illustrate this point.[13] Arrow B–E reflects the differences across the rows of Table 3–4—the fact that those from more affluent backgrounds tend to be more Post-Materialist than others of the same age. Arrow A–E corresponds to the differences up and down the *columns*—the fact that younger groups are more Post-Materialist even when we control for social background. Formative affluence, then, may make an important contribution to the influence flowing through arrow A–E. But variation in formative affluence is only one of the ways in which the age cohorts differ from each other. Another important difference might be described as "formative physical security." Some age groups experienced invasion and devastation during their pre-adult years, while others were brought up in time of peace. These experiences seem to leave visible traces in the attitudes of given age cohorts. For example, among West European publics, those born before World War I are still predominantly distrustful of the Germans; younger groups have predominantly positive feelings. A similar pattern applies to feelings toward the Russians: younger groups show a good deal more trust for them than older groups (although overall levels of trust are much lower than for the Germans). One might argue that this is essentially a life-cycle effect: young people are inherently more trusting toward any foreign people regardless of nationality. But this is simply not the case: feelings toward some nationalities (the Americans or Swiss, for example) have virtually no correlation with age.[14]

In short, the respective age cohorts differ in the amount of both economic and physical security that they experienced during their formative years. Both may contribute to the relatively strong relationship that exists between age and value type.

We have analyzed the hypothesis of inter-generational value change from a variety of perspectives. No one piece of evidence by

[13] Strictly speaking, of course, we should refer to a cross-tabulation of values by age, controlling for father's socio-economic status. But parental socio-economic status and one's own education are so closely correlated that the pattern differs very little from the one shown in Table 3–4.

[14] The foregoing findings are based on analyses of the European Community's 1970 surveys, which included a set of questions concerning trust for various foreign peoples.

itself would prove that such change is taking place. The model we have just examined suggests that communications patterns are important, and that one's *current* level of prosperity may have some impact. But viewed as a whole, the evidence indicates that inter-generational change is occurring.

III. OTHER SOCIAL BACKGROUND INFLUENCES

We have just examined some theoretically crucial social background variables that seem to influence value type. But a number of other variables also have significant effects, including religious affiliation, political party preference, labor union membership, sex, and nationality. The discussion of these variables will be relatively brief because they play a less central role in our theoretical scheme and because their empirical linkages with values are generally less important than the effects of age cohort and educational level.

Frequent church attendance and the female sex role both seem to be conducive to an emphasis on order and economic security. While these findings were not anticipated in our hypotheses, they are compatible with them. Table 3–6 illustrates the relationship between church attendance and value type in the six European countries. Those who belong to some church are more likely to

TABLE 3–6. Values by Church Attendance:
Six European Nations, 1970

	Mats.	P.-Mats.	N
No affiliation	22%	26%	(1,134)
Affiliated, never attend	31	12	(2,077)
Attend a few times a year	40	8	(3,733)
Attend at least weekly	38	11	(3,598)

have Materialist value priorities than those who do not. On the other hand, among those who *do* attend church, those who go only a few times a year are most Materialist. And the relationship may be somewhat spurious: farm families are more likely to attend church than other groups, and the farm population has a lower income and a lower rate of exposure to cosmopolitan communications channels than the population as a whole. Nevertheless, there is some indication that participation in organized religion tends to reinforce adherence to traditional values, which in contemporary industrial society means *Materialist* values. Differences between Catholics and Protestants are less important, and religious factors seem to be less important in the United States than in Europe. There is virtually no difference between the values of Catholics and Protestants in the United States; Jews, on the other hand, show marked differences (they are predominantly Post-Materialist). But Jews make up such a small proportion of the American population that overall relatively little variance is explained by religious variables.

As Table 3–7 illustrates, women are less likely to be Post-Materialist than men. The *direction* of the sex-linked difference is the

TABLE 3–7. Values by Sex in Western Europe and the United States[a]

	Nine European Nations			United States		
	Mats.	P.-Mats.	N	Mats.	P.-Mats.	N
Male	33%	13%	(15,934)	30%	14%	(1,458)
Female	41	8	(16,387)	32	9	(1,806)

[a] European figures based on combined results from the European Community's surveys in 1970, 1971, and 1973; American figures based on results from the SRC economic behavior survey, May, 1972; the University of Michigan Center for Political Studies election survey, November, 1972; and the European Community's American survey, March, 1973.

same in all seven countries; but its size is greatest in France, Belgium, and Italy and weakest in the United States. *Ex post facto*, one can think of various reasons why women would have different value priorities than men. From a very early age, they have, at least in the past, been oriented toward maintaining a home, raising a family and preserving traditional values. And (in the past, at least) their socialization placed less stress on self-expression in the political realm. But there is some evidence that sex-role differences may be declining over time. When we cross-tabulate values by age and by sex, we find that the value distribution among women between ages 16 and 24 closely resembles that of men between ages 25 and 34—as if they lagged a decade behind.[15] But the values of women between ages 25 and 34 resemble those of men between

[15] If one prefers, one could of course view this as evidence that women are a decade more *mature* than men.

ages 45 and 54—the equivalent of a twenty-year lag; the same applies to the next-older cohorts. If change is taking place, the pre-World War II female cohorts lag two decades behind the men; the post-war cohort is only one decade behind. In the United States, these differences disappear among the youngest cohort.

Though these indications of change are interesting, sex is a relatively weak predictor of value type, at least in Western countries. Six of the twelve value priorities items used in 1973 show virtually no differences between the ratings given by men and by women (see Table 3–8). Women are more concerned with crime and

TABLE 3–8. Value Priorities by Sex
(Percent ranking of a given item as first or second out of twelve goals, in combined nine-nation sample, 1973)

Goal	Men	Women	
Fight rising prices	35%	45%⎫	Significantly heavier
Fight crime	19	26 ⎭	emphasis by women[a]
More beautiful cities	6	8	
Strong defense forces	4	4	
Maintain order	18	17	
Less impersonal society	16	16	
Ideas count	6	6	
More say on job	17	14	
More say in government	13	10	
Stable economy	23	20	
Economic growth	27	20 ⎫	Significantly heavier
Free speech	13	9 ⎭	emphasis by men[a]

[a] Significance tests are based on the complete range of ratings (coded from "1" to "6"), not simply on the first and second choices, as shown above; given the extremely large sample size, the items indicated above show differences significant at the .01 level, although the percentage differences are rather small.

rising prices than men; and men place more emphasis on freedom of expression and overall economic conditions than women. The differences seem understandable. In their traditional role as principal purchaser for a family unit, women are apt to be more aware of rising prices; while men, who are more likely to be the principal wage earner, are concerned with economic growth and its implications for full employment. Thus, while both sexes are concerned with economic conditions, their attention tends to focus on different aspects of the economy.

In non-economic domains, there are modest but significant differences in the problems that concern the respective sexes, and the net result is to make women appear somewhat more Materialist than men. Women place more emphasis on fighting crime, perhaps because they feel more vulnerable to it, while men are more apt to emphasize freedom of speech, probably because politics was traditionally considered a man's business. Women did not even obtain the right to vote until the end of World War II in France, Belgium, and Italy; and interestingly enough, these countries show the largest sex differences in value types among the ten countries surveyed in 1973.

It happens that two of the four items that show significant sex differences were included in our original four-item values index. Consequently the twelve-item index is less sensitive to sex role than the original one—another argument in favor of the more broadly-based measure, for most purposes.

The general relationship between values and three other variables can be summarized very briefly. The distribution of value types varies according to nationality, as we have already seen. Yet throughout most of this chapter, the various nationalities have been treated as if they were members of one sample. This has been done because the effects we are examining appear to be transnational. Significant cross-national differences exist, and we have drawn attention to them in Chapter 2; but the basic forces that give rise to value change seem to act similarly across most Western nations.

Labor union members are somewhat more likely to be Post-Materialist than non-members, and people who support conservative political parties are less likely to be Post-Materialist than those who support parties of the Left. Furthermore, those who belong to labor unions are likely to support the parties of the Left. In each case, affiliation with an institution of the Left is linked with a tendency to have Post-Materialist values. The relationship between values and political partisanship is clearly the more important of the two. This linkage will be examined in detail in later chapters. We will pass over it briefly here, since it is viewed primarily as a *consequence* of holding certain values rather than a cause. Nevertheless, we must examine this relationship here in order to satisfy ourselves that one's value priorities are more strongly linked with such factors as age and affluence than with political party preference. If this were not the case, we might be left wondering whether

Post-Materialist values were simply a reflection of one's party preferences.

Table 3–9 gives the results of a multi-variate analysis of the predictors of value type, using data from the six countries surveyed in 1970 and the United States. The independent variables are

TABLE 3–9. Predictors of Value Type in Seven Nations[a]

Value Type	Eta	Beta
Education	.354	.226
Age	.330	.218
Political party	.209	.128
Church attendance	.223	.126
Occupation, head of household	.261	.103
Nationality	.173	.088
Union membership	.092	.082
Sex	.161	.081
	Multiple correlation = .496	

[a] Based on multiple classification analysis of data from the six European surveys of 1970 and the American survey of May, 1972; the two polar value types only were included (N = 5, 425).

ranked from top to bottom according to the strength of their beta coefficients—the measure of how much influence they seem to have on values after we have controlled for the effects of each of the other seven variables. The eta coefficients show the strength of this relationship *before* adjusting for these effects.

The respondent's level of education emerges as the strongest predictor of value type, after controlling for each of the other variables. As we recall, education, when examined *by itself*, was also the strongest predictor in the analysis of our 1971 data. Since we do not attempt to take account of multi-stage causal sequences (such as that between education, information, and values), education now has the highest beta coefficient as well. But it is followed closely by age cohort. These two variables rank far ahead of any others in their impact on value type. It appears that value type is indeed shaped by relative affluence and cohort experiences more than by the other factors. One's political party ranks third, but its beta coefficient is well below that of age, having virtually the same weight as church attendance. It is questionable whether political party preference should be regarded as a cause rather than a consequence of value type. In most cases, political party choice probably comes later in life than the formative experiences that shape one's values. But we have another variable that *could*, much more plausibly, be considered an influence on value type since it is present at an earlier point in time. This variable is one's *parents'* political party preference. When we use it (rather than one's *own* party preference) in a similar analysis, we find that it has a beta coefficient of only .069. The socio-economic status of the family in which one was raised is a fairly strong predictor of one's value type; the *political* preference of that family provides a comparatively weak explanation. The degree of security or deprivation one experienced as a child seems to have more influence on one's values than the political preferences with which one was reared.

In this analysis, occupation and union membership were included as a further check on the relative importance of one's current social class. They seem to have some impact, but it is clearly of secondary importance. The influence of sex role diminishes considerably when we control for the effects of the other variables. Women are more likely to attend church regularly and to support relatively conservative political parties than men are. They are also less educated and a little older, on the average. When we adjust for these factors, the remaining influence of sex role becomes rather modest.

Nationality was treated as a predictor variable in this analysis. Both theoretically and empirically, this is an interesting variable. But nationality *per se* is not one of the most important influences on value type in this analysis. In a similar analysis of our 1973 data, nationality ranks after education as one of the two strongest predictors of value type. This stronger showing may be due to the fact that a larger number of nations was surveyed in 1973, and consequently the range of variation by nationality has been extended. In other respects the 1973 results resemble those in Table 3–9: age, political party preference, and church attendance are the other important predictors. Occupation, union membership, and sex are even weaker predictors than they were in the 1970 analysis. The pattern, furthermore, is fairly consistent from nation to nation: the same predictors tend to play important roles in each of the various countries. A given nation's history and political institutions have important effects on how fast change takes place and on what consequences it may have for political life. But in examining the causes of value change, the same basic process seems to be at work in each of the respective countries.

IV. GENERATION, LIFE-CYCLE, AND EDUCATION: EVIDENCE FROM 1973

In an analysis based on the 1973 survey data, Russell Dalton attempts to sort out the relative impact of generational effects, life-cycle effects, education, and current income. Using the age cohort as his unit of analysis, he undertakes to explain the variance in value priorities across eleven age cohorts in each of eight nations.[16] As an indicator of generational effects, he uses Gross Domestic Product per capita during the period when a given age cohort in a given nation was eight to twelve years old. Performing a multiple regression analysis, Dalton finds that this indicator of prosperity during formative years is his most powerful explanatory variable (the partial correlation with value type is .47). The second strongest predictor of values is the generation unit's mean educational level (partial correlation is .35). Life-cycle effects rank last (the partial correlation between age and values is −.25). Rather surprisingly, current income explains only a little additional variance, controlling for the effects of the other variables. One would certainly expect current income to have an impact on one's priorities. It's partial correlation is only .30 in this analysis.

Several other points in Dalton's analysis are worth noting. Perhaps the most striking is the apparent dominance of *early* socialization over later experiences. Dalton tested several possible formative periods, using economic conditions prevailing when a given cohort was in the age spans eight to twelve, thirteen to seventeen, and eighteen to twenty-two. The *earliest* of these age spans yields the most powerful explanation of value type. Coupled with the fact that the generation unit's *current* income explains a surprisingly small amount of variance, the results suggest that response to our values items reflects early experiences more than current ones.

[16] See Russell Dalton, "Was There a Revolution? A Note on Generational versus Life Cycle Explanations of Value Differences," *Comparative Political Studies*, 9, 4 (January, 1977),459–473. Dalton uses data from seven European Community countries surveyed in 1973. His dependent variable is the original four-item values index, with the Materialist type coded as "1," the mixed types coded as "2" and the Post-Materialists coded as "3."

Dalton also finds evidence of a saturation effect. The impact of rising prosperity seems to be greatest at lower economic levels and diminishes as one reaches higher levels. This accords well with the view that the subjective effects of prosperity follow a law of diminishing returns. But it also suggests, as Dalton points out, that the process of value change is likely to move even more slowly than had been anticipated in our earlier analyses.

One more point seems particularly significant in Dalton's analysis. It is the fact that, using the age cohort as his unit of analysis, he obtains a multiple correlation with the dependent variable of .79. In our own analysis of the *same* set of surveys, using a very similar set of predictors (age, education and income), but taking the *individual* as the unit of analysis, we obtain a multiple correlation of only .41. In other words, Dalton "explains" nearly four times as much of the variance in value type as we do.

This striking improvement in explanatory power may be due, in part, to the fact that Dalton has devised a better indicator of the formative conditions shaping a given generation unit than anything available in the individual-level data. But this can not be the whole explanation, for even such variables as education show significantly stronger correlations with values when aggregated to the cohort level than they do at the individual level. Another probable explanation is that in moving to the aggregate level, we overcome some of the error in measurement that is more or less inevitable in survey data. As we argued in Chapter 2, part of the random noise cancels out when we aggregate the responses of an entire group.

One's basic values are difficult to measure through survey methods, and our indicator of a given individual's value type may be contaminated with a fairly large amount of error. Nevertheless, this finding suggests, our estimate of a given *group's* mean value score may be relatively accurate. Survey data are needed in order to measure attitudinal variables; paradoxically, they may give their most reliable results at the aggregate level.

V. CONCLUSIONS

Formal education, one's current social milieu and perhaps life-cycle effects all seem to help shape one's value priorities. But the impact of a given generation unit's formative experiences seems to be the most significant variable not only empirically but theoretically as well. For the fact that a given milieu emphasizes certain values at a given time is only the first step in explaining the genesis of these preferences. One must ask *why* given goals become paramount for given generation units but not for others. When we seek an answer, an examination of changing formative experiences in different historical periods seems highly relevant. The impact of these experiences is mediated by the communications network surrounding a given individual; but the *content* that is communicated can change over time. Both are crucial.

Moreover, we can safely conclude that inter-generational value change is taking place quite *apart* from other changes in formative experiences. For, as both Dalton's analysis and our own indicate, education has a significant linkage with value type. And varying educational levels are a structural feature of the respective age cohorts: the younger generations are much more highly educated than the older ones and this relationship will not change over time. Thus, differences in cohort experiences and differences in educational level should *both* encourage a shift in basic value priorities.

Ongoing changes in occupational structure seem to reinforce this process. Our data tend to support the thesis developed by Weber, Mannheim, Bell, and Lipset: professionals are, indeed, significantly more apt to have Post-Materialist values than other occupational groups. The growth and professionalization of the service sector is closely linked with rising educational levels and a shift toward more cosmopolitan communications patterns. But the differences we observe between the values of various age cohorts cannot be attributed solely to the increasing prevalence of professionals and "socially unattached intellectuals." It seems necessary to supplement these insights about the changing nature of the work experience with the concept of psychological adaption in response to changing levels of need satisfaction. For there are marked inter-generational differences in the value priorities of *given* occupational groups; we find a pervasive pattern that impinges on virtually every stratum, professional or managerial, manual or non-manual, highly educated or not. Does this pattern reflect the presence of life-cycle effects superimposed on the effects of changing social structure? To some extent it may. But the pattern of cross-national variation makes it virtually impossible to attribute the age differences entirely to the effects of being young or old *per se*. For these differences are markedly larger within those nations that have experienced relatively great recent historical changes in prevailing levels of economic and physical security, and relatively modest in those that have experienced relatively little historical change.

None of these changes are irreversible. But to undo their effects would require sharp declines in prevailing levels of economic security and education. It is not enough that educational expansion be *halted*. For example, the younger cohorts now entering the electorate are so much more highly educated than those dying off that the educational level of the electorate as a whole would continue to rise for at least a couple of decades even if the percentage receiving higher education were permanently frozen at its present level. To halt the long-term process of value change, economic and educational stagnation would have to persist for a sufficiently long time that the cohorts entering political relevance would no longer be more Post-Materialist than those dying off.

CHAPTER 4

Stability and Change in Value Priorities

Evidence in the preceding chapters indicates that the distribution of value types is undergoing gradual inter-generational change; it also suggests that these value types resist change due to short-term fluctuations in the socio-economic environment. The two points are equally important. If there were not at least a certain amount of stability in the face of short-term forces, any long-term trends would be totally submerged by the impact of current conditions.

While we cannot yet make direct measurements of long-term value change, we *can* look for indications of short-term change. In doing so, we must distinguish between two forms of short-term variation: (1) change at the individual level; and (2) aggregate change.

I. INDIVIDUAL-LEVEL CHANGE

Panel survey data are generally considered desirable in order to measure individual-level change. Not much panel data are available; but the original four-item value priorities question was included in a German panel survey carried out in the Saarland in May, 1973, and again in May, 1974.[1] A total of 1,307 individuals were interviewed at both points in time. If we group these respondents into three categories (Materialist, Post-Materialist, and

---

[1] I am greatly indebted to Max Kaase of the Zentrum für Umfragen, Methoden und Analysen at the University of Mannheim for giving me access to the Saarland findings and for carrying out a number of analyses on my behalf. It turns out that the Saarland is not an ideal setting in which to test the stability of these items, for the population is heavily skewed toward the Materialist end of the spectrum. In 1973 only five percent and in 1974 less than three percent of the Saarlanders were Post-Materialists. This level is far below the proportion normally found in the West but it accords with the fact that the Saar is by far the poorest *Land* in Germany. Post-Materialists seem to be a rare, almost abnormal phenomenon in the Saar. This peculiarity in no way diminishes the general usefulness of Kaase's sample, but it obviously does limit the sample's utility as a gauge of value stability over time.

Mixed), we find that 61 percent of those reinterviewed in 1974 place themselves in the same category as in 1973. This was a period of great change in the economic environment, but the 39 percent who shifted represent a disturbing amount of turnover. Some responses show substantially more stability than this. For example, 68 percent of the sample expressed the same political party preference in 1973 and 1974 (categorizing party into four groups: the Christian Democrats, Free Democrats, Social Democrats and non-partisans). Theoretically, value priorities occupy an even more central place in one's world-view than political party preferences and should therefore show greater stability over time. But realistically speaking, it is not surprising that the values indicator shows less stability. One is rarely called on to articulate one's basic values. But one declares oneself either a Republican or a Democrat repeatedly throughout life—and these labels are anchored by numerous group ties and social pressures.

The fact that 39 percent of the sample shifted from one value type to another may reflect problems in measurement rather than the fact that deep-rooted values do not exist. For the stability of value types in the Saarland panel is weakest among those who are less educated and least interested in politics; it is decidedly greater among those who are more educated and interested in politics— probably because they have more facility in articulating their opinions and values. Precisely those groups which show the highest constraint among attitudes at a given time also reveal the greatest constraint *across* time.

Our four-item index is clearly an imperfect measure of one's basic values. We should note, however, that it showed greater stability across time than most of the other items included in both surveys. The Saarland survey asked identical questions about twenty-nine basic attitudes in both 1973 and 1974. Five of them showed significantly higher stability than the values index. In order of descending stability, these items were: political party preference; self-placement on a Left-Right scale; two "political efficacy" items; and a question about virginity before marriage. Political partisanship repeatedly has been found to be an exceptionally stable orientation among mass publics, and Left-Right self-placement is closely related to it.[2] One's sense of efficacy and one's outlook on sexual

[2] See Ronald Inglehart and Hans D. Klingemann, "Party Identification, Ideological Preference and the Left-Right Dimension Among Western Pub-

behavior are generally considered part of one's basic character structure. Only these items proved more resistant to change than the values index.

On the other hand, a large array of attitudes showed *less* stability across time: it included attitudes toward abortion, pornography, student protest, free speech for dissenters, whether communism is dangerous, whether the German social order is unjust, whether hard work pays off and whether big business is too powerful. These are hardly topics of superficial importance, and one might well expect them to be reasonably deep-rooted in the individual's attitudinal structure. The values index showed greater stability than any of them.

The fact remains that our values index falls far short of total stability at the individual level. It reminds us of earlier observations that it is unrealistic to expect high levels of constraint across items or across time in attitudinal research. Nevertheless, if individual measurement error is randomly distributed, the marginal distribution of responses may be accurate even if individual scores are not. Thus, in the University of Michigan Survey Research Center surveys of the American public, the overall distribution of political party identification never varied by more than a few percentage points during the decade from 1952 to 1962. Yet in a panel survey included in this series, 39 percent of the respondents actually changed their responses from 1956 to 1958.[3]

The new twelve-item values index may show greater stability over time than the four-item index that was used in the Saarland study. For the newer index generally shows greater attitudinal constraint than that displayed with the original four-item index. Across the nine European nations as a whole, the new index "explains" half again as much variance in Left-Right self-placement and nearly twice as much variance in job goals. If the broader-based index shows greater constraint across attitudes, it may also demonstrate greater constraint across *time*. Knowledge of whether it actually does or not awaits the results of future research.

lics," in Ian Budge *et al.* (eds.), *Party Identification and Beyond* (New York: Wiley, 1976), 243–273.

[3] See John C. Pierce and Douglas D. Rose, "Nonattitudes and American Public Opinion: The Examination of a Thesis," *American Political Science Review*, 68, 2 (June, 1974), 631. The 39 percent cited above includes only those who expressed an identification in both years; other computations yield even higher turnover figures.

II. AGGREGATE CHANGE, 1970–1976

The Saarland panel data make it clear that there is a good deal of short-term fluctuation in value types at the individual level. But it is not clear how much of this represents systematic change in attitudes and how much of it is due to more or less random fluctuation, or error in measurement. It is quite conceivable that most of the fluctuation represents "noise" rather than genuine attitude change.

On the other hand, there are good reasons why one might expect to find some perfectly genuine attitude change among the Saarland respondents between May, 1973, and May, 1974. The intervening year was one of severe deterioration in the economic environment—a period in which galloping inflation was aggravated by the Arab oil embargo of late 1973, bringing a decline in industrial output and rising unemployment. One might well expect to find a shift toward greater emphasis on Materialist concerns in such a situation. The question is, do we find a systematic shift that can be attributed to these short-term forces?

The Saarland data provide a partial answer. They reveal little systematic shift. In the sample as a whole there is only a slight increase in the proportion of Materialists and a slight decrease in the proportion of Post-Materialists from 1973 to 1974; the total amounts to only a few percentage points.

In order to examine aggregate changes, however, we should return to our various national samples. They provide a broader data base in terms of both time and space, offering data over a span of nearly seven years from the six nations where our four-item values index was administered in early 1970, fall, 1973, and late 1976.

Early 1970 was a period of high prosperity and full employment throughout Western Europe. There had been almost unbroken economic expansion for two decades. But the years 1971–1975 were a period of exceptionally severe inflation; in 1973, prices were rising at rates nearly four times as high as during the 1960's. Following the 1973 oil embargo, a major recession occurred. Real income declined, unemployment rose sharply and economic growth came to a halt. These factors clearly had an impact on the attitudes of Western publics. In December of each year, a national sample of the German public is asked, "Is it with hopes or with fears that you enter the New Year?" In December 1969, just before our first survey, confidence was near its all-time high: 63 percent felt hopeful. There was a marked deterioration of confidence in subsequent years. By December 1973 only 30 percent of those sampled expressed hope; confidence among the German public was at its lowest point since 1950.[4] American consumer confidence also reached the lowest level ever recorded, in early 1974.[5] This collapse of confidence was widespread. In 1974, 84 percent of the Italian public felt that the economic situation had become worse during the previous year, while only 5 percent felt it had improved. The outlook was almost equally gloomy in The Netherlands, Belgium and France.[6]

If such conditions persisted for long, we would expect Western publics to become increasingly materialistic. But the question is, "*How* long?" If our items really do tap an individual's basic value priorities, they should be reasonably resistant to short-term forces.

Let us examine changes in the distribution of value types in the six countries for which we have data from as early as 1970 (see Table 4–1). There is no sign of dramatic decline in the distribution of Post-Materialists from 1970 to 1976: it shows a slight decrease in Italy and The Netherlands, no change in Britain and Belgium and a slight *increase* in Germany and France. The percentage of Materialists does rise in four of the six countries but compared with the calamitous shifts in consumer confidence observed during this period, the net change seems almost incredibly small.

One of our two key hypotheses holds that younger people are relatively malleable. Accordingly, we would expect them to show more change than older groups. This is precisely what we do find, as Table 4–2 indicates. Among the six nations as a whole, the *overall* distribution of value types was virtually unchanged from 1970 to 1976. But this net result conceals two underlying processes that largely offset each other: (1) The youngest category became 5 points more Materialist and 4 points less Post-Materialist, with a net shift toward materialism of 9 percentage points; as hypothesized, the young seem most affected by current condi-

[4] Institut für Demoskopie, annual greeting card (Allensbach, December, 1973).

[5] See *ISR Newsletter*, 2, 2 (Summer, 1974), 2; similarly, in December, 1973, the Sindlinger Consumer Confidence Index (based on the American public's expectations relating to income levels, job security, and business conditions) showed the most pessimistic outlook in more than twenty-five years.

[6] See Commission of the European Communities, "Information Memo: Results of the Sixth Survey on Consumers' Views of the Economic Situation" (Brussels: April, 1974).

TABLE 4–1. Changes Over Time in Distribution of Value Types[a]
(Based on 4-item index used in Feb.–March, 1970; Sept.–Oct., 1973; & Nov., 1976)

	Britain			Germany			France		
	1970	1973	1976	1970	1973	1976	1970	1973	1976
Materialist	36%	32%	37%	43%	42%	41%	38%	35%	41%
Post-Materialist	8	8	8	10	8	11	11	12	12

	Italy			Belgium			Netherlands		
	1970	1973	1976	1970	1973	1976	1970	1973	1976
Materialist	35%	40%	41%	32%	25%	30%	30%	31%	32%
Post-Materialist	13	9	11	14	14	14	17	13	14

[a] Source: European Community surveys. The 1976 data were gathered while this book was in press and are only touched on in this chapter.

TABLE 4–2. Value Shifts from 1970 to 1976 by Age Group
(Combined results from the six European nations shown in preceding table)

	1970		1973		1976	
Ages	Mats.	P.-Mats.	Mats.	P.-Mats.	Mats.	P.-Mats.
15–24	20%	24%	21%	20%	25%	20%
25–34	31	13	28	13	29	16
35–44	35	12	35	9	35	11
45–54	36	9	39	7	39	8
55–64	45	7	43	6	47	6
65 and over	48	3	45	4	52	5
Total:	35	12	34	10	37	12

tions; (2) The *next* youngest category moved in the opposite direction! Formerly composed entirely of persons born before 1945, population replacement brought large numbers of people from the post-war generation into its ranks by 1976. Although these people themselves became somewhat more Materialist as they went through the recession, their cohort was originally so much *less* Materialist than the one they replaced that the process of population replacement more than offset the impact of the recession on this age category: it shows a net shift of 5 points toward the *Post*-Materialist pole. The four older groups were relatively unchanged by the recession.

Figure 4–1 shows these value shifts in graphic form. The ver-

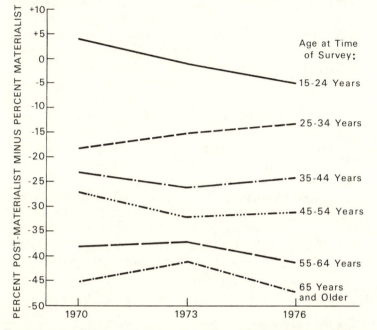

FIGURE 4–1. Change in Value Priorities, 1970–1976: Age-Group Comparison.

Based on results from combined six-nation sample.

tical dimension is based on the difference between the percentage Post-Materialist and the percentage Materialist: The result is positive if Post-Materialists outnumber Materialists and negative if Materialists are more numerous. As we noted earlier, in 1970 there was a major watershed between those who were born before the end of World War II (and thus were 25 or older in 1970) and those who were born afterward. This watershed shows up clearly in Figure 4–1, where we find a 22-point gap between the two youngest groups in 1970. We argued that this gap was due to major differences between the formative experiences of the post-war generation and all older groups. But, of course, it *could* be argued that this gap was simply due to life-cycle effects: people get married in their mid-twenties, start having children and "settle down" to a Materialist outlook. If this life-cycle explanation were correct, we would expect to find a similar gap at age 25 in 1976. But, as Figure 4–1 demonstrates, we find nothing of the kind. By 1976, those born in 1945 were 31 years old. And in 1976 the gap between the two youngest groups had dwindled to only 8 points. But, at the same time, an 11-point gap had opened up between ages 34 and 35: *This* now constituted the largest values gap. Could it be that the World War II watershed was following the post-war generation into their early thirties? This does, indeed, seem to be the case. When we break down our respondents according to year of birth instead of by fixed age categories, we find that at *all three time* points, the largest gap (never less than 13 points) falls between those born in 1945 or earlier, and those who were born later. This watershed must be due to historical changes, rather than life cycle effects.

Projections of the future are always uncertain. But, apparently, it would take a disaster of the first magnitude to greatly reduce the numbers of Post-Materialists. If their overall distribution was held constant but not diminished by the worst recession since the 1930's, it seems likely that with renewed prosperity the upward trend based on population replacement would again go into effect.

III. TIME-SERIES DATA FROM OTHER SOURCES

We have repeatedly stressed the need for time-series data in any conclusive test of whether change is occurring. Thus far we have been able to monitor value change over several years at best. But some data are available on the value priorities of the German public over a period of more than 20 years. A question asked in 1947 helps us put them in comparative perspective: a representative sample of West Germans was asked, "Which of these two forms of government would you personally choose: a government which offers people economic security and a chance to make a good living, or a government which guarantees freedom of speech, suffrage, press, and religion?" Sixty-two percent replied that they favored a government which provided economic security, while 26 percent preferred a government which guaranteed freedom (the rest had no opinion).[7] When the same question was asked

[7] OMGUS Report 74, October 27, 1947, cited in Sidney Verba, "Germany: The Remaking of Political Culture," in Lucian Pye and Sidney Verba (eds.), *Political Culture and Political Development* (Princeton: Princeton University Press, 1965), 131–154.

in the United States, 83 percent chose freedom, while 21 percent chose economic security.[8]

The cross-national contrast is remarkable: An overwhelming majority of Germans chose economic values, while an overwhelming majority of Americans chose expressive ones. And the relationship between these choices and the environment in which the two peoples were living is obvious. German cities had been reduced to rubble and hunger was widespread. America was secure and prosperous.

A similar item was asked of the German people in 1949, and repeated at intervals until 1970. This question was, "Which of the four Freedoms do you personally consider most important— Freedom of Speech, Freedom of Worship, Freedom from Fear or Freedom from Want?" Like our Materialist/Post-Materialist items, this question forces an individual to indicate his priorities among a series of positively valued goals. And because most Germans chose either "Freedom of Speech" or "Freedom from Want," it seems to tap a similar dimension.

In the Germany of 1949, "Freedom from Want" was the leading choice by a wide margin. German recovery was just beginning to get under way. But the years that followed were the years of the *Wirtschaftswunder*. The country rose from poverty to prosperity with almost incredible speed. In 1954, "Freedom from Want" was still narrowly ahead of any other choice, but by 1958 "Freedom of Speech" had moved ahead. In 1970, "Freedom of Speech" was chosen by more people than all other choices combined.[9] Almost unquestionably, these changes in the German population's value priorities reflect changes in their economic environment. And there are strong indications of an age-related lag between economic change and value change. In 1962, 58 percent of the Germans between the ages of 16 and 25 chose "Freedom of Speech"; the figure declines monotonically as we move to older groups, reaching a low of 34 percent among Germans aged sixty-five and older.[10] Here too, we find indications of generational change. But in this case, period effects tend to *reinforce* those of

[8] NORC *Opinion News,* August 1, 1948, cited in Verba, "Germany."

[9] These data are cited in Arnold J. Heidenheimer, *The Governments of Germany*, 3rd ed. (New York: Crowell, 1971), 105.

[10] These figures are from EMNID *Pressedienst,* cited in *Encounter*, 22, 4 (April, 1964), 53. I attempted to track down the original data from earlier years for purposes of cohort analysis: they have been irrecuperably lost. It was a sad illustration of the vital role played by survey data archives.

generational change (rather than neutralizing them, as during 1970–1976) for the magnitude of the overall shift from 1949 to 1970 is so great that the various age cohorts—both old and young—must necessarily have become *less* concerned with economic security as they aged.

In an ingenious secondary analysis of German survey data, Baker, Dalton, and Hildebrandt have examined the issues that were rated as most important by the German public in 1961, 1965, 1969, and 1972.[11] They find that the younger age cohorts place markedly more emphasis on Post-Materialist types of issues than do older groups, as do upper status groups by comparison with lower status groups. They also find that the Materialist issues declined, and Post-Materialist issues became more salient from 1961 to 1972. This period begins well before the appearance of the counter-culture in German universities: The shift in emphasis cannot be attributed to simple imitation of a university-based cultural elite.

Japan is another country that has experienced spectacular economic and social change; and a twenty-year series of data on the value priorities of the Japanese public exists. Logically enough, while British observers tend to be skeptical that anything basic has changed in their own country, authorities on Japanese political culture seem to concur that there *have* been major changes in Japan. Thus Richardson finds evidence of substantial inter-generational differences in the Japanese public's attitudes toward their political system, and in the levels of political involvement.[12]

Ike has addressed himself specifically to the question whether the Japanese have shifted from Materialist toward Post-Materialist priorities, as our hypotheses would predict of a society that has experienced pronounced economic development. To test this hypothesis, he performed a cohort analysis of Japanese "National Character" data from surveys carried out in 1953, 1958, 1963, and 1968.[13] He concludes that generational change is indeed tak-

[11] See Kendall L. Baker, Russell Dalton and Kai Hildebrandt, *Transitions in German Politics* (forthcoming); cf. Baker *et al.*, "The Residue of History: Politicization in Post-War Germany," paper presented at the Western Social Science Convention, Denver, May 1976.

[12] See Bradley M. Richardson, *The Political Culture of Japan* (Berkeley: University of California Press, 1974), 189–228.

[13] See Nobutaka Ike, "Economic Growth and Intergenerational Change in Japan," *American Political Science Review*, 67, 4 (December, 1973), 1194–1203.

ing place, with the younger generation less acquisitive, and more inclined to value freedom than their elders. But his findings also suggest that the process of value change may work somewhat differently in Western and non-Western settings. For the physiological needs are universal; but when we move beyond them, the needs most emphasized may be influenced by the cultural context. In the West, for example, the need for belonging may generally represent the most urgent of the Post-Materialist needs; for modern Western society has placed extreme emphasis on individual economic achievement, even at the expense of group affiliation. But in other societies, such as Japan, the cultural pattern may be such that the belonging needs are satisfied or even surfeited. Ike, at any rate, argues that the most important of the changes in Japanese culture is an inter-generational shift toward greater "individuation," reacting against an excessive subordination of the individual to the group that may be rooted in Japanese traditional patterns. If this is true, Post-Materialists in Japan might place proportionately less emphasis on belonging and more on esteem and self-actualization.

The process of value change may have a distinctive character in Japan; but it clearly *is* taking place and moving in a Post-Materialist direction. Since Ike's study, the National Character surveys have been carried farther extending from 1953 to 1973. They show a continuing erosion of what Ike considered Materialist values and a striking increase in what he viewed as Post-Materialist responses. From 1953 to 1973 a slowly but steadily rising proportion of the Japanese public chose as their life goal: "Don't worry about money or fame, lead a life that suits your own tastes," with the percentage choosing this goal rising from 21 percent to 39 percent. Following given age groups over this twenty-year time span, Sakamoto concluded: "Changes in opinions have not come about because people of a specific generation have changed their opinions over the twenty-year period. Rather, people from a younger generation have carried these new opinions into society."[14] In another analysis of these materials, Suzuki reached similar conclusions.

[14] See Yosiyuki Sakamoto, "A Study of the Japanese National Character —Part V: Fifth Nation-Wide Survey," *Annals of the Institute for Statistical Mathematics* (Tokyo: Institute for Statistical Mathematics, 1975), 33. Cf. Tatsuzo Suzuki, "Changing Japanese Values: An Analysis of National Surveys," paper presented at the twenty-fifth annual meeting of the Association for Asian Studies.

The above studies drew on a rich longitudinal data base containing a number of questions that seem to provide relevant parallels to the Materialist/Post-Materialist items used in the West. But not until 1972 was our original four-item value priorities series actually replicated in Japan.[15] Watanuki's analysis of the results confirms that the Japanese pattern resembles the one found in the West in most respects; yet at the same time it provides further evidence of the impact of a given nation's culture.[16] As our hypotheses might suggest, Japan has a higher proportion of Materialists and a lower proportion of Post-Materialists than any Western nation: the respective figures are 44 percent and 5 percent. This much might be anticipated, since Japan, until recently, has had a lower economic level than any Western country we have studied. Though the Japanese now enjoy a higher standard of living than some European publics, a large share of the Japanese grew up under conditions of severe economic scarcity, by Western standards. But this cross-national contract cannot be attributed entirely to the effects of economic history. For Watanuki's results also indicate that sex role plays a more important part in Japan than in the West. While women are somewhat less Post-Materialist than men in each of our Western samples, the differences are generally on the order of a three-to-two ratio. In Japan, the sex-linked differences seem both larger and more persistent. The Post-Materialist type is less than *half* as prevalent among Japanese women as among Japanese men. Furthermore, these differences do not disappear among the youngest groups in Japan, as they tend to do in the West. As Table 4–3 indicates, among the youngest cohort of Japanese males, Post-Materialists are nearly as numerous as Materialists; among the youngest *female* cohort, Materialists are seven times as prevalent as Post-Materialists—and less than one quarter as prevalent as they are in the corresponding male cohort. No western country shows an equally extreme sex ratio. The female sex-role, in the Japanese setting, seems to have a powerful inhibiting effect on the development of Post-Materialist values.[17]

[15] This survey was sponsored by the Association for Promoting Fair Elections, with fieldwork carried out in December, 1972. A total of 2,468 interviews were executed with a random sample of the Japanese population.

[16] See Joji Watanuki, "Japanese Politics: Changes, Continuities and Unknowns" (Tokyo: Sophia University Institute of International Relations, 1973), mimeo.

[17] It also seems to inhibit Japanese women from expressing *any* opinion about society—an effect that is especially pronounced among the older cohorts. Among those aged fifty and over, 25 percent of the males gave no

TABLE 4–3. Value Type by Age and Sex in Japan, 1972[a]
(Percentage classified as pure type on original four-item values index)

Ages	Men			Women		
	Mats.	P.-Mats.	N	Mats.	P.-Mats.	N
20–24	23%	21%	(57)	35%	5%	(113)
25–29	29	17	(189)	41	6	(152)
30–39	28	8	(212)	44	1	(289)
40–49	45	1	(188)	50	4	(222)
50–59	48	5	(155)	57	3	(129)
60+	50	3	(154)	72	2	(83)
Total spread across cohorts	45 points			40 points		

[a] Joji Watanuki, "Japanese Politics: Changes, Continuities and Unknowns" (Tokyo: Sophia University Institute of International Relations, 1973, mimeo), Table A. Percentages have been recalculated to eliminate missing data from the percentage base, as has been done throughout this book.

The relationship between age cohort and value types suggests that Japan may be undergoing a process of inter-generational value change similar to that in the West—but women are lagging behind the men by a sizeable distance. If we compare the pattern found among Japanese males with that among Western publics, the two are rather similar. The total percentage spread across the Japanese male cohorts amounts to 45 points—substantially larger than that found among the British or American publics (where the figures are 17 points and 26 points, respectively, as shown in Table 2–2). Indeed, in a comparison of males only (using age categories similar to those in Table 4–3), Japan ranks ahead of nine of our eleven Western nations in the amount of apparent inter-generational change (only Germany and France show larger age-differences). Once again, we find that those countries which have experienced relatively drastic recent historical change, manifest relatively large inter-generational value differences.

The Japanese results parallel the Western ones in another important respect: Japanese Post-Materialists are far more likely to support the Left than Materialists. Watanuki reports that among the Materialist type, 65 percent support the dominant Liberal Democratic Party; among Post-Materialists, only 33 percent do

response to the Materialist/Post-Materialist questions. This figure is high in comparison with young males, but small in comparison with women in the same age bracket—*41 percent* of whom gave no response.

so. Thus, there is an interesting combination of contrast and similarity: contrast, in the greater importance of sex role in Japan; and similarity, in that a substantial shift from Materialist to Post-Materialist values seems to have taken place in Japan, as in the West, and appears to have similar consequences.

IV. VALUE CHANGE IN THE UNIVERSITIES

Was the student activism of the late 1960's simply an interesting but transient outlet for youthful rebelliousness? It would be rash to dismiss it as such. The high energy level needed to sustain certain kinds of political activism may be a feature of youth. But a movement's *goals* are important, as well as the amount of energy behind them, and the goals pursued by youth movements seem to have changed in rather significant ways. Again, the German case is particularly striking.

Loewenberg provides a devastating refutation of the notion that youth are inherently more Leftist or Liberal than their elders. According to Loewenberg, the Nazi rise to power in the closing years of the Weimar Republic was largely due to the disproportionate attraction which the Nazis had for *young* voters, large numbers of whom began to vote for the first time during this period. The Nazi appeal was not limited to lower middle-class or *lumpenproletariat* youth. Nazi candidates won absolute majorities in student elections at numerous German universities several years before the Nazi Party rose to power on a national scale. Loewenberg traces the Nazis' success among younger voters to distinctive formative experiences undergone by the age cohort that went through childhood during World War I. Typically, this experience combined absence of the father with extreme hunger bordering on starvation.[18]

One need scarcely dwell on the Rightist and authoritarian aspects of student movements in Germany and Italy in the 1930's. Though it is less widely recognized, the predominant thrust of political activism among *French* students also had a markedly Right-wing character at that time. Their most crucial intervention in politics took place in 1934, when Monarchist and quasi-Fascist youth (many of them from the universities) provided the man-

---

[18] See Peter Loewenberg, "The Psychohistorical Origins of the Nazi Youth Cohort," *The American Historical Review*, 77, 1 (December, 1971), 1456–1503.

power for a series of riots that nearly overthrew the Third Republic.

The inter-generational contrast is less extreme on the American side of the Atlantic. But it seems clear that the prevailing norm on the elite campuses two or three decades ago required one to identify with the Republican Party.[19] It is equally clear that the pressure of conformity in these settings now favors the Democrats.

The campus is relatively quiet today. But protest does not take place in a vacuum; it may spring from values inside people, but it is constrained by the system in which they live in and relates to problems in the external world. Relevant issues must be at stake if an individual is going to act on his values, and the individual must perceive some possibility of getting the political system to respond to his goals. The disappearance of the Vietnam issue and a declining sense of political efficacy (or even a feeling that activism was counter-productive) seem to have contributed to the decline of political activity in the student subculture. Moreover, one would expect the recent economic decline to have a dampening effect on the Post-Materialist phenomenon. Nevertheless, certain underlying values that were linked with political activism in the late 1960's seem to have become *more* widespread, even as activism itself was declining. A series of surveys of American youth provides relevant evidence. In his analysis of the results, Yankelovich finds two contrasting patterns of change.

On one hand, he finds a trend *away* from political activism. For example, the proportion which believes that campus radicalism is growing dropped from 67 percent in 1970 to 34 percent in 1971; and in the latter year, 61 percent of the students said they were more involved in their own private life and concerns than they were a year ago.

On the other hand, the data show a trend toward increasing acceptance of "new" cultural values relating to work, money, sex, authority, religion, drugs, etc. The belief that "hard work will always pay off" showed an astonishingly sharp decline in the student subculture, falling from endorsement by 69 percent in 1968 to 39 percent in 1971. The same trend can be seen among non-college

---

[19] Bennington was an interesting exception—but an exception. For a view of the Yale political culture in the 1950's and early 1960's, see Robert Lane, *Political Thinking and Consciousness* (Chicago: Markham, 1969). For a sharply contrasting view a decade later, see Kenneth Keniston, *Young Radicals: Notes on Uncommitted Youth* (New York: Harcourt, Brace, and World, 1968); or Reich, *Greening of America*.

youth, though it moved more slowly. In 1969, 79 percent of this group believed in hard work; in 1973 the figure declined to 56 percent. Increasing proportions of both groups said that they would welcome less emphasis on money. In 1968, 65 percent of college youth did so, and the proportion rose to 80 percent in 1973. The comparable figures for non-college youth were 54 percent and 74 percent. On the other hand, students began to place considerably more emphasis on job security during this period— no doubt a reflection of the extremely tight job market in 1973. Finally, there was a sharp decline among both groups in the proportion who felt that patriotism was a very important value. In 1969, 35 percent of the college students emphasized patriotism; in 1973 only 19 percent did so. Among non-college youth the figure fell from 60 percent to 40 percent.[20]

Evidence from a variety of sources points to value change in advanced industrial societies. There is nothing inevitable about these changes: they seem attributable to specific conditions and would be expected to continue only insofar as those conditions are present. If rising affluence contributed to the emergence of relatively numerous Post-Materialists among the younger cohorts, one would expect the disappearance of prosperity to lead to the disappearance of the Post-Materialists. And at the time of this writing, the Western world is undergoing its most serious economic crisis since World War II. A return of widespread economic insecurity—or a war which resulted in the invasion of these countries —could end the conditions that led to the Post-Materialist phenomenon. The process of value change might reverse its present direction. We cannot exclude that possibility. Some observers argue that the prosperity from 1950 to 1970 was an extraordinary aberration and that Western society is now entering a period of long-term economic decline. If that is the case, we would indeed expect the proportion of Post-Materialists to dwindle. Being concentrated among the youngest and most malleable cohorts, the Post-Materialist ranks are probably more vulnerable to short-term forces than those of the Materialists (which are concentrated among older and less flexible cohorts). The Post-Materialist phenomenon, and the issues and type of protest associated with it, might be re-

[20] See Daniel Yankelovich, *The Changing Values on Campus* (New York: Washington Square Press, 1973), 39–41. Cf. Yankelovich, *Changing Youth Values in the 1970's* (New York: JDR 3rd Fund, 1974).

membered only as an intriguing historical incident of the late 1960's.

Or we might witness a renaissance of prosperity that endured a few more decades and were *then* followed by economic collapse (the basic forecast of *The Limits to Growth*).[21] In that case, we would eventually find the *opposite* relationship between age and value type from that which prevails today: the older cohorts would manifest vestiges of a bygone Post-Materialist era, while the younger cohorts would begin to emerge as materialistic, money-grubbing barbarians.

But it seems probable that advanced industrial societies will find solutions to the current economic crisis, just as they have surmounted past ones. This would not necessarily involve an exponential increase in the consumption of raw materials—merely a pattern in which economic and physical security were assured for all or most of the population. If this holds true, we would expect a long-term increase in the proportion of Post-Materialists —bringing a distinctive outlook and set of priorities to the politics of Western nations.

[21] See Donella Meadows *et al.*, *The Limits to Growth* (New York: Universe, 1972).

CHAPTER 5

Values, Objective Needs, and the Subjective Quality of Life

I. Introduction

SPECULATION on the sources of human satisfaction has an ancient history. One of the simplest and seemingly most plausible hypotheses was voiced by Plato: Those who are materially well-off are likely to be satisfied, while those who are impoverished are apt to be dissatisfied and a source of political instability. But as early as de Tocqueville it was noted that, paradoxical as it seemed, the French Revolution occurred *not* at a point of maximum impoverishment but during a period of relative prosperity.

The tendency to assume a one-to-one relationship between objective conditions and subjective satisfaction was questioned by such observations, but by no means ended. During the 1950's and early 1960's, one of the key concepts underpinning belief in the decline of ideology and sharp political conflict was the assumption that the more people have, the more satisfied they are. Rising levels of economic welfare, it seemed reasonable to suppose, should lead to rising levels of public satisfaction.

Yet by the late 1960's it was apparent that something was wrong. The traditional principles of welfare economics did not seem to be working. The real income of the American public rose very markedly between 1957 and 1973, but their reported levels of happiness actually declined slightly.[1] Never before had Western publics had so much material welfare, as measured by all objective indicators. Yet not since the 1930's had there been so much manifest discontent. These circumstances led to an increasing aware-

---

[1] See Angus E. Campbell *et al.*, *The Quality of American Life: Perceptions, Evaluations and Satisfactions* (New York: Russell Sage, 1976). Cf. James A. Davis, "Does Economic Growth Improve the Human Lot? Yes, Indeed, About .0005 per Year." Paper prepared for the International Conference on Subjective Indicators of the Quality of Life, Cambridge, England, September 8–11, 1975; and Otis Dudley Duncan, "Does Money Buy Satisfaction?" *Social Indicators Research*, 2 (1975), 267–274.

ness of the need to understand and measure *subjective* well-being, in addition to the now-familiar economic indicators.

II. Environment, Aspirations, Values and Satisfaction: Some Hypotheses

There has been a remarkable flowering of social indicators research in recent years. Building on the pioneering studies of Gurin, Veroff and Feld,[2] of Cantril,[3] and of Bradburn,[4] major investigations of the perceived quality of life have been undertaken in the United States and at least a dozen other Western countries.

This research has been fruitful in a variety of ways. But for present purposes the most interesting result is a finding that is far from obvious yet turns up repeatedly in various investigations: the fact that there is remarkably little variation in Overall Life Satisfaction from one group to another within a given society. For example, in an analysis of American data, Andrews and Withey find that the combined effects of age, sex, race, income, education and occupation account for only 8 percent of the variance in a carefully validated index of Overall Life Satisfaction.[5]

Just as one would expect, the rich are more satisfied with their *incomes* than the poor are, and the highly educated are more satisfied with their *education* than the less educated. But the differences are smaller than one might expect; and when we analyze satisfaction with one's life as a *whole*, even income (which is the strongest social background predictor in almost every country) shows only a modest relationship.

Why does satisfaction with one's life as a *whole* vary so little across groups whose circumstances vary greatly? The global nature of Overall Life Satisfaction may itself be an important contributing factor. For, as Andrews and Withey demonstrate convincingly, satisfaction with one's life as a whole is additive—it reflects the sum of one's satisfaction in various domains (such as income, housing, leisure activities, family life, and so forth)

[2] Gerald Gurin *et al.*, *Americans View Their Mental Health* (New York: Basic Books, 1960).

[3] Hadley Cantril, *The Pattern of Human Concerns* (New Brunswick: Rutgers University Press, 1965).

[4] Norman Bradburn, *The Structure of Psychological Well-Being* (Chicago: Aldine Press, 1969).

[5] See Frank M. Andrews and Stephen B. Withey, *Social Indicators of Well-Being in America* (New York: Plenum, 1976).

weighted according to the relative importance of the given domain. There is a definite tendency for satisfaction in one domain to go together with satisfaction in other domains; but the correlations are far from perfect. Consequently, satisfaction in one domain sometimes compensates for dissatisfaction in another. Satisfaction with one's family life, for example, is one of the most important components of Overall Life Satisfaction but it is largely unrelated to income. This fact tends to dampen the correlation between income and satisfaction. The relationship between income and Overall Satisfaction may not be particularly strong; but there is even less variation in satisfaction levels across most other social categories.

Averaging satisfaction from one domain to another may reduce the variation in satisfaction from group to group; but another process seems even more important. Campbell, Converse and Rodgers also find surprisingly weak relationships between social background variables and satisfaction in analyses of American data, and propose an interesting explanatory model. They argue that one's subjective satisfaction with any given aspect of life reflects the gap between one's *aspiration level* and one's *perceived situation*; but aspiration levels gradually *adjust* to changed life conditions. If this is true, then one is unlikely to find large differences between the subjective satisfaction levels of given social groups *provided* that these groups have reasonably stable membership: for in the long run, the aspiration levels of stable groups will have time to adjust to their respective external circumstances.

This pattern of low inter-group variance should apply most faithfully to groups defined by genetic or ascriptive characteristics, since these are particularly stable attributes of a given individual. It would *not* necessarily hold true of social categories having a fluctuating membership—particularly those for which a change in category tends to coincide with a change in satisfaction level. One's income level, for example, can change a good deal even over short periods of time—and when it does, the individual concerned is likely to move simultaneously from one income category to another *and* from one satisfaction level to another. Consequently, the portion of the public that shifts upward (or downward) will tend to show distinctively high (or low) levels on *both* variables. Thus we would expect to find comparatively strong correlations between satisfaction and *income*. Education predicts most attitudes better than income does; but education is a decidedly more stable attribute of given individuals, and should show weaker relationships with Overall Life Satisfaction. One's sex is perhaps the most stable characteristic for which we have cross-national data; accordingly, we would generally expect to find minimal variation in satisfaction levels by sex, despite the various disadvantages women face.

These expectations may seem counter-intuitive at first; everyone *knows* that when you get something you wanted, you are more satisfied than you were before you got it; it would seem obvious that Subjective Satisfaction *must* respond to external circumstances. Indeed, it does—at least in the short term. A person who has been lost in an arid desert, no doubt, is delighted when he finally reaches an oasis. But would we expect an ample water supply to give rise to continual expressions of delight after weeks or months have passed? Hardly. One probably would take the supply for granted and start to worry about other things. And for those who have *always* lived in an environment where water is plentiful, it may seem virtually valueless, so that the quantity available is unrelated to the Subjective Quality of Life.

Thus, differences in subjective satisfaction levels reflect the impact of *changes* over time, more than absolute *levels* of external conditions. Within any large sample one finds a wide range of satisfaction levels, reflecting the fact that some people's recent experiences have exceeded their expectations, while others' have fallen short. When a need is suddenly fulfilled, one feels a heightened sense of satisfaction, but after a time, one begins to take one's situation for granted; aspirations and objective circumstances come into balance. Upon reflection, it seems obvious that some such mechanism would be necessary in order for humans to function as they do. If it were otherwise, fulfillment of given goals would lead to a state of satiated immobility.

We view man as a goal-seeking organism, similar to any other animal in his pursuit of biological survival, but unique in his degree of adaptability and in the wide range of non-physiological goals he pursues. He can survive from the equator to the arctic and from the ocean floor to the surface of the moon. His goals range from food and oxygen to knowledge and beauty. Mankind seeks his goals under widely varying conditions, and paradoxically, this immensely varied activity is regulated by a drive for inner homeostasis. Like other animals, man seeks to maintain a constant percentage of water in the body, a constant percentage of oxygen and sugar in the blood. When this inner balance is upset, he strives, sometimes desperately, either to reposition himself in the environment or to change the environment in ways that redress the balance.

Man's pursuit of non-material goals seems to work in analogous fashion. Here it is no longer a question of maintaining a physiological homeostasis; but one's feelings of psychological satisfaction or dissatisfaction help guide the conscious pursuit of man's varying needs just as on a less conscious level sensations of pleasure and pain help direct one toward physiological survival. Gratification of either material or non-material needs produces a sense of subjective satisfaction, but it persists for only a limited time. In an environment where given needs are satisfied in a secure and continuing fashion, the salience of these needs declines and new sources of dissatisfaction become important. The net result is that in the long run one's overall sense of subjective satisfaction tends toward homeostasis.

Though everyone seeks happiness, contentment or a sense of Overall Satisfaction, these goals are elusive. For Overall Satisfaction is not a substance, but a continually moving balance. Yet people *are* aware of being generally satisfied or dissatisfied at a given moment and can report these feelings. Analysis of such reports indicates that satisfaction is additive: one's sense of Overall Satisfaction apparently reflects a weighted average of satisfaction in all those domains that are important to the given individual. But the weights vary from individual to individual and from culture to culture. A sense of Overall Satisfaction does not automatically result from obtaining optimal physiological conditions. For better or for worse, man is not simply an animal but has a vast range of higher-order goals. In any society, social, intellectual, and aesthetic needs seem to be present. Given some respite from the pursuit of subsistence, people create art and ceremony, and seek an explanation of the universe. The relative weight of the various needs is influenced by the physical environment, no doubt, but not determined exclusively by it.

The process of adjustment is complex. For the balance between needs or aspirations, on the one hand, and fulfillment, on the other, is continually being upset and readjusted. Satisfaction of a given need can provide intense pleasure; but in days or months or years (depending on how long and intensely one has sought the given goal) one aspires to more or to different things.

But which will it be: more of the same or a shift to different goals? The distinction seems crucial, for the two types of response have quite different implications, and they seem to have different time frames. On the one hand, we are dealing with a quantitative adjustment of aspirations; it does not take place immediately. Campbell *et al.* conclude that aspiration levels adjust themselves only "slowly and in the rather long term."[6] Nevertheless, the evidence indicates that given individuals can and do adjust their aspirations to their situation, shifting them upward with prosperity and (somewhat more slowly) downward with adversity. Over the course of one's lifetime, one tends to achieve a progressively better fit between aspirations and external circumstances, according to Campbell *et al.* with the result that the oldest respondents are the most satisfied age group among their samples of the American public.

This process of incremental quantitative changes may take considerable time, but the other process—a qualitative shift from one type of goal to another—seems to work even more slowly. Once he has reached adulthood, a given individual's aspirations may be firmly linked to certain types of goals. It seems easier to raise one's sights to more income or a larger house than to shift them to different kinds of goals or different ways of life. Major changes in value priorities can take place in a society, but they seem to occur largely as a matter of inter-generational population replacement.

Thus, changes in the economic and social environment can have three different types of impact, each with its own time frame:

1. In the short term, changes in one's objective circumstances can produce an immediate sense of satisfaction or dissatisfaction.

2. Changes that persist for some time gradually raise or lower an individual's aspiration levels in a given domain.

3. Changes that persist for the very long term can lead to inter-generational value changes, with the result that different domains come to be given top priority by the population of a given society.

The existence of these different processes has important implications concerning the levels of subjective satisfaction that prevails in a society. They suggest that we are not likely to find a simple one-to-one relationship between indicators of objective welfare

[6] Campbell *et al.*, *Quality of American Life*, 209.

and subjective satisfaction. Although the immediate impact of short-term changes would work along the lines of "the more you get, the better you feel," it would tend to be offset by the two other processes. For the adjustment of aspiration levels could neutralize much of the relatively high gratification that otherwise would be associated with relatively high levels of objective welfare.

Changes in value priorities could lead to still greater disparities between objective welfare and subjective satisfaction. They could even produce situations in which groups that ranked high on indicators of objective welfare actually were satisfied *less* than those who ranked lower. This could happen if, for example, a high-income group had distinctive value priorities that emphasized non-economic domains more heavily than economic ones; and were less *satisfied* with conditions in their top-priority domains than lower-income groups were with conditions in *their* top-priority domains. Such an inversion of the normal relationship between objective conditions and subjective satisfaction is not just a theoretical possibility, it actually seems to be taking place. As we will see below, Post-Materialists tend to manifest relatively *low* levels of satisfaction with many aspects of their lives, despite the fact that they rank far above average in income, education, and occupational status.

Because of these counter-balancing processes, we ordinarily would expect to find only modest differences in Overall Satisfaction levels across stable social categories within given nations. Short-term variation, of course, will occur. At any given moment, some people have done better than usual, while others have done worse. But when we compare large groups, the effects of short-term variation are likely to cancel out. Does this mean that the effects of *all* short-term variation simply vanish in a sort of Brownian Movement that is visible at the individual level but has a resultant of zero? Certainly not. One readily can conceive of certain infrequent but powerful events that would be capable of suddenly raising or lowering the satisfaction levels of entire *groups* of people. But such events that come to mind most readily, such as war or economic depression or political collapse, are apt to have their impact on an entire nation or even several nations. Thus they could cause large changes in the satisfaction level of a given nationality from one year to the next or could bring about large disparities between one nation and another; but within any given national cross-section, we might find little variation between social groups.

We might ordinarily find only modest differences in Overall Satisfaction levels within given nations. But, let us hasten to add, this pattern should not be viewed as an iron law—it is merely a relatively probable condition. For the impact of economic or political disaster is sometimes heavily skewed. Such an event would tend to depress the Overall Satisfaction level of everyone in a given nation, but if the impact were extremely skewed, some groups might be forced down so much faster than others that large intergroup differences would open up. One can even conceive of major events that would be expected to *raise* the Overall Satisfaction level of one large group, while *lowering* that of others. The victory of the Republican Presidential candidate, for example, might bring cheer to all Republicans and dismay to all Democrats. Knowing the peripheral role that politics usually plays in the lives of most people, such an event might have only a marginal impact on one's Overall Satisfaction level. But let us push the example to an extreme. Imagine a situation in which one group had just triumphed over another group in a civil war. Would we expect the former group to show higher levels of global satisfaction? Certainly. Under such circumstances we would anticipate very sizeable inter-group differences within a given nation. Our point is simply that such situations probably occur much less frequently than major changes that have a similar impact on most people in a given region or nation—with good times (or hard times) bringing favorable (or unfavorable) changes to both rich and poor, Protestant and Catholic, male and female. Even though the absolute positions of the respective groups remain quite different, they move in the same direction, and it is *change* that seems to be crucial in shaping subjective satisfaction.

The foregoing hypotheses may seem to contradict part of the literature on relative deprivation. Would not feelings of relative deprivation work against any tendency toward minimum inter-group variation? The term "relative deprivation" has been used in a variety of ways. In the classic study on the American soldier,[7] findings were presented to the effect that soldiers could endure very substantial degrees of objective deprivation and maintain

[7] See Samuel Stouffer *et al.*, *The American Soldier* (Princeton: Princeton University Press, 1949).

good morale, provided that they did not experience a sense of *relative* deprivation. The crucial factor seemed to be whether one was treated at least as well as one's reference group. But military populations constitute a rather special case. Enlisted men live in exceptionally close contact with each other, under exceptionally uniform norms and conditions, and in relative isolation from the more heterogenous outer world. Reference-group comparisons are exceptionally salient and compelling under such circumstances. More recent research (based on civilian samples) continues to employ the term "relative deprivation" but has given it new meanings. Instead of emphasizing reference-group comparisons, this literature has emphasized the importance of comparisons across time and comparisons with abstract norms and expectations. Individuals compare how well-off they are at present with their own conditions in the past, or their expectations for the future.[8] Efforts to explain satisfaction or dissatisfaction in terms of diachronic comparisons have taken a variety of forms. Cantril measured the discrepancy between one's perception of his actual level of achievement and the best possible situation he could imagine.[9] Other analysts have focused on the discrepancy between perceived achievement and the level to which one feels rightfully entitled,[10] and between perceived level of achievement versus aspiration levels.[11]

Our own interpretation emphasizes the latter type of comparisons. Nevertheless, reference-group comparisons probably do have some impact. The adjustment of one's aspirations to one's circumstances is never perfect. Those with lower incomes and less education *are* less satisfied with their incomes and education than those who are objectively better off. But, as we shall see, the differences are smaller than one might expect; and when averaged in with

---

[8] For an example of this approach, see James C. Davies, "Toward a Theory of Revolution," *American Sociological Review*, 6, 1 (February), 5–19.

[9] See Hadley Cantril, *Pattern of Concerns*, cf. Don R. Bowen *et al.*, "Deprivation, Mobility and Orientation toward Protest of the Urban Poor," in Louis H. Masotti and Don R. Bowen (eds.), *Riots and Rebellion: Civil Violence in the Urban Community* (Beverly Hills: Sage, 1968); and Joel D. Aberbach and Jack L. Walker, "Political Trust and Racial Ideology," *American Political Science Review*, 64, 3 (September, 1970), 1199–1219.

[10] See Bradburn, *Structure of Well-Being*; and Ted Gurr, *Why Men Rebel* (Princeton: Princeton University Press, 1970).

[11] See Campbell *et al., Quality of American Life.*

other domains, their impact on Overall Life Satisfaction becomes even smaller.

Let us summarize the ideas that have just been outlined. We hypothesize the following:

1. One's Overall Life Satisfaction can be viewed as the sum of one's satisfaction with each of the various aspects of life, weighted by each domain's importance to the given individual. Satisfaction tends to be generalized from one domain to another, but only to a limited extent.

2. One's satisfaction with a given aspect of life is determined by the size of the gap between:

a. One's perception of his or her current situation; and

b. One's level of aspirations.

3. Aspirations tend to adjust to one's circumstances. People adjust them in two ways:

a. By upward or downward shifts in the *level* of aspirations—that is, by aspiring to more or less of the *same* things. One's aspirations rise with prosperity and fall with adversity; but the process is gradual so adjustment is rarely perfect.

b. By changing the *weights* accorded to various aspects of life—that is, through changes in value priorities. This process can neutralize or even reverse the normal relationship between material conditions and subjective satisfaction, causing a group with given value priorities to be less satisfied than another group that objectively seems less favorably placed. The time lags associated with change in value priorities seem to be very sizeable, probably involving inter-generational population replacement.

4. Hence, within any given culture, Overall Subjective Satisfaction will usually show only modest variation across stable social categories:

a. Short-term effects tend to cancel out because those who have had unusually favorable recent personal experiences are likely to be balanced off by those who have had unusually unfavorable recent experiences, in any large social category.

b. Structural differences tend to be offset by the fact that aspiration levels and values gradually adjust to *long-term* differences in objective circumstances.

5. Nevertheless, we may find relatively large *cross-national* differences in satisfaction levels:

a. Insofar as a nation constitutes a distinct cultural unit, its people may display a relative homogeneity of values and expectations, by comparison with members of other cultures. Since different cultures may assign different weight to given domains, satisfaction levels may vary a great deal even among societies facing similar external circumstances.

b. Moreover, the people of different societies tend to face *different* circumstances. National boundaries still define a key unit of socio-economic experience. The impact of short-term changes is often more sharply differentiated according to nationality than according to other social categories.

III. OVERALL LIFE SATISFACTION: A TEST OF THE LOW INTER-GROUP VARIATION HYPOTHESIS

Our hypotheses imply that one is likely to find only modest differences in the Overall Life Satisfaction levels of various social groups within given nations. How accurate is this prediction? Let us examine actual data from nine countries.

The 1973 European Community surveys asked a series of cross-nationally standardized questions about how satisfied one was with a number of important aspects of life, and with one's life as a whole. Table 5–1 shows the percentage "very satisfied" with

TABLE 5–1. Percentage "Very Satisfied" with Their Lives as a Whole, by Family Income: Combined Nine-Nation Sample, 1973

Under $200/month	28%	(1,618)
$200–399	24	(2,665)
$400–599	29	(2,640)
$600–799	30	(1,695)
$800–999	31	(1,428)
$1,000 and over	37	(824)

their lives as a whole in the combined nine-nation sample. Satisfaction does increase somewhat as one moves from the lowest income group to the highest, but the change is not dramatic—an increase of nine percentage points. The modest size of this change has nothing to do with the fact that we have, for simplicity of presentation, pooled data from nine different countries. The same pattern appears when we examine the results from each country separately.

Table 5–1 gives a concrete idea of the relationship between one social background variable (income) and one measure of satisfaction (with one's life as a whole): the relationship proves to be rather weak, as hypothesized. Does this finding reflect an isolated fluke, or is it the prevailing pattern? In order to answer this question, we looked at the relationships between every available indicator of subjective satisfaction and a large array of social background characteristics, in each of our nine countries. We found that Table 5–1 was, in fact, indicative of the general pattern. To demonstrate this fact, we will examine the relationship between a broadly based multi-item index of subjective satisfaction, and an entire set of background variables, simultaneously controlling for the effects of each background variable in a multi-variate analysis.

Our first step in doing this is to analyze the way in which the responses to our various questions about satisfaction go together empirically. Otherwise, we would be in danger of adding apples to oranges when we summed up an individual's responses to produce an index of satisfaction. The 1973 surveys inquired about each respondent's satisfaction in twelve different domains.[12] Table 5–2 shows the results of a factor analysis of responses to these questions. Again, in order to summarize a large bulk of material, we will show the results for our combined nine-nation European sample.

The items fall into two main clusters. The first factor clearly taps an Overall Satisfaction dimension. The highest-loading item is satisfaction with one's "life as a whole," which has a loading

[12] The wording was: "I would like to ask you how you regard certain aspects of your present situation. I will read out a number of aspects and for each of them I would like you to say whether you are very satisfied, fairly satisfied, not very satisfied, or not at all satisfied?" The respondent was asked about: "The house, flat or place where you live; your income; your work (as a housewife, in a job, at school); education for children; your leisure (spare time); the social welfare benefits you would receive if you became ill or unable to work; in general terms, your relations with others; the kind of society in which we live in (Britain) today; relations between the generations; the way democracy is functioning in (Britain)." Respondents were then asked: "On the whole, are you very satisfied, fairly satisfied, not very satisfied, or not at all satisfied with the life you lead?" Finally, they were asked: "Do you think, generally speaking, that people give you the respect which you deserve, or not?"

TABLE 5–2. Dimensions of Subjective Satisfaction in Nine
European Countries, 1973
(Loadings above .300 in conventional factor analysis)

First Factor: Overall Satisfaction (32% of variance)		Second Factor: Socio-Political Satisfaction (10% of variance)	
Life as a whole	.722	How democracy	
Leisure time	.622	functions in (Britain)	.625
Personal income	.616	Kind of society in which	
Work—at job, home, school	.613	we live	.580
Kind of society in which		Relations between	
we live	.577	generations	.393
Relations with others	.572	Work—at job, home,	
House, apartment in which		school	−.342
we live	.551		
Education for children	.538		
How democracy functions			
in (Britain)	.518		
Relations between generations	.486		
Social welfare benefits	.479		
Respect people give you	.406		

of .722. But all twelve of the domains have loadings of at least .400 on this factor. The pattern tends to support the conclusion reached by Andrews and Withey that satisfaction is additive, and that satisfaction with "your life as a whole" reflects a summed-up response to a variety of other domains.

Satisfaction seems to be generalized from one domain to another to a considerable extent, for all of the bivariate correlations are positive—in most instances rather strongly so. Consequently, the first factor alone explains 32 percent of the total variance among these items—a substantial amount, although part of it is no doubt due to response set (these items were not asked in forced-choice format, but in a uniform series). If you are satisfied in one domain, it apparently tends to pull up your score in other areas.

Separate country-by-country factor analyses also were performed. The pattern is remarkably similar from one nation to another, which suggests that these questions have similar meanings throughout the nine nations. In each country, the items fall into two clusters, the first of which accounts for about three times as much variance as the second. The first and larger cluster in every country can be described as an Overall Life Satisfaction group, similar to the one shown in Table 5–2.

The second cluster is dominated by one's satisfaction with two other domains: "the kind of society in which we live" and satisfaction with "the way democracy is functioning in (Britain, France, etc.)." Satisfaction with these domains is positively correlated with one's Overall Life Satisfaction, but the linkage is weaker than for the other domains. Socio-political Satisfaction (as we will call it) is a relatively autonomous aspect of the quality of life, and it varies in a distinctive fashion. Furthermore, let us note that our nine European publics give predominately positive responses to the items in the Overall Life Satisfaction cluster; but the number of "dissatisfied" responses actually outweighs the "satisfied" responses concerning Socio-political Satisfaction.

This analysis enables us to identify two groups of items that tap two rather distinct aspects of subjective satisfaction. These items cluster together in much the same way cross-nationally. It seems that we can combine one's responses to items from a given cluster in order to obtain a measure of satisfaction with a specific broad aspect of life. We constructed an index of Overall Life Satisfaction by summing the responses to the four highest-loading items on the first factor in Table 5–2. Scores range from "1" ("very dissatisfied" with all four items) to "13" ("very satisfied" with all four items). A similar index was constructed using a set of almost identical items included in a survey of consumer attitudes among the American public conducted by the Survey Research Center in May, 1972.[13] Using this index as our dependent variable, we then tried to "explain" relative levels of satisfaction in terms of the following social background variables: age, sex, income, occupation, education, religious denomination, church attendance, political party identification, political information, labor union membership, region, size of community in which the respondent lives, mother tongue (in Belgium), race (in the United States), and value type.

We used the foregoing variables as predictors of Overall Satisfaction in Multiple Classification Analyses (MCA).[14] The results

[13] For a description of this survey, see the appendix to Burkhard Strumpel (ed.), *Economic Means for Human Needs* (Ann Arbor: Institute for Social Research, 1976). I am indebted to Strumpel and to Frank Andrews and Stephen Withey for sharing these data with me.

[14] We used the OSIRIS II Multiple Classification Analysis program for this purpose. See John A. Sonquist, *Multivariate Model Building: The Val-*

of this analysis confirm the impression one gets from Table 5–1. In both the European countries and in the United States, our battery of social background variables explains relatively little variance in subjective satisfaction. As Table 5–3 indicates, the average figure is only 10 percent across our nine countries, with the figures for given countries ranging from a low of 8 percent to a high of 13 percent. These figures are surprisingly low. For comparison,

TABLE 5–3. Attitudinal Variance Explained by Social Structure in Nine Nations[a]

(Percent of total variance explained by multiple classification analysis model using standard social background predictor variables)

Nation:	Left-Right Self-Placement	Political Party Identification	Voting Intention	Value Priorities	Overall Life Satisfaction
France	51%	37%	28%	35%	12%
Netherlands	41	43	35	22	10
Belgium	16	49	43	23	12
Italy	58	25	25	24	10
Denmark	35	28	23	28	11
Britain	45	25	26	12	13
Germany	31	27	23	28	8
Ireland	10	2	4	15	12
United States	8	37	27	17	6
Mean, all nations	33	30	26	23	10

[a] This analysis not run for Luxembourg because of inadequate sample size.

we might note that the same set of background variables explains 30 percent of the variance in political party identification on the average across the nine countries, with the figure rising to 49 percent in given cases. To further put our findings into perspective, Table 5–3 also shows the results of similar analyses using three other dependent variables. In connection with voting intention, value priorities and self-placement on a Left-Right scale (or a Liberal-Conservative scale in the United States), our predictor variables explain two or three times as much variance as they do with our Overall Satisfaction index. In short, there is a tendency

idation of a Research Strategy (Ann Arbor: Institute for Social Research, 1970).

for satisfaction levels to remain relatively constant across all of the social characteristics included in our analyses.

There are a variety of possible explanations for this striking lack of variance according to age, sex, income, education, and so forth. For example, our items simply might not do a very good job of measuring subjective satisfaction. But most of these items were adapted from previous studies in which they had been tested and validated exhaustively. Another explanation might be that no real attitude exists to be measured here. In response to questions about which they know or care very little, people some-times give meaningless answers more or less at random. Such re-sponses would tend to show null relationships with social back-ground characteristics. But surely people must know and care whether they are satisfied with their own incomes, leisure, work, and life in general; these are immediate concerns that involve them directly. One indication that a question seems remote or mean-ingless to one's respondents is an abnormally high non-response rate—sometimes running as high as 30 percent of a sample. But non-response rates here were extremely *low*, averaging less than 4 percent regarding one's income, leisure, and work, and less than *1* percent regarding one's life as a whole. It would seem that inter-group differences really are relatively small and, by implication, that a process of accommodation is taking place.

Still, we do explain *some* variance. Which variables account for it? Table 5–4 shows the mean satisfaction scores for a number of the social groups included in a Multiple Classification Analysis of the combined nine-nation sample. It reveals an interesting fact. When nationality is used as a predictor it explains more variance than any other variable. Indeed, nationality explains more variance than *all* our other variables combined. Alone it accounts for 13 percent of the total variance. As Table 5–4 indicates, mean satis-faction scores range from a low of "7.1" among the Italian public to a high of "10.4" among the Danes. These cross-national differ-ences are substantial and quite intriguing. We will explore them in some detail in the following chapter. Here we will simply note that the nation seems to be a key unit of analysis for the study of the Quality of Life.

After nationality, one's family income proves to be the second strongest predictor of satisfaction scores—in keeping with our hypothesis that relatively fluctuating characteristics such as income would be linked with greater variation than fixed characteristics

TABLE 5-4. Overall Satisfaction Scores by Social Background in Nine European Countries, 1973 (Mean scores on Overall Satisfaction index)[a]

Nationality

Denmark	10.4	(1,171)
Netherlands	9.9	(1,388)
Belgium	9.9	(1,214)
Luxembourg	9.8	(300)
Ireland	9.5	(1,171)
Britain	8.8	(1,904)
Germany	8.2	(1,894)
France	8.1	(2,122)
Italy	7.1	(1,832)

Family Income

Under $200/month	8.2	(1,570)
$200–$399	8.3	(2,582)
$400–$599	8.8	(2,586)
$600–$799	9.1	(1,658)
Over $800/month	9.4	(2,368)
Not ascertained	9.0	(2,232)

Education (age at which respondent left school)

15 years or younger	8.5	(7,091)
16–19 years	9.1	(4,295)
20 years or older	9.2	(1,610)

Sex

Male	8.8	(6,294)
Female	8.8	(6,699)

Value Type

Materialist	8.8	(6,765)
Score = 1	8.9	(2,338)
Score = 2	9.0	(1,742)
Score = 3	8.9	(1,106)
Score = 4	8.8	(749)
Post-Materialist	8.7	(673)

Age

15–19	8.8	(1,013)
20–24	8.8	(1,394)
25–34	8.8	(2,496)
35–44	8.7	(2,390)
45–54	8.8	(2,140)
55–64	8.9	(1,759)
65+	9.0	(1,801)

Occupation, Head of Family

Non-manual	9.1	(4,617)
Farm	8.6	(1,014)
Manual	8.6	(4,634)
Retired; housewife	8.6	(2,731)

Church Attendance

At least once/week	9.0	(4,136)
At least a few times per year	8.7	(4,406)
Never; no church	8.7	(4,427)

Party Identification

Respondent feels closest to a party of the:

Right	9.1	(3,573)
None; Center	8.8	(5,339)
Left	8.6	(4,084)

[a] A score of 13.0 (the maximum) indicates that the individual is "very satisfied" with his or her income, work, leisure and life as a whole; a score of 1.0 indicates that the respondent is "very dissatisfied" with all four; a score of 7.0 is neutral. Mean for total sample is 8.8. Figures in parentheses indicate the number of cases on which the given mean score is based.

such as sex. Let us note, in the latter connection, that we find literally no variation *whatever* in satisfaction levels according to sex. Similarly, we find almost none connected with value type, despite the fact that Post-Materialists tend to have relatively high incomes. None of the other variables shows large differences in satisfaction from one group to another. Education, occupation, and political party preference do appear to have some impact, but it is considerably weaker than that linked with income. Even income makes a rather modest contribution to explaining levels of Overall Satisfaction. From those with incomes under $200 a month to those with incomes over $800 a month, satisfaction levels vary by only 1.2 points—which is slightly less than half a standard deviation. In no country does it account for more than 3 or 4 percent of the total variance.

Our findings, based on data from eight European Community countries and the United States, are consistent with the hypothesis that there is a long-term tendency for Overall Subjective Satisfaction to remain constant across social categories of a given society. Similarly, in an analysis of data from four Nordic countries, Allardt reports that "A striking fact is revealed when the satisfaction measures are related to common background variables such as . . . occupation, education, sex, age, etc. It appears that within each country the overall satisfaction level tends to be surprisingly constant across categories defined by social characteristics."[15] The distribution of prosperity, prestige, and opportunities for self-expression is uneven across these categories. Yet we find remarkably little variation in Overall Satisfaction from one category to another.

The phenomenon is not intuitively obvious. Everyone *knows* that women earn less money than men and suffer from a variety of disadvantages; yet the Overall Subjective Satisfaction levels of the two sexes appear to be identical. Everyone knows that in the United States the objective conditions of blacks are considerably worse than those of whites. Yet the Overall Satisfaction levels of the two races differ to only a modest degree. The latter finding is truly astonishing; but it has been established not only here but

[15] See Erik Allardt, "The Question of Interchangeability of Objective and Subjective Social Indicators of Well-Being." Paper presented to the 1976 Congress of the International Political Science Association, Edinburgh, August 16–24, 1976, 5.

also in several other American surveys.[16] Even more astonishingly, a recent study indicates that individuals with severe physical handicaps—muscular diseases, paralysis, missing limbs, or blindness—do not differ significantly from other people in their subjective satisfaction levels.[17] Surprising as it may seem, but in keeping with our hypotheses, Overall Subjective Satisfaction tends to remain constant across social categories within a given culture.

IV. Change and Satisfaction

We argued that subjective satisfaction is influenced by recent *changes*, more than by absolute levels of need satisfaction. A conclusive test of this hypothesis will, of course, require a substantial longitudinal data base. But some of the items in the 1973 surveys permit us to make a quasi-longitudinal test. Our respondents were asked:

> If you think back to your life five years ago, would you say that you are:
>
> —More satisfied now than you were five years ago?
> —Less satisfied?
> —No change?

If we add this item to our multi-variate analysis, we find that it explains Overall Satisfaction levels rather well. It is a far stronger predictor than any of the social background variables (apart from nationality). Our new MCA model now accounts for 29 percent of the variance in Overall Satisfaction—nearly three times as much as that explained by social background variables alone, in the country-by-country analyses.

The linkage between perceptions of recent improvements and Overall Satisfaction is hardly surprising. Response set may account for some of this relationship. Those who are currently well satisfied probably tend to take a rosy view of recent developments. But the relationship is by no means tautologous. For one's perceptions of *recent* change are a much stronger predictor of current satisfaction than are one's expectations of *future* improvements; and the latter variable should be at least equally vulnerable to

---

[16] See Andrews and Withey, *Social Indicators*, and Campbell *et al.*, *Quality of American Life*.

[17] See Paul Cameron, "Social Stereotypes: Three Faces of Happiness," *Psychology Today* (August, 1974), 62–64.

response set. The former refers to actual experience; the latter must depend, in large part, on one's current general feelings. The question cited above was followed by the query:

Do you think that your everyday conditions will improve over the next five years or not?

—Yes, a lot.
—Yes, a little.
—No, will not.

Table 5–5 shows the variation in satisfaction according to perceptions of *recent* change, and according to expectation of *future* change. We find a spread of 1.7 points across the former variable

TABLE 5–5. Overall Satisfaction by Perception of Recent Change and Expectations of Future Change (Mean scores on Overall Satisfaction index)

By perceptions of recent change:		
More satisfied now than five years ago	9.3	(5,526)
No change	9.1	(4,242)
Less satisfied now than five years ago	7.6	(2,963)
By expectations of future change:		
Will improve a lot over next five years	9.1	(1,891)
Will improve a little over next five years	8.7	(4,555)
Will not improve over next five years	8.5	(4,549)
Don't know	8.3	(2,001)

and one of only .8 points across the latter (interestingly enough, in the latter case the most dissatisfied group are not those who have low expectations, but those who are uncertain). For the nine nations as a whole, perceptions of recent change account for over three times as much variance as do expectations of future improvement. It would seem that recent short-term changes play an important and independent role in shaping one's Overall Satisfaction.

Our data on the effects of short-term changes must be considered with caution. An individual's report of recent changes is less reliable than direct measurements at a series of time points would be. But our data certainly tend to support those theorists who have emphasized the importance of relative deprivation based on longitudinal intra-personal comparisons. Our findings are not inconsistent with the interpretation that a sense of relative deprivation also can spring from cross-sectional comparisons with other groups —but the latter effect seems relatively weak. In general, one's aspiration level seems to be shaped by one's personal experiences more than by the achievement levels of other groups in the same society.

V. Value Priorities and Subjective Satisfaction

Our findings tend to support the hypothesis that aspiration levels gradually adjust to external conditions, with longitudinal intra-personal comparisons playing a key role in shaping subjective satisfaction. Insofar as favorable changes outpace one's aspirations, one experiences a sense of satisfaction.

We have given little attention thus far to possible long-term change in the *nature* of the aspirations prevailing in a society. Such changes could have very important implications. Insofar as people's values change to emphasize new goals, given processes of "favorable" change may no longer produce a sense of satisfaction among that population. Moreover, as long as different groups have different value priorities, a set of conditions that satisfies one group may leave another group relatively dissatisfied. Thus the interplay between external conditions, values and subjective satisfaction is complex and sometimes paradoxical.

A recent study by Alan Marsh illustrates this complexity.[18] Analyzing a 1971 British survey that included our original four-item values index, Marsh found that Post-Materialists did not express higher levels of satisfaction with their material conditions than the Materialists—a fact that is anything but obvious, for the Post-Materialists have substantially higher levels of income and education and more desirable jobs. At first, this finding might seem to contradict any interpretation based on the concept of a need hierarchy. For we have argued that the Post-Materialists have distinctive goals because their lower-order needs have been relatively well satisfied. Does it not follow, therefore, that they should express relatively great satisfaction with their incomes, housing, jobs, health, and so forth?

[18] See Alan Marsh, "The 'Silent Revolution,' Value Priorities and the Quality of Life in Britain," *American Political Science Review*, 69, 2 (March, 1975), 21–30. This is a critique of Ronald Inglehart, "The Silent Revolution in Europe: Intergenerational Change in Post-Industrial Societies," *American Political Science Review*, 65, 4 (December, 1971), 991–1017.

As we have seen, the answer is no. The assumption that they would rests on an understandable but crucial error: the failure to distinguish between the satisfaction of external needs and sub-jective *feelings* of satisfaction. A large body of recent evidence indicates that the relationship between the two is surprisingly loose, and the tendency to equate them can be very misleading. Nevertheless, the word "satisfaction" is generally used to refer to both things, and Marsh equates them, perhaps unconsciously. If the events and the research of recent years have taught us anything in this connection, it is that people can be very well-off objectively, and very dissatisfied subjectively. Let us consider how this happens.

The need-hierarchy concept implies that human beings pursue one goal after another in a more or less predictable order, starting with those which are most crucial to physiological survival; if a given need is satisfied, they tend to move on to pursuit of other "higher-order" needs. "Erst Kommt das Fressen, dann Kommt die Moral," as Brecht put it. It may seem reasonable to assume (as Marsh does) that those who have attained satisfaction of the needs for economic and physical security would be likely to express relatively great *subjective* satisfaction with these domains. But *would* they? The need-hierarchy model states that those who have attained satisfaction of a given set of objective needs will, after a time, shift their priorities, giving greater attention to the pursuit of other needs—not that they would necessarily manifest relatively great *subjective* satisfaction concerning the "lower-order" domains. Maslow states, "What I have observed is that need gratifications lead to only temporary happiness which in turn tends to be succeeded by another and (hopefully) higher discontent."[19] In the short run, gratification of a given need *does* lead to increased subjective satisfaction; in the long run, it does not, and my hypotheses about inter-generational value change very explicitly are concerned with long-term effects. They imply that Post-Materialist value priorities will be found mainly among those who have experienced economic and physical security for a long period of time—throughout their formative years, to be specific. In short, the Post-Materialists are Post-Materialist precisely because they do *not* derive relatively great subjective satisfaction from their relatively favorable material conditions.

[19] Abraham H. Maslow, *Motivation and Personality*, 2nd edition (New York: Harper & Row, 1970), 15.

Marsh's critique helps clarify the nature of value change in Western societies. As he points out, the emergence of a large Post-Materialist minority among the younger age cohorts does not reflect the appearance of an essentially nobler, more altruistic generation. Like everyone else, they are pursuing the needs most salient to them. The change lies in the fact that the Post-Materialists are trying to maximize *different* values from those most emphasized by earlier generations. Marsh argues that Post-Materialists simply are trying to capture the admiration and esteem of their peers in endorsing a change-oriented ideology and supporting the Left. Their behavior reflects nothing more than a desire for Radical Chic. Probably this interpretation captures part, though not the whole, of what has been taking place, and it is entirely consistent with the implications of the Maslovian model on which our interpretation was based. For according to Maslow, needs for a sense of belonging and the esteem of others are precisely what we would *expect* to receive emphasis when the needs for sustenance and physical safety have been secured. It is probable that at least *some* of the Post-Materialists are motivated by a need for self-esteem or self-actualization (which, in practice, might be difficult to distinguish from altruistic behavior). But even if we discount that possibility altogether, Marsh's findings seem to support rather than undermine a Maslovian interpretation.[20]

Most important, Marsh has emphasized a fact that has far-reaching implications. Although their distinctive value priorities may be due to a relatively high level of objective need-satisfaction during formative years, the Post-Materialists do *not* show high levels of subjective satisfaction. On the contrary, they are relatively sensitive to the non-economic shortcomings of advanced industrial society and tend to manifest slightly *lower* levels of satisfaction with many aspects of their lives than other groups.

At first, this finding may seem surprising. Why do the Post-Materialists fail to show higher satisfaction levels? In a thoughtful discussion of the Maslovian need hierarchy, Haranne and Allardt (1974) point out one of its implications: that those who have attained (objective) satisfaction of their lower-order needs should be relatively *dissatisfied* with some of their higher-order needs.[21]

[20] For a detailed analysis and refutation of Marsh's argument, see Ronald Inglehart, "Values, Objective Needs and Subjective Satisfaction among Western Publics," *Comparative Political Studies* (January, 1977), 429–458.
[21] See Markku Haranne and Erik Allardt, *Attitudes Toward Modernity*

One would expect this result if, and only if, the group in question had shifted their value priorities, demanding more in the realm of higher-order needs. Haranne and Allardt have no measure of an individual's value priorities; consequently they are unable to identify any group that ranks high on material need satisfaction yet is relatively dissatisfied with higher-order needs. But if our interpretation is correct, the Post-Materialists should correspond to their description. This group has a high level of material welfare, which they largely take for granted. Consequently, they place more intense emphasis on non-material aspects of life. In contrast to the materialistic majority—for whom a high degree of material welfare casts a favorable halo over all other aspects of life—the Post-Materialists may manifest a relatively *low* level of satisfaction with certain higher-order domains.

Is there any evidence that they do so? The dimensional analysis shown in Table 5–2 reveals two broad types of satisfaction— "Overall Satisfaction" and "Socio-political Satisfaction." This latter dimension taps precisely the type of domain in which we might expect the satisfaction levels of Materialists to differ from those of Post-Materialists. In the first place, these items form a smaller cluster than the broad "Overall Satisfaction" group; response to these two items should have a weaker tendency to be averaged in with other responses than the items in the "Overall Satisfaction" group. Relatively free from the inertia of the much larger cluster, we might expect Socio-political Satisfaction to be more influenced by short-term forces having a differential impact on groups with different values. Moreover, the *content* of these items enhances the likelihood of different types of response. By their very nature, Post-Materialists are presumably less preoccupied with immediate personal needs such as those emphasized in the first cluster, and more sensitive to societal problems; and, theoretically, they evaluate societal performance by different criteria than those emphasized by other value types. While there is no theoretical reason why the Post-Materialists necessarily would be less satisfied with governmental and societal performance than other groups, we know that they constitute a minority in all Western nations. As a relatively small group that has only recently emerged in significant numbers, they live in societies that predominately are oriented

and Modernization: An Appraisal of an Empirical Study (Helsinki: University of Helsinki Press, 1974), 63–71.

toward Materialist goals. There is a rather high probability that they would be overruled frequently.

Finally, the political domain is, as we suggested earlier, one in which entire groups as a whole may experience sharply differentiated changes in their circumstances. For example, in our 1973 British survey, those who supported the Conservative Party showed higher levels of political satisfaction than those who supported any other party. This was consistent with a broader pattern in which supporters of the parties of the Right were more satisfied than those who favored the Left. But it *also* seems to reflect the fact that the Conservatives were the party in power at that time. In Germany, where the Left was in power, the electorate of the Social Democratic Party was more satisfied politically than any other group. And a 1975 survey shows that after the Labour Party had come to power its adherents ranked higher on political satisfaction than any other constituency in Britain.

Is Socio-political Satisfaction more salient to Post-Materialists than to Materialists? We argued that if material needs attain long-term satisfaction, other needs become increasingly relevant to one's Overall Subjective Satisfaction. Thus the *overall* satisfaction levels of the Materialist and Post-Materialist value types are virtually indistinguishable; but the various *components* of Overall Satisfaction may not be equally important for the two groups.

That they are not becomes evident when we perform separate factor analyses of satisfaction levels for each value type. In these analyses all of the items have rather high loadings, as was the case in Table 5–2: there is a fairly strong tendency to generalize satisfaction across domains. Moreover, satisfaction with one's "life as a whole" emerges as the highest-loading item on the first factor among both the Materialist and Post-Materialist subsamples. This factor taps Overall Satisfaction in both cases. But beyond this point, two distinct patterns appear. Among Materialists, satisfaction with one's job, leisure time, and income are the three next highest-loading items—the domains most intimately linked with Overall Satisfaction. Among the Post-Materialists, on the other hand, the second highest-loading item is "the kind of society in which we live," followed by "education for children," "leisure time," and "how democracy is functioning." What happens in the social and political spheres seems to have more impact on the Overall Satisfaction of Post-Materialists than of Materialists.

The relationship between *objective* income and satisfaction with one's life as a whole also shows quite different patterns for the respective value types. Income has less impact on the Overall Satisfaction levels of Post-Materialists than of Materialists. Among the pure Materialist type in our nine-nation sample as a whole, the association between actual family income and Overall Life Satisfaction shows a gamma of .130; among the Post-Materialists, there is a very faint *negative* relationship (gamma $= -.002$).[22] Table 5–6 shows the percentage "very satisfied" with their lives as a whole by income, among the two polar value types. Among

TABLE 5–6. Satisfaction with Life as a Whole by Family Income: Materialists vs. Post-Materialists (Percentage "very satisfied" among combined-nation European sample)

Family Income per Month	Mats.		P.-Mats.	
Under $200	27%	(933)	33%	(55)
$200–399	26	(1,397)	16	(111)
$400–599	30	(1,297)	20	(102)
$600–799	31	(787)	23	(120)
$800–999	31	(728)	24	(98)
Over $1,000	40	(391)	23	(57)

Materialists, Overall Satisfaction increases as we move from low to high family income. Among Post-Materialists there is no clear pattern and the poorest group is *more* satisfied than the wealthiest group. This pattern reappears in the respective national surveys: among Materialists, there is invariably a positive relationship between income and Overall Life Satisfaction. Among the Post-Materialists, the linkage is consistently weaker and we actually find a *negative* relationship in four of the nine countries.

We hypothesized that Post-Materialists are relatively likely to be dissatisfied with their nation's social and political life. As Figure 5–1 illustrates, there is a clear overall tendency for Post-Materialist values to be linked with political dissatisfaction. Satisfaction with income or one's life as a whole shows little relationship with value type; but the linkage between values and political satisfac-

[22] These coefficients are based on the relationship between family income and the item concerning satisfaction with "your life as a whole." Value type is measured by the twelve-item index, hence the "pure" types are the groups at the two extremes among our six categories; respective Ns for Materialists and Post-Materialists are 5,533 and 543.

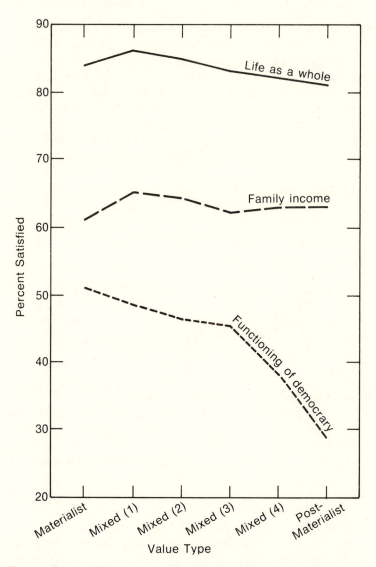

FIGURE 5–1. Satisfaction in Three Domains by Value Type: Europe, 1973.

Percent "satisfied" or "very satisfied" among the combined nine-nation European Community samples, in 1973. Missing data excluded from percentage base.

tion is substantial. In the nine European Community countries as a whole 51 percent of the polar Materialist type are "satisfied" or "very satisfied" with the way democracy is functioning in their country; only 29 percent of the Post-Materialists are satisfied.

Political dissatisfaction is not *inherent* in Post-Materialist values; however, as Figure 5–2 indicates, the strength of the relationship varies a great deal from one nation to another. In seven of the eight countries shown, the most Post-Materialist group is less satisfied than any other group—sometimes by wide margins. But we do have one deviant case (Denmark) where Post-Materialists are not particularly dissatisfied. There may be an overall likelihood that the Post-Materialists will find themselves disappointed by the outputs of their political institutions. But these institutions vary from country to country; and at any given time, relatively conservative forces may hold office in one, while relatively progressive groups hold office in another. Thus, one can find intense political dissatisfaction at either the Materialist or Post-Materialist end of the continuum.

Without question, the most striking illustration of this fact is provided by the Italian neo-Fascists. The supporters of this party are more heavily skewed toward the Materialist extreme than any other electorate among fifty-two parties for which we had data in 1973. At the same time, they were politically the *least* satisfied of the fifty-two groups. The neo-Fascists are not the only example of a dissatisfied Materialist group. In Denmark, a long reign by the Social Democrats instituted one of the most advanced (and expensive) welfare states in the world. Here, the more or less Poujadist "Progress Party" provides another example of a Materialist but relatively dissatisfied constituency.

Political dissatisfaction can be found at either end of the values continuum. Yet the global tendency is clear: Dissatisfaction is most prevalent among the Post-Materialists. A relatively small minority in predominately Materialist societies, they are relatively apt to perceive a disparity between their own values and the society that surrounds them.

Satisfaction with "the society in which we live" shows a pattern quite similar to that of satisfaction with "the way democracy is functioning." To permit a more reliable analysis of this dimension, we constructed an index of "Socio-political Satisfaction" based on responses to these two items.[23] Using this as our dependent var-

[23] This index simply sums each individual's satisfaction levels for the two

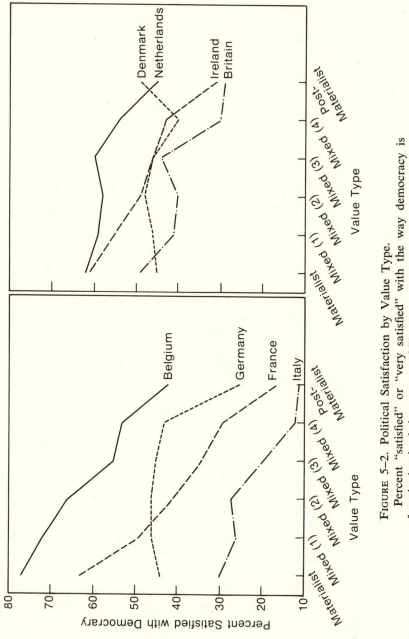

FIGURE 5–2. Political Satisfaction by Value Type.
Percent "satisfied" or "very satisfied" with the way democracy is
functioning in their country, 1973.

iable, we then carried out Multiple Classification Analyses similar to the one shown in Table 5–4 for each national sample and for the combined nine-nation European Community sample. Results from the latter analysis are shown in Table 5–7. Once again, nationality is the strongest predictor of satisfaction. But in other respects, the pattern is quite different from that governing Overall Satisfaction scores. For one thing, the mean score is slightly on the *negative* side. While European publics seem to be predominately satisfied with their lives as a whole (and with the material aspect in particular) there is more dissatisfaction than satisfaction with social and political life. Furthermore, there is virtually no variance in Socio-political Satisfaction according to income. In contrast with what we found in connection with Overall Satisfaction, the higher income groups are no more satisfied than the lower income groups. The same holds true of occupation; in fact, while those with non-manual occupations showed the highest *Overall* Satisfaction, they have the lowest *Socio-political* Satisfaction.

We have already pointed out a fact that helps explain the weakened or reversed relationships with income and occupation. Post-Materialists (who have better incomes and occupations) are decidedly less satisfied than Materialists. The average Socio-political Satisfaction score for the Materialists is 4.0—which happens to be the neutral point between satisfaction and dissatisfaction. The intermediate value types fall toward progressively lower levels of satisfaction; while the group at the Post-Materialist pole has a mean score of 3.2—which makes them less satisfied than eight of the nine nationalities—only the Italians rank lower. Our multivariate analysis indicates that value type is the second strongest predictor of Socio-political Satisfaction. Only nationality explains more variance among the predictors shown in Table 5–7. As was true with Overall Satisfaction, the percentage of total variance explained in this analysis is modest: merely 12 percent. As we suggested above, a process of accommodation probably dampens the variation in satisfaction ratings. Nevertheless, the relationship between values and Socio-political Satisfaction is unquestionably significant. And though it varies a good deal from one setting to another, this analysis indicates that the relationship is not spurious: after adjusting for the effect of income, education, age, politi-

---

items, producing an index with scores ranging from "1" ("Very dissatisfied" with both) to "7" ("Very satisfied" with both).

TABLE 5–7. Socio-Political Satisfaction Scores by Social Background in Nine European Countries
(Mean scores on political satisfaction index: Maximum = 7.0)[a]

Nationality

Belgium	4.6	(1,253)
Luxembourg	4.6	(323)
Ireland	4.3	(1,198)
Netherlands	4.1	(1,423)
Denmark	4.0	(1,199)
Germany	4.0	(1,946)
Britain	3.8	(1,931)
France	3.7	(2,166)
Italy	3.1	(1,903)

Family Income

Under $200/month	3.9	(1,616)
$200–$399	3.8	(2,639)
$400–$599	3.9	(2,644)
$600–$799	4.0	(1,700)
Over $800	3.9	(2,414)
Income refused, not ascertained	4.0	(2,329)

Education (age at which respondent left school)

15 years or younger	3.9	(7,212)
16–19 years	4.0	(4,379)
20 years or older	3.7	(1,674)

Value Type

Materialist Score = 1	4.0	(6,765)
Score = 2	4.0	(2,338)
Score = 3	3.9	(1,742)
Score = 4	3.7	(1,106)
	3.5	(749)
Post-Materialist	3.2	(673)

Age

15–24	3.8	(3,619)
25–34	3.9	(2,448)
35–44	3.9	(2,273)
45–54	3.9	(1,913)
55–64	3.9	(1,771)
65+	4.1	(1,176)

Occupation, Head of Family

Farm	4.2	(1,055)
Retired; housewife	3.9	(2,806)
Manual	3.9	(4,741)
Non-manual	3.8	(4,740)

Sex

Male	3.8	(6,514)
Female	4.0	(6,823)

Church Attendance

More than once/week	4.0	(685)
Weekly	4.1	(3,599)
Several times/year	3.9	(4,512)
Never; no church	3.7	(4,546)

Party Identification

Respondent feels closest to a party of the:

Right	4.0	(3,677)
None; center, other	3.9	(5,475)
Left	3.8	(4,190)

[a] A score of 7.0 on this index indicates that the individual is "very satisfied" with "the kind of society in which we live in (Britain) today" and with "the way democracy is functioning in (Britain)." A score of 1.0 indicates that the individual is "very dissatisfied" with both; a score of 4.0 is neutral.

cal party, and so forth, we find that values account for more variance than any other explanatory variable within a given nation.

As Marsh discovered, Post-Materialists are not any more satisfied with their lives or even with their incomes than Materialists; they may sometimes even be a little less so, partly because higher economic expectations offset the effects of their higher objective level. But it seems equally important that the Post-Materialists have shifted emphasis among the criteria by which satisfaction is gauged to the point where income has little relationship to subjective satisfaction. Conversely, the political and social life of their nation is a relatively important component of their Overall Satisfaction and tends to be judged negatively.

VI. Conclusion

Overall Subjective Satisfaction varies surprisingly little from one social group to another—a seemingly negative finding that actually must reflect an immense human capacity to adapt and change— for high satisfaction levels appear to be inherently fragile. Favorable changes in external conditions may raise an individual's satisfaction level, but in the long run rising aspirations—and in the still longer run, changing values—tend to neutralize the effects.

While increased prosperity may produce a short-term sense of gratification, an individual gradually adjusts his aspiration level to his external circumstances; after a certain time lag, one takes a given level of prosperity for granted and aspires to more. Thus, structural differences in material welfare among groups with a stable membership are linked with surprisingly small differences in subjective satisfaction. Furthermore, generation units that have never been deprived of given needs apparently shift their value priorities to emphasize qualitatively different goals. For such groups, relatively high levels of material need satisfaction may actually be associated with relatively *low* levels of Overall Satisfaction if they experience frustration in the pursuit of their most highly valued goals.

Thus it is only an apparent paradox that Post-Materialists fail to show relatively high levels of subjective satisfaction with their lives as a whole or even with the material aspects of life. For by its very definition, this group has distinctive value priorities. It places less emphasis on material welfare and more on qualitative aspects of society than other groups.

Under the circumstances prevailing in the 1970's, Post-Materialists tended to show lower levels of Socio-political Satisfaction than Materialists. The implications of this fact may be far-reaching. While in earlier periods of Industrial society, political dissatisfaction usually may have had its origins in material conditions and been concentrated among low income groups, our findings suggest that the relatively prosperous Post-Materialists may now comprise the leading center of political dissatisfaction. Partly as a consequence of this development, Socio-political Dissatisfaction was no longer concentrated primarily among the working class. While those with non-manual occupations show the highest Overall Satisfaction, they have the *lowest* Socio-political Satisfaction. Accordingly, Post-Materialist elements of the middle class may offer a base of new support for parties of the Left and a key potential source of political protest.

Protest does not automatically result from dissatisfaction. It requires appropriate organizations, leaders, issues, skills, and a sense of efficacy before it is put in practice. Political protest was at a low ebb in Western countries in the mid-1970's. But political *dissatisfaction* had by no means disappeared. It apparently had shifted its center of gravity to a new social base, but remained widespread.

CHAPTER 6

Subjective Satisfaction: Cross-Cultural and Cross-Temporal Variations

In the preceding chapter we hypothesized that satisfaction with one's life as a whole tends to remain constant across the social categories of a given culture; and the evidence supports this assumption. But the qualifying phrase, "of a given culture," is extremely important, for while Overall Life Satisfaction shows only modest variation from group to group *within* any given nation, it shows a great deal of variation from one country to another.

I. CROSS-NATIONAL DIFFERENCES IN OBJECTIVE WELFARE

There are many ways in which one could conceivably explain this cross-national variation. One of the most obvious possibilities (and one which seems intuitively plausible) is that given nations show different levels of subjective satisfaction simply because they are better-off than others: their populations enjoy higher incomes, better housing, better medical care, more agreeable climates, and so forth. In short, better objective conditions lead directly to greater subjective satisfaction.

But this temptingly simple explanation of the cross-national differences is virtually identical to the explanatory model that has just proven spectacularly inadequate in explaining individual-level differences in life satisfaction. Objective conditions do have an impact on individual life satisfaction; but the relationship is shaped in crucial ways by internal aspirations and values that can themselves change (though with important time lags). A moment's reflection makes it apparent that the objectively determined model is not likely to provide an adequate explanation of the cross-national differences either.

True, the Italian public ranks lowest on Overall Life Satisfaction and Italy is one of the poorest and most troubled countries in our sample; thus far, the model seems promising. But beyond this point we run into gross inconsistencies. Ireland is poorer than Italy; and at the time of our survey the Irish not only were subsisting on the lowest per capita income to be found among these countries but also were suffering one of the highest inflation rates (as high as the Italian) *and* one of the highest unemployment rates (far higher than the Italian). As if this were not enough, a virtual civil war was taking place in Northern Ireland;[1] yet the Irish public (and also the public of Northern Ireland!) shows a relatively high level of overall satisfaction, ranking well above the Italians, French, Germans, and British. Conversely, the Danes (with the second highest per capita income, though with high unemployment) were the most satisfied public; but the Germans (with the *highest* per capita income of the nine and a remarkably good overall economic performance) ranked seventh among the nine countries in overall satisfaction. Easterlin reports a similar finding based on analysis of Cantril's cross-national data. He finds little positive association between income and happiness levels among countries.[2]

We suspect that threshold effects may be involved. In extremely impoverished societies like India, with per capita revenues around $100 per year and millions of people literally starving, Overall Life Satisfaction may be very low. But as one rises above the subsistence level, economic factors probably become less relevant to overall satisfaction and happiness. *All* of the European Community countries have per capita revenues at least fifteen times as high as India's. Some of these countries are less prosperous than others, but are far above the subsistence level. Within the industrialized West, then, it is virtually impossible to interpret the observed cross-national life satisfaction levels as a direct reflection of objective welfare. Do the cross-national differences reflect the influence

[1] In 1975, for the first time, the European Community surveys gathered data from Northern Ireland as well as the rest of the United Kingdom. Furthermore, Northern Ireland was oversampled, in order to provide enough cases to permit a reasonably accurate estimate of opinion in that region (N = 300). Satisfaction levels in Northern Ireland were closer to those in the Republic of Ireland than to those in Great Britain, although all of these interviews were carried out in English. As noted above, the Irish public ranked surprisingly high on Overall Life Satisfaction; but the public of Northern Ireland ranked slightly *higher* on this characteristic than their neighbors to the South. Northern Ireland is not included in Table 6–3, below, since it was not surveyed in 1973; if it were, it would rank tenth out of 56 regions, with a mean score of "16.04."

[2] See Richard A. Easterlin, "Does Economic Growth Improve the Human Lot? Some Empirical Evidence," in Paul A. David and Melvin W. Reder (eds.), *Nations and Households in Economic Growth* (New York: Academic Press, 1974), 89, 126.

of long-term cultural factors? Or could it be that they reflect nothing more than a transient fluke, attributable perhaps to sampling error?

Time series data are needed in order to determine whether we are dealing with an accident or a deep-seated pattern, and fortunately some such data are available.[3] Figure 6–1 shows responses to the question concerning satisfaction with "your life as a whole" from surveys carried out in nine European Community countries at three points in time. The pattern shows extremely high stability across time for the nine nations as a whole—although there is a very gradual, almost glacial, movement downward across the two-year period. The proportion "very satisfied" moves from 21 percent to 20 percent to 19 percent with a corresponding increase in the proportion that is "very dissatisfied." The four categories of response at each point in time are summed up in a weighted index that mirrors this downward trend: it stands at 2.97 in September, 1973, at 2.94 in May, 1975, and 2.90 in October-November, 1975.

How stable are the relative positions of given nations across these three points in time? Figure 6–2 depicts the pattern, using the index just described, to sum up a given nation's responses.[4] The stability of both absolute and relative positions is impressive. Apart from the fact that in May, 1975, the Belgian sample shows a slight upward fluctuation while the Irish show a small downward fluctuation, the rank orders of all eight countries are identical at all three points in time. None of the four larger countries shows any variation whatsoever in rank order. In absolute terms, all eight publics were a little less satisfied in the Fall of 1975 than they were

[3] The European Community sponsored nine-nation surveys in May, 1975, and October-November, 1975, as part of a program to take regular readings of public opinion. In this series of surveys, slightly more than one thousand interviews were carried out in each of the European Community countries, except Luxembourg (where N = 300); and, as noted above, the British sample is supplemented by an additional 300 interviews in Northern Ireland. Fieldwork was carried out by IFOP (France), Nederlands Instituut voor de Publieke Opinie (NIPO-Netherlands), DOXA (Italy), Irish Marketing Surveys (Ireland), Gallup Markedsanalyse (Denmark), INRA (Belgium and Luxembourg), Gallup Polls, Ltd. (Britain), and EMNID-Institut (Germany).

[4] The results from Luxembourg show greater fluctuations than any of the larger countries, due to the small number of interviews gathered in that country (approximately 300 at each point in time). Accordingly, Luxembourg is not depicted in Figure 6–2. Even this relatively unreliable sample fluctuates within rather narrow limits, remaining between the Danish and British levels.

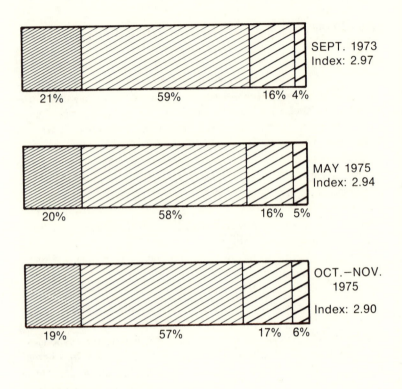

| SEPT. 1973 | |
| Index: 2.97 | |

21% 59% 16% 4%

MAY 1975
Index: 2.94

20% 58% 16% 5%

OCT.–NOV.
1975

Index: 2.90

19% 57% 17% 6%

 Fairly Satisfied
Very Satisfied
Not Very Satisfied
Not at All Satisfied

FIGURE 6–1. Overall Life Satisfaction in the Nine-Nation European Community Combined at Three Points in Time.

Index is calculated by scoring "very satisfied" responses as "4," "fairly satisfied" as "3," "not very satisfied" as "2," and "not at all satisfied" as "1," in response to the question about satisfaction with one's life as a whole.

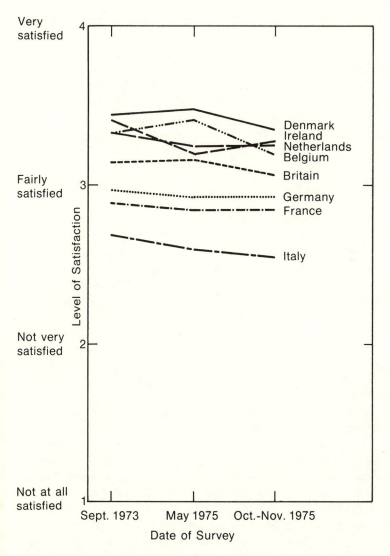

FIGURE 6–2. Overall Life Satisfaction Levels in the Eight Larger European Community Countries.

Levels are based on mean satisfaction indices for the given country, calculated as in Figure 6–1. An index of 4.00 would indicate that everyone in the given sample was "very satisfied"; an index of 1.00 would mean that everyone was "not at all satisfied" with his life as a whole.

in September, 1973, but the change is small in every case. Unmistakeably, the cross-national differences do not reflect an accident, but a real and remarkably deep-seated attribute of the respective publics.

But what is the nature of this attribute? Are the French and Italians really less satisfied with their lives than the Danes and Irish? Or is there simply some pervasive tendency for Frenchmen and Italians to *say* they are less contented than people in other countries? Or could we be dealing with an artifact of translation?

II. LANGUAGE AND SATISFACTION

Let us consider the latter possibility first. Translation from one language to another rarely if ever achieves perfect equivalence, so it is always somewhat hazardous to compare absolute response levels cross-nationally if the surveys were carried out in different languages. It is conceivable that subjective satisfaction tends to remain constant across nationality, as across other social characteristics, but that *measurement* is especially prone to distortion on a cross-national basis. For example, "très satisfait" may mean something quite different from and more demanding than "very satisfied" or "sehr zufrieden" or "molto soddisfatto." This is possible. But the available evidence indicates that the cross-national differences are *not* artifacts of translation.

One indication derives from the fact that about half of our Belgian interviews were conducted in French and the other half in Dutch. It turns out that the Francophone Belgians show satisfaction levels that are not only higher than those from France as a whole but also higher than those from any *region* within France. Both French-speaking and Flemish-speaking Belgians are more satisfied with their lives than the French. Thus, the line of demarcation seems to follow national rather than linguistic frontiers.

The 1972 Swiss survey provides an even richer source of comparisons, since its interviews were conducted in German, French, and Italian. The questions posed in Switzerland were not identical to those used in the European Community, and did not include a question about satisfaction with one's life as a whole. But some of the Swiss questions are close approximations of those asked elsewhere, and should permit rough comparisons. For example, in both Switzerland and the European Community, our respondents were asked how well satisfied they were with their incomes.

The Swiss questionnaire contained the alternatives "very satisfied," "fairly satisfied," "satisfied," "not very satisfied," and "not at all satisfied." The European Community questionnaire offered only the first two and last two alternatives. If we are willing to assume that "satisfied" is a basically positive response, whereas the alternatives "not very satisfied" and "not at all satisfied" can be grouped together as negative ones, we can make cross-national comparisons in which nearly every language employed was used in more than one country. Table 6–1 shows the results. The Ger-

TABLE 6–1. Satisfaction with Income in
Western Europe
(Percentage ''not very satisfied'' or
''not at all satisfied'')[a]

Switzerland (German)	11%
Netherlands	16
Belgium (Dutch)	16
Switzerland (French)	18
Denmark	19
Switzerland (Italian)	25
Belgium (French)	28
Luxembourg (German dialect)	31
Ireland (English)	37
Germany	41
Britain	43
France	45
Italy	53

[a] In Switzerland the question about income had five alternatives: ''very satisfied,'' ''fairly satisfied,'' ''satisfied,'' ''not very satisfied,'' and ''not at all satisfied''; in the European Community countries, only the first two and last two categories were offered; thus, the ''satisfied'' answer in Switzerland has been treated as a positive response, for purposes of this table. For countries with more than one official language, the language in which the interviews were conducted appears in parentheses. Swiss data are from 1972, data for other countries from 1973.

man-speaking Swiss rank far higher than the Germans as a nation and higher than the respondents of any *region* in Germany; similarly, the French-speaking Swiss rank far higher than the French of any region; and the Italian-speaking Swiss rank far above the Italians. The low rating of the Italians cannot be attributed to the hypothesis that "soddisfatto" indicates a more demanding cutting point than "satisfied," for the Italian-speaking Swiss rank well above both the Irish and British, who were interviewed in English. In addition, every one of the nine groups living in small nations ranks above the populations of each of the four large nations. It appears that there might be a shred of support for the hypothesis that a given language may tend to bias responses downward or upward, however, for the Italian-speaking Swiss rank substantially lower than their compatriots, while the German-speaking Swiss rank at the top—just as, among the large nations, the Italians rank lowest and the Germans rank highest. Can we conclude that (holding nationality constant) it is inherently easier to be "per niente soddisfatto" than to be "gar nicht zufrieden?" It would be rash to do so. For the Italian-speaking region of Switzerland happens to be economically less developed than the German-speaking region, and our Italian-speaking Swiss have a substantially lower average income than the German-speaking Swiss we interviewed; since satisfaction with one's income is related to one's actual income, this rather than anything inherent in the respective languages might explain why the Italian-speaking Swiss rank relatively low in Table 6–1.

Another set of comparisons may help us solve the riddle. In the preceding question, each person interviewed was asked a question that referred to his or her *own* income. Now let us turn to a question in which everyone interviewed in a given nation was asked to respond to the *same* stimulus: the way the country is being run. Again the question asked in Switzerland is not identical to the one asked in the European Community, but this time the same four response categories were offered in Switzerland and in the European Community. The Swiss were asked, "How do you judge the way the Swiss government is running the country? Are you very satisfied, rather satisfied, not very satisfied, or not at all satisfied?" In the European Community, the respondents were asked how well satisfied they were with "The way democracy is functioning in (your country)." The alternatives were "very satisfied," "fairly satisfied," "not very satisfied," and "not at all satisfied." In both Switzerland and the European Community, the political satisfaction question was preceded by a series of items concerning satisfaction with one's housing, job, income, and so on. In response to this item, the Italian-speaking Swiss prove to be *more* satisfied than their German-speaking countrymen. Indeed, they are the

TABLE 6–2. Political Satisfaction in
Western Europe
(Percentage "fairly satisfied" or
"very satisfied")[a]

Switzerland (Italian)	79%
Switzerland (French)	70
Switzerland (German)	68
Belgium (Dutch)	63
Belgium (French)	62
Ireland (English)	55
Luxembourg (German dialect)	52
Netherlands	52
Denmark	45
Germany	44
Britain	43
France	41
Italy	27

[a] The alternatives offered (in every country) were:
"very satisfied," "fairly satisfied," "not very satisfied" and "not at all satisfied."

most satisfied of the thirteen groups; but *all three* of the Swiss
groups rank above any of the others; and both Belgian groups rank
above any of the remaining ones. Nationality rather than language
proves to be the decisive variable in this comparison, and there
is no reason whatever to believe that the cross-national differences
result from the languages used.

III. REGIONAL POLITICAL CULTURES AND SATISFACTION

It appears that distinctive levels of Overall Life Satisfaction are
linked with given geographic or political units rather than with
any particular language. If so, we should examine the effect of one
of the most important institutions linked with given political units,
the political party.

France and Italy are the two countries that rank lowest in life
satisfaction, and these two nations happen to have by far the
largest Communist parties in Western Europe. Could this fact
account for their low satisfaction levels?

Not in any simple and direct fashion—for even when we remove
all Communist party supporters from our samples, the remaining French and Italian respondents *still* rank lower on Overall Life
Satisfaction than any other publics. If a strong Communist im-

plantation leads to dissatisfaction, the effect seems remarkably diffuse. It influences non-Communists (and even anti-Communists) as well as Communists. We cannot rule out this factor altogether; for it is conceivable that a strong Communist presence might, over a period of years, tend to legitimize the *expression* of dissatisfaction among all portions of the political spectrum. Thus, these publics may not actually be less satisfied than any other nationality: they are merely more ready to *say* they are.

The latter hypothesis is difficult to disprove but most analysts would probably attribute widespread support for the Communists to dissatisfaction, rather than the other way around. And indeed, the increased Communist vote in Italy's 1976 elections was preceded by rising political dissatisfaction (see page 172).

The classic studies of regional political cultures in Southern France and Southern Italy by Wylie, Banfield, and Tarrow have concluded that these subcultures are characterized by pervasive distrust and pessimism.[5] While these attributes cannot be equated with subjective satisfaction, they may be related. If they are, our data tend to confirm the conclusions reached by these writers. For Southern Italy ranks lower on overall satisfaction than any other region in the nine nations (with Sicily and Sardinia next above it); and Southeastern and Southwestern France rank lower than any other part of France except the Paris region.

Furthermore, distinctive levels of overall satisfaction seem to be stable attributes of given geographic units, as Wylie, Banfield, Tarrow and others might argue. The region, province, or *Land* in which a respondent lives proves to be a relatively good predictor of overall satisfaction. In nation-by-nation analyses only income ranks above it as an explanatory variable, and given geographic units show distinctively high or low levels of overall satisfaction with an impressive degree of consistency across time. Table 6–3 shows the relative positions held by 55 different geographic units within the European Community, first in September, 1973, and then in May, 1975.[6]

[5] See L. Wylie, *Village in the Vancluse* (Cambridge: Harvard University Press, 1957); Edward C. Banfield, *The Moral Basis of a Backward Society* (Glencoe: Free Press, 1958); and Sidney Tarrow, *Peasant Communism in Southern Italy* (New Haven: Yale University Press, 1967).

[6] The scores shown for 1975, in Table 6–3, are based on responses to *two* questions about satisfaction with "your life as a whole," which have been combined for greater reliability. The first question was identical to the one used in 1973; the second was asked considerably later in the interview

In 1973 the top ranking region in terms of Overall Life Satisfaction was the Dutch province of Drenthe; Denmark's Jutland peninsula ranked second; while the lowest rank, among the fifty-five regions for which we have reliable data, was held by the South of Italy. In 1975, these three regions held exactly the same positions: Drenthe was first, Jutland second, and Southern Italy last. Among the fifteen regions ranking highest in 1973, nine were still in the top fifteen in 1975. Stability is even *more* impressive at the opposite end of the scale. Of the eleven regions that ranked lowest in 1973, nine occupied *exactly* the same rank in 1975, or one adjacent to its previous rank.

In part, this extraordinary stability might be due to the fact that given nations hold their relative positions virtually without change. But there is also a great deal of stability *within* given nations. In The Netherlands, for example, the provinces of Drenthe, Friesland, and Overijssel rank among the four highest provinces in both 1973 and 1975; North Holland, South Holland and Limburg are the three lowest in both years (falling well down the list, around the midpoint of the fifty-five regions). Curiously enough, the Belgium province of Limburg—adjacent to the Dutch province of the same name and similar in language and religion—is one of the two *highest* ranking Belgian provinces in both years, ranking twenty-three places above its Dutch namesake in 1973 and twenty-four places higher in 1975. In Britain, Yorkshire-Humberside, the East Midlands, and the Southeast constitute three of the four highest-ranking regions in both years. Similarly in Germany, Schleswig-Holstein, Lower Saxony, and North Rhine-Westphalia constitute three of the top four in both years; in Italy, the Northeastern and Northwestern regions rank respectively first and second both times; and in France, the seven regions have virtually identical ranks both times, the only change being that the regions which were sixth and seventh in 1973 traded places in 1975.

The French regions contain another interesting case where political boundaries run across linguistic frontiers: in Alsace-Lorraine, a large part of the population speaks German as its native language. Though the interviews were conducted in French, this region manifests a higher satisfaction level than any other part of France. Yet it is uncertain whether one can attribute Alsace-Lor-

---

and uses an eleven-point semantic differential scale, running from "very satisfied" to "completely dissatisfied."

TABLE 6-3. Satisfaction with "Life as a Whole" by Region, 1973 and 1975[a]

	1973[b]			1975[c]	
Rank	Nation, Region, or Province	Mean Score	Rank	Nation, Region, or Province	Mean Score
1.	Netherlands-Drenthe	3.58	1.	Netherlands-Drenthe	17.00
2.	Denmark-Jutland	3.56	2.	Denmark-Jutland	16.94
3.	Belgium-Limburg	3.54	3.	Belgium-Antwerp	16.81
4.	Netherlands-Overijssel	3.54	4.	Denmark-Sealand	16.70
5.	Denmark-Funen	3.52	5.	Netherlands-Friesland	16.57
6.	Ireland-Dublin	3.51	6.	Belgium-Limburg	16.36
7.	Netherlands-Friesland	3.48	7.	Ireland-Munster	16.31
8.	Netherlands-North Brabant	3.48	8.	Netherlands-Zealand	16.28
9.	Belgium-East Flanders	3.48	9.	Ireland-Leinster	16.24
10.	Belgium-Antwerp	3.46	10.	Belgium-West Flanders	15.96
11.	Netherlands-Groningen	3.46	11.	Netherlands-Overijssel	15.85
12.	Ireland-Munster	3.40	12.	Netherlands-Utrecht	15.85
13.	Belgium-West Flanders	3.40	13.	Belgium-Brabant	15.82
14.	Ireland-Leinster	3.40	14.	Britain-East Midlands	15.78
15.	Netherlands-Gelderland	3.39	15.	Ireland-Connaught-Ulster	15.76
16.	Britain-Yorkshire, Humberside	3.37	16.	Belgium-Hainaut	15.60
17.	Denmark-Sealand	3.35	17.	Belgium-Namur	15.60
18.	Netherlands-Utrecht	3.35	18.	Netherlands-Groningen	15.59
19.	Netherlands-Zealand	3.32	19.	Netherlands-North Brabant	15.54
20.	Netherlands-South Holland	3.28	20.	Denmark-Funen	15.42
21.	Belgium-Liege	3.27	21.	Britain-Southwest	15.31
22.	Luxembourg	3.25	22.	Netherlands-Gelderland	15.29
23.	Belgium-Brabant	3.25	23.	Germany-Schleswig-Holstein	15.28
24.	Britain-East Midlands	3.25	24.	Britain-Yorkshire, Humberside	15.26
25.	Netherlands-Limburg	3.20	25.	Britain-London and Southeast	15.21
26.	Belgium-Hainaut		26.	Ireland-Dublin	15.12

No.	Region (1973)[b]	Score	No.	Region (1975)[c]	Score
27.	Netherlands-North Holland	3.1?	27.	Belgium-Liege	
28.	Belgium-Namur	3.19	28.	Britain-Scotland and Wales	14.89
29.	Britain-Scotland and Wales	3.17	29.	Netherlands-Limburg	14.88
30.	Ireland-Connaught-Ulster	3.17	30.	Netherlands-North Holland	14.80
31.	Britain-London and Southeast	3.16	31.	Netherlands-South Holland	14.79
32.	Britain-North	3.16	32.	Luxembourg	14.60
33.	Britain-West Midlands	3.14	33.	Germany-Lower Saxony	14.56
34.	France-Alsace-Lorraine	3.12	34.	Britain-North	14.55
35.	Germany-Hamburg and Bremen	3.11	35.	Britain-West Midlands	14.54
36.	Germany-Schleswig-Holstein	3.09	36.	Britain-Northwest	14.51
37.	Britain-Southwest	3.06	37.	Belgium-East Flanders	14.43
38.	Germany-North Rhine-Westphalia	3.05	38.	Germany-Hesse	14.27
39.	Germany-Lower Saxony	3.03	39.	France-Alsace-Lorraine	13.84
40.	Germany-Hesse	3.03	40.	Germany-North Rhine-Westphalia	13.82
41.	Britain-Northwest	2.99	41.	Germany-Bavaria	13.75
42.	France-Northwest	2.99	42.	Germany-Baden-Wurttemberg	13.70
43.	Germany-Bavaria	2.96	43.	France-Northwest	13.59
44.	Germany-Baden-Wurttemberg	2.96	44.	Germany-Rhine-Palatinate	13.38
45.	France-North, Pas de Calais	2.96	45.	France-North, Pas de Calais	13.37
46.	France-Southeast	2.96	46.	France-Southeast	13.27
47.	France-Paris Basin	2.94	47.	France-Paris Basin	13.03
48.	France-Southwest	2.92	48.	France-Metropolitan Paris	13.03
49.	Italy-Northeast	2.88	49.	France-Southwest	13.00
50.	Germany-Rhine-Palatinate	2.87	50.	Italy-Northeast	12.89
51.	Italy-Northwest	2.78	51.	Germany-Hamburg and Bremen	12.72
52.	France-Metropolitan Paris	2.77	52.	Italy-Northwest	12.51
53.	Italy-Central	2.71	53.	Italy-Islands	12.23
54.	Italy-Islands	2.56	54.	Italy-Central	12.19
55.	Italy-South	2.54	55.	Italy-South	10.63

[a] The Irish regions for 1975 are only approximately comparable with those used in 1973. In several instances, geographic units with small numbers of cases have been combined with other units: thus, Bremen is grouped with Hamburg, Wales with Scotland, and East Anglia with the London and Southeast Unit.

[b] For 1973, mean score on scale ranging from "1" (very dissatisfied) to "4" (very satisfied).

[c] For 1975, mean score on Index ranging from "1" (very dissatisfied) to "20" (very satisfied).

raine's relatively high satisfaction levels to her cultural ties with Germany, for this region also ranks markedly higher than the adjacent regions of Germany and higher than Germany as a whole. Germany herself contains one spectacular anomaly: Hamburg-Bremen ranked first among the German regions in 1973 and last in 1975. But this is the least populous unit included for that country, and consequently the number of interviews is smaller and less reliable than for the other *Länder*.

With reference to Table 6–3 generally, we must bear in mind that we have only a fraction as many interviews from any given region as we have from a given nation. Hence, considering that we have a wider margin of error at this lower level of aggregation, the stability of rankings *within* nations is almost as impressive as the stability *between* nations.

There is no readily apparent linkage between overall satisfaction levels and economic levels among these regions (just as was true at the national level). Southern Italy is one of the poorest regions, and it ranks at the bottom in both years. But Drenthe is the poorest province in a nation of only middling prosperity. Yet it ranks at the *top* in both years. Conversely, metropolitan Paris is France's richest region by far, but it ranks relatively low on subjective satisfaction. We find no simple and obvious explanation for the pattern observed here; it probably reflects the interplay of history, social context and current economic changes.

It seems safe to conclude that relatively stable features of the political cultures of given nations—and of given subnational regions—help influence the level of life satisfaction expressed by the people living in these ecological units. But a full explanation will probably also require data on recent *changes* in such things as per capita income, housing and cost of living, as well as various non-economic aspects of life for those living in a given nation or region. At present, adequate data for such an analysis are not available. Further research combining ecological data with survey data might help us understand the reasons underlying the differences in subjective satisfaction from one geographic unit to another. It seems eminently worthwhile.

IV. Size and Satisfaction

The cross-national differences in satisfaction show a striking characteristic that we have scarcely mentioned but that has probably intrigued the reader: in virtually every instance, the small nations show higher satisfaction levels than the large ones. The remarkable consistency with which the publics of the smaller nations rank above those of the larger nations suggests that life in a small polity may be more satisfying than life in a large one. But smallness *per se* is not the answer. Once we have observed the dichotomy between the four "large" and six "small" nations, there is no relationship between size and satisfaction. Switzerland has a larger population than Denmark or Ireland, and is a positive giant in comparison with Luxembourg, but seems to rank above them all in both economic and political satisfaction. Similarly, Germany is the largest of the four "large" nations but ranks highest in both kinds of satisfaction (and only a trifle below the "small" nations). Furthermore, the United States is several times larger than France or Germany. Yet the American public seems relatively satisfied. Directly comparable data are not available for the United States, but rough comparisons suggest that the American public is *at least* as satisfied as the German, and perhaps has as high a rank as the publics of some smaller nations.

The data just examined show a 1.00 correlation between living in a "small" rather than a "large" nation (as dichotomized above) and relative satisfaction. But unfortunately, we probably have not discovered an eternal verity. It strains one's credulity to assume that the Belgians would have reported relatively high levels of satisfaction during World War I, when their country was the hapless battleground for a war between her neighbors. It seems likely that the people of larger but less devastated nations such as the United States or Great Britain would have shown higher levels at that time. One could multiply such hypothetical examples, from World War II to the war in Indochina; though data are sparse, common sense suggests that small nations are not *necessarily* in an enviable position, though they may have certain advantages under certain conditions.

Some data from a cross-national survey carried out in 1948 help illustrate this point.[7] The study covered several of the same nations that were surveyed more than a quarter-century later by the European Community, and included a question that can be taken as at least a rough indicator of Overall Life Satisfaction. The question was, "How satisfied are you with the way you are getting

---

[7] See William Buchanan and Hadley Cantril, *How Nations See Each Other* (Urbana: University of Illinois Press, 1953).

on now?" The questions immediately preceding it have reference to job security, prospects for world peace, and human nature. In this context, the item would seem to refer to satisfaction of a rather general nature. Table 6–4 shows the responses to this question in five of the European Community countries, Norway, and the United States. As this table illustrates, both Britain and the United States show higher satisfaction levels than The Netherlands, although The Netherlands is far smaller than either of them.

TABLE 6–4. Overall Satisfaction Levels in Seven Western Nations, Summer, 1948[a]

"How satisfied are you with the way you are getting on now?"						
Norway	United States	Britain	Nether- lands	Germany	Italy	France
Very satisfied						
21%	15%	12%	8%	2%	5%	2%
All right 68	58	54	56	53	47	32
Dissatisfied 10	27	34	35	45	48	66

[a] The German sample was drawn from the British zone of occupation only. Figures are based on data in William Buchanan and Hadley Cantril, *How Nations See Each Other* (Urbana: University of Illinois Press, 1953), 135–213.

The finding is simple and far from surprising: both Britain and the United States escaped the trauma of invasion and occupation that recently had afflicted all of the other countries in Table 6–4. On the Continent, the ravages of World War II had not yet been repaired; devastation and poverty were still widespread. The data demonstrate that it *is* possible for the people of a small nation to be less satisfied than those of large ones—and it would be rather astonishing if this were not the case.

But at the same time, Table 6–4 shows a surprising degree of *continuity* with the pattern found in the 1970's. To be sure, the *absolute* level of dissatisfaction was much higher in 1948 than it was a generation later: the percentage saying that they were generally dissatisfied was about two or three times as large in 1948 as in our recent surveys. But the *relative* positions of the given countries remain rather similar.

The Italians and French rank at the bottom in both periods—although they exchange places. The Germans ranked next above them—in 1948 as in the 1970's, despite the fact that in the former year many of them were literally hungry, their cities were in ruins, and the land was occupied by foreign armies. As we have noted, the Dutch ranked below the British in 1948; but aside from this, Britain held her place as the most satisfied of the four "large" European countries. Finally, there may be one more similarity between 1948 and 1975, though it depends on a speculative leap. Let us assume (on grounds of cultural similarities and parallel experiences in World War II) that in 1948, the Norwegian public showed a satisfaction level comparable to what the Danes would have shown if they had been surveyed. If we assume this, it becomes more than an interesting coincidence that the Norwegians ranked at the top of this particular list—just as the Danes did a generation later. But regardless of whether we wish to view the Norwegians as possible surrogates for the Danes, one's overall impression is that underlying the fluctuations in absolute levels there is a certain stability of relative position that may be due to cultural factors.

Another kind of evidence indicates that the subjective quality of life is not always and inevitably higher in small countries than in large ones. The May, 1975, European Community surveys asked each respondent: "Taking all things together, how would you say things are these days—would you say you're very happy, pretty happy or not too happy these days?" Happiness is not the same thing as Overall Life Satisfaction. "Satisfaction" implies a rational evaluation of one's situation, weighed against reasonable expectations. "Happiness" implies an absolute state of being, something more emotional and less cognitive. Nevertheless, Happiness and *Overall* Satisfaction overlap a good deal conceptually, and they have a strong empirical tendency to go together. The May, 1975, survey contained questions about both of them, and responses to the two items correlate at about the .6 level in all nine countries. Table 6–5 shows the levels of happiness reported by the publics of nine European Community countries, plus responses to an identical question asked earlier in the United States.

In their levels of reported happiness, the nine European nations show almost exactly the same rank order as was displayed in connection with Overall Life Satisfaction. There is one striking exception: the Irish, who generally rank second in Life Satisfaction, drop all the way to eighth place in reported happiness (here again, respondents from Northern Ireland behave like the Irish rather than like the British: if treated as a separate nation, Northern Ireland would have ranked second in Overall Life Satisfaction—

TABLE 6-5. Reported Happiness of Publics in Ten Western Countries [a]

	Denmark	Belgium	Nether-lands	United States	Luxem-bourg	Britain	Germany	Ireland	France	Italy
Very happy	41%	37%	33%	24%	26%	22%	12%	17%	16%	6%
Pretty happy	52	54	57	67	52	51	66	54	56	49
Not too happy	7	10	11	9	22	27	22	30	28	45

[a] American figures are based on the mean of two surveys carried out by the SRC in 1972, cited in Campbell, Converse and Rodgers, *The Perceived Quality of Life*, Chapter 2. European data are from the May, 1975, European Community Survey.

and *sixth* on happiness).[8] This drop, of course, puts the Irish much closer to where one would expect them to be, in terms of their objective material circumstances (though they still rank higher than they should). If happiness is a more absolute condition than satisfaction, less prone to be gauged against one's long-term expectations, it could explain why the Irish ranked relatively low on happiness, though high on satisfaction, in 1975.

A similarly worded question was asked in a 1965 cross-national survey that included five of the countries in Table 6–5.[9] Ranked from happiest to least happy, these countries were: Great Britain, the United States, West Germany, France, and Italy. Except for an exchange of positions between Britain and the United States, the rank order in 1975 replicates that of 1965.

Do the cross-national differences shown in Table 6–5 mean that the Belgians, Danes, and Dutch really are happier than the Germans, Italians, and French? Or are we merely dealing with some invisible factor that always induces the Belgians, Danes, and Dutch to *say* they are more satisfied and happier?

The question is academic. By definition we cannot measure this invisible factor, if it exists (though future research might uncover some perfectly mundane explanation for the cross-national differences). In either case, we seem to be dealing with a deep-seated feature of given cultures that may have important political implications.

Table 6–5 demonstrates another exception to the general rule that the publics of small nations are more contented than the publics of large ones. But even here, the rule remains valid for most countries: Ireland is an exceptional case.

Dahl and Tufte have probed deeply into the advantages and disadvantages of being large or small, in connection with a nation's prospects for becoming and remaining democratic.[10] They con-

[8] The only relevant data I have seen from Switzerland would put the Swiss in first place, a trifle ahead of the Danes. This, of course, is entirely consistent with our data on Overall Life Satisfaction, which also indicates that the Swiss are our most contented public. The Swiss data, however, were gathered a decade earlier than the data in Table 6–4. With the obvious reservation that things may have changed, they indicate that among the Swiss, 42 percent were "very happy," 52 percent "happy" and 6 percent "not very happy." Cited in Denis de Rougemont, *La Suisse: L'Histoire d'un Peuple Heureux* (Paris: Hachette, 1965), 172.

[9] Based on analysis of Cantril's World Survey III, cited in Easterlin, "Economic Growth," 107.

[10] See Robert A. Dahl and Edward R. Tufte, *Size and Democracy* (Stanford: Stanford University Press, 1974).

clude that no single type of unit is optimal for achieving the twin goals of citizen effectiveness and system capacity: smaller nations may provide more opportunity for a citizen to participate effectively in that nation's decisions; but what *happens* in that country may be largely determined by decisions made in other larger nations.

But under *current* conditions, the publics of the small nations of Europe may have the best of both worlds. They have the good fortune to live within an international framework that has provided peace, because of a local stalemate between the superpowers and the growth of a European Community; and this Community has also provided access to a large economic unit without loss of a sense of identity. Perhaps the optimal arrangement would be a loosely federated Europe, modeled roughly along the lines of the Swiss cantons in which a maximum of decision-making is decentralized to regional authorities but which maintains central institutions charged with key financial and peace-keeping functions.

VI. CHANGING LEVELS OF SOCIO-POLITICAL SATISFACTION

The relative positions of the various nationalities show a remarkable stability when we trace Overall Satisfaction levels across time, even fairly long periods of time; and even when we shift our focus from Overall Life Satisfaction to a less cognitive attribute, Happiness.

This stability is intriguing, for it points to the existence of some inadequately understood but potentially important characteristic that seems to be deeply woven into the political cultures of the given nations. But at the same time, this stability has a frustrating aspect, for it seems unreasonable that the cross-national pattern should bear so little relationship to the distinctive economic environments in which the respective publics live; it seems counterintuitive that the subjective experience of these publics should be so impervious to current conditions.

As we saw in the previous chapter, satisfaction with one's society and political system constitutes a second basic dimension, distinct from the Overall Life Satisfaction cluster. And this second type of subjective satisfaction seems much less tightly constrained by long-term cultural factors. Socio-political satisfaction can show substantial changes in relative cross-national position, even in a relatively brief period, and they seem intuitively accessible, moving in the direction an informed observer would expect. Thus, the two main dimensions of subjective satisfaction show contrasting patterns over time. With one the relative standing of various nations is astonishingly (almost dismayingly) stable and shows little relationship to current conditions; with the other, relative positions seem to respond to current events in an easily interpretable fashion. Let us examine levels of Political Satisfaction in 1973 and 1975, for an example of the second type of pattern. Table 6–6 presents the relevant data. Even here, we find a fair degree of stability.

TABLE 6–6. Satisfaction with "The Way Democracy Is Functioning" in Respondent's Nation, 1973 and 1975[a]

1973 (four-point scale)			1975 (eleven-point scale)		
Rank	Nation	Mean Score	Rank	Nation	Mean Score
1.	Belgium	2.70	1.	Germany	6.26
2.	Luxembourg	2.66	2.	Luxembourg	6.09
3.	Netherlands	2.56	3.	Belgium	6.03
4.	Ireland	2.49	4.	Denmark	5.76
5.	Germany	2.38	5.	Netherlands	5.67
6.	Denmark	2.35	6.	Ireland	5.11
7.	France	2.33	7.	France	4.80
8.	Britain	2.32	8.	Britain	4.66
9.	Italy	1.99	9.	Italy	2.83

[a] For 1973, mean scores are based on a scale that runs from 1 ("very dissatisfied") to 4 ("very satisfied"). For 1975, mean scores are based on a scale that runs from 0 ("very dissatisfied") to 10 ("very satisfied").

But there is also considerable change, including one really spectacular shift: it involves Germany.

On all our measures of *Overall* Life Satisfaction, the German public ranked at the low end of the scale, together with the publics of the four other "large" European nations. To be sure, the Germans ranked well above the French and Italians; but they fell below the publics of the five "small" countries in all domains connected with the Overall Life Satisfaction cluster. Even in satisfaction with their incomes, for example, the Germans ranked sixth —although they had the highest per capita revenues in the Community.

The Socio-political dimension tells a different story. In their ground-breaking comparative study of political culture, Almond and Verba found that in 1959 the British public were particularly proud of their political system. In response to the question, "What are the things about this country that you are most proud of?" fully 46 percent of the British sample mentioned their political institutions—the leading choice, by a wide margin. At the same time, only 7 percent of the Germans mentioned their political institutions, making them the seventh-ranking choice.[11] Though pride and satisfaction are not identical, it seems safe to assume that the British would have expressed the higher level of political *satisfaction* as well.

If so, this relationship had already changed by 1973. After decades of national decline and indecisive government, the British ranked low on political satisfaction—while the Germans ranked relatively high, somewhat above the British and even ahead of one of the smaller nations. Between 1973 and 1975, the Germans greatly widened the gap, vaulting all the way from fifth to first place. The pariah nation of the post-war era had finally regained her self-respect. This relative sense of well-being was not limited to the political domain. As Table 6–7 shows, Germany ranked

TABLE 6–7. Satisfaction with "The Kind of Society We Live In (France, Denmark) Today," 1973 and 1975

1973 (four-point scale)			1975 (eleven-point scale)		
Rank	Nation	Mean Score	Rank	Nation	Mean Score
1.	Belgium	2.91	1.	Luxembourg	6.56
2.	Luxembourg	2.88	2.	Germany	6.42
3.	Ireland	2.78	3.	Belgium	6.37
4.	Denmark	2.68	4.	Ireland	6.02
5.	Germany	2.61	5.	Denmark	5.88
6.	Netherlands	2.56	6.	Netherlands	5.55
7.	Britain	2.48	7.	Britain	5.14
8.	France	2.33	8.	France	4.68
9.	Italy	2.13	9.	Italy	3.31

above every country except Luxembourg in response to the question about satisfaction with "The Kind of Society We Live In

[11] See Gabriel A. Almond and Sidney Verba, *The Civic Culture: Political Attitudes and Democracy in Five Nations* (Princeton: Princeton University Press, 1963), 102.

Today." It was not only *Time* magazine that viewed Germany as "Europe's Most Successful Society."[12]

Germany's remarkable rise from 1973 to 1975 is not surprising in itself. It is perfectly consistent with the fact that, while her neighbors were suffering annual inflation rates of 15 to 25 percent, the German rate was a relatively mild 6 percent—the Germans actually made a net gain in purchasing power. While nearby countries had unemployment rates as high as 12 percent, the German rate stayed below 5 percent. While most European countries had alarmingly large balance-of-payment deficits stimulated by skyrocketing oil prices, Germany was showing a large surplus.

Conversely, the public of Ireland (and of Northern Ireland) behaved as expected in the face of economic and political difficulties. The Republic of Ireland dropped from fourth to sixth place in political satisfaction. Northern Ireland was not surveyed in 1973, but her mean score in 1975 was 3.00, far below any nation in Table 6–6 except Italy. The Italians themselves were suffering from runaway inflation, endless strikes, and political violence under a government that apparently could not govern or even maintain order. These conditions continued during the years from 1973 to 1975, but in 1973 the Italians *already* ranked lower in political satisfaction than any other nationality—their relative position could not drop any lower. But it is possible to estimate roughly equivalent *absolute* levels for 1973 and 1975, although different scales were used in the two years.[13] A comparison of

[12] See the cover story on Germany entitled "Europe's Most Successful Society," *Time* (International Edition), May 12, 1975.

[13] For methodological reasons, eleven-point scales were used in 1975, instead of the four-point scales used in 1973, though the wording of the questions was not changed. But the question about Overall Life Satisfaction was asked in *both* formats in May, 1975. It turns out that, empirically, the life satisfaction levels as measured on the four-point scale, if multiplied by the constant 2.40, are virtually identical to the life satisfaction scores generated by the eleven-point scale in each of our nine countries. Using this method, we can also transform the four-point life satisfaction scores from *1973* into their eleven-point equivalents. They prove to be a trifle higher than the corresponding eleven-point scores shown for 1975—which they *should* be, since life satisfaction actually did decline slightly between 1973 and 1975. As a comparison of the four-point scale scores reveals, we used this method to calculate eleven-point scale equivalents for each of the satisfaction variables measured in 1973, and compared these results with the corresponding data for 1975. The items in the Overall Life Satisfaction cluster show only small changes (generally in a downward direction). The two Socio-political Satisfaction items reveal considerably larger changes. The eleven-point equivalents of the Political Satisfaction scores for 1973 shown in Table 6–6 are as follows:

these absolute levels indicates that from 1973 to 1975 political satisfaction declined in all but two of the nine European Community countries—and that the decline was larger in Italy than anywhere else. In Denmark there was little change; while in Germany, political satisfaction showed a modest but definite increase.

None of these changes would astonish a well-informed observer. Even the quite spectacular rise in Germany's relative position is perfectly consistent with the assumption that the various publics were aware that most governments seemed to be performing poorly, while the German system was doing rather well by comparison.

What *is* paradoxical, however, is the fact that the various publics behaved as if they were making well-informed, rational judgments about current events, and then applied them *only* to their evaluations of Socio-political Satisfaction. In regard to Overall Life Satisfaction, long-term cultural factors apparently continued to exercise a dominant influence on the relative positions of the various nationalities.

This is even more surprising when we consider the following: a given nation's *economic* performance seems to furnish a major part of the explanation why Socio-political Satisfaction increased in some countries, but decreased in most of them. Yet satisfaction with one's income, job, and other economic aspects of life is *not* linked with Socio-political Satisfaction; instead, it falls into the Overall Life Satisfaction cluster. And like the other items in this cluster, Income Satisfaction shows great stability of national positions. In both 1973 and 1975, the rankings of the various nations remained virtually identical to the Life Satisfaction pattern shown in Figure 6–2.

In short, a review of the evidence concerning Socio-political Satisfaction makes the stability of national rankings on the Overall

	1973 Score	Change from 1973 to 1975
Belgium	6.49	−.46
Luxembourg	6.39	−.30
Netherlands	6.15	−.47
Ireland	5.98	−.77
Germany	5.72	+.54
Denmark	5.64	+.12
France	5.60	−.80
Britain	5.57	−.91
Italy	4.78	−1.95

Satisfaction dimension seem all the more remarkable. For it is clear that the satisfaction levels of given nationalities *can* vary in response to current conditions; mass publics *do* perceive and respond to important economic and political events. If this is true, then the cultural component linked with Overall Satisfaction must be strong indeed, to preserve the continuity we have observed.

By the same token, the publics' apparently logical and predictable response to current conditions, in regard to Socio-political Satisfaction, helps restore one's faith in the potentially rational behavior of mass publics. The public *does* seem to be aware of current socio-economic conditions and capable of assigning credit or blame for them to the authorities in office.

Table 6–8 presents some evidence on this score. It demonstrates the fact that supporters of the party or parties currently in office in a given country virtually always show higher Socio-political Satisfaction scores than supporters of non-incumbent parties. Overall, forty parties are listed in each year. Among the twenty most satisfied electorates in 1973, thirteen were supporters of parties in power; among the twenty least satisfied parties, only three were in power. In 1975 the pattern was similar: of the top twenty parties on the list, twelve held office; among the bottom twenty, only four were in office. In a few instances, a given party left office between the 1973 and 1975 surveys; this was true of the Belgian Socialists and British Conservatives. In both cases, the satisfaction scores of the parties that left office show a decline relative to the parties that took office or continued in office.

There could, of course, be two different explanations for this phenomenon. The first is that the adherents of the party in power are relatively satisfied simply *because* their party is in office. The second is that those who are dissatisfied turn against the incumbent party and give their support to the opposition. In all probability, both factors play a part; panel survey data would be needed in order to determine their relative importance.

VII. CONCLUSION

The implications of our findings are pessimistic in a sense: apparently no government can make its people permanently happy. Even the most enlightened policies may have only a limited impact on Overall Life Satisfaction, one that lasts for only a limited time. But neither this nor the relatively low correlations usually

TABLE 6–8. Satisfaction with "The Way Democracy Is Functioning in Your Country" by Political Party, 1973 and 1975 (Ranked according to mean score from very satisfied to very dissatisfied)[a]

		October, 1973				May, 1975	
Rank	Nation	Party	Mean Score	Rank	Nation	Party	Mean Score
1.	[b]Netherlands	Catholic People's	3.33	1.	[b]Germany	Social Democrat	6.62
2.	[b]France	Gaullist	3.21	2.	[b]Belgium	Social Christian	6.51
3.	[b]Netherlands	Socialist	2.98	3.	Denmark	Radical	6.48
4.	[b]Belgium	Social Christian	2.97	4.	[b]Germany	Free Democrat	6.27
5.	Netherlands	Christian Historical	2.94	5.	Germany	Christian Democrat	6.26
6.	Belgium	Francophone Nationalist	2.94	6.	Belgium	Liberal	6.15
7.	[b]Belgium	Socialist	2.90	7.	[b]France	Gaullist	6.14
8.	[b]Netherlands	Anti-Revolutionary	2.87	8.	Denmark	Conservative	6.13
9.	Belgium	Liberal	2.79	9.	[b]Denmark	Social Democrat	6.10
10.	[b]Ireland	Fine Gael	2.74	10.	[b]Netherlands	Socialist	6.09
11.	France	Reform Movement	2.70	11.	Denmark	Liberal	6.02
12.	Netherlands	Liberal	2.69	12.	Netherlands	Christian Historical	5.93
13.	[b]Britain	Conservative	2.67	13.	[b]Belgium	Francophone Nationalist	5.92
14.	[b]Denmark	Social Democrat	2.65	14.	[b]France	Reform Movement	5.86
15.	[b]Netherlands	Democrats, 1966, Radical, Pacifist Socialist Party	2.64	15.	Belgium	Socialist	5.84
16.	[b]Germany	Social Democrat	2.62	16.	[b]Netherlands	Democrats, 1966, Radical, Pacifist Socialist Party	5.81
17.	Ireland	Fianna Fail	2.55	17.	[b]Netherlands	Catholic People's	5.78

18.	France	Socialist	2.52
19.	bIreland	Labour	2.50
20.	bGermany	Free Democrat	2.46
21.	Belgium	Flemish Nationalist	2.41
22.	Denmark	Liberal	2.41
23.	Denmark	Radical	2.40
24.	bItaly	Christian Democrat	2.31
25.	Britain	Labour	2.29
26.	Denmark	Socialist People's	2.28
27.	Britain	Liberal	2.25
28.	Denmark	Conservative	2.24
29.	France	Left Radical	2.22
30.	Germany	Christian Democrat	2.20
31.	Britain	Scot-Welsh Nationalist	2.06
32.	France	Communist	2.06
33.	Denmark	Progress	2.06
34.	bItaly	Social Democrat	1.97
35.	bItaly	Liberal	1.93
36.	Italy	Socialist	1.92
37.	Italy	Republican	1.77
38.	France	Unified Socialist	1.65
39.	Italy	Communist	1.63
40.	Italy	Neo-Fascist	1.47

18.	bNetherlands	Anti-Revolutionary	5.66
19.	Belgium	Flemish Nationalist	5.61
20.	bIreland	Fine Gael	5.57
21.	Ireland	Fianna Fail	5.47
22.	Netherlands	Liberal	5.32
23.	Denmark	Socialist People's	5.21
24.	Denmark	Progressive	5.19
25.	bBritain	Labour	5.01
26.	France	Left Radical	4.85
27.	Britain	Liberal	4.17
28.	Britain	Conservative	4.41
29.	bIreland	Labour	4.36
30.	bItaly	Christian Democrat	4.19
31.	France	Socialist	4.14
32.	Britain	Scot-Welsh Nationalist	4.11
33.	bItaly	Republican	3.52
34.	France	Communist	3.40
35.	Italy	Social Democrat	2.80
36.	Italy	Socialist	2.51
37.	Italy	Neo-Fascist	2.36
38.	Italy	Liberal	2.26
39.	France	Unified Socialist	1.92
40.	Italy	Communist	1.77

a In 1973 a four-point scale was used, on which "1" represents "very dissatisfied" and "4" represents "very satisfied." In May, 1975 an eleven-point scale was used, on which "0" represents "very dissatisfied" and "10" represents "very satisfied."
b Indicates a party in power at time of survey.

found between satisfaction levels and a people's readiness to rebel can be taken as evidence that mass publics are insensitive to the socio-economic environment or slow to respond to it. On the contrary, as our data on *Socio-political* Satisfaction suggest, Western publics are quite aware of socio-economic conditions, and perfectly capable of assigning credit or blame for them. The low correlations found with Overall Satisfaction measures reflect the fact that socio-economic conditions are only one component among many, including a long-term cultural component.

No government can make its people permanently happy. In the long run, each successful regime digs its own grave: new needs become salient, leading to new demands and new types of dissatisfaction. But ultimately this may be a fortunate state of affairs. A society in which dissatisfaction were absent would be a society frozen in *rigor mortis*.

PART III

Political Cleavages

CHAPTER 7

Political Cleavages in Industrial Society

I. INTRODUCTION

A GRADUAL but deep-rooted and pervasive process of value change seems to be taking place in Western societies. What implications does this have for mass political behavior? Or rather, one might ask, does it *have* any such implications?

In the light of a large body of empirical research it may seem unrealistic to even *expect* that an individual's value priorities would have much influence on how he or she votes. The landmark studies in voting behavior have emphasized the extent to which social background variables (and political party identification in particular) are the dominant influences on electoral choice. What inherited political loyalties and social milieu fail to explain can largely be attributed to candidate perceptions (or misperceptions) rather than issues.[1] The relatively minor role played by political *attitudes* might be attributed to the fact that, among the mass public, they seem to be vague and unstructured, and lack stability over time.[2] If there is little linkage between voting behavior and issue-preferences, we might expect to find an even weaker relationship with one's underlying values.

Materialist values reflect a relatively strong attachment to maintaining order and preserving economic gains. Post-Materialist values emphasize individual self-expression and achieving a more participant, less hierarchical society. Western nations have been

[1] See Paul F. Lazarsfeld *et al., The People's Choice: How the Voter Makes Up His Mind in a Presidential Campaign* (New York: Columbia University Press, 1944); Bernard Berelson *et al., Voting: A Study of Opinion Formation in a Presidential Campaign* (Chicago: University of Chicago Press, 1954); and Angus E. Campbell *et al., The American Voter* (New York: Wiley, 1960); and Donald E. Stokes, "Some Dynamic Elements of Contests for the Presidency," *American Political Science Review*, 60, 1 (March, 1966), 19–28.

[2] See Philip E. Converse, "The Nature of Belief Systems in Mass Publics," in David E. Apter (ed.), *Ideology and Discontent* (New York: Free Press, 1964), 202–261.

successful in achieving economic growth during the past couple of decades, but they have given relatively little attention to the attainment of Post-Materialist goals. We might, therefore, expect Materialists to be more likely to support the established order, and Post-Materialists to be relatively change-oriented.

On the other hand, Materialists tend to be recruited from lower income groups, which traditionally have supported the Left—while the Post-Materialists come mainly from middle-class families, which generally have been more likely to support conservative parties. Social class background might neutralize any tendency for Post-Materialist values to be linked with support for change-oriented parties. Moreover, while average income levels have risen, relative *shares* have changed very little. If shares are crucial to the public rather than levels, economic growth might have had little impact on traditional voting patterns.

Furthermore, political behavior does not occur in a vacuum; it is shaped in crucial ways by the political context in which one lives. Even when the public does have relatively strong policy preferences and potentially *could* engage in policy-voting (as may be increasingly true in the United States), they may be unable to do so because the major party candidates adopt Tweedledee-Tweedledum positions on the key issues. If there is not any perceptible policy difference between the alternatives offered them, the public's voting behavior can not be greatly influenced by values or attitudes. For this reason, the stand one took on American involvement in Vietnam apparently had little impact on whether one voted for Nixon or Humphrey in 1968. On the other hand, in 1972 there *was* a clear-cut difference between the positions of McGovern and Nixon—and a powerful relationship between how the American electorate felt about the issues they contested and how they voted.[3]

[3] See Benjamin I. Page and Richard A. Brody, "Policy Voting and the Electoral Process: The Vietnam War Issue," *American Political Science Review*, 66, 3 (September, 1972), 979–995. For related evidence, see Herbert F. Weisberg and Jerrold G. Rusk, "Dimensions of Candidate Evaluation," *American Political Science Review*, 64, 4 (December, 1970), 1167–1185. A number of scholars argue that issue voting became increasingly important during the 1960's, however; for an excellent sampling of this literature, see Gerald M. Pomper, "From Confusion to Clarity: Issues and American Voters, 1956–1968," *American Political Science Review*, 66, 2 (June, 1972), 415–428; *idem*, "Rejoinder," *ibid.*, 466–467; Richard W. Boyd, "Popular Control of Public Policy: A Normal Vote Analysis of the 1968 Election," *ibid.*, 429–449; *idem*, "Rejoinder," *ibid.*, 468–470; Richard A. Brody and

At least some of the available parties must take noticeably different stands on the relevant dimension in order for the individual to have an *opportunity* to act on his values. No matter how intensely the values are held, if political elites offer no real choice the individual can do little except feel frustrated—unless he is prepared for the arduous task of organizing a new political party or taking over an existing one.

Let us assume, for a moment, that political elites and institutional constraints pose no problems. One's preferences on the Materialist/Post-Materialist dimension are still by no means the only influence shaping one's vote. To a large extent, the electoral decision has been pre-empted by the milieu in which an individual is born. Often, one inherits a sense of political party identification from one's parents. Evidence from several countries indicates that this can be a powerful influence on how a person votes.[4] Our own data confirm, in a still wider range of national settings, the pre-eminent role played by party preferences transmitted from generation to generation.

But even if one's parents fail to transmit any deeply rooted sense of political party identification, a number of background factors may influence voting. From a developmental perspective, these variables might be classified under three headings:

1. *"Pre-Industrial"* *variables*—such as religion, language group, race. These variables are more or less ascriptive; the characteristic is usually transmitted from generation to generation with little change.

2. *"Industrial"* *variables*—the factors underlying the pattern of industrial class conflict, such as income, occupation, education, membership in labor unions. There is a tendency for sons' occupations to resemble their fathers', but educational level and occupation reflect an achieved rather than ascribed status; inter-

Benjamin I. Page, "Comment," *ibid.*, 450–458; and John H. Kessel, "Comment," *ibid.*, 459–465. Miller *et al.* present persuasive evidence that issue voting took on exceptional importance in America's 1972 Presidential election: see Arthur H. Miller *et al.*, "A Majority Party in Disarray: Policy Polarization in the 1972 Election," *American Political Science Review*, 70, 3 (September, 1976), 753–758.

[4] See David Butler and Donald Stokes, *Political Change in Britain* (New York: St. Martin's, 1969); Angus Campbell *et al.*, *American Voter*; M. Kent Jennings and Richard Niemi, "The Transmission of Political Values from Parent to Child," *American Political Science Review*, 62, 1 (March, 1968), 169–184.

generational changes occur far more frequently here than with Pre-Industrial variables.

3. *"Post-Industrial" variables*—reflecting individual-level values, particularly those based on post-economic needs. In comparison with the other two types of variables, these value preferences are less likely to take an institutional form. Yet if they are deeply internalized in given individuals, they may be the basis of predictable patterns of long-term political cleavage. Our value priorities indicator is intended to tap this dimension of political conflict.

The importance of the first two types of cleavage has been widely recognized. Rokkan, Lipset, Rose, and Dahl and their colleagues have analyzed a series of historical crises which took place prior to industrialization, and which set the pattern for much of what we find in modern political cleavages.[5] They emphasize the persistence of religious, linguistic, and regional political differences over time.

The development of Industrial society in the West led to the emergence of an enfranchised working class, pitting its interests against those of the proprietors and managers. The literature on this subject is immense. To a large extent, the politics of Industrial society have revolved around social class conflict, with the groups which rank lower in income and occupation tending to vote for change-oriented parties, or parties of the Left, in opposition to the middle and upper classes, which tend to defend the status quo.

The nature of Post-Industrial cleavage is (for obvious reasons) less clearly understood. We suspect that the politics of Post-Industrial society will, to an increasing extent, be motivated by an individual's life-style preferences and values rather than by either ascriptive or social class-based cleavages.

It may seem strange at first to put an individual's value priorities on an analytic level with the familiar ethnic and class-based variables. One's values are intangible—invisible until measured by the techniques of social science. But let us remember that such variables as social class are *also* analytic constructs—shorthand terms used to sum up the results of a variety of early and ongoing ex-

[5] See Seymour M. Lipset and Stein Rokkan, "Cleavage Structures, Party Systems and Voter Alignments," in Lipset and Rokkan (eds.), *Party Systems and Voter Alignments* (New York: Free Press, 1967); cf. Rokkan, *Citizens, Elections and Parties* (Oslo: Universitetsforlaget, 1970); and Robert Dahl (ed.), *Political Oppositions in Western Democracies* (New Haven: Yale University Press, 1966); and Richard Rose (ed.), *Comparative Electoral Behavior* (New York: Free Press, 1974).

periences; they too may be intangible until measured by appropriate instruments.

To be sure, religion and social class tend to be reinforced by outwardly visible institutional ties, such as church or labor union —while one of the characteristics of the Post-Materialist seems to be a relative *aversion* to traditional bureaucratic institutions. Nevertheless, certain basic value orderings may be deep-rooted and long-lasting enough to serve as useful predictor variables. Even without formal institutional ties they may, like political party identification, be enduring enough to be considered part of a nation's social structure.

Does one's value type influence voting behavior? The answer must be a carefully qualified "sometimes." There are no inexorable trends governing electoral results. There may be underlying tendencies, but what elites do is so important that we can only make probabilistic statements about the influence of changes in the social infrastructure. The emergence of a De Gaulle or an Eisenhower—or the advent of a major war—can affect outcomes tremendously. Furthermore, certain patterns of electoral behavior are already well established and have shown impressive persistence over time. They can inhibit the translation of an individual's values into voting.

The impact of value change is limited by institutional and social constraints, but let us venture to make a few generalizations about its probable long-term effects, other things being equal. In an increasingly Post-Materialist society one might expect the most salient political questions to shift from economic to life-style issues; along with this would come a change in the political meaning of Left and Right, and we might also anticipate a fundamental shift in the social bases of political partisanship.

One of the most striking characteristics of Post-Materialist individuals in every country is the fact that they are recruited mainly from the more affluent strata of society. Yet they tend to vote disproportionately for the parties of the Left. Conversely, the Materialist type tends to come from lower income backgrounds but is more likely to vote for the more conservative parties.

It is conceivable that the apparent influence of values on party preference is spurious. One could imagine various reasons why only those working-class respondents, who would have voted conservatively anyway, express Materialist values. Perhaps our values indicator merely serves to identify those workers who come from politically conservative family backgrounds, for example. Or maybe certain people prefer traditional values *and* conservative political parties simply because they have religious ties. Multi-variate analysis will be required in order to deal with these possibilities.

But if the relationship between values and party preference is *not* spurious, it could gradually neutralize (or even reverse) the traditional alignment of the working class with the Left, and the middle class with the Right. We hypothesize that such a process *has* been taking place during the past two or three decades.

Conclusive findings can only come from observing changes over a long span of time. But we will examine the data now available in an effort to determine whether an individual's value priorities seem to have a significant influence on electoral choice, controlling for the effects of other variables. If this proves to be the case, the polarization of populations along a Materialist/Post-Materialist axis should tend to reduce the incidence of social class-voting. The Industrial basis of political cleavage would gradually decline. We would expect the importance of Pre-Industrial cleavages to diminish also—but (for reasons to be developed later) at a slower rate than that prevailing for Industrial cleavages.

For the time being, both Industrial and Pre-Industrial cleavages retain great importance; indeed, they continue to dominate political cleavages in most, though not all, circumstances. We will examine the role of each of these three types of variables, as an influence on Left-Right voting. The patterns found among a number of different countries may provide some clues about the kinds of political conflict we may expect in Post-Industrial society. But before we can proceed with this analysis, we need to define our dependent variable—Left-Right voting—with reference to each of the eight countries that will be considered here.[6]

II. How To Tell Left from Right

An analysis of the impact of values on voting raises the question, "Why does an individual vote for one party rather than another?"

---

[6] This section will be based on data from the eight countries surveyed from 1970 to 1972 since certain background variables (such as one's parents' party preference) were not included in the 1973 surveys. Consequently we must use the original four-item values index rather than the twelve-item index developed later. Though the latter tends to be a somewhat stronger predictor of voting preference, the basic patterns are similar.

In the United States, this question is relatively simple: one asks "Why did he or she vote for the Republicans rather than the Democrats?" But in a society like The Netherlands, where fourteen different parties won seats in Parliament in the 1972 elections, one might ask, "Why did he vote for the Labor Party rather than the Catholic Party? Or the Radicals? Or the Fundamentalist Calvinists? Or the Pacifist Socialists?" and so on. With fourteen parties in a system, there are ninety-one pairs of parties to compare. To reduce the question to manageable proportions, in a multi-party system one tends to ask: "Why did he vote for one of the Socialist parties rather than one of the religious parties?" Or, more broadly still, "Why did he vote for the Left rather than the Right?" These broad labels serve a useful function, although they necessarily sacrifice some precision. Their meaning may vary somewhat from country to country and, as we have suggested, may change over time within a given country. Broadly speaking, the term Left refers to change-oriented political forces, and Right to those which seek to preserve the existing socio-political pattern. More specifically, the Left generally implies change in an egalitarian direction; and in the politics of Industrial societies it has tended to refer to greater *economic* equality above all.

The Left-Right dimension could be compared to the first factor in a conventional factor analysis: it is a useful data-reduction device that helps the public sum up party differences. In a recent exploration of Swiss politics, a factor analysis was made of preference rankings for each of the eleven leading Swiss parties.[7] The first factor underlying these preferences did, indeed, correlate strongly with the respondent's self-placement on a Left-Right scale. Analysis of data from ten other countries showed that in most cases, the individual's political party preference was closely related to where one placed oneself on a Left-Right scale.[8] The proportion of variance which the Left-Right dimension explains— and the number of additional dimensions which are important—undoubtedly varies from country to country and from time to time. But the Left-Right dimension seems to be a useful first approximation to a complex reality.

[7] See Ronald Inglehart and Dusan Sidjanski, "The Left, the Right, the Establishment and the Swiss Electorate," in Ian Budge *et al.* (eds.), *Party Identification and Beyond* (New York: Wiley, 1976).

[8] See Ronald Inglehart and Hans D. Klingemann, "Party Identification, Ideological Preference and the Left-Right Dimension Among Western Publics," in Ian Budge *et al.*, *Party Identification.*

Janda has drawn up a detailed list of the major issues on which political parties disagree and has undertaken to code actual party positions, on the basis of over 3,500 documents on party politics in fifty countries. According to his coding scheme, the parties of the Left tend to be relatively favorable to government ownership of the means of production; a major government role in economic planning; redistribution of wealth; extensive social welfare programs at public expense; alignment with the Eastern rather than the Western bloc; the secularization of society; higher allocations to the military; independence from foreign control; supranational integration; national integration; extension of the franchise; and protection of civil rights.[9] Janda's factor analysis of the issue positions actually taken by twenty-six political parties indicates that only the first six issues listed above correlate highly with a single underlying Left-Right dimension: their factor loadings range from .91 for government ownership of the means of production to .68 for secularization of society. A party's stance for or against religion is less highly correlated with the Left-Right dimension than some of the other issues, but it can be regarded as an aspect of that dimension. The other issues are relatively weakly related to the Left-Right dimension. Support for higher military allocations turns out to be linked with the Right rather than the Left, but the association is very moderate; and protection of civil rights also shows a faint negative polarity. Janda's codings are based on the period from 1957 to 1962, but in general they seem to stand up fairly well today—at least in regard to the large established parties.

In an unambiguous world, Left-Right voting would occur when:

1. Certain parties supported all the policies of the Left and others opposed them.

2. Implementing these changes were the dominant goal of all parties of the Left; consequently, they would be likely to ally with other parties of the Left rather than with those of the Right.

3. The electorates perceived these policy differences and voted *because* they were for or against them.

In this neat, logical, and unidimensional world, a voter would support the party that was nearest to his own position on a Left-

[9] See Kenneth Janda, *A Conceptual Framework for the Comparative Analysis of Political Parties* (Beverly Hills: Sage Professional Papers in Comparative Politics, 1970), 96–98; and Janda, "Measuring Issue Orientations of Parties Across Nations" (Evanston: International Comparative Political Parties Project, 1970 [mimeo]).

Right continuum; if he shifted his vote, it would be to one of the nearby parties.

Unfortunately, the real world is not this simple. Survey data indicate that it was impossible to identify any one major dimension of electoral choice in the America of the 1950's—although in the period preceding the Civil War there possibly *was* a "strong ideological focus," as Stokes puts it.[10] It seems, however, that with the shift from the bland politics of the 1950's to the relatively ideological late 1960's and early 1970's, the concept of Left versus Right (or Liberal versus Conservative) has become more applicable to American politics.[11] Similarly, it has often been noted that French political parties during the Third and Fourth Republics were divided along two distinct major axes: one related to religion and the other related to social class. During the Presidency of De Gaulle, a single Gaullist–anti-Gaullist dimension tended to dominate French political life.

Recognizing that no single dimension can fully describe all the differences between political parties in Western countries, we nevertheless suggest that, as a first approximation, we can attempt to group them under two broad categories (with several subcategories) as indicated in Table 7–1.[12] This table is intended to suggest that there is a rough similarity between given political parties in various countries, and to show the relative strength of these parties.

Many well-informed observers will not agree with all the details of how these parties are arranged from Left to Right. Some would argue, for example, that the New Left is actually to the *Left* of the Communist parties, on the grounds that the former are now making a more fundamental critique of existing society than the Communists generally do. Where there might be controversy, the table conforms to available information about how the *electorates* of multi-party systems perceive the given parties.[13] Voters' percep-

[10] See Donald E. Stokes, "Spatial Models of Party Competition," in Angus E. Campbell *et al., Elections and the Political Order* (New York: Wiley, 1966), 161–179.

[11] See Arthur Miller *et al.*, "Majority Party in Disarray."

[12] We will not analyze Danish or Irish political cleavages here: the available data for these countries (from the 1973 survey) do not include one of our key variables—parents' political preference. Luxembourg is also omitted due to the small number of cases.

[13] See Emeric Deutsch *et al., Les Familles Politiques Aujourd'hui en France* (Paris: Minuit, 1966); Samuel H. Barnes and Roy Pierce, "Public

TABLE 7-1. Political Party Configurations in Eight Countries

Nation	Left				Right	
	Communist	New Left	Center-Left	Center	Center-Right	Radical-Right
Great Britain (Vote Oct. 1974)			Labor 39%	Liberals 18%	Conservatives 36%	
West Germany (Vote in 1976)			Social Democrats 43%	Free Democrats 8%	Christian Democrats 49%	
France (Vote in 1973, first round)	Communists 21%	United Socialists 3%	Socialists 19%	Reform Movement 12%	Gaullist Coalition 38%	
Italy (Vote in 1976)	Communists 34%	Radicals 1%	Socialists 10% Social Democrats 3%	Republicans 3%	Christian Democrats 39% Liberals 1%	Neo-Fascists 6%
Belgium[a] (Vote in 1974)	Communists 3%		Socialists 27%	Liberals 15%	Social Christians 32%	
Netherlands (Vote in 1972)	Communists 5%	Radicals 5% Democrats, 1966 4%	Labor 26%	Democratic Socialist, '70 4%	Catholic Party 18% 2 Protestant parties 14% Liberals 14%	Farmers Party 2% Protestant Right parties 4%
Switzerland (Vote in 1975)	Communists 2%		Socialists 27%	Independents 6%	Radicals 22% Christian parties 23% People's 10% Liberals 2%	National Action 3% Republican movement 3%
United States (Vote in 1976) (Party Identification in parentheses)			Democrats 51% (Democrat I.D. = 42%)	(Independents I.D. = 37%)	Republicans 49% (Republican I.D. = 21%)	

[a] In Belgium's 1974 elections, Flemish and French-speaking nationalist groups polled 21% of the vote; we did not attempt to place them

tions may lag behind reality, but they are obviously an important factor in electoral choice.

Several alternatives to the Left-Right classification have been proposed, and they emphasize significant features of given systems. Sartori, for example, points out the importance of a "system/anti-system" party dichotomy.[14] Such a dichotomy might place the Italian Communists, Proletarian Socialists and Neo-Fascists together in the latter category, on the grounds that these parties do not merely work to achieve reforms under existing institutions, but seek to overthrow the system altogether. Similarly, one might argue that the really important line of cleavage in French politics lies between the Communists (perhaps together with the Unified Socialists) and the other parties which seem willing to work within existing institutions. Clearly, the system/anti-system dichotomy marks an important line of cleavage in Italy and France. But it is one that seems less significant in other countries: it would contrast a tiny handful of anti-system voters with a vast majority, in most cases.

The gulf between system and anti-system parties has by no means disappeared, however. As of 1976, the Communists had not participated in government coalitions of any major Western country since the Cold War got under way, though they seem to be moving in that direction. In the 1973 parliamentary elections, France's Communists and Socialists were allied as "The Union of the Left." But despite the existence of a common platform and a common electoral strategy linking the two parties at the elite level, about half of those who planned to vote Socialist on the first ballot said they would *not* vote for a Communist candidate on the second ballot.[15] In the 1974 Presidential elections, the Communists and Socialists backed a common candidate—a Socialist, and very nearly won the election. But in the wake of the abortive Commu-

---

Opinion and Political Preferences in France and Italy," *Midwest Journal of Political Science*, 15, 4 (November, 1971), 643–660; Hans Klingemann, "Testing the Left-Right Continuum on a Sample of German Voters," *Comparative Political Studies*, 5, 1 (April, 1972), 93–106; and A.-P. Frognier, "Distances entre partis et clivages en Belgique," *Res Publica*, 2 (1973), 291–312; and Inglehart and Klingemann, "Party Identification."

[14] See Giovanni Sartori, "European Political Parties: The Case of Polarized Pluralism," in Joseph LaPalombara and Myron Weiner (eds.), *Political Parties and Political Development* (Princeton: Princeton University Press, 1966), 137–176.

[15] IFOP survey cited in *L'Express*, January 8, 1973.

nist *coup* in Portugal, cooperation between the two main parties of the Left became uneasy.

Nevertheless, in terms of the number of voters involved, the system/anti-system dichotomy is not the dominant line of political cleavage in Western countries. Even in France and Italy, where it seems to be most important, it is highly questionable whether the Communist parties really *are* anti-system parties today. They have adopted an increasingly moderate tone in recent years, with the Italians in particular emphasizing the argument that they would not overthrow the major institutions of representative democracy if they came to power. Since the mid-1960's, the French Communist Party has engaged in rather effective electoral alliances with the other parties of the Left. In the crisis of 1968, the Communist elite did not perform as revolutionaries. Ironically, it was the Gaullists who alleged that the Communists were a revolutionary party, while the Communist leaders strove to project an image of sober respectability. They have continued to cultivate this image in recent electoral campaigns, running on a platform not a great deal more radical than that of the British Labour Party.

Another alternative (or supplement) to the Left-Right scheme is the "territorial-cultural" dimension emphasized by Rokkan and Lipset.[16] In addition to the Left-Right contrast, important territorial cleavages exist, especially in Belgium. Nationalist parties rooted in the Flemish-speaking and French-speaking subcultures have shown impressive vitality in recent years: rising from an almost negligible level a dozen years previously, they won 21 percent of the Belgian vote in the early 1970's. It would be difficult to group these parties with either the Right or the Left without giving rise to heated disagreement. While linked with specific territorial and cultural bases, they might also be viewed as a special case of Sartori's "anti-system" parties: in Belgium, they have sometimes threatened the basic political arrangements in a more immediate way than the various Communist parties of other countries.[17]

The following analyses will be based primarily on a distinction

[16] See Lipset and Rokkan, "Cleavage Structures," 9–13; cf. Rokkan, *Citizens.* The territorial-cultural dimension is seen as one of two major axes of cleavage—the other one being the "functional" cleavage (which is roughly equivalent to what others call the Left-Right dimension).

[17] See Martin O. Heisler, "Institutionalizing Societal Cleavages in a Co-optive Polity," in Heisler (ed.), *Politics in Europe: Structures and Processes in Some Postindustrial Democracies* (New York: McKay, 1974).

between the parties of the Left and those of the Right in each of eight countries, but they do not depend on the assumption that Table 7–1 is correct in all details. They depend on a much simpler assumption: that in France, for example, there is a major difference between the Communist, Socialist, and Radical parties, on one hand, and the Gaullist coalition, on the other. In other words, our analysis will be based on a dichotomy between two sets of parties. We need not even agree on how to label the two sets. The reader may think of them as "Liberal vs. Conservative" or "Group 1 vs. Group 2," if he prefers, so long as he or she agrees that there *is* an important difference between the two groups. Because the terms have a widespread familiarity (and remain meaningful), we will use the terms "Left" and "Right" to describe the two sides of the dichotomy. Operating in this manner, we need not assume that political conflict in a given country is unidimensional. Empirically, almost any number of dimensions may prove useful in explaining the reasons for choice between the two main alternatives. We have dichotomized our dependent variable for two reasons:

1. For convenient cross-national comparison: in this way, one can indicate the proportion of working class, middle class, Catholic, Protestant, and other types of respondents voting for the Right or the Left by presenting a single figure for each group. Because we are dealing with as many as fourteen parties in each of eight countries, we would be overwhelmed by details if we were to show the percentage voting for each of the respective parties, among each of the respective social groups in each country. In simplifying, we inevitably lose some information, but the circumstances warrant it.

2. For multi-variate analysis (which will be undertaken in Chapter 9), technical and theoretical considerations require that we dichotomize. An alternative, in the French case for example, might be to code the Gaullists as 1, the Independent Republicans as 2, the Centrists as 3, the Radicals as 4, Socialists as 5, Communists as 6, and Unified Socialists as 7. This implies that there is a single dimension underlying all of the parties—and that the Socialists are precisely five times as "Left" as the Gaullists, and two and one-half times as "Left" as the Independent Republicans. Such assumptions would be untenable.

The difficulty of dichotomization varies from country to country. In several cases it is quite easy: an obvious and natural dichotomy is present in the "two-party" systems. In fact, more than two parties are present in all of these countries, but in three cases (Britain, West Germany, and the United States) the two leading parties obtained about three-quarters of the vote in the most recent national elections. Our dichotomy simply contrasts the two leading parties in these cases.

The other five countries have multi-party systems in which no combination of two parties received as much as 75 percent of the vote. In four of these cases, a reasonably clear basis for dichotomization nevertheless exists, although there is a certain amount of ambiguity at the center. France has a fairly clear-cut boundary between government and opposition that coincides with our Left-Right dichotomy, as indicated in Table 7–1. At the time of our surveys, the Center was divided between government and opposition, and its supporters are excluded (as is done with third parties in a "two-party" system).[18] This dichotomization *does* imply that the Communists are closer to both the Socialists and Unified Socialists than to the Gaullists—an assumption which most, though not all, observers would doubtlessly accept. The leaders and electorates of these parties seem to accept such a dichotomization. The Gaullist coalition has shown a considerable degree of cohesion throughout the Fifth Republic, while the parties of the Left have begun to institutionalize a set of ties among themselves during the last several national elections. In The Netherlands, we group together the parties of the Left (as indicated in Table 7–1) in contrast with the coalition based on the Liberals and Confessional parties, which was in power in the late 1960's and early 1970's. Not long ago, one might have considered grouping the church-related parties together, in contrast with the secular parties—which would have put the Liberals (who are conservative on economic issues) together with the Left. Recently, the Dutch Left has moved toward institutionalizing itself as an alternative government; the Left-Right distinction seems more meaningful than any other.

The Italian situation is problematic. At the time of our 1970 survey, the Christian Democrats were governing in coalition with the Republicans, Socialists, and Social Democrats. After the 1972

---

[18] To be more precise: in the 1971 survey, Centrist respondents were asked which faction they supported—the one in the government or the one in opposition—and were included in our dichotomy accordingly. In 1970, this distinction was not made, and Centrists were excluded from our dichotomy on grounds of ambiguity. Radicals were grouped with the Left.

elections the Christian Democrats were allied with the Liberals and Social Democrats, with the Republicans supporting the new government but not joining it. As one can see, in the Italian case coalition partnerships do not provide a clear guide for a dichotomy: they are shifting and cut across conventional Left-Right boundaries. Moreover, Italy is a country in which the system/anti-system dichotomy suggests itself with particular force. Even if one grants that the Communist Party is on its way to becoming a "system" party, there remain such phenomena of the extreme Right as the Neo-Fascist party or MSI (Italian Social Movement). One could, very plausibly, argue that the Neo-Fascists should be treated as a separate political force, rather than being grouped with the rest of the Italian Right.[19] The problem is, where does the Left end and the Right begin, in Italian politics? One could make a respectable case for including the Republicans with the Left. On the other hand, one could argue that, on the basis of their policies and past behavior, not only the Republicans but also the Social Democrats as well "really" belong to the Right. Faced with this problem, we dichotomized according to the perceptions of the Italian electorate. The Italian voter *sees* the Social Democrats, Socialists, Proletarian Socialists, and Communists as parties of the Left; and views the other parties as located on the Right half of a Left-Right continuum. Moreover, one's placement on this continuum tends to be linked with one's policy preferences and party choice.[20] Accordingly, our dichotomy contrasts the Left (as shown in Table 7–1) with all other parties.

The Belgian case is still more difficult to deal with. The two largest parties—the Social Christians and the Socialists—might once have been considered the basis of a two-party Left-Right dichotomy. As recently as 1958, they got 85 percent of the total vote. But their vote has been declining in recent years, falling to 61 percent of the total in the 1974 elections. Moreover, it is not easy to see which parties might be grouped with them in order to form a more comprehensive but still meaningful dichotomy. The

[19] In addition to the analyses which are reported here, I ran a parallel analysis of Italian data which excluded the MSI from the Right. Partly because of the relatively small number of MSI supporters, the results do not differ fundamentally from those of analyses based on a broader Left-Right dichotomy.

[20] See Samuel H. Barnes, "Left-Right and the Italian Voter," *Comparative Political Studies*, 42 (July, 1971), 157–175; cf. Barnes and Pierce, "Public Opinion"; and Inglehart and Klingemann, "Party Identification."

Liberals might conceivably be combined with the Social Christians to form a Left-Right dichotomy, but this would still leave a major share of the electorate excluded—those who voted for one of the linguistic nationalist parties. These parties are almost impossible to place in a natural unit with any of the three main traditional parties. Their ethnocentric flavor might tempt one to place them on the Right. Weil describes them as "ultra-conservative" and stresses the fact that they are, in a sense, descendants of the pre-World War II Rexist Party, which eventually became pro-Nazi.[21] Yet today these groups present themselves as parties of emancipation, use the rhetoric of the Left, and unquestionably are change-oriented. Therefore, one might also consider placing them on the Left. Other complications include the significant differences between the Flemish-speaking and French-speaking parties. The latter are, in part, a reaction against the former. It would seem that we cannot dichotomize the Belgian political parties in a way which is both comprehensive and coherent. Our solution has been a compromise. The "Left-Right" dichotomy for Belgium simply contrasts the electorates of the two leading parties. Admittedly, this excludes a large share of the electorate from analysis. To help complete the picture, we will also carry out a parallel analysis designed to explain why an individual votes for an ethnic nationalist party rather than one of the traditional parties.

In the Swiss case, the analysis cited earlier revealed that all of the parties could be meaningfully placed on a dominant Left-Right dimension, except for the Alliance of Independents (which was placed almost precisely at the midpoint of this dimension and has been excluded from analysis); and the Swiss Republican Movement and National Action (two small anti-foreign parties which most observers would place on the extreme Right). Support for the latter two parties taps another dimension, which is quite distinct from the major Left-Right axis. Like the ethnic nationalist parties of Belgium, these two parties must be analyzed separately, and they have been excluded from our analysis of Left-Right voting.[22]

[21] See Gordon L. Weil, *The Benelux Nations: The Politics of Small-Country Democracies* (New York: Holt, Rinehart, and Winston, 1970), 100–108.

[22] For an interpretation of the two principal dimensions of Swiss politics and the role of National Action and the Swiss Republican Movement, see Inglehart and Sidjanski, "Left, Right."

III. FAMILY TRADITION AND INDUSTRIAL POLITICAL CLEAVAGES:
SOME ZERO-ORDER RELATIONSHIPS

We will use various analytical techniques to understand why an individual votes for a given kind of political party and, more specifically, whether his or her value priorities influence the choice. Our first step will be to examine the relationship between social background and vote, using simple cross-tabulations. We will examine a number of these tables, gaining a detailed view of the basic relationships so that we will be able to grasp the much more complex pattern that will be summarized in the results of our multivariate analyses.

The respondents in each of our European samples were asked:

"If there were a General Election tomorrow, for which party would you be most likely to vote?"[23]

In multi-party systems, the responses were dichotomized as indicated above.

In the United States, two different questions were asked, one concerning political party identification and the other, how the respondent actually voted in the 1972 Presidential election. Both questions will be useful—one as a baseline indicator of long-term party loyalties and the other as a measure of actual behavior in the peculiar circumstances of 1972. The respective items were:

"Generally speaking, do you think of yourself as a Republican, a Democrat, an Independent, or what?"

The American sample was also asked if they had voted in the 1972 elections and if they had:

"Who did you vote for in the election for President?"

Our respondents were also asked what their *parents'* political party preference had been, if any.[24] There were important cross-

[23] In Switzerland the respondent was asked to rank the eleven leading parties from first to last choice, according to how much he liked them.

[24] In the United States the wording was: "Do you remember when you were growing up whether your father was very much interested in politics, somewhat interested, or didn't he pay much attention to it?" (unless "Don't Know"): "Did he think of himself mostly as a Democrat, as a Republican, as an Independent, or what?" (The same question was asked concerning one's mother.) In the European countries, respondents were asked: "Do you know if your parents had a preference for any particular political party?" (If "Yes"): "What was your parents' political preference?" The question referred to the past but because of problems related to the Fascist period in Germany and Italy, we felt that we could not tie the question to a specific period in the respondent's past.

national differences in the percentage able to report their parents' political party preference. It was highest in the United States and Great Britain, where 75 percent or more of the total sample reported such a preference; it was fairly high in Belgium and The Netherlands, where 60 to 65 percent reported one; lower in Italy and France, where the figures were 56 and 53 percent, respectively; and markedly lower in West Germany, where only 38 percent reported a parental political preference.

Nothing about this cross-national pattern is particularly surprising. Great Britain and the United States both have relatively long-established political party systems, which are dominated by only two parties. The likelihood that one's parents *were* consistently linked with a given party label would be higher in such systems. France's present party system has emerged only since De Gaulle came to power in 1958; prior to that time, the Right and Center of the French political spectrum fluctuated. In all probability, fewer parents *had* stable party preferences. Italy and Germany both suffered periods of Fascist rule when free competition between political parties was suspended—and in Germany one is under an especially powerful pressure to repress any awareness of parental political affiliation, if the parent had been associated with the Nazi Party.

These cross-national differences obviously affect the extent to which one can be influenced by political preferences inherited from one's parents. Yet, as Table 7–2 indicates, there is a pronounced relationship between parental preference and one's own voting intention in all seven countries. The effect seems quite important even in Germany and Italy. We should bear in mind that by 1970 (when the question was asked) all those respondents who were less than 45 years old had passed at least some *part* of their youth and childhood in the post-war era. But even for those who are older, reported parental preferences seem to have a measurable impact on voting intention.

It appears that political preferences transmitted from one's parents may play a key role in shaping electoral choice in all seven countries. We will be attentive to this possibility throughout our analysis. For the moment, let us move on to an examination of the "Industrial" category of variables.

Social class has long been regarded as a major influence—perhaps *the* key influence—on political behavior. Lipset summarized a large body of findings from many countries with the comment,

TABLE 7–2. Voting Intention by Party Parents Supported[a]
(Percent preferring parties of the Right)

Britain			Germany		
Labour	30%	(567)	Social Democrats	6%	(232)
Don't know parents'			Free Democrats	25	(8)
preference	56	(426)	Don't know parents'		
Liberal	63	(111)	preference	47	(906)
Conservative	86	(410)	Christian Democrats	64	(290)

France			Italy		
Left	17%	(336)	Left	18%	(226)
Center	18	(28)	Don't know	61	(554)
Don't know	51	(624)	Extreme right	82	(68)
Right	82	(305)	Christian Democrats,		
			PRI, Liberals	86	(374)

Netherlands			Belgium		
Left	11%	(262)	Socialist and		
Don't know	42	(414)	Communist	7%	(116)
Confessional,			Liberal	50	(16)
Liberals	72	(454)	Don't know	62	(241)
			Christian Social	90	(250)

United States: Party Identification			United States: Vote in 1972		
Democrats	17%	(1,575)	Democrats	57%	(1,362)
Don't know	34	(427)	Don't know	61	(257)
Independent, mixed	45	(75)	Independent, mixed	70	(150)
Republicans	76	(756)	Republicans	81	(789)

[a] Figures for European countries are based on European Community 1970 survey. United States figures for party identification are based on Institute for Social Research May, 1972, omnibus survey, Center for Political Studies 1972 election survey and European Community March, 1973, survey; vote in 1972 is based on the two latter surveys only. This variable was not available in the Swiss data.

"The most impressive single fact about political party support is that in virtually every economically developed country the lower income groups vote mainly for the parties of the Left, while the higher income groups vote mainly for the parties of the Right."[25] More recently, he concluded that "there has been a reduction in the intensity of class-linked political struggles in most of Europe,"[26] but not of class voting. "A comparative look at the pattern of work-

[25] Seymour M. Lipset, *Political Man: The Social Bases of Politics* (Garden City: Doubleday, 1960), 223–224.
[26] Seymour M. Lipset, *Revolution and Counter-Revolution: Change and Persistence in Social Structures* (New York: Basic Books, 1968), 215.

ing-class voting in contemporary Europe reveals that with the exception of Holland and Germany, the Leftist parties secure about two-thirds or more of the working-class vote, a much higher percentage than during the depression of the 1930's."[27] Similarly, after analyzing the relationship of occupation to party vote in a total of thirty-three surveys carried out from 1936 to1962 in Great Britain, Australia, the United States and Canada, Alford found that in nearly every case manual workers were more likely to vote for parties of the Left than non-manual workers. He calculated a "class-voting index," obtained by simply subtracting the percentage of non-manual respondents voting for the Left from the percentage of manual respondents voting for the Left. The mean index of class voting ranged from $+8$ in Canada to $+40$ in Great Britain. The United States had a mean index of $+16$.[28] Campbell *et al.* had presented evidence that class polarization was highest among the Depression generation and lower among both older and younger age groups;[29] One might therefore expect social class-voting to fade out gradually. Alford disputed this interpretation, arguing, on the basis of his own evidence, that "there had been no substantial shift in the class basis of American politics since the 1930's, despite the prosperity since World War II and despite the shifts to the Right during the Eisenhower era."[30] Hamilton, more recently, reached similar conclusions: there had been no weakening of social class voting in the United States.[31]

Our hypotheses imply that this may have been true in the recent past; it is less likely to be true today and in the immediate future. Let us look at our data. Table 7–3 shows the relationship between social class (as indicated by the occupation of the head of family) and vote.

There is a clear and consistent zero-order relationship between social class and voting intention or party preference. In every country, people with manual occupations (and their families) are more likely to vote for the Left than those from white-collar backgrounds. In some cases the relationship is quite strong. In Great

[27] *Ibid.*, 223. As noted above, Lipset has also devoted considerable attention to the importance of cultural and territorial variables.

[28] See Robert R. Alford, *Party and Society: The Anglo-American Democracies* (Chicago: Rand McNally, 1963).

[29] Campbell *et al., American Voter*, 356–361.

[30] Alford, *Party and Society*, 226.

[31] See Richard Hamilton, *Class and Politics in the United States* (New York: Wiley, 1972).

TABLE 7-3. Social Class and Political Partisanship[a]
(Percent supporting the parties of the Right)

Britain

Middle class	78%	(442)
Working class	44	(1,066)
Alford index:	+34	

Germany

Middle class	50%	(1,208)
Working class	37	(1,039)
Alford index:	+13	
Farm	64%	(120)

France

Middle class	50%	(467)
Working class	35	(419)
Alford index:	+15	
Farm	67%	(148)

Italy

Middle class	63%	(758)
Working class	48	(524)
Alford index:	+15	
Farm	67%	(272)

Netherlands

Middle class	55%	(985)
Working class	40	(541)
Alford index:	+15	
Farm	78%	(149)

Belgium

Middle class	70%	(468)
Working class	54	(502)
Alford index:	+16	
Farm	90%	(114)

Switzerland

Middle class	74%	(581)
Working class	53	(395)
Alford index:	+21	
Farm	93%	(123)

United States: Party Identification

Middle class	44%	(1,565)
Working class	29	(1,401)
Alford index:	+15	
Farm	53%	(168)

United States: Vote in 1972

Middle class	67%	(1,382)
Working class	59	(842)
Alford index:	+8	
Farm	79%	(117)

[a] Social class is based on occupation, head of family: those in non-manual occupations are categorized as middle class; those in manual occupations are considered working class, except for farm families. The Alford index is simply the difference in the percentage voting for the Left, between the first two groups. Data from 1970 and 1971 European Community surveys are combined in this table for all countries except Britain (where 1971 survey data were not available). Swiss data are from a 1972 survey by the Universities of Geneva and Zurich. American data for party identification are from the Institute for Social Research May, 1972, omnibus survey, Center for Political Studies 1972 election survey and European Community March, 1973, survey; vote in 1972 is based on the two latter surveys only. These sources are also the basis of the following tables in this chapter, except as noted.

Britain, for example, there is a difference of 34 percentage points between working class and middle class in likelihood of voting for the Left (in other words, we have an Alford class-voting index of +34). Britain provides an illustration of the fact that social class voting is by no means a myth: in some settings, the middle class *does* vote overwhelmingly for the Right, while a clear majority of the working class votes for the Left. Switzerland also shows a rather impressive class-voting index of +21.

In the other six countries, the tendency toward social class-voting is much weaker, however. In five of them the class-voting index ranges from +13 to +16—only half the size of the British figure. In the sixth—the United States—the index for class-*voting* (as opposed to party identification) is less than one-fourth as large as the British index. One might be tempted to conclude that Britain shows a relatively high rate of class-voting simply because she has undergone relatively slow economic change lately, but reality is never that simple. Britain's high rate of class-voting seems to date back at least several decades, and perhaps as far back as the era when the working class first became fully enfranchised. Like the Scandinavian countries (which show even higher rates of class-voting) she was able to polarize predominantly along class lines because of the absence of competing religious cleavages. Relatively widespread and deep-rooted political party loyalties probably have been more important in maintaining this class polarization than has her slow rate of economic change.

Nevertheless, the evidence indicates that a decade or two ago class-voting was considerably stronger and more widely prevalent than it was in the 1970's. The class-voting index that we obtain for Britain is somewhat smaller than the mean figure reported by Alford. And the index for the United States is only half the size of Alford's mean value. One's impression that social class-voting has declined receives additional reinforcement when we compare the American class-voting index for 1972 with a similar index based on the respondent's sense of political party *identification*. Party identification indicates a general sense of affiliation, which may have been instilled by one's family of orientation. It does not necessarily reflect current voting intention (as the results of the 1972 election made abundantly clear). The Alford index based on political party identification is +15—almost as large as the average class-voting index obtained by Alford for the period from 1936 to 1960. Despite the persistence of these traditional ties linking the working class to the Left and the middle class to the Right, the index based on actual *vote* in 1972 was only +8.

Independent analyses of large bodies of time series data by Glenn and by Abramson demonstrate rather conclusively that there has been a long-term decline in class-voting in the United States.[32] The trend did not take the form of a straight line moving ever downward. Class-voting indices dropped to a temporary low point of about +11 during the Eisenhower years and then rose somewhat in the next two elections. But the long-term pattern is clear: class voting shrank from an average of about +18 from 1936 to 1948, to +8 or lower in 1972. More significantly, the trend seems deep rooted. Both Abramson and Glenn conclude, on the basis of cohort analysis, that the pattern reflects generational change. A given rate of social class voting seems to persist over time within a given age cohort; it remains high among the older groups but is low or negligible among the younger ones. Indeed, in 1968, both authors actually detected faintly *negative* class-voting indices among the youngest American age cohort; in 1972, Abramson found negative indices among his *two* youngest cohorts.[33] We can expect continuing fluctuation in future elections, as parties change their strategies, and as the Democratic Party recovers from the debacle of 1972. But it will probably be the fluctuation of a variable that now has secondary importance in American politics.

Equally reliable data are not available for most European countries, but what we have tells a similar story. Goldthorpe *et al.* argued that class conflict is not declining in Britain, and they are correct in a relative sense: the decline in that country has been smaller than elsewhere; but recent evidence suggests that there has been a decline even there.[34]

How can we reconcile these findings with the conclusions reached by Alford, Hamilton, and others after careful analysis of

[32] See Norval D. Glenn, "Class and Party Support in the United States: Recent and Emerging Trends," *Public Opinion Quarterly*, 37, 1 (Spring, 1973), 1–20; and Paul R. Abramson, "Generational Change in American Electoral Behavior," *American Political Science Review*, 68, 1 (March, 1974), 93–105. Cf. Abramson, *Generational Change in American Politics* (Lexington, Mass: Lexington Books, 1975).

[33] See Abramson, *Generational Change*, 35. Furthermore, although the relationship between social class and party *identification* remained relatively strong among the older cohorts, there was no correlation whatever between these variables among those who first voted in 1972. See *ibid.*, 52.

[34] See David Butler and Donald E. Stokes, *Political Change in Britain*, 2nd ed. (New York: St. Martin's, 1974), 139–154.

a large number of surveys? I suggest that the answer lies in the fact that the change has been relatively recent (while their data took them only as far as 1964, at the latest).

Let us assume that economic issues were more salient and social class conflict more intense in the 1930's than before or since.[35] It would seem logical, at first glance, to conclude that *if* social class-voting were going to decline, it would have done so during the relatively calm and prosperous 1950's. Yet the evidence examined by Alford, Lipset, and others showed no such decline. On the contrary, in both Europe and the United States, social class-voting indices actually seem to have been *higher* in the 1950's than in the 1930's. But the expectation that class-voting would have declined by the 1950's is based on the implicit assumption that people would respond almost *immediately* to the changed economic environment. This assumption sounds plausible enough, but it is contradicted by the evidence. It appears that relatively few individuals changed their party identification during these years. The shift in the American electorate from a Republican majority to a Democratic majority was overwhelmingly due to population replacement—the effects of which did not become fully manifest until decades after the historical events that set this transformation in motion. For similar reasons, the incidence of social class-voting did not reach its peak until long after the Great Depression. It reflects the political and economic situation prevailing during one's formative years, not just the immediate situation. The age cohorts socialized during the Depression and Recession did not become fully incorporated into the electorate until the 1950's. Only then did the cohorts entering the electorate start to be *less* class polarized than their elders. Once again, the process of population replacement entailed a considerable delay between historical event and the manifestation of its impact on the electorate.

The evidence that social class-voting is gradually declining in the United States is rather conclusive. But we may expect further ups and downs. Just as class-voting rates made a partial recovery after Eisenhower's charisma was no longer a factor, the election of

[35] A recent analysis by W. Phillips Shively indicates that the rate of social class-voting in the United States was relatively low prior to 1936—but that a shift took place in that year which linked low-income groups to the Democratic Party and upper-income groups to the Republican Party. His findings give new support to the concept of a "generation of the New Deal"; see Shively, "A Reinterpretation of the New Deal Realignment," *Public Opinion Quarterly*, 35, 4 (Winter, 1971–1972), 621–624.

1972 must be regarded as an abnormal phenomenon: never in recent history have so many Americans voted against their own sense of party identification. Short-term forces could be expected to raise the class-voting rate in the near future—though not to the level found by Alford. Furthermore, if the prosperity of recent decades diminished the salience of economic issues, one would expect that the Recession from 1973 to 1975 would have reinstated them at least partially. Let us compare the class-voting rates of 1970 and 1971 with those of 1973 and 1975, in the six European countries for which we have the necessary data. Table 7–4 shows the vote by class in our 1973 and 1975 surveys, with Alford indices for both the earlier and later periods. We find that in four of the six countries, the class-voting indices are higher at the later time than they were in the earlier one, though only in The Netherlands and France are the increases at all substantial. In two countries (Belgium and Italy) the index actually *declined*. Overall, the impact of the Recession seems to work in the anticipated direction, but with rather modest results. The inconsistency of the pattern suggests that the recent changes reflect local circumstances more than a general reversion to social class-voting.

Our analysis up to this point has used occupation of head of family as an indicator of social class. Perhaps we have simply failed to measure the real basis of class conflict. Many skilled manual workers now earn substantially more than lower-grade white-collar employees; it has been argued that the latter now constitute part of the Proletariat. Perhaps the most important political cleavage today lies between the lower-paid workers (in both manual and non-manual occupations) and those with higher incomes (whether manual or non-manual). If we analyze our data according to income rather than occupation, will we find evidence of stronger class cleavages? Table 7–5 shows the relationship between income and voting intention for six of our eight countries.[36] In general, the relationship between income and vote is *not* stronger than that between occupation and vote. Indeed, in Germany, France, and Italy, the lowest income groups seem to be the most *conservative*! This paradoxical finding is largely due to the fact that older people and farm families tend to have low incomes, and tend to support the parties of the Right. But income does not seem to provide stronger evidence of class voting than occupation did.

[36] Data on income was obtained in the 1971 European surveys only; Great Britain was not surveyed in that year.

TABLE 7–4. Social Class and Political Partisanship, 1973–1975[a]

(Percent supporting the parties of the Right by occupation of head of household)

Britain			**Germany**		
Middle class	68%	(545)	Middle class	49%	(803)
Working class	33	(839)	Working class	35	(648)
Alford index:	+35	(+34)[b]	Alford index:	+14	(+13)
Italy			**Netherlands**		
Middle class	54%	(650)	Middle class	57%	(721)
Working class	40	(545)	Working class	36	(518)
Alford index:	+14	(+15)[b]	Alford index:	+21	(+15)
			France		
			Middle class	47%	(914)
			Working class	28	(663)
			Alford index:	+19	(+15)
			Belgium		
			Middle class	65%	(324)
			Working class	55	(425)
			Alford index:	+10	(+16)

[a] Based on the combined data from the 1973 and May 1975 European Community surveys. The samples are merged to provide reasonably reliable class-voting indices.

[b] Class-voting indices from 1970 to 1971 appear in parentheses, to the right of the indices from 1973 to 1975.

TABLE 7–5. Voting Intention by Family Income[a]
(Percent supporting parties of the Right)

Germany		
Under $250/month	54%	(157)
$250–$320	48	(204)
$320–$400	47	(266)
$400–$475	52	(217)
Over $475/month	50	(366)

Netherlands		
Under $170/month	57%	(75)
$170–$270	55	(120)
$270–$370	62	(231)
$370–$530	68	(247)
Over $530	72	(184)

United States: Party Identification		
Under $333/month	33%	(706)
$333–$833	31	(1,561)
Over $833	43	(1,675)

France		
Under $160/month	52%	(183)
$160–$350	42	(520)
$350–$500	44	(242)
$500–$600	41	(164)
Over $600/month	49	(90)

Belgium		
Under $160/month	70%	(119)
$160–$250	57	(155)
$250–$350	58	(143)
$350–$500	68	(80)
Over $500	82	(38)

United States: Vote in 1972		
Under $333/month	58%	(364)
$333–$833	60	(831)
Over $833	69	(1,482)

Italy		
Under $200/month	70%	(310)
$200–$300	58	(323)
$300–$420	60	(195)
$420–$580	61	(82)
Over $580	70	(40)

[a] European data are from 1971 survey only; American data from same sources as for Table 7–3.

Education is another important indicator of social class. Its relationship with the vote is shown in Table 7–6. Here also we find curvilinear relationships. In Britain, West Germany, France, and the United States, the most educated group was *less* likely to vote for the Right than those with a secondary school education. In

TABLE 7–6. Political Party Preference by Education, 1970 and 1971
(Percent supporting the parties of the Right)

Britain			Germany			France		
Primary	49%	(1,125)	Primary	50%	(2,161)	Primary	47%	(1,380)
Secondary	77	(274)	Secondary	55	(452)	Secondary	50	(954)
University	63	(65)	University	33	(124)	University	43	(263)
Italy			*Netherlands*			*Belgium*		
Primary	63%	(1,531)	Primary	53%	(1,282)	Primary	62%	(811)
Secondary	63	(428)	Secondary	54	(842)	Secondary	66	(353)
University	67	(205)	University	61	(138)	University	80	(63)
			United States:			*United States:*		
Switzerland			*Party Identification*			*Vote in 1972*		
Primary	63%	(526)	Primary	32%	(967)	Primary	62%	(436)
Secondary	73	(582)	Secondary	35	(2,038)	Secondary	68	(1,360)
University	73	(67)	University	43	(1,077)	University	63	(915)

France, this group is actually the most *Left*-oriented of all three categories.[37] Across the eight countries, the respondent's education does not seem to be linked with political party preferences to a significantly greater extent than occupation of the head of family.

To complete the picture, let us look at another one of the important variables underlying class conflict in Industrial society:

---

[37] A number of observers have attributed student radicalism (particularly in France) to the fact that employment opportunities for the university-educated in France had deteriorated seriously by 1968, the year of the massive student uprising. This may have contributed to unrest, but it scarcely provides a sufficient explanation. The most radical students were very often among the academically most successful and those with the best family connections—precisely the ones who had least reason to fear unemployment or underemployment. They may, nevertheless, have sought radical change because of fears for the economic situation of their peers, but this is quite another type of motivation from that underlying conventional class conflict. The interpretation that a declining job market produces student radicalism becomes a good deal more implausible when applied to the United States. In this country, student radicalism rose during a period when the demand for Ph.D.'s was exceptionally strong, and declined during a period when the job market had collapsed.

labor union membership. Table 7–7 shows how this variable relates to voting intention in each of our seven countries. It has been
demonstrated repeatedly that affiliation with a labor union is associated with support for the parties of the Left.[38] The data in Table
7–7 simply confirm these findings. In all eight countries, union

ABLE 7–7. Political Party Preferences by Labor Union or *Syndicat* Membership
(Percent supporting the parties of the Right)

itain			*Germany*			*France*		
ember	41%	(367)	Member	27%	(591)	Member	31%	(635)
on-member	60	(1,147)	Non-member	51	(2,236)	Non-member	51	(2,062)
aly			*Netherlands*			*Belgium*		
ember	51%	(289)	Member	43%	(465)	Member	62%	(374)
on-member	64	(1,884)	Non-member	57	(1,822)	Non-member	69	(860)
			United States:			*United States:*		
witzerland			*Party Identification*			*Vote in 1972*		
ember	43%	(133)	Member in			Member in		
on-member	71	(1,042)	household	26%	(953)	household	58%	(712)
			Non-member	40	(3,092)	Non-member	68	(1,991)

membership is linked with a preference for the Left; in some cases,
the relationship is quite strong. Labor unions provide a major
institutional reinforcement to the Industrial pattern of political
cleavage. Nevertheless, there is reason to believe that it may be in
decline. In the United States the linkage between union affiliation
and support for the Democratic Party was far stronger from 1948
to 1956 than it was in 1972.[39] Furthermore, the proportion of the
_labor force made up of union members has been declining for some
time in most Western countries.

Our data on occupation, income, education and labor union
membership make it clear that the Industrial pattern of political
cleavage has by no means disappeared. Nevertheless, it probably

[38] See Campbell *et al.*, *American Voter*, 301–332; Butler and Stokes,
Political Change in Britain, 151–170; Klaus Liepelt, "The Infra-Structure
of Party Support in Germany and Austria," in Mattei Dogan and Richard
Rose (eds.), *European Politics: A Reader* (Boston: Little, Brown, 1971),
183–201; and Morris Janowitz and David R. Segal, "Social Cleavage and
Party Affiliation: Germany, Great Britain and the United States," *American
Journal of Sociology*, 72, 6 (May, 1967), 601–618.

[39] For data on the earlier period, see Campbell *et al.*, *American Voter*,
302.

is declining in importance. There are two main reasons: first, the working class feels less incentive to vote for change-oriented parties than it did a generation ago; second, a growing segment of the middle class feels *more* incentive to do so. Let us examine some evidence supporting the first point.

In the early phases of Industrial society, the population tends to be divided between a large mass of poorly paid workers and a relatively small number of owners and managers having much higher incomes and a radically different life style.[40] In advanced Industrial societies, the ranks of the middle class are greatly increased by growth in the number of people in managerial, technical, clerical, and sales occupations; the relative number of manual workers diminishes but their income levels rise and the amount of leisure time at their disposal increases with the result that many of them are able to adopt a life style relatively close to conventional middle class standards.

The much criticized "middle majority" theory held that as this process takes place, there will be a decline in class conflict and a narrowing of party differences. As Lipset put it in an often cited and controversial article, "In the long run, however, the remaining bases of ideologically intrinsic politics will continue to decline due to the contradiction between reality and their definition of the situation, and because of the irrelevance of their call to action in terms of a situation which will no longer exist."[41] During the 1950's and early 1960's, writers with viewpoints as diverse as those of Aron, Bell, Keniston, and Marcuse called attention to the decline of ideological conflict with various degrees of approval or dismay. Implicit in the discussion was the assumption that radical protest movements could be based *only* on the working class. This assumption has been a continuing source of confusion, in what

[40] In most such societies, there is also a substantial number of farmers, but both from the standpoint of Marxist theory and empirically, they tend to be marginal to the principal social conflicts of Industrial society.

[41] Seymour M. Lipset, "The Changing Class Structure and Contemporary European Politics," *Daedalus*, 93, 1 (Winter, 1964), 271–303. See also Robert E. Lane, "The Politics of Consensus in an Age of Affluence," *American Political Science Review*, 59, 4 (December, 1965), 874–895. For a good example of the many vigorous criticisms directed at this interpretation, see Joseph LaPalombara, "Decline of Ideology: A Dissent and an Interpretation," *American Political Science Review*, 60, 1 (March, 1966), 5–16. More recently, Lipset has summed up his side of the argument in "Ideology and No End: The Controversy Till Now," *Encounter*, 39, 6 (December, 1972), 17–24.

became the "End of Ideology" debate. Alternative bases of radicalism (such as the younger middle class and students) were scarcely considered; it was taken for granted that they would be conservative or apathetic. As Marcuse stated: "Everywhere and at all times, the overwhelming majority of students are conservative and even reactionary."[42] If the working class were no longer radical, therefore, we had necessarily reached the "End of Ideology."

If the foregoing phrase is interpreted to imply the end of all conflict based on politically-relevant world views, the diagnosis was manifestly false, as anyone who has lived through the past decade must be aware. But in a narrower sense, the implications of the "middle majority" thesis were correct. There is still plenty of conflict, and much of it is ideological; but it is *not* the conventional conflict of working class against middle class. Protest comes from different sources, and for different motives. The working class is no longer a revolutionary force. Data from the 1970 surveys bear this out.

Respondents in five countries were asked to rate their family's economic position on a seven-point scale, ranging from rich to poor. This is a measure of *subjective* economic position, in contrast to the data on actual family income shown in Table 7–5. In one respect, the results support the concept that politics are economically determined, to a greater extent than do the data in Table 7–5. Those who see themselves as poor or near the bottom end of the economic spectrum are very likely to vote for the Left, while those who consider themselves rich are likely to vote for the Right. But only a relative handful *see* themselves as falling at either extreme. The vast majority place themselves at the midpoint or one of the two adjacent points (see Table 7–8). This self-defined "middle majority" is smallest in Italy—where it nevertheless amounts to 78 percent of the total sample. In the other countries it ranges from 86 to 94 percent. Not many Europeans consider themselves poor, even in Italy—the country having the largest stratum that *is* poor by objective standards. These perceptions may be based on comparisons between one's own economic circumstances today and in the recent past, more than on comparisons between oneself and others in the same society, for the relative distribution of incomes has not become appreciably more egalitarian in recent years. But absolute levels of income *have* risen,

[42] Marcuse, interview in *Le Monde*, April 11, 1968.

TABLE 7–8. The Middle Majority: Distribution of Economic Self-Perceptions by Nation[a]

(Percent rating selves as rich, poor, or in-between)

Rate selves as:	Germany		Belgium		France		Netherlands		Italy	
Poor	1%	(21)	1%	(18)	3%	(56)	5%	(55)	2%	(26)
	2	(36)	3	(39)	3	(89)	3	(36)	7	(80)
Mid-point	94% {14	(289)	91% {24	(306)	89% {36	(735)	86% {32	(356)	78% {13	(160)
	33	(671)	27	(355)	32	(657)	26	(290)	45	(547)
	47	(950)	40	(512)	21	(424)	28	(311)	20	(247)
Rich	2	(44)	3	(42)	2	(42)	2	(23)	11	(138)
	.1	(3)	1	(9)	.4	(8)	4	(50)	1	(13)

[a] Data are from the 1970 European Community survey; comparable data are not available for the other countries.

and the majority of both Europeans and Americans seem to think they are materially better-off than they were in the past.[43]

To some extent, the "End of Ideology" debate is based on false alternatives. One side emphasizes the importance of rising *levels* of income; the other emphasizes the persisting inequality of income *distribution*; and one variable is sometimes emphasized almost to the exclusion to the other. Furthermore, an empirical analysis tends to get confused with a normative analysis. Carried to an extreme, the middle majority theorists are alleged to be *opposed* to a more egalitarian income distribution. Morally speaking, an egalitarian distribution may well be the only thing that counts. But empirically, it seems that income *levels* are also important. In my view, an awareness of reality cannot be pernicious; it is essential to any effective program of social change.

Even in relative terms, the West European working class has reason to feel well-off in one respect. In all of these countries except Italy, a large proportion of the unskilled manual jobs are now filled by foreign laborers. The economies of Western Europe have pulled in millions of Spaniards, Portuguese, Algerians, Indians, Turks, Greeks, Yugoslavs, and others. In each of these countries, the most poorly paid and economically insecure group consists of foreign laborers, who do not have the right to vote and consequently do not figure in any analysis of class-voting.

Our expectation is that the working class of Western countries no longer desires radical social change. An item in our surveys

[43] See Reader's Digest Association, *A Survey of Europe Today* (London: Reader's Digest, 1970), 166–167. Survey data for all six of our European countries indicate that both in 1963 and in 1969, strong majorities felt that they were better off than they had been five years earlier. Scammon and Wattenberg present related evidence for the United States. They cite Gallup surveys which show that from 1949 to 1969 there were substantial increases in the percentage of Americans who said they were satisfied with their work, their family income, and their housing. By the later year, 88 percent were satisfied with their work, 67 percent with their family income and 80 percent with their housing. See Richard M. Scammon and Ben J. Wattenberg, *The Real Majority* (New York: Coward McCann, 1970), 102. Frank E. Myers argues that *relative* income distribution is what counts, not *absolute* levels; since the former has not changed significantly, the working class will remain as dissatisfied as ever, and therefore favorable to radical change. See Myers, "Social Class and Political Change in Western Industrial Systems," *Comparative Politics*, 2, 2 (April, 1970), 389–412. Myers' contention that increasing affluence will not necessarily bring an end to social conflict is clearly correct. But the foregoing evidence strongly suggests that relative level is not the only important variable; absolute levels of income may have important effects on levels of satisfaction and on *who* is protesting and *what* they are protesting.

provides a test of this hypothesis. The 1970 European Community surveys and the 1972 Swiss survey included the following item:

On this card are stated three basic attitudes toward the society in which we live. Would you tell me which one comes closest to your own view?

1. We must change the entire organization of our society by revolutionary action.

2. We must improve our society gradually by intelligent reforms.

3. We must defend our present society courageously against all subversive forces.

This question was also included in the 1973 American survey, in modified form. The options were:

1. We must radically change our whole society.

2. We must improve our society by gradual reform.

3. We must defend our present society from being undermined.

Table 7–9 shows the responses to this item in the seven countries for which we have data. Once again, we find evidence of a large middle majority. More than three-quarters of the European respondents and a clear majority of Americans favor gradual reform. A similar pattern appears when we ask these publics to place themselves on a Left-Right scale (or, in America, a Liberal-Conservative scale): a solid majority locate themselves in the center range.[44] As we saw in Chapter 5, those with manual occupations show no more dissatisfaction with society and politics than those in non-manual occupations. A similar pattern emerges here. Working-class and middle-class respondents support the revolutionary or radical alternative in about equal proportions, but in none of the countries is it favored by more than one-eighth of any group. In six of the seven countries, the workers are *more* likely to favor a resolute defense of the present society than the middle class! If support or opposition to social change is the essence of the Left-Right dimension, the working class appears to be as conserva-

[44] In the United States, for example, among those interviewed in the 1972 Center for Political Studies election survey, 72 percent placed themselves in one of the three center spaces of a seven-block Liberal-Conservative scale. For details of how various European publics were distributed in 1973, see Inglehart and Klingemann, "Party Identification."

Germany

	Present Society	Gradual Reform	Revolutionary Change	N
Middle class	17%	80%	2%	(699)
Working class	22	76	2	(725)
Farm	24	74	2	(170)

Italy

	Present Society	Gradual Reform	Revolutionary Change	N
Middle class	9%	82%	9%	(654)
Working class	11	81	9	(392)
Farm	15	80	6	(206)

Belgium

	Present Society	Gradual Reform	Revolutionary Change	N
Middle class	11%	85%	4%	(522)
Working class	20	76	4	(370)
Farm	24	75	2	(55)

Switzerland

	Present Society	Gradual Reform	Revolutionary Change	N
Middle class	23%	75%	2%	(857)
Working class	32	65	2	(547)
Farm	46	54	1	(127)

France

	Present Society	Gradual Reform	Revolutionary Change	N
Middle class	9%	84%	7%	(737)
Working class	15	79	6	(605)
Farm	13	84	4	(223)

Netherlands

	Present Society	Gradual Reform	Revolutionary Change	N
Middle class	13%	81%	6%	(722)
Working class	17	75	9	(330)
Farm	27	65	9	(71)

United States

	Present Society	Gradual Reform	Radical Change	N
Middle class	28%	63%	9%	(603)
Working class	28	59	13	(682)
Farm	40	55	5	(88)

[a] European data from 1970 European Community survey, American data from 1973 survey; British data not available.

tive in its attitudes as the middle class. It seems quite conceivable that the working class remains more likely to *vote* for the Left primarily because of traditional party loyalties. If this is the case, one would expect a gradual decline in class-voting as time goes by.

As we noted earlier, the class-voting index that we obtained for Britain in 1970 is somewhat below the figure found by Alford using data from 1943 to 1962; and our index for the United States in 1972 is far below his figure. Time-series data for the six other countries are in comparatively short supply; national opinion surveys did not even begin to be carried out in them until about a decade later than in the United States. Alford did not calculate class-voting indices for these other countries, but we can obtain an idea of their magnitude during the period from 1956 to 1959 in a study by Lijphart. He obtains an average class-voting index of +24 for Germany, France, Italy, The Netherlands, Belgium, and Switzerland.[45] The combined results of our surveys from 1970 to 1972 produce a mean class-voting index of +16 for the same six nations. In other words, the class-voting index was about half again as large in the 1950's as in the early 1970's.

A relatively good time-series data base is available for Germany. In a fascinating analysis of political change that draws on these data, Baker, Dalton and Hildebrandt find that the German social class-voting index dropped from +30 in 1953 to +17 in 1972.[46]

[45] See Arend Lijphart, *Class Voting and Religious Voting in the European Democracies: A Preliminary Report* (Glasgow: University of Strathclyde, 1971). We must be cautious about placing too much emphasis on a class-voting index obtained from a single survey; Alford very prudently based his analysis on the mean result obtained from a number of surveys. Sampling error may amount to only a few percentage points for the overall results of a national survey; but when the results are broken down by occupational category, the sampling error (even for a good sample) may amount to several points. Moreover, the class-voting index is obtained by *comparing* the voting pattern of two such categories. In the unlikely event that sampling error has biased results for the two categories in opposite directions, one could obtain a class-voting index as much as 10 or 12 points from the true value. Hence, we report the mean index from Lijphart's six samples for this cross-time comparison. Lijphart's data contain what seems to be an anomalously low class-voting index of +15 for France in 1956. Indices of +31 and +25 are obtained for the years 1947 and 1955, respectively, from data in Duncan MacRae, Jr., *Parliament, Parties and Society in France; 1946–1958* (New York: St. Martin's, 1967), 257–258. And data in Lipset, *Political Man*, 164, yield an index of +29 for the year 1958.

[46] See Kendall L. Baker, Russell J. Dalton and Kai Hildebrandt, "Political Affiliations: Transition in the Basis of German Partisanship," paper presented at the sessions of the European Consortium for Political Research, London, April 7–12, 1975. Cf. Baker, Dalton and Hildebrandt, *Transitions in German Politics* (forthcoming).

Part of this decline is undoubtedly due to macro-political events, in particular the middle-of-the-road program adopted by the Social Democrats in 1959. But the decline does not seem to be simply a consequence of this policy shift. For one thing, no particularly marked decline in class-voting took place immediately after 1959 (the biggest drop took place in 1969). For another thing, the decline in class-voting seems to reflect a generational change more than an immediate response to changes in elite positions. For, as the authors demonstrate, there was virtually *no* decline in class-voting among the older German cohorts; it was only among the post-war German age cohorts that class-voting diminished over time—and there it has all but disappeared.

Drawing on another body of data, Abramson argues that class-voting is diminishing in France, Germany, and Italy—though not in Great Britain.[47] We would conclude that class cleavages have been declining in each of the eight nations dealt with in this chapter except (possibly) for Britain.

The notion that social class polarization may be declining tends to be received by orthodox Marxists with all the enthusiasm that a fundamentalist Christian would have for reports that the millennium will not come. Yet in Post-Industrial society, strong social class-voting spells doom for the Left. A generation ago, it was true in many countries that the Left was sure to win, if only all the manual workers would vote along class lines. But the blue-collar share of the population has been shrinking steadily; for many years they have been outnumbered by white-collar workers in the United States. By 1980 this will be true throughout most of Western Europe. The Left *must* go beyond a working-class base if it hopes to win elections. The emergence of a relatively large Post-Materialist section of the middle class offers the Left a new opportunity—if it can appeal to the emerging group without alienating its traditional base.

[47] See Paul R. Abramson, "Social Class and Political Change in Western Europe: A Cross-National Longitudinal Analysis," *Comparative Political Studies*, 4, 2 (July, 1971), 131–155.

CHAPTER 8

Pre-Industrial and Post-Industrial Political Cleavages

IF class-linked voting is declining, common sense might seem to suggest that voting patterns based on Pre-Industrial variables must be declining even more rapidly. Universalism rather than particularism and achieved rather than ascribed status are widely considered to be hallmarks of modern political systems. Religion, race, and other ethnic ties seem improbable and inappropriate bases for political cleavage in societies supposedly characterized by a legal-rational style of authority. Religion, in particular, has been an important basis of political conflict since the Reformation, but religious issues have faded in intensity during the twentieth century. Moreover, church attendance has shown a sharp decline in most Western countries during the past decade. One might expect the influence of religion on political behavior to have dwindled in similar fashion.

Indeed, there is some evidence that it has. The proportion of the vote going to religious parties in The Netherlands has fallen spectacularly in recent years. In 1922, 59 percent of the Dutch electorate voted for parties linked with the Protestant or Catholic churches. Religious voting remained remarkably stable for decades; as recently as 1963, the figure was 52 percent. By the 1972 elections, it had dropped to 36 percent. In Belgium, the vote for the Social Christians has shown a similar recent decline from 47 percent in 1958 to 34 percent in 1974.

In France's June, 1946, elections, the church-backed Popular Republican Movement won 28 percent of the vote, making it the largest of France's political parties at the time. By 1956 its vote had declined to 11 percent of the total; in 1967 it was dissolved. On the other hand, the vote for religious parties has been quite stable in Germany and Italy. In both countries, the share of the vote going to the Christian Democrats in 1976 was about the same size it had been 25 years earlier. But underlying this stability, there are indications of a possible future decline: church attendance is falling in both countries. Schmidtchen finds a markedly lower rate of church attendance among younger Germans, and it is linked with the presence of secular values which seem to persist through the life-cycle; and Barnes finds a sharp decline in favorable attitudes toward the clergy among younger Italians, as compared with older Italians.[1]

Gabriel Almond has spoken of political cultures based on religion as Pre-Industrial survivals, "outcroppings of older cultures" which persist due to a "failure on the part of the middle classes in the nineteenth century to carry through a thoroughgoing secularization of the political culture."[2]

The religious factor seems to have persisted far beyond its time; its disappearance could be expected to lead to a sharp increase in polarization along class lines. Is the current change in values and mores an indication that the secularization of Western political culture is finally being completed?

Apparently not—at least not yet. Paradoxical as it may seem, Pre-Industrial cleavages appear to be *more* persistent than Industrial political cleavages. There are two principal reasons for this: (1) a family tends to transmit certain Pre-Industrial characteristics to its offspring with higher rates of fidelity than those applying to Industrial characteristics; (2) the relationship of value change to the two respective types of cleavage. Let us consider each of these reasons in turn.

As we have seen, the political party which one's parents supported seems to be a very powerful predictor of how the individual himself votes. Let us assume, for the moment, that both class-linked and religious and ethnic issues had entirely ceased to operate as contemporary influences on the vote; and that the individual's choice between the parties of the Left and those of the Right were shaped exclusively by preferences inherited from one's family. Obviously, these are assumptions which we would reject—

[1] See Gerhard Schmidtchen, *Zwischen Kirche und Gesellschaft* (Freiburg: Herder Verlag, 1972); and Samuel H. Barnes, "Religion and Class in Italian Electoral Behavior," in Richard Rose (ed.), *Electoral Behavior: A Comparative Handbook* (New York: Free Press, 1974), 171–225. Evidence of an inter-generational decline in religiosity on the American scene is reported in M. Kent Jennings and Richard G. Niemi, "Continuity and Change in Political Orientations," *American Political Science Review*, 69, 4 (December, 1975), 1316–1335.

[2] Gabriel Almond, "Comparative Political Systems," *Journal of Politics*, 18, 3 (August, 1956), 391–409. Reprinted in Roy C. Macridis and Bernard E. Brown (eds.), *Comparative Politics: Notes and Readings*, 4th ed. (Homewood, Ill.; Dorsey, 1972).

along with everyone else. But they enable us to put an important influence on political behavior in clear perspective.

In a world governed by these assumptions, both class-linked and Pre-Industrial types of variables would continue to be correlated with voting behavior, insofar as they were transmitted from generation to generation along with political party preference. But different characteristics tend to be transmitted from generation to generation with varying degrees of fidelity, and the rate seems to be a good deal lower for Industrial characteristics than for most Pre-Industrial characteristics.

Social class does tend to be inherited, but the tendency is weakened by social mobility. In the United States in 1962, 24 percent of the male population consisted of middle-class males whose fathers had had working-class occupations; an additional 10 percent were working-class sons of middle-class fathers.[3] The rate of social mobility seems somewhat lower in Great Britain: 28 percent of those interviewed by Butler and Stokes in 1963 had experienced inter-generational social mobility (21 percent upward and 7 percent downward).[4] In some European settings, the rate of inter-generational mobility seems to be even higher than in the United States.[5] Similarly, in view of the great educational expansion of recent decades, the educational level of a good many children must be higher than that of their parents.

Although we have no data on inter-generational transmission rates for Pre-Industrial political cleavage characteristics, it seems safe to make certain generalizations. Such characteristics as race and language group are undoubtedly transmitted with a far higher rate of fidelity than holds true for social class: the correlation between parent and child for race and language probably approaches 1.00 in most countries. Religious characteristics are somewhat more problematic. Actual conversion from one denomination to another may be quite rare, but simply ceasing to participate in the religious life of one's denomination seems fairly widespread. Rates of church attendance in many Western countries

[3] See Peter Blau and Otis Dudley Duncan, *The American Occupational Structure* (New York: Wiley, 1967), 496.

[4] See Paul R. Abramson, "Intergenerational Social Mobility and Electoral Choice," *American Political Science Review*, 66, 4 (December, 1972), 1291–1294. Applying a more stringent definition of social mobility (based on both objective *and* subjective criteria), Butler and Stokes, *Political Change in Britain*, obtain a still lower rate.

[5] See Roger Girod, *Mobilité Sociale: Faits établis et problèmes ouverts* (Geneva and Paris: Droz, 1971), 52–53.

have declined in recent years. But in general, religious ties tend to be instilled relatively early in life and have a pre-rational basis which may be more enduring than affiliations based on economic position. Furthermore, parents usually encourage their children to adhere to their own religious pattern, whereas working-class parents often encourage their children to "move up" from their own economic status. Thus, religious denomination is probably transmitted from parent to child with substantially greater fidelity than social class; the same probably holds true of church attendance (or non-attendance), at least until quite recently.

We must concede, however, that certain *other* Pre-Industrial characteristics show a relatively low rate of inter-generational transmission. Lipset and Rokkan speak of "territorial-cultural" differences as one of two main axes of political cleavage.[6] The cultural aspect of this dimension may have a high probability of being transmitted from generation to generation, but the territorial aspect, a much lower one. A great deal of geographical mobility has taken place in Western countries in the past few decades. In Germany and France, inter-generational geographic mobility is probably about as common as social mobility.[7] And if we regard sex as a Pre-Industrial basis of political cleavage, we are at the opposite extreme from race: the correlation between sex of parents and children is .00. If our Pre-Industrial and Industrial variables were ranked according to fidelity of inter-generational transmission, then, they would have the following order:

> Race
> Language Group
> Religious Denomination
> Church Attendance
> Region Where Respondent Lives
> Industrial Cleavage Variables
> Sex.

Insofar as contemporary electoral behavior were based exclusively on preferences inherited from one's family, the above ranking

[6] Seymour M. Lipset and Stein Rokkan, "Cleavage Structures."

[7] Our 1971 surveys show that in both Germany and France, at least a third of the population no longer lived in the region in which they had been born. The regions referred to were the *Länder* for Germany, and the *regions de programme* (such as Brittany, Burgundy, Lorraine) for France. The figures ranged from 14 percent to 26 percent in Belgium, The Netherlands, and Italy.

would indicate how strongly the respective variables would be correlated with party preference. If social class, for example, is transmitted with a lower degree of fidelity than religious denomination, it would now show a weaker correlation with party preference than, say, religious denomination, even if we assume that they both had equally strong correlations with party preference a generation ago. Figure 8–1 illustrates this point with a simple causal model. It assumes that class and religion had .5 correlations with party preference in Generation 1, but are transmitted to Generation 2 (the children of Generation 1) with correlations of .4 and .9, respectively. In Generation 2, religious denomination would have more than twice as strong a linkage with party preference as would social class.

The assumptions of the foregoing model do not correspond to reality. Current issues *do* affect the way people vote, and economic issues seem to be much more widespread and salient than religious issues, which would weaken the effect shown in the model. Furthermore, some of those who experience inter-generational social mobility shift to the party that prevails in their new milieu, although it appears that most do not.[8] Finally, the model gives no consideration to the possibility that inter-generational value change might have an impact on political preferences.

The emergence of a Materialist/Post-Materialist value dimension *would* influence political choice. But it could have quite different effects on Industrial and Pre-Industrial types of cleavages. It would tend to neutralize the former cleavage, for reasons outlined earlier: the Post-Materialist type is recruited disproportionately from middle-class sources, but is disproportionately likely to vote for the parties of the Left. The process works to reduce the linkage between middle-class background and support for the parties of the Right.

The emergence of a Post-Industrial basis of cleavage does *not* necessarily have this effect on Pre-Industrial cleavages. In fact,

[8] Britain would seem to be the country in which pressures to conform to the party of one's class are greatest. But in his secondary analysis of Butler and Stokes' British data, Paul Abramson indicates that a majority of downwardly mobile respondents whose parents were Conservatives, and a majority of upwardly mobile respondents from Labour backgrounds, retained their family's political party preference in their new milieu. Most of those whose parents were Liberals did not, but this was true regardless of whether or not one was mobile. Abramson disagrees with Butler and Stokes about the *rate* of social mobility, but not about the foregoing finding. See Abramson, "Intergenerational Social Mobility."

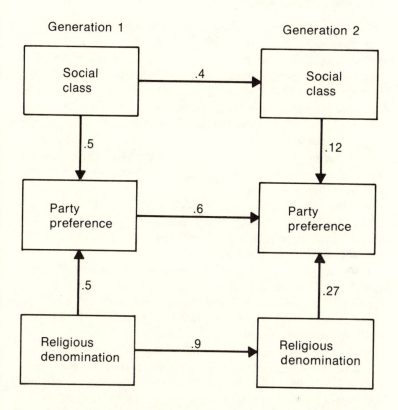

FIGURE 8–1. Inter-Generational Transmission of Social Class, Party Preference, and Religious Denomination.

with religious cleavages the reverse might sometimes hold true. The Post-Materialist type is disproportionately likely to be recruited from those who are low on religious involvement; but this group *already* tends to vote for the Left. Conversely, those who are most intensely affiliated with the established religions tend to vote for the Right, and adhere to traditional values and life-styles. Thus, the emergence of a Post-Materialist counter-culture could even temporarily strengthen the correlation between religion and electoral behavior. Accordingly, the rise of a Post-Industrial cleavage does not inherently tend to cancel out Pre-Industrial cleavages as it does Industrial ones.

For the foregoing reasons, we might expect Pre-Industrial variables to retain a relatively strong relationship with political behavior, even in societies that are entering a Post-Industrial phase. Let us look at some of the evidence.

Using political parties as their unit of analysis, Rose and Urwin found that, among seventy-six parties studied, thirty-five were "cohesive" on religion while only thirty-three were "cohesive" on social class. "Religion, not class, is the main social basis of parties in the Western world today," they conclude.[9]

Our survey data indicate that both religious denomination and frequency of church attendance are strongly related to party preference (see Tables 8–1 and 8–2). In most countries, the percentage differences linked with religion are larger than those linked with social class (as we see when we compare Tables 7–3 and 8–1). Britain is the one clear-cut exception to this pattern. In West Germany, on the other hand, 63 percent of the Catholics and only 37 percent of the Protestants support the Christian Democrats— a spread of 26 percentage points; the difference between working class and middle class shown in Table 7–3 was only half as large as this.

In France, Italy, and Belgium, the vast majority of the popula-

---

[9] See Richard Rose and Derek Urwin, "Social Cohesion, Political Parties and Strains in Regimes," *Comparative Political Studies*, 2, 1 (April, 1969), 7–67. The definition of "cohesion" used here varies from case to case; in most instances it means that at least two-thirds of a given party's supporters share the same characteristic. The authors also examined two other variables, "communalism" and region; eight parties were found to be cohesive on each of these characteristics. Rose and Urwin use the party as the unit of analysis, rather than the individual; one consequence of this approach is that the tiny Farmer's Party in The Netherlands is given the same weight as the Labor Party in that country, or the Democratic Party in the United States. Nevertheless, their basic conclusion seems to be correct.

TABLE 8-1. Political Party Preference by Religious Denomination
(Percent supporting the parties of the Right)

Britain			Germany			France		
Non-Anglican	52%	(535)	No religion	20%	(108)	No religion	11%	(303)
Anglican	57	(961)	Protestant	37	(1,388)	Protestant,		
			Catholic	63	(1,212)	Other	47	(157)
						Catholic	52	(2,179)
Italy			Netherlands			Belgium		
No religion	17%	(188)	No religion	25%	(754)	No religion	11%	(165)
Catholic	66	(1,964)	Liberal			Catholic	73	(1,059)
			Calvinist	57	(540)			
			Catholic	73	(766)			
			Fundamentalist					
			Calvinist	89	(214)			
			United States:			United States:		
Switzerland			Party Identification			Vote in 1972:		
No religion	36%	(33)	Jewish	12%	(107)	Jewish	36%	(75)
Protestant	63	(602)	Catholic	23	(991)	Catholic	61	(719)
Catholic	78	(518)	Protestant	43	(2,706)	Protestant	70	(1,774)

tion is Roman Catholic; it makes little sense to discuss differences between religious denominations. But the difference between practicing Catholics and non-practicing Catholics or Atheists tends to be quite impressive (see Table 8-2). In all eight countries, those who attend church regularly are a great deal more likely to vote for the parties of the Right than those who attend rarely or never. In the United States this holds true *despite* the fact that Catholics are traditionally linked with the Democratic Party, and have relatively high rates of church attendance.

One finding is striking and rather surprising in terms of class conflict theories: Britain has quite modest religious cleavages, but by far the highest level of social class polarization among these countries. Yet her political life in recent years has been less violent than any of the others except Switzerland, which has the second highest class-voting index. A similar pattern characterizes the Scandinavian countries. They have relatively moderate religious cleavages, but even higher levels of social class polarization than Britain, and they, too, are characterized by relatively consensual politics. Rose and Urwin conclude that in countries where political cleavages are based on social class, regime strains are likely to be relatively low; if politics is based on religious or other ethnic

TABLE 8-2. Political Party Preference by Church Attendance[a]
(Percent supporting the parties of the Right)

Britain			Germany			France		
Never attend	49%	(530)	Never attend	27%	(800)	Never	31%	(1,061)
Attend monthly			Monthly or			Monthly or		
or less	57	(769)	less	42	(1,149)	less	55	(955)
Attend weekly	58	(142)	Weekly	73	(696)	Weekly	68	(523)
More than			More than			More than		
once a week	73	(63)	weekly	90	(93)	weekly	74	(62)
Italy			*Netherlands*			*Belgium*		
Never	28%	(382)	Never	37%	(959)	Never	28%	(353)
Monthly or			Monthly or			Monthly or		
less	53	(686)	less	55	(393)	less	52	(214)
Weekly	79	(845)	Weekly	81	(770)	Weekly	87	(581)
More than			More than			More than		
weekly	92	(260)	weekly	92	(64)	weekly	97	(95)
			United States: Party Identification			*United States: Vote in 1972*		
Switzerland								
Never	48%	(149)	Never	34%	(277)	Never	53%	(263)
Rarely	61	(272)	Monthly or			Monthly or		
Sometimes	67	(319)	less	37	(736)	less	63	(634)
Nearly every			Almost weekly	41	(197)	Almost weekly	66	(206)
week	74	(166)	Every week	36	(500)	Every week	72	(478)
Weekly	88	(242)						

[a] European data from 1970 and 1971 European Community surveys; American data from Center for Political Studies 1972 election survey.

cleavages, regime strains are apt to be high. They argue that this tends to be true because economic controversies "are typically expressed in terms of money. Money is a continuous variable capable of indefinite subdivision for providing incremental adjustments in the distribution of economic benefits. In short, it is something that is very easy to bargain about."[10] Religious claims, on the other hand, tend to be non-bargainable; conflict is more likely to be seen in dichotomous, moralistic terms: one is right or wrong, good or evil. When these are involved, even the British are perfectly capable of getting embroiled in bitter and intractable disputes, as the conflict in Northern Ireland demonstrates.

We would agree with this analysis, with one important reserva-

[10] Rose and Urwin, "Social Cohesion," 39. Also see Richard Rose, *Governing without Consensus: An Irish Perspective* (Boston: Beacon, 1971). Lipset and Rokkan present a similar argument: see Lipset and Rokkan, *op cit.*, 6.

tion: economic conflicts may be comparatively easy to resolve in the Western world *today*; they have not always been so. Under conditions of economic scarcity, one may not be able to make concessions without endangering one's very survival. In the past, the margin for maneuver was far narrower. As recently as the middle of the nineteenth century, food riots were the principal form of political protest in Western Europe; they continued to play a major role in the politics of Spain and Italy well into the twentieth century.[11] Survival is *not* something easy to bargain about. The idea that economically based conflicts are relatively easy to bargain about (*today*, at least) has one disturbing implication: conflicts based on an individual's value priorities do not have this same incremental quality. Like religious conflicts, they tend to take on a moralistic tone. If conflicts based on value priorities are likely to play an increasingly important role in Post-Industrial society, we may be far from the politics of consensus in an age of affluence. Ideological conflict is likely to remain, possibly with a *diminishing* toleration for opposing viewpoints.

What has just been said about religious cleavages seems to apply in equal measure to racial and communal conflicts. In the present phase of development, they can give rise to political conflicts far more divisive than those based on social class. Table 8–3 shows the relationship between language group and political preference, and between race and political preference, in Belgium, Switzerland, and the United States, respectively. In Belgium and the United States, the percentage differences associated with these Pre-Industrial characteristics are far larger than those associated with social class. Flemings are nearly twice as likely to vote for the Social Christian Party as are Walloons. And whites were more than three times as likely as blacks to vote for the Republicans. These differences are so widely discussed that little additional comment seems necessary. Our data merely confirm once more that they are extremely important and persistent. Switzerland is a remarkable deviant case. Her complex linguistic and religious cleavages have been minimized by a set of institutions consciously designed to provide maximum autonomy for the group which is numerically predominant in a given region, while avoiding the dominance of any one group at the local, cantonal or federal

---

[11] See Charles Tilly, "Food Supply and Public Order in Modern Europe," in Charles Tilly (ed.), *The Formation of National States in Western Europe* (Princeton: Princeton University Press, 1975).

TABLE 8–3. Political Preference by Language Group and by Race: Belgium, the United States, and Switzerland

Belgium (percent supporting Social Christian Party)		
Mother-tongue is French	42%	(223)
Mother-tongue is Flemish	75	(402)

Switzerland (percent supporting the parties of the Right)		
Mother-tongue is French	56%	(246)
Mother-tongue is Italian	68	(63)
Mother-tongue is German	72	(855)

United States (percent supporting Republican Party)

Party identification			Vote in 1972		
Blacks	8%	(414)	Blacks	16%	(222)
Whites	41	(3,518)	Whites	70	(2,466)

level.[12] We will not discuss these peculiar institutions in the present general study. But it is noteworthy that *even* in Switzerland, linguistic differences are linked with quite substantial differences in partisan preference.

Territorial cleavages are among the key Pre-Industrial variables discussed by Lipset and Rokkan, but they do not seem to have transmitted themselves to contemporary generations with the same force they once had. Only a decade or so ago, it was possible to divide France into two large zones, one of which tended to vote predominantly for the Left, and the other predominantly for the Right in a pattern that had persisted for generations. There are still sizeable regional differences in French politics, but their magnitude has diminished noticeably.

The electronic communications revolution put television into most French homes during the 1960's, and the public seems less likely to rely on local *notables* to relay political views and information: one sees what is happening in Paris on the television screen, and has a sense of direct, personal communication that was never possible with the printed media. This development has been reinforced by a very substantial amount of geographic mobility. In the eighteenth century, it was fairly common for a peasant to live out his entire life without ever traveling more than ten miles from the spot where he was born. Today, travel is relatively rapid and

[12] For an insight into the Swiss pattern of decision-making, see Jurg Steiner, *Amicable Agreement versus Majority Rule: Conflict Resolution in Switzerland* (Chapel Hill: University of North Carolina Press, 1974).

widely accessible, and it seems to reduce the importance of regional political cultures.

We will not present a region-by-region breakdown of voting patterns for each country. Electoral statistics show them with greater precision than our survey data can provide. But it does seem worthwhile to present some findings concerning the two countries in which regional differences seem to retain the most importance. The countries happen to be Belgium and the United States, the two nations in which linguistic and racial cleavages are most powerful.

As Table 8–4 indicates, large regional political differences exist in Belgium and they coincide closely with the Flemish-Walloon ethnic cleavage. Although there are certain Walloon districts that vote predominantly for the Christian Social Party and vice versa, it seems safe to say that the persistence of regional cleavages in Belgium owes much to the reinforcing effect of ethnic cleavages.

TABLE 8–4. Political Preference by Region and Language Group

Belgium (percentage supporting Christian Social Party)

Four Walloon provinces	45%	(341)
Brabant (mixed province)	57	(219)
Four Flemish provinces	75	(683)

United States (percentage supporting Republican Party)

	Party Identification		Vote in 1972	
Midwest	45%	(1,096)	67%	(836)
Northeast	39	(919)	60	(689)
West	37	(684)	63	(464)
South	28	(1,293)	69	(729)

Similarly, regional cleavages in the United States have been heavily influenced by racial factors. The South still stands out from the rest of the United States by its markedly lower proportion of Republican Party identifiers, an alignment dating back to the Civil War era. But the pattern is changing. A majority of blacks now live outside the South, and the Republican Party is no longer seen as the party of Emancipation. In the 1972 election, the South was the region which voted *most* heavily for the Republican candidate for President. It seems possible that political party identification will also eventually shift, although this type of change seems to occur very gradually, as the 1976 election illustrated.

One additional variable might be placed in the Pre-Industrial category, somewhat arbitrarily: the variable is sex. Sexual cleavages are too important to leave out of discussion and, needless to say, they predate the Industrial cleavage. Furthermore, the pattern of sex differences that we find today seems to reflect Pre-Industrial role of women—one that generally discouraged them from taking part in movements aimed at social change. As Table 8–5 shows, sex has a consistent and, in some cases, pronounced relationship with vote. In seven of the eight countries, women are

TABLE 8–5. Political Party Preference by Sex
(Percent supporting the parties of the Right)

Britain			Germany			France		
Male	50%	(699)	Male	40%	(1,328)	Male	44%	(1,321)
Female	59	(810)	Female	53	(1,532)	Female	51	(1,280)
Italy			Netherlands			Belgium		
Male	56%	(1,096)	Male	53%	(1,221)	Male	60%	(624)
Female	70	(1,077)	Female	55	(1,069)	Female	64	(617)
			United States: Party identification			United States: Vote in 1972		
Switzerland								
Male	66%	(637)	Male	37%	(1,670)	Male	68%	(1,245)
Female	70	(535)	Female	37	(2,322)	Female	63	(1,473)

more likely to support the parties of the Right than men. Although sex differences in France do not seem to be particularly large at present, during the earlier years of the Fifth Republic sex was one of the most powerful predictors of vote: women were significantly more Gaullist than men.

We might expect the magnitude of sex differences to vary according to a country's level of economic development. In a Pre-Industrial society, economic production depends largely on sheer muscular strength, in respect to which sex differences are relatively large; and the role of women tends to be sharply differentiated from that of men.[13] In Industrial society (and still more in Post-Industrial society), achievement depends largely on intellectual

[13] There are important variations among specific types of Pre-Industrial societies. In both hunting-and-gathering societies and agrarian societies, the status of women tends to be far below that of man. In simple horticultural societies, however, the female is the main provider, and tends to have a decidedly higher status than in other Pre-Industrial societies. See Gerhard E. Lenski, *Power and Privilege: A Theory of Social Stratification* (New York: McGraw-Hill, 1966).

qualities; sex differences are unimportant, except insofar as a society's role expectations lag behind technological and economic change. We would not, of course, expect sex differences to reflect a country's *present* level of economic development; it would reflect the level prevailing during the average respondent's formative years: for a sample as a whole, it should correspond to the conditions which prevailed roughly a generation ago.

The size of the sex differences in the respective countries does, indeed, seem to correspond to these expectations. The differences are greatest in Italy, which was decidedly the least developed country a generation ago, and are smallest in the United States, which has long been the economically most advanced. Indeed, our data indicate that in the United States' 1972 Presidential election, the usual polarity may have been *reversed*: women apparently were more likely to vote for the Democratic candidate than men.

We might conclude that sex differences in politics tend to diminish as a society reaches an advanced Industrial phase. Or, going beyond our data, one could interpret the cross-national pattern as reflecting a continuous shift to the Left on the part of women: in the past they were more conservative than men; in Post-Industrial society, they may be more likely to vote for the Left. The relative conservatism of women is probably disappearing.

I. POST-INDUSTRIAL POLITICAL CLEAVAGES

On the basis of the foregoing evidence, we can conclude that *both* Pre-Industrial and Industrial variables influence political choice. The question is, "How much?" Thus far, we have limited ourselves to cross-tabulations of party preferences by one variable at a time, making no effort to control for other variables. Until we carry out multi-variate analyses, it will be difficult to say how great an impact a given variable actually has on the vote.

But before we do so, we should look at a third type of variable: the values indicator that, we hypothesized, taps a characteristically Post-Industrial influence on voting. This indicator is, of course, only a provisional way of measuring an individual's value priorities. Extensive additional exploration will be needed before we would have an instrument that might be regarded as the definitive way to measure politically relevant value priorities. Nevertheless, this simple indicator, based on rankings of four goals, does seem to tap a pervasive aspect of an individual's outlook. Let us examine

its apparent impact. Our expectation, of course, is that Post-
Materialist values will be an influence toward voting for the Left.
The relationship between value type and voting intention is shown
in Table 8–6.[14] The results seem to confirm our expectations and
are remarkably consistent cross-nationally. In every one of the

TABLE 8–6. Political Party Preference by Value Priorities[a]
(Percent supporting the parties of the Right)

Britain			Germany			France		
Post-			Post-			Post-		
Materialists	50%	(115)	Materialists	30%	(256)	Materialists	18%	(299)
Mixed	52	(835)	Mixed	46	(1,181)	Mixed	48	(1,236)
Materialists	60	(533)	Materialists	53	(1,168)	Materialists	61	(1,019)
Italy			Netherlands			Belgium		
Post-			Post-			Post-		
Materialists	45%	(263)	Materialists	34%	(330)	Materialists	52%	(125)
Mixed	57	(1,023)	Mixed	56	(1,199)	Mixed	63	(556)
Materialists	73	(888)	Materialists	62	(720)	Materialists	68	(403)
			United States:			United States:		
Switzerland			Republican Party I.D.			Vote in 1972		
Post-			Post-			Post-		
Materialists	56%	(125)	Materialists	27%	(275)	Materialists	41%	(193)
Mixed	67	(626)	Mixed	39	(1,600)	Mixed	63	(978)
Materialists	74	(348)	Materialists	39	(911)	Materialists	76	(655)

[a] Based on original four-item values index.

eight countries there is a neat, monotonic pattern: the Materialists
are *least* likely to vote for the parties of the Left and the Post-
Materialists are *most* likely to do so; the mixed types (which are
theoretically ambivalent) fall between the two extremes.

The differences are relatively modest in the British sample, reinforcing one's impression that in recent years things have changed
rather slowly in Britain—politically as well as economically. Only
10 percentage points separate the Materialists from the Post-
Materialists, as far as party preference is concerned. This difference is not insignificant, of course: it is larger than some of the
other percentage differences we have just reviewed. But it is

[14] A more detailed table, giving the percentage of Materialists and Post-
Materialists voting for each sizeable party or political tendency appears as
an appendix at the end of this chapter.

dwarfed by what we find in comparable cross-tabulations for certain other countries.

Belgium and Switzerland are closest to Great Britain in the apparent impact of values on Left-Right voting: the Post-Materialists are respectively 16 and 18 percentage points more likely to vote for the Left than are the Materialists. In Germany, the difference is larger. The Social Democrats run 23 percentage points ahead among the Post-Materialists with the Christian Democrats doing better among the Materialists by a corresponding amount. In both Italy and The Netherlands, there is a 28-point gap between the two polar value types in likelihood of voting for the Left.

France is at the opposite extreme from Great Britain among our European countries. There is a difference of fully 43 percentage points between the Materialists and the Post-Materialists in support for the Gaullist coalition! The mixed types are almost evenly balanced between Left and Right; and a heavy majority of the Materialists favors the Gaullists who are supported by less than one in five of the Post-Materialists. The French electorate is polarized according to individual value priorities to an exceptional degree. For reasons we will discuss in Chapter 10, the crisis of May-June, 1968, may have accentuated this polarization, impelling Materialists to the Right and Post-Materialists to the Left. If so, the pattern has persisted into the 1970's.

Despite the presence of widespread and stable feelings of political party identification—which is only weakly associated with value type—the United States showed a powerful linkage between value type and Presidential vote in 1972. Post-Materialists were more likely to vote for McGovern by a margin of 35 percentage points. Only in France was the impact of values on vote greater.

Our expectations about the linkage between values and vote are amply confirmed thus far: there is a clear, monotonic and often strong relationship between the two, with Post-Materialists preferring the Left in every country. In regard to party *identification* in the United States, the pattern breaks down. The difference between value types is much weaker, and the mixed types are as likely as the Materialists to be Republicans. Far from undermining our interpretation of the role of value change, this finding strengthens it. For we regard value type as a potential impetus for *change*, and a factor that has attained importance relatively recently. Party identification, on the other hand, presumably reflects the accumulated residue of *past* experiences, and family traditions shaped by events that may have taken place before the individual was born. The relatively weak (and irregular) relationship between party identification and values suggests that the electorate did not "always" polarize along these lines—that the value cleavage is, in fact, something relatively recent.

On the whole, the relationship between values and voting intention is impressive. We view it as a source of change in the basis of political partisanship. To what extent is this interpretation plausible? The relationship we have just observed could, conceivably, be spurious: some third variable might account for the presence of *both* Post-Materialist values and Leftist political preferences in given individuals. Among the possible causes of such a spurious association, family political background seems the most likely candidate. We know that it is a powerful influence on political party preference. It is also related to value type. Perhaps the data in Table 8–6 simply indicate that certain families instill in their children a preference for libertarian values *and* Leftist parties.

We will control for the effects of family political background and several other variables in a broad multi-variate analysis. But to get a concrete illustration of how these three key variables affect each other, let us examine the relationship between values and vote, controlling for the political party preference of one's parents; for simplicity we will limit ourselves to the two extreme cases—Britain and France. As Table 8–7 indicates, even when we control for family political background, substantial differences persist between the voting intentions of Materialist and Post-Materialist respondents. The apparent influence of values remains modest in the British case, but does not disappear; and it remains strikingly large in the French case.[15]

Table 8–7 could be read as an intriguing illustration of the influence of value type on inter-generational change in party preferences. Looking at it from that perspective, two things are evident:

1. In Britain, the great majority of respondents continued to support the Labour Party, if their parents were Labourites; or the

[15] The number of cases in Table 8–7 is relatively small because parental political background was asked only in 1970. Hence, the table deals only with those members of our 1970 samples who reported a party preference of their own and were either Materialist or Post-Materialist types; and whose parents *had* a party preference—which was *known* to the respondent and which was not Liberal or Centrist.

TABLE 8–7. Inter-Generational Party Shifts in Britain and France
by Value Type[a]
(Percent supporting Conservatives and Gaullists)

Britain

Value type:	Parents supported Labour Party		Parents supported Conservative Party	
Materialists	33%	(185)	86%	(171)
Post-Materialists	23	(47)	78	(31)
Difference	+10		+ 8	

France

Value type:	Parents supported "Left": Communists, Socialists		Parents supported "Right": Independents, Popular Republican Movement, Gaullists	
Materialists	29%	(106)	85%	(131)
Post-Materialists	6	(52)	19	(57)
Difference	+23		+66	

[a] Based on 1970 European Community survey.

Conservative Party, if their parents were Conservatives. But among those who shifted, values *did* seem to make some difference—with Post-Materialist types more likely to move to the Left and Materialists to the Right.

2. In France, inter-generational continuity was predominant also, but there was much more shifting. Indeed, among Post-Materialists who had been raised in a family which supported the Right, the great *majority* deserted that half of the political spectrum! According to our data, 81 percent of this group moved away from the political orientation of their parents, leaving only 19 percent still supporting the Right. It seems clear that rebellion against one's parents cannot explain these shifts by the Post-Materialists, because those who were raised in a family of the Left showed an astonishing rate of *fidelity*: 94 percent of them continued to support the Left, with only 6 percent shifting to the Right. Leftist gains among the Post-Materialists were largely balanced by Gaullist gains among the Materialists. But the data indicate that inter-generational shifts greatly increased the extent to which political choice polarized according to value priorities, rather than social class.

The overall pattern seems clear: the presence of Post-Materialist values is linked with a tendency to remain loyal to the Left, if

234 — Political Cleavages

one were brought up in that tradition, and a tendency to *shift* to the Left among those who were raised in a relatively conservative milieu. Jennings and Niemi have found that recall data (such as ours) may tend to exaggerate the degree of consistency between the political preferences of parent and child.[16] A child's report of his parents' party preference seems to be reasonably accurate, but where there *is* error it tends to fall on the side of consistency. This finding implies that, if anything, our data may *understate* the degree to which inter-generational party shift is taking place.

We have now reviewed the zero-order relationships between a whole series of background variables and party choice, as reflected in a Left-Right dichotomy. But we have not yet examined partisan choice from the perspective of system/anti-system cleavages or regional-cultural cleavages. These cleavages tend to be less important than the Left-Right dimension in sheer quantitative terms: that is, relatively few voters support anti-system parties or regional-cultural parties. Still, we should not ignore the possibility that analysis from other perspectives may help us understand the impact of value change on Post-Industrial politics. The connotations of the conventional Left-Right dimension are largely economic. Yet the emerging Post-Materialist group seems to be primarily concerned with life-style issues, which may be particularly relevant to other types of cleavage. Let us turn our attention to a country where other cleavages besides Left and Right are manifestly important: Belgium.

II. REGIONAL-CULTURAL CLEAVAGES: THE FLEMISH AND WALLOON NATIONALISTS

Up to this point, our analysis of Belgian data has focused on a Left-Right dichotomy similar to that used in the other countries. But Belgium is an exceptional case. Applying such a dichotomy excludes an unusually large share of the electorate from consideration. Fully 21 percent of the Belgian vote went to Flemish- or French-speaking linguistic nationalist parties in 1971. Moreover, this electorate is particularly interesting from a theoretical viewpoint. It reflects a type of Pre-Industrial cleavage that (like race in the United States) has been increasing in salience, while else-

[16] See M. Kent Jennings and Richard G. Niemi, "The Transmission of Political Values from Parent to Child," *American Political Science Review*, 62, 1 (March, 1968), 169–184.

where, ascriptive cleavages seem to be declining in importance or at best remaining stable. Furthermore, it is extremely difficult to place these parties on the Left-Right dimension if we use conventional definitions. The position of the New Left parties may be ambiguous, but most observers would at least agree that they belong somewhere on the Left. Similarly, one might well question the legitimacy of grouping the neo-Fascists or National Democrats with the Christian Democrats in their respective countries, but practically everyone would agree that they are parties of the Right. The ethnic nationalists simply do not seem to fit on our main dimension. One might view the contrast between these groups and the traditional Belgian parties as reflecting either a system/anti-system or a territorial-cultural cleavage.

The conflict between French-speaking and Flemish-speaking groups is deeply rooted in Belgian history. As early as 1815, the country's socio-economic elite had become largely French-speaking, partly as a result of twenty years of French rule. A fifteen-year period of Dutch domination began in that year, but with Belgian independence, Dutch and its Flemish variations were excluded from use in administration, the law courts, the army, the secondary schools, and the universities. Upward social mobility became virtually impossible for anyone who was not fluent in French. Business, industry, and public life were completely dominated by Francophones throughout the nineteenth century and well into the twentieth, despite the fact that Flemings make up a majority of the country's population.

Membership in the Flemish-speaking community still carries a connotation of lower social status. Even in recent years, Flemish families in the Brussels region have had a tendency to learn French and "pass" into the Walloon community. Over the decades this has contributed to making Brussels, located on the Flemish side of the linguistic boundary, a predominately French-speaking city.

The French-speaking region (Wallonia) had been decidedly the wealthier part of Belgium since that country's Industrial Revolution in the first half of the nineteenth century. But in recent years the Flemish-speaking region has moved ahead rapidly, finally surpassing Wallonia in the 1960's. With the emergence of an industrialized and prosperous Flanders, a Flemish nationalist movement began to expand its strength rapidly. In its present form, the Flemish *Volksunie* could be viewed as an emancipation movement, seeking social equality commensurate with the economic gains already made. Francophone nationalist movements have emerged as important forces still more recently, partly as a reaction against what were felt to be the excesses committed by the Flemish nationalists. By the time of our 1970 survey, Flemings and Walloons were about equally likely to support a nationalist party. Thus, although one's native language obviously determines *which* type of ethnic nationalist party one supports, it is a weak predictor of *whether* one supports a nationalist party. When we examine the background characteristics of ethnic nationalists, as shown in Table 8–8, several facts seem significant:

TABLE 8–8. Social Bases of Nationalist Parties in Belgium[a]
(Percent supporting Flemish or Walloon nationalist parties)

Parents' party			Value priorities		
Left	5%	(136)	Materialists	9%	(275)
Christian	13	(314)	Mixed	12	(462)
Liberal	12	(58)	Post-Materialists	35	(131)
Don't know	17	(365)			
Nationalist party	81	(21)			

Occupation, head of household			Age			Education		
Middle class	23%	(385)	16–24	29%	(158)	Primary	8%	(413)
Working class	8	(308)	25–34	11	(149)	Secondary	20	(380)
Farm	9	(54)	35–44	16	(164)	University	27	(86)
Retired, inactive	10	(147)	45–54	14	(133)			
			55–64	12	(133)			
			65+	7	(157)			

Church attendance			Union membership		
Never attend	14%	(250)	Member	11%	(294)
Monthly or less	14	(163)	Non-member	17	(599)
Weekly	17	(415)			
More than weekly	7	(66)			

[a] Based on 1970 European Community survey.

1. Support for these parties is not primarily the result of youthful extremism or rebellion. The nationalist parties get a higher proportion of their support from the young than from the old. But support is spread across all age groups; a majority of their supporters are thirty-five or older. Moreover, while only a handful of the nationalists had parents who supported nationalist movements,

the pattern is one of inter-generational *continuity* rather than rebellion: the children of ethnic nationalists are far more likely to support a nationalist party than those from other political backgrounds.

2. Ethnic nationalism seems to be predominately a middle-class phenomenon. Substantial numbers of workers and farmers support these parties, but the bulk of their vote seems to come from the middle class. This is true of both the Fleming and Walloon movements.

3. Although it has a middle-class base, ethnic nationalism is obviously not just a university fad: there are not nearly enough university students to provide the votes which these parties have polled. University students have often been the most salient advocates of these movements, and the university-educated are over-represented among the ethnic nationalists. But they comprise a small minority of the nationalist electorate.

4. The ethnic nationalists seem to be recruited among those who are not closely affiliated with the major established institutions, but the pattern is somewhat ambiguous. On the one hand, they seem less likely to be members of labor unions; and (apart from the children of ethnic nationalists) they are likely to have received no clear parental cue concerning party preference. On the other hand, they have a fairly high rate of church attendance, although they are *not* likely to be among those whose ties with the church are most intense.

5. Among those with Post-Materialist value priorities the ethnic nationalists are heavily over-represented. They are more than three times as prevalent among Post-Materialists as among Materialists. This tendency is more applicable to the Flemish than the Walloon nationalists, but it holds true for both groups. The latter are over-represented among the Post-Materialists by a ratio of two to one; the former by a ratio of *five* to one!

We could not describe these parties as *primarily* Post-Materialist. They receive some important components of their support from traditional sources: from descendants of pre-war nationalists; from regional political cultures; and from individuals with Materialist value priorities. Yet it is also clear that Post-Materialists support them in quite disproportionate numbers.

These findings may help explain why it is so difficult to classify the ethnic nationalist movements—why some observers view them as reactionary and ethnocentric, emphasizing historical links with proto-Fascist movements of the pre-war era; while others view one side or the other (or even both sides) as liberation movements.

One reading of the data would be that the Post-Materialist type is capable of turning to *either* the extreme Left or extreme Right. This possibility has serious implications, and we must not dismiss it lightly. But the validity of this interpretation is doubtful. The degree of continuity between the contemporary ethnic-nationalist movements and their pre-war quasi-Fascist counterparts is very tenuous: the earlier movements had all but died out before the present resurgence of Flemish and Walloon parties. Moreover, their communal emphasis does not seem to reflect a parochial ethnocentrism, so much as a desire for self-expression in a particular cultural style. They are *not* ethnocentric in the pattern of the Authoritarian Personality. We asked a battery of questions concerning support for European integration, and it turns out that the ethnic nationalists are *more* favorable to international integration than the supporters of the three traditional parties. Again, there is a difference in degree between the French-speaking and Flemish-speaking nationalists. The former are only slightly more European in outlook than those who support the traditional parties, while the latter are quite markedly more so. But both groups deviate in the same direction. Ethnic nationalism in Belgium is a new type of communalism, even if it appears in an old and sometimes disheartening guise. Probably it is becoming increasingly Post-Materialist in character.

And paradoxical as it may seem, both Flemish and Walloon nationalists are change-oriented and, in this sense, located on the Left. The question immediately arises, "How could two movements which seem diametrically opposed *both* be on the Left?" In part, the answer is that they are *not* total opposites. Their goals are rather similar and they agree on one major aspect of the means to attain these goals: greater autonomy for their respective communities. In other respects, they have sharp differences about how to attain their goals, as different factions of the Left often do.

The struggle for cultural emancipation is a major goal of the Flemish nationalists. They have been a heavily disadvantaged group, seeking to achieve equality. One important Flemish demand was that French-speaking children who live in the Flemish half of the country not be permitted to attend school in their native language. For a time, this actually was prohibited by law. The measure was aimed at preventing further penetration of the French culture in Flanders; the desire to have Flemish and Walloon children attend the same schools was not a paramount consideration. On the contrary, another Flemish demand was for the expulsion of all French-speaking students from a major bilingual university which happened to be located in Flanders, a few miles from the linguistic frontier.

It is not always easy to say who are the oppressors and who the oppressed. The French-speaking Belgians are less numerous than the Flemish and, except in the Brussels region, they tend to be poorer. The two perspectives are so different that it is possible for *both* sides to see themselves as emancipation movements. Belgium's nationalist groups provide a tragic example of divisions that are possible, perhaps even likely, within Post-Industrial societies. The Flemish and Walloon nationalists represent a new Left, for their concerns are primarily cultural rather than economic. Indeed, the present-day nationalists seem prepared to make quite considerable economic sacrifices in order to achieve cultural autonomy.

And they represent the Left, rather than the Right, for they are oriented toward cultural change rather than cultural traditionalism —more toward fulfillment of needs for self-expression than toward the safety needs. It might seem tempting (because parsimonious) to argue that the explanation is very simple: the Post-Materialists give a low priority to order and therefore are relatively ready to support *any* anti-system party whether of the Right or Left. But this does not seem to be empirically true. Parties of the anti-system Right exist in both Italy and Germany, and the Post-Materialist type seems unlikely to support either of them. In Italy, for example, the neo-Fascists were backed by 11 percent of the Materialists and by only 3 percent of the Post-Materialists. In the late 1960's, a more or less neo-Nazi party, the National Democrats, seemed to be making great inroads among the German electorate. By 1970 and 1971, support for them had fallen to a very low level, so the number of cases in our sample is small. But our data show that slightly better than 2 percent of the Materialists supported them as compared with barely 1 percent of the Post-Materialists.

In my view, then, the Belgian ethnic nationalist groups today are parties of the cultural-change-oriented Left. As such, they constitute part of a new Left and have a tendency to clash not only with conservative parties but also, under certain conditions, with those of the established Left.

III. ETHNIC NATIONALISM AND THE POST-INDUSTRIAL LEFT

In Industrial society, the parties of the Left have sought change in the direction of *economic* equality above all—even, if necessary, by means of increased governmental interference with the liberty of the individual.

The Post-Industrial Left is distinguished by an emphasis on the self-development of the individual—even, if necessary, at the cost of further economic expansion. Thus, the goals of the Industrial and Post-Industrial Left, while not inherently incompatible, can sometimes collide with each other. One of the main reasons why the Industrial Left sought increased economic equality was because this would mean a higher economic level for the working class. But economic growth can *also* contribute to this result, and the Post-Industrial Left tends to give a relatively low priority to economic growth; indeed, insofar as economic growth is seen as leading to a deterioration of the quality of life, the new Left is often *opposed* to growth. When these different goals are forcefully juxtaposed, the two Lefts have clashed.

The Industrial Left generally has accepted a considerable degree of organizational discipline and hierarchy as necessary for effective political change and economic progress. The Post-Industrial Left, more oriented toward individual self-expression, tends to view party bureaucrats as machine hacks or Stalinist bastards. Suspicious of the State, they are far more sympathetic to both individualism *and* communalism than to the norms of rational bureaucracy. For the individual, in part, is that which he is born. While emphasizing egalitarianism, the Post-Industrial Left seems particularly concerned with permitting the individual to express himself in a variety of life-styles rather than a standardized mode. Thus, one might choose to live as part of a radically new counter-culture or as part of a traditional particularistic culture.

According to Janda's coding scheme, the Left tends to support increased national integration. Belgium's ethnic nationalists clearly *de*-emphasize national integration. Here again, they form part of a new Left, which is likely to emphasize local autonomy from the central political authority.

Under certain conditions, the Post-Materialists seem especially likely to support anti-system parties. For an important latent function of such parties may be to satisfy the need for belonging. While we acknowledge and emphasize the importance of the manifest goals of a given movement in a given context, it is also significant that anti-system movements which are in radical conflict with their environment can provide their members with a sense of belonging. In the middle of large, anonymous societies, these movements may become tight little communities bound together all the more closely because of the hostility isolating them from the surrounding society. Insofar as the need for belonging is an important component of these movements, their ideological content could vary widely. They might be Flemish, Walloon, or New Left.

In numerous Western countries, recent years have seen the emergence of political parties and movements that represent a new kind of Left. Among the various labels applied to them, the phrase "New Left" gained widespread currency, but was inherently doomed to obsolescence: nothing remains forever new. We believe that there was, indeed, something distinctive about these movements, however—above all, a tendency to be inspired by Post-Materialist goals and to recruit among a Post-Materialist constituency. *Is* support for the New Left particularly likely to polarize along the Materialist/Post-Materialist dimension? Whether or not we can answer this question depends on how one defines the New Left. In France, the Unified Socialist Party (PSU) emerged from the crisis of May and June, 1968, as the political embodiment of the New Left—the only significant party that had unambiguously supported the May Revolt. Today, some French Leftists consider it a very stodgy old party. The *real* New Left, they would contend, begins with various splinter groups to *its* Left. The difficulty with accepting such a definition of the New Left is that support for the groups in question is so small as to be invisible in a national sample. If one *is* willing to consider the PSU a party of the New Left, as many people would, we can answer the question. Although this party was supported by only 2 percent of the Materialists in our French samples, fully 24 percent of the Post-Materialists backed it (see Table 8–9).

The respective value types differ immensely in the degree to which they support the new or Post-Industrial Left. By comparison, the other parties of the French Left enjoy only a relatively small advantage among the Post-Materialists, getting 14 percentage points more support there than among the Materialists. A similar

TABLE 8–9. Support for New Left and Ethnic Nationalist Parties
by Value Type[a]

Value type	France Unified Socialists	N	Italy Proletarian Socialists	N
Materialists	2%	(1,072)	1%	(888)
Post-Materialists	24	(324)	7	(263)
	Netherlands Radicals + Democrats, 1966	N	Belgium Ethnic Nationalists	N
Materialists	9%	(720)	9%	(508)
Post-Materialists	27	(330)	29	(236)

[a] 1970 and 1971 European Community survey data combined.

pattern applies to support for three other parties that might be said to have a more or less New Left coloring: in Italy, the Proletarian Socialists; and in The Netherlands, the Radical Party and Democrats, 1966. In both countries, the Post-Materialists prefer the New Left parties to a much greater extent than they do the other parties of the Left.[17] The pattern resembles the one we found in our examination of Belgium's ethnic nationalists.

Our conclusion is that radical political oppositions today are more likely to arise from differences along the Materialist/Post-Materialist dimension than from cleavages along the conventional Left-Right dimension. In Italy, both an anti-system Right and an anti-system Left are present, and their bases of support tend to be concentrated at opposite ends of the value priorities dimension. The contemporary anti-system parties are rooted in cultural differences more than in economic differences.

There seems to be a certain curvilinearity to the process of value change. In its emphasis on individual self-development

[17] In the Italian case, however, the Communist Party *also* seems to enjoy a relative preference within the Post-Materialist constituency: the Italian Communist Party (PCI) and Italian Proletarian Socialist Unity Party (PSIUP) combined are supported by 7 percent of the Materialists and by 30 percent of the Post-Materialist group (leaving the two socialist parties only a slightly greater proportion of support from the Post-Materialist group than from the Materialists). It appears, then, that members of our Italian sample react to the PCI almost as if it were a New Left party—an interesting finding in view of the fact that support for the French Communist Party does *not* show a similar pattern. One wonders if the PCF cut itself off from Post-Materialist support in repudiating the May Revolt.

rather than a powerful government, and on the value of a community's way of life rather than economic rationality, the New Left resembles the classic Right. While we earlier suggested that Pre-Industrial cleavages have been gradually declining in importance, in a sense this was too broad a generalization. In most countries, regionalism *does* seem to have lost its importance, and institutionalized religion seems to be in gradual decline. But the Post-Materialist quest for something absolute, together with its downgrading of economic and scientific rationality, gives that search a certain similarity to Pre-Industrial patterns of thought. The recent revival of interest in religious or pseudo-religious communities and the effort to revive or develop tribal bonds may reflect a yearning for ascriptive ties that are stronger than legal-rational ones. This curvilinear aspect should not be exaggerated. In many ways Post-Materialist values are novel: in regard to the role of women, for example, or the way in which they tend to be simultaneously global and tribal in perspective. Nevertheless, there seems to be a partial re-emergence of Pre-Industrial values among the Post-Materialists.

At this point one might well ask, "In view of the fundamental differences between old Left and new, does the concept of Left and Right retain any meaning?" Insofar as the two Lefts emphasize a common concern with social change in an egalitarian direction, it does. The divergences are profound, but they can be bridged. The German Social Democrats illustrate the fact that the two forces can be held together in one party even in a society undergoing very rapid change. The strains between the traditional base and a New Left wing of this party have been acute, but a judicious mixture of idealism, compromise and firmness among its leadership have maintained the party's cohesion, making possible some significant accomplishments.

The Post-Materialist type seems much more attracted to a new Left than the old; but it is relatively sympathetic to *both*, and the goals of the Materialist Left are not fundamentally incompatible with those of the Post-Materialists.

CHAPTER 9

Multi-variate Analysis of Political Cleavages

W E now have a general overview of the relationship between partisan choice and various background variables. So far, our analysis has been based entirely on simple percentage tables, usually tables showing the relationship between voting intention and only one other variable. These tables tell us to what extent the more educated, for example, prefer the parties of the Right; but by themselves they tell us nothing conclusive about what causes an individual to vote for the Right or the Left. For higher levels of education, higher incomes and middle-class occupations all tend to go together. Furthermore, they all tend to be associated with Post-Materialist values. To obtain a clearer sense of whether a given variable actually influences party choice we must carry out multi-variate analyses.

We will use two complementary computer programs for this purpose: the Automatic Interaction Detection (AID) technique and Multiple Classification Analysis (MCA).

The AID procedure splits a survey sample into progressively smaller groups, on the basis of the relative power of a given predictor variable (religion, education, occupation, age, sex, and so on) to "explain" variance in the dependent variable (political party preference).[1] This form of analysis is particularly useful in indicating whether the effects of given predictor variables are additive or interactive.

Examination of the AID output for each of our eight countries indicates that interaction effects seem to have relatively little importance. This is a negative finding, but an important one. For status inconsistency theory suggests that interactions between two or more variables might play an important role in shaping political party choice. Our AID analyses reveal few if any instances of groups giving disproportionate support to the Left (or the Right)

---

[1] For a more complete description of the AID analysis, see John A. Sonquist and James N. Morgan, *The Detection of Interaction Effects* (Ann Arbor: Institute for Social Research, 1964).

as a result of interaction effects; in the few cases in which there is a hint of interaction according to the status inconsistency model, the effects are so weak that they could easily be due to sampling error. These results corroborate a series of recent findings that status inconsistency explains little, if anything, beyond what might be attributed to the impact of the respective variables.[2] Given a set of essentially additive predictor variables, we can move on to a more conclusive form of analysis: Multiple Classification Analysis (MCA).

MCA could be considered a form of dummy variable multiple regression. Like AID, the MCA technique is based on non-metric assumptions about the predictor variables. But whereas AID merely shows us major lines of cleavage based on the strongest predictor of party preference at given points in the breakdown, MCA gives us an indication of the explanatory power of each predictor variable across the sample as a *whole*.

The MCA output provides two useful statistics for each predictor variable. The first is the Eta coefficient, an indicator of how much of the variation in party preference can be explained by the given predictor. The second is the Beta coefficient, which indicates whether the given predictor can still explain a significant portion of the variation when we *control* for the effects of all the other predictors. The output also specifies how much of the variation in the dependent variable can be explained by an entire set of predictor variables.[3]

Table 9–1 shows the results of MCA analyses for each of the eight countries. The predictor variables are ranked from top to bottom, according to the relative strength of their Beta coefficients. The dotted line across each table indicates a threshold below which the given predictors are considered to have a negligible effect on political party preference, when the effects of other variables are taken into account. We have (somewhat arbitrarily) set this threshold at a Beta coefficient below .075. The difference between Eta and Beta coefficients is often substantial. Thus, although certain predictors have a reasonably strong zero-order relationship with political party preference, the relationship may largely disappear when we take other variables into account.

---

[2] For an excellent interpretation of the literature on this subject, see David R. Segal, *Society and Politics: Uniformity and Diversity in Modern Democracy* (Glenview, Ill.: Scott, Foresman, 1974), 91–97.

[3] See John A. Sonquist, *Multivariate Model Building: The Validation of a Search Strategy* (Ann Arbor: Institute for Social Research, 1970).

TABLE 9–1. Predictors of Political Party Preference Ranked According to Relative Strength in Additive Model[a]

Variable	Eta (Zero-order relationship)	Beta (Partial relationship)
Britain		
Parents' party	.448	.375
Social class	.322	.196
Church attendance	.124	.103
Religious denomination	.049	.084
Education	.212	.081
Region	.174	.076
Union membership	.164	.075
Value priorities	.092	.071[b]
Age cohort	.048	.044
Sex	.093	.033
Germany		
Parents' party	.364	.258
Church attendance	.381	.241
Religious denomination	.289	.140
Occupation, head of household	.188	.105
Age cohort	.175	.104
Union membership	.201	.101
Economic self-perception	.105	.089
Value priorities	.174	.087
Land	.141	.085
Education	.081	.074[b]
Size of town	.144	.070
Sex	.132	.033
France		
Parents' party	.463	.349
Value priorities	.368	.265
Church attendance	.363	.133
Occupation, head of household	.173	.115
Economic self-perception	.127	.111
Age cohort	.113	.102
Syndicat membership	.148	.101
Region	.161	.086
Religious denomination	.287	.062
Size of town	.103	.046
Sex	.054	.041
Education	.040	.033

TABLE 9-1. *(Continued)*

Variable	Eta (Zero-order relationship)	Beta (Partial relationship)
Italy		
Parents' party	.492	.405
Church attendance	.415	.341
Value priorities	.276	.121
Religious denomination	.227	.119
Economic self-perception	.133	.115
Age cohort	.165	.086
Occupation, head of household	.181	.067
Region	.130	.057
Size of town	.040	.026
Education	.023	.022
Union membership	.100	.010
Sex	.146	.010
Netherlands		
Parents' party	.479	.309
Church attendance	.486	.253
Religious denomination	.456	.165
Age	.164	.155
Value priorities	.250	.145
Economic self-perception	.140	.105
Education	.075	.090
Occupation, head of household	.171	.087
Union membership	.068	.050
Province	.146	.049
Sex	.050	.027
Size of town	.110	.021
Belgium		
Church attendance	.672	.397
Parents' party	.620	.344
Province	.393	.183
Size of town	.369	.103
Occupation, head of household	.196	.090
Religious denomination	.491	.086
Value priorities	.199	.082
Fleming v. Walloon	.334	.073
Union membership	.152	.039
Economic self-perception	.207	.033
Age cohort	.059	.030
Education	.092	.016
Sex	.068	.002

TABLE 9–1. *(Continued)*

Variable	Eta (Zero-order relationship)	Beta (Partial relationship)
Switzerland		
Church attendance	.272	.200
Subjective social class	.183	.198
Occupation, head of household	.271	.197
Religious denomination	.210	.157
Union membership	.232	.126
Value priorities	.141	.111
Language	.149	.110
Age	.079	.084
Education	.103	.045
Sex	.057	.017
Belgium (Nationalist Parties)		
Parents' party	.307	.250
Value priorities	.264	.190
Province	.173	.157
Occupation, head of household	.202	.115
Age	.199	.104
Church attendance	.072	.080
Union member	.075	.076
Economic self-perception	.132	.070
Education	.185	.054
Size of town	.075	.054
Sex	.043	.037
Fleming v. Walloon	.039	.027
1. *United States: Political Party Identification* (Multiple Classification Analysis)		
Parents' party	.494	.409
Religious denomination	.190	.190
Race	.225	.175
Union member in family	.146	.130
Church attendance	.079	.117
Region where respondent lives	.145	.109
Family income	.122	.104
Occupation, head of family	.158	.102
Value priorities	.164	.101
Age	.121	.101
Education	.124	.095
Sex	.032	.060
Size of Community	.109	.027

TABLE 9–1. *(Concluded)*

Variable	Eta (Zero-order relationship)	Beta (Partial relationship)
2. *United States: Vote in 1972*		
Race	.311	.281
Parents' party	.282	.224
Value priorities	.273	.202
Religious denomination	.222	.147
Age	.160	.122
Region	.095	.104
Size of community	.166	.097
Church attendance	.162	.087
Sex	.060	.074
Union member in family	.086	.068
Family income	.113	.065
Occupation, head of family	.075	.050
Education	.044	.044

[a] Based on 1970 European Community survey data.

[b] Variables with a Beta below .075 are considered to have a negligible impact on party preference, controlling for the effect of the other variables. The elimination from the model of *all* such variables usually reduces the percentage of variance explained by less than three percentage points.

Our central interest here is in the impact of values on party choice. In including age and education in our multi-variate analysis, we are, in a sense, *over*controlling. Our theory implies that these two variables should be strongly associated with value type, and data from eight countries make it clear that they *are*. Hence, when we control for education we are, in considerable part, controlling for an individual's value type. When we control for *both* age and education, we have greatly reduced the variance in value type and, consequently, its explanatory power as reflected by the Beta coefficient. If value change *is* influencing political party preferences, then age and education *should* show comparative strong correlations with political party choice.

Unfortunately, for the simplicity of our analysis, age and education are powerful but ambiguous variables. The former, for example, can indicate life-cycle effects as well as the generational effects that interest us. The latter can reflect cognitive development and communication networks, as well as how wealthy one's parents were. In our multi-variate analyses we include age and education as predictors. This gives a conservative estimate of the impact of value priorities on political party choice.

Let us quickly review the MCA results country by country. In Britain, the relationship between values and voting intention is negligible and in Germany it is quite modest when we control for the effects of other variables, even though the zero-order relationship is substantial. Our Swiss data suggest that value type has a significant impact on party choice, but the Swiss results are not entirely comparable with those from other countries. One of the most powerful explanatory variables (parents' party) was not available. Its inclusion might have reduced the Beta for value priorities to a lower level. The zero-order linkage *is* relatively low. In Belgium, an individual's value priorities have relatively little influence on one's choice along the conventional Left-Right dimension, but are very important in deciding whether one votes for one of the traditional parties or for one of the ethnic nationalist parties.

In The Netherlands and Italy, one's value priorities seem to constitute a very important influence on Left-Right party choice. Their fragmented party systems may facilitate this state of affairs, for in both countries, various small parties have emerged which make distinctive appeals to the respective groups on the Materialist/Post-Materialist continuum: Italy's Proletarian Socialists and neo-Fascists; and Holland's Radicals and Democrats, 1966. To a certain extent, the conventional Left-Right dimension has been modified to accommodate the Materialist/Post-Materialist dimension in these countries.

When we examine the comparable analysis for France, we find a striking contrast with the British pattern. Value priorities, which play a negligible role in Britain, rank next after parental influences for our French sample. Religion is important too; in fact its Eta coefficient is as strong as the Eta associated with value priorities. This reflects the fact that family political traditions are the most important single influence on the vote, and as a result of these inherited patterns France's well-known clerical/anti-clerical split retains a strong zero-order relationship with voting. But its source seems to be hereditary more than contemporary. When we control for parental political preferences, religion proves to be a much weaker influence on the vote than an individual's value priorities. One's values also appear to have a markedly greater influence on political preferences than the various class-linked variables.

A new party system has developed in France under the Fifth Republic. The recent vintage of her largest political party (the Gaullists and their allies), and the relative weakness of inherited party loyalties, may help to explain why France's dominant Left-Right dichotomy coincides with the Post-Industrial cleavage more closely than in any other country.

The distinction between inherited political preferences and contemporary influences comes into particularly sharp focus when we turn our attention to the United States where inherited political loyalties are particularly strong. As an influence on one's sense of political party *identification*, value priorities are relatively weak (although by no means negligible). This is what we would expect if we view party identification as largely a reflection of traditional ties. Family inheritance is by far the strongest predictor of party identification, followed by religious denomination and race. Social class variables, region, and church attendance come next; value priorities rank far down the list (in ninth place).

When we examine the influences on how one actually *voted* in the 1972 Presidential election, an entirely different picture emerges. Race is the strongest predictor of vote. Although blacks made up less than 10 percent of the electorate, they provided almost a quarter of McGovern's votes. In almost all of the other countries, parents' party preference was the strongest predictor of vote, and it was the strongest predictor of party *identification* in the United States. But the election of 1972 was an exceptional one. It offered a real choice between candidates representing distinctly different philosophies. Large numbers of voters deserted their traditional party allegiances; many voted against the party their parents had supported. Parents' party dropped to second place as a predictor of vote in 1972—with value type being a very close third.

By comparing the sizes of the Eta and Beta coefficients for a given variable, one can see to what extent its zero-order association with political party preference may be due to the effects of other variables. In the table for Britain, for example, we see that social class has a zero-order association of .322 with party preference. This declines to .196, still a rather strong linkage, when we control for the other variables. On the other hand, education, which has an Eta coefficient of .212, drops to a Beta coefficient of .081 when we control for the other variables. The explanation may be that much of the association between social class and party preference in Britain may be due to the fact that middle-class

Britons are likely to inherit both middle-class status and a Conservative Party preference from their parents; nevertheless, one received rather strong cues from one's social-class milieu, which influence one to vote Labour (if one is working class) or Conservative (if one is middle class) *regardless* of family tradition. Education, on the other hand, has a rather strong zero-order relationship with political party preference in Britain but it is *not* primarily due to education in itself, so much as to the fact that the more educated are likely to have been raised in Conservative families and to live in a middle-class milieu. Value priorities have a comparatively weak zero-order relationship with party preference in Britain (as we saw in Table 8–6); when we control for the other variables, this relationship is negligible. The same is true of sex and age.

The pattern in our German sample is somewhat similar. Parental influences are weaker than in Britain (or in any of our other countries) but they nevertheless rank first. Religious influences are much more important than in Britain. Indeed, they are virtually as important as one's parents' party. The influence of social class is substantially weaker, although both the occupation of the head of household and labor union membership are significant independent influences on party choice. In Britain and Germany, family background, social class and religion do most of the work in accounting for variation in party preference. In Belgium we have a rather different configuration: Pre-Industrial cleavages are clearly predominant. Whether one supports the Christian Social Party or the Socialists depends primarily on how closely one is linked with the church. But a regional cleavage is also important. This regional cleavage is closely related to the fact that Belgium has two main language groups, but it *is* a genuine regional cleavage. French-speaking individuals are far more likely to vote for the Left than Flemish-speaking persons, but the region one inhabits is an even *stronger* predictor of party preference than mother-tongue. An ecological effect seems to be at work. Flemish-speaking people who live in the predominately Flemish region are substantially more likely to support the Christian Social Party than are Flemings who live in Wallonia. Consequently, although there is a strong zero-order relationship between mother-tongue and party preference, its strength diminishes greatly when we control for region.

Among our eight countries, the United States and Belgium are the only ones in which genuine regional differences still play an important role. Oddly enough, our largest and smallest countries are the two most affected by regionalism. Marked regional differences in party preferences exist in other countries. Bavaria is much more heavily Christian Democratic than the rest of Germany, for example. This difference is largely attributable to the fact that Bavaria is overwhelmingly Roman Catholic and has relatively many farmers (categories favoring the Christian Democrats), while it has relatively few unionized industrial workers and non-church-goers (categories favoring the Social Democrats). Much, though not all, of the regional difference disappears in multi-variate analysis; a comparatively modest ecological effect persists. The diminished role of regional cleavages may indicate that physical distance in itself is no longer very important in an age of almost instantaneous electronic communication and considerable geographic mobility.

The multi-variate analyses enable us to test an hypothesis which has very significant implications: Do the Post-Materialists tend to vote for the Left simply because they are relatively young, or is it the values *themselves* that influence the vote? If value type influences political choice, then insofar as different age groups tend to have different values, age would *also* be correlated with party preference. In countries where there had been particularly rapid value change, the predictive power of age might be greatly enhanced, provided that the available political parties took opposing positions on the Materialist/Post-Materialist dimension. But age would be a transient basis of cleavage, gradually disappearing as the respective value types became more evenly distributed across the population. In a country like the United States, where the relationship between age and value type is comparatively weak, values might have a much greater impact on vote than age.

The results of the multi-variate analyses suggest that value type itself, rather than age, is the key influence. Germany appears to be exceptional. When we compare the size of the respective Beta coefficients, age itself seems to have more impact than value type, although even here value type has a significant independent effect, when we adjust for the impact of age. In The Netherlands, the influence of values appears to be about equal to that of age, adjusting for the effects of the latter variable. In the other six countries, value type seems to have considerably more impact than age. In the United States, age *per se* is a *far* weaker explanatory variable than value type. In 1972, age showed a stronger relationship with vote than in any Presidential election since the New Deal realignment, but this phenomenon apparently reflects an exceptionally strong *value* polarization in the 1972 election rather than life-cycle effects.

Table 9–1 contains a rich variety of other findings. We will not attempt to comment on them all. To summarize the pattern that emerges from the foregoing analyses, let us classify our eight countries according to the types of political cleavages which have the greatest impact on voting.

The party preferences inherited from one's parents are a key influence everywhere. They are immensely important, but by reason of their pervasiveness they do not aid us in differentiating between countries. Furthermore, they constitute a force working for continuity with the past. Insofar as we are interested in change, we must focus our attention on other variables—influences which may be less powerful than family tradition at any given time, but may bring about significant changes in the long run. Our typology, therefore, is based on these other variables, grouped into three categories: Industrial, Pre-Industrial and Post-Industrial.

The relative importance of each of these three categories of variables is summarized in Table 9–2. For the European Community countries, this table is based on the 1973 survey data. We replicated the multi-variate analyses presented earlier in this chapter, using the newer data base. The results are very similar at the two points in time—indeed, almost interchangeable. For the United States and Switzerland, we continue to draw on the 1972 and 1973 data.

Great Britain and Denmark constitute the only countries where the classic pattern of Industrial cleavage is predominant. Pre-Industrial variables play a secondary role; and Post-Industrial influences have, as yet, a negligible impact.

In all of the other countries, Pre-Industrial cleavages—and in many cases, Post-Industrial cleavages as well—outrank all of our various social class indicators. One would hardly have expected this finding, judging by much of the literature in the field. Could it be that some *other* type of economic variable would provide a stronger predictor? Perhaps. Segal and Knoke find that one's occupational category bears a weaker relationship to political party choice than one's position in the credit market or one's position in the commodity market: in a credit- and consumer-oriented econ-

TABLE 9-2. Predictors of Left-Right Voting in Eleven Countries, 1972–1973
(The five strongest predictors, ranked according to strength of Beta coefficients in MCA analysis)

I. Value type ranks second to a "Pre-Industrial" variable but outranks any "Industrial" variable

Rank as Predictor:	United States	France	Italy	Netherlands
1st	Race	Church attendance	Church attendance	Church attendance
2nd	Values	Values	Values	Values
3rd	Religious denomination	Occupation, head of family	Union membership	Income
4th	Age	Economic satisfaction	Region	Education
5th	Region	Income	Age	Economic satisfaction

II. Value type is of tertiary importance

	Industrial Cleavage Dominant		Pre-Industrial Cleavage Dominant			
Rank:	Britain	Denmark	Germany	Ireland	Belgium	Switzerland
1st	Union membership	Occupation, head of family	Church attendance	Region	Church attendance	Church attendance
2nd	Region	Church attendance	Occupation, head of family	Church attendance	Religious denomination	Occupation, head of family
3rd	Economic satisfaction	Education	Religious denomination	Values	Region	Religious denomination
4th	Religious denomination	Size of town	Age	Age	Values	Union membership
5th	Values	Income	Region	Economic satisfaction	Union	Values

omy, these markets may become more important than one's relationship to the means of production.[4] Alternative indicators of social class might, therefore, provide a somewhat more powerful prediction of political behavior. But it seems unlikely that they would enhance the explanatory power of Industrial cleavage variables by any wide margin, for Segal and Knoke find that *none* of their indicators of economic class provides predictions of political party choice as strong as those provided by religion, race or region.

Among the countries we have analyzed, Pre-Industrial cleavages seem to dominate the scene, even today. In most cases these Pre-Industrial influences work to reinforce rather than to neutralize the cues received from one's parents. This is not equally true of our Post-Industrial variable.

Yet in all of these countries, a Post-Industrial type of cleavage seems to have significant impact. In Germany, Switzerland, Ireland, and Belgium (as analyzed from a conventional Left-Right perspective), individual value priorities are weaker than both Pre-Industrial and Industrial variables. In our supplementary Belgium analysis, based on a dichotomy between system parties and anti-system parties, the values indicator ranked *first*. If we had analyzed our Italian data on the basis of a dichotomy between the anti-system Right and anti-system Left, a similar finding probably would have emerged (we did not do so because of the small number of respondents involved). In Italy, The Netherlands, France and the United States, the Post-Industrial category ranks second, below Pre-Industrial variables, but clearly ahead of the indicators of Industrial class conflict. In the United States an individual's value type was an especially crucial influence on voting: despite the deeply engrained partisan loyalties which characterize this country, values ranked second only to race—and a very close second. France is the country where the impact of values on political partisanship is greatest. As was true in connection with the 1970–1971 data, religion and values have about the same direct relationship to voting intention. But the former reflects the politics of the past, while the latter relates to current issues, so that when we control for parental preferences, value type proves to be more important. The 1973 data do not permit us to apply such controls, however.

[4] See David R. Segal and David Knoke, "Political Partisanship: Its Social and Economic Bases in the United States," *American Journal of Economics and Sociology*, 29, 3 (July, 1970), 253–262.

Our earlier findings imply that economic and physical security will lead to an increasing proportion of Post-Materialists among the electorate. And, as we have just seen, Post-Materialists tend to vote for the Left. Does this mean that economic growth can be expected to produce an automatic and never-ending increase in the percentage voting for the Left? Of course not. Not even party identification has a 1.00 correlation with one's vote, and the link between values and vote is much less direct than that between party identification and vote. The evidence indicates that value priorities *are* a significant influence on electoral behavior, but this fact must be interpreted in the context of a given election in a given party system. The emergence of a new distribution of values may, itself, stimulate a given country's parties and candidates to shift their relative positions in response to new forces. It may even re-define the meaning of Left and Right (or other dimensions of party space).

The 1972 Presidential election in the United States provides an example. In that year, the proportion of votes going to the party of the "Left" shrunk to an unprecedented low. Yet this apparently resulted from a split within the Democratic Party that was linked with the *growing* impact of new values. In a penetrating analysis of the forces involved in this election, Miller and Levitin demonstrate that in 1972, even as the American public's *vote* was shifting sharply to the Right to produce a Nixon landslide, their underlying political values were moving to the *Left*. On such key issues as equality for blacks, women's role in society, societal responsibility for the poor, and intervention in Vietnam, the American electorate was becoming progressively more liberal, as a result of generational change. Miller and Levitin conclude that, "Contrary to the popular impression that the electorate either did not respond or, at most, was moved to conservative reaction against the values and issues of the New Politics, this book documents the fact that public sentiment moved sharply to the Left between 1970 and 1972 in ways that supported New Politics and New Left themes."[5]

The result of the 1972 election seems to reflect a series of tactical mistakes by the Democratic candidate rather than an ideological

[5] Cited from Warren E. Miller and Teresa E. Levitin, *The New Liberals: Political Leadership and Generational Change in American Politics* (Cambridge, Mass.: Winthrop, 1976), Introduction. Cf. Arthur H. Miller *et al.*, "A Majority Party in Disarray: Policy Polarization in the 1972 Election," *American Political Science Review*, 70, 3 (September, 1976), 753–778.

shift by the American public. Figure 9–1 illustrates what happened. It is based on one of the most dramatic issues of the campaign, the hawk versus dove conflict over intervention in Vietnam, but the pattern shown here applies to a number of other key issues. In the public's perceptions, President Nixon's position on Vietnam changed very little from 1968 to 1972. But the attitude of the American public as a whole shifted appreciably from a position slightly on the hawk side of the continuum to one clearly on the dove side of the midpoint. This in itself would have favored McGovern. But his own position (as perceived by the public) was that of a dove extremist, much farther away from the median voter than that of the President. The result (here and on various other key issues) was a strong net preference for Nixon.

The election presented a choice between candidates offering visibly different positions on a set of issues clearly relevant to one's value priorities. But the choice was posed on terms needlessly disadvantageous to the Post-Materialist side.

An individual's value priorities have a significant independent influence on voting in eight of the ten countries shown in Table 9–2. This influence varies from nation to nation in a manner that is constrained by existing institutions and elite strategies.

The impact of value change on voting is limited by at least four factors:

1. The extent to which a sense of identification with the existing political parties is widespread and deep-rooted.

2. The positions taken by the leaders of established political parties on the most salient contemporary political issues. If they do not differ perceptibly, the individual's values are irrelevant.

3. The number of political parties in the system. As a rule, it is probably easier for new forces to take over a small party than a large one. The existence of many parties provides a larger number of entry-points for expression of a given ideology.

4. The level and rate of economic development and value change in the given country.

Table 9–3 summarizes the relationship between the party system and the degree to which voting is polarized according to the individual's value priorities. Elite tactics change from year to year, which can greatly affect the result, as we have just seen. Nevertheless, in the early 1970's there was a manifest overall tendency for value priorities to have a relatively modest impact on how the public voted in "two-party" (or 2½-party) systems; where the

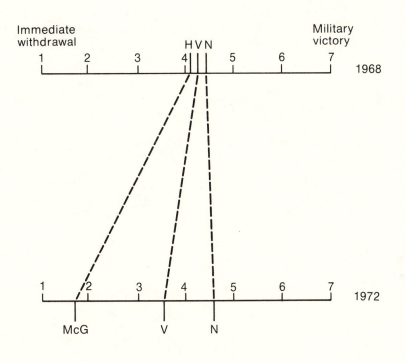

FIGURE 9–1. Issue Positions of Average Voter and the Two Presidential Candidates in 1968 and 1972, as Perceived by the Average American Voter.

"V" indicates mean self-placement of American public on Vietnam policy preference scale ranging from support for "Immediate Withdrawal" to support for goal of "Military Victory." "N" indicates mean placement of Nixon, "H" indicates that of Humphrey, "McG" indicates that of McGovern. Adapted from Miller, Miller, Raine and Brown, *op. cit.*

TABLE 9–3. Importance of Post-Industrial Cleavage and Party System

Polarization of vote according to values was high, 1972–1973

France	multi-party system (7)[a]	dates from 1958
Italy	multi-party system (7)	dates from 1946
Netherlands	multi-party system (14)	of pre-war origin, but marked decline of religious parties since 1967.
United States	2½ party system	dates from 1860's; Democratic Party captured by its Left wing in 1972.

Polarization of vote according to values was low, 1972–1973

Great Britain	2½ party system	of pre-war origin
Germany	2½ party system	dates from 1949; Great Coalition 1966–1969
Ireland	2½ party system	of pre-war origin
Luxembourg	multi-party system (4)	of pre-war origin
Denmark	multi-party system (5)	of pre-war origin
Belgium	multi-party system (7)	was virtually a 2½ party system as recently as 1958, when upset by rise of ethnic nationalist parties; the latter are not included in Left-Right coding, but *do* polarize strongly according to individual value priorities.
Switzerland	multi-party system (11)	in theory. In fact, has been dominated by the same coalition almost continuously since 1943.

[a] The number of parties represented in parliament appears in parentheses.

impact of values was strong, there usually was a large number of parties. A multi-party system does not automatically lead to re-polarization along Post-Industrial lines, however. First, the pluralism must be genuine: multi-party systems facilitate the emergence of Post-Industrial cleavages because they increase the number of alternatives available to the electorate—and hence, the likelihood that some reasonably eligible and credible candidate will take a distinctive stand on Post-Industrial issues. But this is not always the case, of course. In Switzerland, though there are many parties, there is far less pluralism than meets the eye. The five most important ones form a governing cartel that has been in office almost continuously since 1943. The respective members of this coalition generally take a common stand on key policy matters, which may contribute to the remarkable stability of Swiss political life, but which scarcely maximizes the number of alternatives presented to the public.

But it is not only a matter of making a variety of alternatives available to the public. The public must also be available to respond to new alternatives. Insofar as they are committed in advance to given political parties, it may be futile to offer distinctive policies. Hence, as Table 9–3 shows, the impact of values tends to be greater in the new party systems than in long-established ones.

The United States remains a deviant case. Possessing a "two-party" system with exceptionally deep historical roots, the American public was, nevertheless, highly polarized according to value type in 1972. This illustrates the fact that one can not interpret a nation's political life by *merely* counting the number of major parties and their age. These are significant factors, no doubt. But the tactics of given leaders can not be ignored.

By and large we would expect long established and deeply rooted political party systems (such as those of Britain and the United States) to be relatively resistant to the process of realignment described above. Similarly, countries experiencing relatively rapid economic and social change should undergo this process of realignment more rapidly than countries experiencing relative stagnation. Finally, countries in which the established parties take opposite positions on the Post-Industrial issues dimension should undergo a shift from class-based to value-based alignment more rapidly than countries in which this dimension cuts across established party lines. Among the countries in our study, Great Britain comes nearest to providing an example of the ideal type in which all conditions are conducive to *slow* realignment. Loyalties to established parties have deep historical roots, economic growth and value change have both been relatively slow, and there are two major parties that tend to take similar centrist positions on important political issues.[6] France comes close to providing the opposite ideal type in all four respects, and it is interesting to note that these two countries represent the opposite extremes in the degree to which values are related to political party choice.

The impact of values is mediated by structural and tactical constraints. But within these limits, changing value priorities seem to be gradually reshaping the social basis of political conflict in advanced Industrial societies.

[6] The question of membership in the Common Market was a partial exception: The Labour Party opposed membership at one point and remains divided on this issue; but since 1975 both major parties have officially supported membership.

CHAPTER 10

The Post-Materialist Phenomenon

A NEW Politics emerged throughout advanced industrial societies during the late 1960's. It was not without historical precedent; few things are. But it embodied a significant change from established patterns in two respects. It emphasized new issues (indeed, in a confused fashion, it seemed to be groping toward a new vision of society); and it reflected a change in the social basis of protest.

There was protest in the middle of affluence and to a considerable degree the groups calling for change were no longer the economically deprived but the affluent. The emergence of a new type of protest in a time of high prosperity was not a matter of sheer coincidence. Economic collapse may have produced a swing to the Left in the 1930's, but a prolonged period of affluence and physical security led to the rise of a new Left in the late 1960's and early 1970's. This wave of protest had subsided by the mid-1970's: ironically enough, in a period of economic contraction, there was relative political calm. Great Britain constitutes the one striking exception to this pattern—a country in which things remained relatively calm during the wave of student protest, but where the politics of class confrontation were rather speedily revived in the 1970's.

This chapter will undertake a retrospective view of politics in the late 1960's and early 1970's. We will touch on the example nearest at hand, the American one. But America was by no means unique in her political upheavals; one finds striking parallels in other countries that were neither at war nor in the grip of racial conflict. Our objective is to distinguish between pervasive patterns and phenomena linked with a specific time and place. In order to do so, it will be useful to review events in other advanced industrial societies. For underlying the events which took place in specific countries, we may find certain common forces at work.

In seeking basic themes, the French case history seems particularly useful. A process that was diffuse and scattered over many times and places in countries such as the United States or Germany was concentrated in a relatively brief but remarkably intense crisis in France. The attention of the French public was riveted on the questions posed by the New Politics. At the height of the crisis, it looked as if France might be on the brink of civil war. There was an extraordinary amount of soul-searching and a massive re-polarization of the French public along new lines.

Let us attempt to recapture the mood and some of the key events of this era in the recent past.

I. The New Politics in the United States and West Germany

The American Presidential election of 1968 was preceded by a spectacular and often violent drama in which a movement demanding radical change was led (symbolically at least) by Senator Eugene McCarthy. His troops consisted largely of younger members of the upper middle class, especially university students. Although the insurgents were turned back at the Chicago Democratic Party Convention, it was only after they had administered a series of shocks sufficient to bring about the virtual abdication of the Chief Executive.

Four years later a broader but rather similar coalition went a step farther—it actually captured the Democratic Party's Presidential Nomination. Using a variety of novel tactics, a cadre of young, well-educated militants wrested control of the nation's largest party from the hands of more experienced bosses and kingmakers, many of whom had been in power before some of their key adversaries were born. The subsequent election produced a landslide victory for the Republican candidate and deep disillusionment for many of the McGovernites. Nevertheless, they had pulled off an astonishing *coup*. And the electoral results showed significant changes from previous patterns.

For one, age became an important basis of political cleavage. As Axelrod points out, "The young, who were previously not part of anyone's coalition, made a large contribution to the Democratic coalition in 1972. In each previous election since 1952 people under thirty years of age accounted for only 13 percent to 15 percent of the Democratic votes, but in 1972 they accounted for fully 32 percent of the Democratic votes. . . . Their loyalty which had never been more than 3 percent pro-Democratic since 1952 went up in 1972 to 12 percent pro-Democratic."[1]

Another change that took place from 1968 to 1972 concerns the role of social class. Lipset has provided impressive documentation of the fact that in the 1940's and 1950's, lower income groups voted mainly for the Left, while higher income groups voted mainly for the parties of the Right.[2] Similarly, Alford furnishes evidence that in the English-speaking democracies, manual workers were much more likely to support the Left than those in non-manual occupations: from 1952 to 1962 the American public showed a mean class-voting index of +16.[3]

The 1968 Presidential campaign saw the emergence of a third-party candidate who might be termed conservative or even reactionary. Starting with a Southern base, George Wallace built up a Northern following that was unprecedented for such a candidate in this century—threatening, for a time, to win as much of the normally Democratic vote as the official candidate of the Democratic Party. While his support in the South might be regarded as largely traditional, the inroads Wallace was making in the North were apparently based on his strong stand for "law and order." He was, in a sense, a defender of the established order, but his support came not from the economically most privileged strata, but chiefly from working-class whites. Survey data gathered during this campaign reveal a decline in class voting. Although strenuous efforts by organized labor brought large numbers of labor union members back to Humphrey at the end of the campaign, the percentage of this group which voted Democratic was the lowest since the start of the New Deal.[4] Most of the loss went to George Wallace. The class-voting index fell by about four points, from approximately +15 in 1964 to approximately +11 in 1968.[5]

[1] Robert Axelrod, "Communication," *American Political Science Review*, 68, 2 (June, 1974), 717–720.

[2] Seymour M. Lipset, *Political Man* (Garden City: Doubleday, 1960), 223–224.

[3] Alford's index is computed by subtracting the percentage of non-manual workers voting for "Left" parties from the percentage of manual workers voting for "Left" parties. See Alford, *Party and Society: The Anglo-Saxon Democracies* (Chicago: Rand McNally, 1963).

[4] See Gallup report of December, 1968, cited in The Republican National Committee, *The 1968 Elections* (Washington, D.C., 1969), 216.

[5] Class-voting indices based on data from the 1964 and 1968 election surveys carried out by the SRC/CPS, University of Michigan. For a discussion of the long-term trend in class voting, see Paul R. Abramson, "Gen-

Wallace's campaign was aborted in 1972 by an attempted assassination, but his electorate did not return to the Democratic fold. In 1972 the impact of issues was stronger than that of established party loyalties, an extraordinary phenomenon on the American scene; most of the former Wallace voters shifted their support to the Republican candidate.[6] And the index of class-voting fell three points below the 1968 level.[7]

Clearly, some of the most important factors relating to the American Presidential elections of 1968 and 1972 were exceptional and nation-specific—in particular the war in Vietnam and the civil rights struggle.[8] Other Western countries were not at war and do not have the degree of racial heterogeneity found in the United States. Yet there is evidence that an important component of American politics in this era reflected phenomena that are widespread in economically developed societies. The dynamics of protest were remarkably parallel in Germany, France and other Western countries.

During this period, West German secondary and university students, mainly of middle-class origin, showed a pattern of behavior similar to that of American students. In a 1968 survey of 2,500 male students, ages seventeen to twenty-six, a mere 32 percent of those interviewed declared themselves satisfied with the present German political party system, while 60 percent indicated that they would like to vote for other parties; more than a third said they would like to vote for a party to the Left of the Social Democrats, the only important existing party on the Left. The leading political party among the electorate as a whole (the Christian Democrats) ranked *third* among the students.[9]

---

erational Change in American Electoral Behavior," *American Political Science Review*, 68, 1 (March, 1974), 93–105.

[6] See Arthur H. Miller *et al.*, "A Majority Party in Disarray: Political Polarization in the 1972 Election," *American Political Science Review*, 70, 3 (September, 1976), 753–778.

[7] See Chapter 7 above.

[8] While much of the discontent in the American case focused on a group which *is* relatively deprived economically, we must distinguish between the motivations of the black civil rights advocates themselves, and their white sympathizers. Charles Hamilton has characterized the behavior of the former as predominantly "instrumental" and that of the latter as largely "expressive." Cited in Seymour M. Lipset, "The Activists: A Profile," *The Public Interest*, 13 (Fall, 1968), 39–52.

[9] See *EMNID-Informationen* number 8/9 (August-September, 1968). German students continue to lean to the Left. From 1973 to 1974, 4,000 of

While the students themselves were leaning toward the Left, German student activism seems to have contributed to a right-wing reaction rather similar to the one seen in the United States. A series of clashes took place between student demonstrators and police, the most important of them in Cologne, Bremen, Nuremberg, and West Berlin. These clashes reflected protest against a variety of objects, ranging from the conservative Springer press empire to the Shah of Iran and the war in Vietnam. They apparently fueled a gradual but growing anti-student reaction. In November, 1966, after a demonstration in Cologne, only 8 percent of the West German adult population said they felt the police had been "too lenient" toward the student demonstrators. In a survey of February, 1968, 15 percent of the adult German respondents said that the police had been "too lenient" toward demonstrators in Bremen. After a series of large and destructive demonstrations, a survey in May, 1968, found that 32 percent of German adults felt the police had been "too lenient"; 34 percent felt that the police had acted properly; only 17 percent felt they had been "too harsh." The young and the upper socio-economic groups were more sympathetic to the demonstrations than the older and lower income groups.[10] On several occasions West German workers had to be restrained from attacking demonstrating student radicals.

For a time in the late 1960's the neo-Nazi National Democratic Party (NPD) was making alarming electoral progress, winning up to 15 or 20 percent of the vote in state elections. The rise of this party seems to have been encouraged by the spread of violent student demonstrations. The NPD leaders obviously viewed anti-student reaction as a promising source of support. Their 1969 campaign was largely directed against the students and their slogan has a familiar ring: "Sicherheit in Recht und Ordnung" ("Security in Law and Order"). The bulk of the NPD supporters had working-class occupations; elements of the *traditional* middle class (small merchants and craftsmen) were also over-represented. But the *modern* middle class (those owning or employed in large

---

them were asked, "Which political party is closest to your views?" Forty-five percent of the sample chose the Social Democrats, while the Christian Democrats again ranked third (with only 14 percent of the choices); 5 percent named the Communists and 16 percent said that none of the existing parties represented their views. See Infratest survey cited in "Studenten: Jeder Dritte Resigniert," *Der Spiegel*, July 8, 1974, 98.

[10] See *EMNID-Informationen*, number 7 (June, 1968).

enterprises) was under-represented among the ranks of NPD supporters.[11]

Fears of a Fascist comeback in Germany turned out to be exaggerated; the lesson of the Nazi era was not forgotten. The Social Democrats managed to avoid a complete break between their young Socialist wing and their traditional bases of support, and took office following the 1969 elections. The NPD fell short of the 5 percent threshold required for representation in the national legislature in 1969 and their support dwindled away.

The rise of support for the NPD in Germany and for George Wallace in the United States have rather striking similarities; and the parallel apparently extends to the *new* strength won by De Gaulle in 1968.

II. THE MAY 1968 UPRISING IN FRANCE

The Post-Materialist phenomenon manifested itself with unusual clarity in France. From about 1965 until as late as 1972, youth protest and other forms of the New Politics burst forth intermittently in the United States, Germany, Italy, The Netherlands, Sweden, Japan, and most other advanced industrial nations. France's peculiar institutions and structure tended to inhibit such manifestations from surfacing. But when they did, the result was a larger and more concentrated explosion that paralyzed the entire nation.

The French upheaval came as a surprise to nearly everyone. In his New Year address for 1968, President De Gaulle congratulated the French people and himself on the fact that France (unlike some of her neighbors) seemed calm and stable and likely to remain so. There were some apparently trivial difficulties with students at the new university at Nanterre, having to do with whether men could visit in the women's dormitory, but nothing serious.

In the early months of 1968 the students became more troublesome, interrupting scheduled classes in order to hold meetings of their own. In March they briefly occupied the administrative building. In April there was heated disagreement over a proposal to hold an anti-imperialist session at the university and the dean finally decided to temporarily close the university.

[11] See Ronald Inglehart, "Revolutionnarisme Post-Bourgeois en France, en Allemagne et aux États-Unis," *Il Politico*, 36, 2 (July, 1971), 216–217.

On May 3, several hundred students gathered in the courtyard of the Sorbonne (the focal point of the French university system) to protest against the closing of Nanterre and the prospective expulsion of eight student leaders. The police were called and a fight broke out that escalated into a battle involving thousands of students. Skirmishes continued over the next few days. Public buildings were occupied and automobiles were pulled across the streets to build barricades in the student quarter of Paris. The police stormed the barricades and were repulsed with stones; they attacked again and broke through, clubbing down students in a display of force that shocked public opinion. Within a week the crisis spread over all of France. The educational unions and labor unions condemned the government for its "brutal repression" and called a general strike for May 13.

The strike was the biggest France has ever known. And the labor leaders repeatedly found themselves being left behind by their followers. On May 14 young workers, not content with a token gesture of solidarity, occupied a large aviation plant near Nantes and locked in the manager. The pattern was repeated at a number of other major factories on the following day and they remained occupied. On May 16 all Renault plants went on strike. Sit-in strikes spread throughout the chemical and engineering industries. Trains and subways came to a halt and the post offices ceased to function. By the third week of May millions of workers went on strike. Teachers, doctors, architects, government officials, and young executives joined the strike. The air lines stopped flying, and radio and television workers went on strike. Many of those who did not strike could not get to work for lack of transportation. France was paralyzed.

But there was an immense outpouring of conversation, books, and pamphlets. Paris was covered with posters depicting stalwart workers raising clenched fists against bloated capitalists, brutal policemen, or a caricatured De Gaulle. Where there were no posters the walls were covered with slogans, some of them citations from Marx or Lenin or Mao, but many of them original expressions of an individual's reaction to what was happening:

It is forbidden to forbid.
Millionaires of all countries, unite: the wind is changing.
The dream is reality.
Comrades, arm yourselves!

Imagination to Power.
To exaggerate is to begin to invent.
Don't take the elevator, take power.
To be free in 1968 is to participate.
The Mandarin is within you.
I have something to say but I don't know what.

In the occupied universities, factories, and office buildings, there were endless discussions of how to reorganize that enterprise or the entire society. Strangers spoke to each other in the streets. When the government tried to forbid the return to France of Daniel Cohn-Bendit (a student leader of German nationality and Jewish background) a hundred thousand students marched in the streets chanting "We are all German Jews!" There was euphoria in the air.

The euphoria was not universal. Barricades had sealed off the student quarter of Paris. Scores of prominent public buildings were occupied in open defiance of the state; the tricolor was hauled down, to be replaced by the red flag of revolution or the black flag of anarchy. There were runs on grocery stores and banks. A survey made immediately after the crisis indicates that a clear majority of the French public actually thought that civil war might break out. Fear began to change the atmosphere.

The leaders of organized labor and the government reached an agreement on various social reforms, including a 14 percent wage increase. On May 29, President De Gaulle disappeared for six hours. He was consulting French military commanders in Eastern France and Germany, ensuring that he would have their support if needed. The next day he addressed the French public by radio, announcing that general elections would be held in June. He called on the people to organize "civic action" and to help the government in its struggle against subversion and "totalitarian communism." Immediately after his speech there was, for the first time, a massive demonstration by Gaullists, marching down the Champs Élysées. Elections to the National Assembly took place on June 23 and 30. The result was an overwhelming Gaullist victory.

III. RESULTS OF THE 1968 FRENCH ELECTIONS

The 1968 French elections offer a rare opportunity to study the impact of a major social upheaval on electoral behavior. A previous legislative election had been held in 1967; the 1968 election was called in response to the cataclysm of May and June, and was held in its immediate aftermath. To an exceptional degree, the French public was aware of, and involved in, the crisis that precipitated the election. Far more than is usually the case, we can point to a specific set of events as the probable cause of voting shifts.

The predominant pattern was continuity. Most people voted for the same party in 1968 as in 1967. Nevertheless, a large amount of shifting took place. About one-fifth of the electorate changed parties and important numbers of voters moved to the *Left*, as well as to the Right. The elections reflected a polarization of the electorate; but what was its nature?

Initially, our expectations were based on a model that was widely accepted at the time. Very briefly stated, our hypothesis was that the most deprived group of a society should most eagerly welcome radical change; conversely, the class holding the most property under the existing order, having the most to lose, should be most resistant to an upheaval having overtones of social revolution. This hypothesis led us to expect a political polarization based on class lines in which the working class would shift to the Left responding to appeals for social change, while the middle class would shift to the Right in support of the Gaullist regime and the established order.

The elections to the National Assembly showed a dramatic change from the patterns that had appeared after the elections of 1967. Voting statistics revealed that the parties of the Left lost about 5 percent of their 1967 vote, while the center lost over one-fifth of its vote; at the same time, the Gaullist coalition's vote increased enough to give them a huge majority in the National Assembly that they had marginally controlled the year before. The Gaullist victory has frequently been attributed to a shift toward the Gaullists on the part of the (largely middle-class) electorate of the Center—an interpretation which fits in well with the hypothesis outlined above: it was supposedly a social class polarization in which a frightened bourgeoisie closed ranks against the workers.[12]

[12] See, for example, François Goguel, "Les Elections Legislatives des 23 et 30 Juin, 1968," *Revue Française de Science Politique*, 18, 5 (October, 1968), 837–853. This interpretation of the 1968 Gaullist victory as the result of a frightened middle class rallying to the Right seems to have entered

Analysis of survey data gathered immediately after the second round of voting casts grave doubt on this interpretation.[13] The data indicate that the decline of the Center was *not* a case of the bourgeoisie rallying behind De Gaulle. About as many of its former voters moved to the Left as to the Right.[14] This tended to conceal the fact that a surprisingly large number of former Leftist voters had shifted to the Gaullist coalition. Indeed, former Communist and Socialist voters apparently contributed more to the Gaullist gains than did the Center.

The impression that the 1968 election did not primarily reflect a process of class conflict is strengthened when we directly examine the relationship between social class and vote, controlling for age group. As we see from Table 10–1, the working class contin-

---

into the mores; in a background article on the elections of March, 1973, the *New York Times* was reporting it as an established fact.

[13] The analysis which follows is based on a nation-wide representative survey of the French population sixteen years of age or older (N = 1,902). Field work was carried out by the Institut français d'opinion publique during the week of July 1, 1968.

Our measure of vote shift is based on the response to two questions that asked, respectively, what party the respondent had voted for in 1967 and in 1968. A respondent's recall of his own vote is generally subject to various distortions. Frequently, there is a "bandwagon" effect that tends to exaggerate reported vote for the winner. Moreover, the respondent's memory of how he voted (even as recently as a year ago) is apt to be distorted by pressures toward cognitive consistency; especially if he were strongly committed, we would expect that he would tend to modify his report of past vote to make it consistent with his present position: vote *shift* (especially toward the winner) would thus be under-reported. It is somewhat reassuring to note that we nevertheless find a substantial amount of vote-shifting reported. In France, the problem is further complicated by a consistent tendency for Communist Party vote to be under-reported. Given the degree of political isolation and suspicion which still surrounds the French Communist Party (PCF), many of its supporters are reluctant to disclose their choice to a (usually middle-class) interviewer.

All of these factors work to reduce the reliability of our measure of vote shift. In addition most voters continued to vote for the same party in 1968 as in 1967. Consequently the number of cases for which we have a reported vote shift is relatively small (about one-fifth of our sample) and the reliability of this subsample is accordingly diminished. Thus, we will present evidence relating to the factors that influenced the 1968 vote within the entire sample (which is much larger and which presumably includes cases of unreported shift) as well as an analysis of reported vote *shift*. Certain patterns which emerge seem to be so pronounced as to minimize the suspicion that they could be due to sampling error in measurement.

[14] Among our sample, 11 percent of those who had voted for the Democratic Center in 1967 shifted to the Left in 1968 (nearly half of them to the Unified Socialist Party [PSU]) and 12 percent shifted to the Gaullist coalition.

TABLE 10–1. Percent Voting for the Gaullists vs. the Left in 1968
by Social Class and Age Group[a]

	Ages 21–39		Ages 40+	
Working class	50%	(402)	57%	(358)
Modern middle class	59	(339)	67	(264)
Traditional middle class	74	(58)	85	(99)
Farm	81	(142)	78	(235)
Retired, inactive			74	(411)

[a] In this and succeeding tables, we dichotomize between two groups of parties: the Gaullists and their allies, the Independent Republicans; and the parties of the Left (Communist, Federation of the Left and Unified Socialist Party). Those supporting the Center (Progress and Modern Democracy) are eliminated from the percentages on the grounds that a vote for it was ambiguous—indicating neither clear support nor clear opposition to the government. Based on combined data from Institut Français d'Opinion Publique pre-election survey D 101 and my post-election survey. Social class categories are based on occupation of head of household.

ued to vote more heavily for the parties of the Left than other social groups. To a considerable extent, this seems to reflect the persisting influence of early socialization. Even in 1968, there was a pronounced tendency for Frenchmen to support the political party that had been favored by their fathers. But Table 10–1 reveals another important aspect of the 1968 election: a larger number of French working-class votes went to the Gaullist coalition than to the Left! The existence of a working-class Gaullist vote in the early 1960's had already been noted. Dogan, for example, found that approximately 40 percent of France's industrial workers supported the Gaullist position in the referendum of 1962.[15] To put this fact into perspective, however, we should remember that De Gaulle won 62 percent of the total vote in that

[15] See Mattei Dogan, "Le Vote ouvrier en France: Analyse écologique des élections de 1962," *Revue française de Sociologie*, 6, 4 (October-December, 1965), 435–471. Cf. Dogan, "Political Cleavage and Social Stratification in France and Italy," in Seymour M. Lipset, *Party Systems and Voter Alignments* (New York: Free Press, 1967), 129–195.

Other writers have discussed the converse idea. In the French context, for example, Bon and Burnier recently argued that a lower strata of the modern middle class—technicians, middle management, etc.—provide a potential reserve of support for parties of the Left because they are relatively remote from the command posts of society. See Frédéric Bon and Michel-Antoine Burnier, *Les Nouveaux Intellectuels* (Paris: Cujas, 1966). The explanatory basis of this book (and hence its implications) are rather different from our own. We would argue that higher social levels provide an *at least* equally promising area of recruitment, and our data seem to bear this out.

referendum; the Gaullist minority among the workers was no doubt significant, but the working class was still heavily under-represented on the Gaullist side.

Although the Gaullist margin of victory was smaller than in the 1962 referendum, the 1968 election was the first in which Gaullist candidates won a larger number of working-class votes than did Communist candidates. Gaullist gains among the workers were substantial indeed at a time when the traditional rhetoric of social class conflict was pervasive.

Conversely, another aspect of Table 10–1 is also significant: the relatively high level of support given to the Left by members of the modern middle class. This support is strongly related to age; thus, the younger members of the modern middle class gave nearly as high a proportion of their vote to the Left as did the older members of the working class. Again, the findings are not wholly new: a tendency for younger voters to be less Gaullist than older voters had been noted throughout the 1960's, but the age variable was of relatively modest importance then. Various analyses of survey data from 1962 to 1965 indicate a spread of several percentage points between the youngest and oldest age groups in relative support for the Gaullists. But the age difference was overshadowed by such factors as sex differences (women were notably more Gaullist than men). In 1968, the age variable was a far stronger predictor of vote than was sex—and fully as important as social class. When we break down our respondents into ten-year age groups, we find a steady increase in the Gaullist vote as we move to older groups. The Gaullists enjoyed a three-to-one advantage among voters in their seventies; but they received a minority of the vote from those in their twenties. The crisis of 1968 was a generational conflict more than a class conflict. To the extent that vote shifting took place, it emphasized the former factor at the expense of the latter.

If we use the respondents' *education* as an indicator of social class rather than our occupational categories, we find an even more striking reversal of class roles among different age groups (see Table 10–2). Comparing the "middle class" (the two more educated groups, as defined in this fashion) with the "working class," we would obtain a positive Alford index of +18 among respondents aged 40 and older—the normal polarity by traditional expectations. Among the younger group, we would actually obtain a *negative* index. Clearly, the age-linked differences are not simply

TABLE 10–2. Vote in 1968 by Education, Age Controlled
(Percent voting Gaullist in two-way split)

Social Class, as indicated by education	Ages 21–39		Ages 40+	
Working class & lower middle class (Primary or middle school education)	53%	(209)	63%	(490)
Middle class (Technical and secondary school education)	54	(145)	72	(117)
Upper middle class (University education)	39	(44)	69	(35)

due to the higher levels of education among the younger group. The effect of education seems to be *reversed* between older and younger generations.

Returning to Table 10–1 we note that the traditional middle class gave markedly less support to the Left than did the modern middle class; its older members especially voted as if class conflict were the issue, and they were intent on protecting their interests. But the increasingly numerous and prosperous modern middle class (especially its younger members) gave a surprisingly large share of their vote to the parties of the Left, considering that France was purportedly on the brink of proletarian revolution.

One might argue that middle-class support for the Left in general did not mean much because by 1968, the French Communist Party and Federation of the Left were scarcely revolutionary parties. We would not deny the latter half of this assertion: the French Communists, in particular, may have won support a generation or two earlier because they promised a Russian-style revolution, but in 1968 this was clearly not the case. Both the Communists and Federation of the Left acted with notable restraint, condemning violent acts of protest and taking great pains to avoid giving the impression that they contemplated seizing power through any means other than by elections. One could argue therefore that members of the middle class could vote for the two main parties of the Left because they were acting as essentially conservative forces.

This objection has a certain amount of truth to it, and it directs our attention to two groups that reflect the dynamics of the crisis in a relatively unambiguous way. These two groups consist of those who shifted to provide *new* support for the Gaullists, on the one hand; and those who voted for the Unified Socialist Party in 1968, on the other.

The Unified Socialist Party was the only party to support the

May Revolt openly and to the end of the crisis. It paid a certain price for this stand. Fully one-third of those who had voted for the Unified Socialist Party in 1967 deserted it in 1968. On the other hand, the Unified Socialist Party gained many new recruits. About half of those who voted for it in 1968 were new supporters. Although it polled only about 4 percent of the total vote, its electorate is especially interesting because, in a much clearer fashion than was true of any other party, a vote for the Unified Socialist Party represented a vote for the May Revolt.

It seems significant, therefore, that the Unified Socialist Party electorate shifted from one which was made up of roughly equal numbers of working-class and middle-class voters in 1967 to one composed overwhelmingly of middle-class voters in 1968 with less than a quarter of its support coming from the working class. Only a handful of voters came from other social categories. The Unified Socialist Party's big gains from 1967 to 1968 were made among the younger members of the modern middle class; its big losses were among older workers.

Vote shifts to and from the Gaullist Union for Defense of the Republic (UDR) were a mirror image of what happened to the Unified Socialist Party. Despite the strong overall trend favoring the UDR in 1968, that party suffered a net *loss* among the younger modern middle class. In that category, 41 percent of our respondents under forty years of age voted for the UDR in 1967, whereas 32 percent did so in 1968. The UDR made gains between 1967 and 1968 among all other groups. Because of its relative size, the working class provided the numerically most important Gaullist gains.

For an event that was billed as a revolutionary class conflict, the results run contrary to expectations. The younger cohorts of the economically most favored strata showed a net shift in favor of the revolution; the workers (with declining elements of the middle class) rallied behind the forces of the established order.

IV. The Impact of the Crisis: Fear of Violence and the Appeal of a New Social Order

In France, as in Germany and the United States, the politics of the late 1960's reflected a change in the social bases of protest. The crucial question is *why* the various social groups acted as they did.

The crisis of 1968 gave rise to two contrasting reactions which, superimposed on previous party preferences, induced given individuals to shift their support to the Right or to the Left. On the one hand, there was widespread fear of violence. A majority of our sample said they thought civil war might break out. On the other, certain groups cherished hopes that a better society might emerge from the May Revolt.

A flood of articles, pamphlets, and posters appeared in May and June. While many were couched in traditional Marxist or Anarchist jargon, frequently they also stressed the theme of "participation." The meaning of this term was diffuse, but for the protesters it seemed to imply a more humane, less hierarchical social order in which decisions would be reached on the basis of warm, personal face-to-face interaction rather than through the impersonal and hierarchical authority relationships inherent in large bureaucratic organizations.

The reaction against violence apparently had the greater net impact on the elections, but we must remember that the May Revolt had a strongly positive meaning for a substantial part of the population.

Fear of civil violence was widespread. Fifty-eight percent of those interviewed said that they thought the strikes and demonstrations of May and June might lead to civil war. This fear was strongly related to the way they voted. Seventy-three percent of those who expressed a dread of civil war voted for the Gaullist coalition, the advocates of law and order ("Pour les réformes dans la légalité," as the Gaullist slogan put it). Only 31 percent of those who were not intimidated by the threat of civil war voted Gaullist. Although the anti-Gaullist demonstrators actually carried out little violence against people, there had been much talk of "strangling the last capitalist with the guts of the last bureaucrat." It was mere rhetoric and the great majority of protesters did not really mean it, no doubt, but it was apparently taken seriously by many among the older generations.

Fear of civil war did not seem to be merely part of a pro-Gaullist rationale, but was expressed by large numbers of people who normally voted for the opposition, as well as by Gaullist sympathizers. An individual's family background seemed to shape his interpretation of the May events, however. Those who had been raised in the milieu of the Left were considerably less likely to perceive a danger of civil war than were those raised in a family oriented toward the Right. Votes in the 1968 election could be viewed in part as the resultant of two key forces: fears engendered by the current crisis, balanced against political pre-dispositions growing out of earlier family socialization. When the two forces worked in the same direction the electoral outcome was overwhelmingly one-sided (see Table 10–3). Among those who re-

TABLE 10–3. Vote in 1968 by Perception of Current Danger
and Family Political Tradition
(Percent voting Gaullist in two-way split)

	Father-Left		Father's Preference Not Known		Father-Center		Father-Right	
"Danger?"—No, Don't Know	13%	(116)	46%	(193)	42%	(55)	76%	(49)
"Danger?"—Yes	48	(115)	72	(301)	80	(96)	95	(115)

ported that their father had voted for a party of the Left, *and* had perceived no danger of civil war, only 13 percent voted for the Right; whereas those whose father was for the Right and who feared a civil war voted for the Right by an immense margin (95 percent). Those who received ambiguous cues or who were cross-pressured, fell in between.

Knowledge of these two variables alone gives us a fairly powerful ability to predict an individual's vote in 1968. By comparison, such standard variables as occupation, income, education, religious practice, trade union membership, and sex fade into relative insignificance (they account for, at most, half as much of the variance in vote as either of the two above-mentioned variables). But let us trace the causal process a little farther. Fear of civil war need not in itself lead to a Gaullist vote. Whatever his reaction to a current crisis, an individual must first draw some politically relevant conclusion. As it happened, fear of civil war led many people to see De Gaulle as the strong man needed to handle the situation. In the atmosphere of June, 1968, a heavy majority of our sample agreed with the statement, "France will always need a strong leader like De Gaulle to avoid disaster." Needless to say, agreement with this statement was very closely related to vote in 1968.

Working-class respondents were relatively likely to come from families of the Left. But *despite* the influence of family socialization just described, working-class respondents were more likely to have felt a danger of civil war than were members of the modern middle class. We suspect that this finding may reflect the presence of relatively high needs for safety and economic security among the workers, as compared with the modern middle class.

The traditional sector of French society, the traditional middle class and farmers, dreaded civil war the most. It is not surprising that the traditional middle class reacted strongly: the operator of a small business is particularly vulnerable in the face of civil disorder. Yet farmers felt an almost equal degree of anxiety. The great bulk of the violence took place in the cities, especially Paris; one might expect that the farmers, being physically distant, would feel relatively secure. However, the rural population's greater sense of threat may have been heightened by their very isolation. At the peak of the crisis they were largely cut off from normal communications channels. The farmers were aware that a great crisis had paralyzed France, knew that violent confrontations were taking place, but could not learn the details. Their imaginations, or rumor, must have filled in the outlines—and they apparently accepted the revolutionary rhetoric at face value. The great majority of rural voters feared that civil war might erupt; they were very likely to shift to the Gaullist side if they were not already Gaullist in 1967.

The younger cohorts were less likely to have perceived a danger of civil war than were the older cohorts, but only moderately so. The age differences on this item are markedly smaller than those connected with actual vote. Only to a limited degree can the low Gaullist vote among the younger age groups be attributed to their lesser tendency to perceive grave danger in the events of May and June. Moreover, their less Gaullist disposition persists even when we control for perceived danger of civil war. Younger voters were not only less likely to have seen danger in what was happening, but were more hospitable to the Left *regardless* of how they saw the situation. It seems that the *positive* aspects of the May Revolt had a relatively strong appeal for the younger cohorts.

Acceptance or rejection of the idea that "France will always need a strong leader like De Gaulle" was even more closely related to actual vote and more closely influenced by family background than was perception of the danger of civil war. Do responses to this question produce a similar reversal of social class roles among our two most important groups, with members of the working class more ready to endorse this explicitly pro-Gaullist statement than the modern middle class? The answer is "yes," as Table 10–4 demonstrates. If votes had been cast on the basis of this attitude alone, uninhibited by traditional party allegiances, we would have found a clearly *negative* index of class-voting instead of the positive one that actually existed. In their reaction to the May Revolt, the French working class took a position to the Right of the modern middle class (or even the middle class as a whole) overwhelmingly in support of the established order. The retired and farm populations, once again, were still farther to the Right. By contrast, the middle class was far less Gaullist in its response to this item than its traditional political behavior might suggest. To understand these findings, we must examine the psychological rewards of participation in the May Revolt.

TABLE 10–4. Agreement with Statement "France Will Always Need a Strong Leader like De Gaulle To Avoid Disorder" by Occupation (Percent saying "agree" or "agree strongly" among those answering)

Modern middle class	57%	(472)	Class-voting index = −7
Working class	64	(615)	
Traditional middle class	65	(113)	
Retired	73	(299)	
Farm	79	(262)	

Participation in the strikes and demonstrations of 1968 was extraordinarily widespread and by no means limited to students and workers: fully 20 percent of our respondents reported having taken part in some form of protest activity. Although workers were numerically the most important group, large numbers of young executives, professionals, and white-collar employees were caught up in the enthusiasm of the movement. Those who participated in the May protest activities felt a rewarding sense of direct human contact and solidarity. One of the recollections most often mentioned by those who had taken part was the fact that "people talked to each other." Suddenly, barriers were broken, workers were masters in their factories, employees were talking to the *patron* as equals, strangers spoke to each other on the bus. For a brief period, there was a feeling that something unprecedented had happened, that the world was going to be different from now on. This enthusiasm seems to have been most intense among the younger members of the modern sector of society—the sector that has the greatest economic security but is, at the same time, most heavily bureaucratized. Suddenly, anonymous numbers had become people.

Support for the May Revolt was originally drawn from *both* of the major groups in the modern sector, the middle class and the industrial working class. But the two groups were apparently motivated by different values. Having identified those who took some type of action against the government, we asked, "What did you hope to obtain?" Each respondent was given three choices from a list of twelve possible goals that had been selected in an open-ended pre-test. We attempted to include a number of items that (in terms of face content) seemed to tap motivations relating to limited economic gains, as well as a number of items which referred to some kind of radical restructuring of society and hence which might draw on the need to belong and expressive, as opposed to instrumental, motivations.

Sixty-two percent of the working-class respondents (N = 205) named limited economic goals exclusively—the four leading choices being "higher wages," "job security," cancelling "the changes in social security," and lowering "the retirement age." In response to the same question, only 30 percent of the middle-class respondents gave reasons which fell within this category; most of them gave mixed responses, but 16 percent gave answers indicating that they acted entirely in hopes of fundamental political or socio-economic changes (a pattern found among only 2 percent of working-class respondents). The leading choices that we regarded as "radical" were: "a change in government and politics," support of "the workers' and students' movement," "participation in decisions and management of enterprises," "the end of capitalism" (in that order). Overall, the mean number of "radical" reasons cited by middle-class participants was 1.15 (N = 168); for working-class participants the mean was .51 (N = 205).[16]

Similarly, there was a disparity of motivations between the younger and older cohorts among the participants: the younger generation was substantially more likely to report "radical" or expressive motivations than the older cohorts.

When we control for both age and occupation of head of family, a regular progression appears. The younger middle-class group is

[16] The larger number of reasons for support of "radical" positions given by middle-class respondents is not an artifact caused by this group's simply giving more answers. Each respondent was asked to select three choices from the list of alternatives; almost none of the participants failed to select the full number, and they have been eliminated from the present analysis.

by far the most "radically" oriented, and the younger working-class respondents are considerably more so than their elders. But even the older middle-class participants appear to have been motivated by "radical" considerations more than the younger working-class participants; and among the older workers, "radical" motivations are almost totally absent (see Table 10–5).

TABLE 10–5. Mean Number of "Radical"
Reasons Given for Protest Participation
by Age and Occupation
(Participants only)

Age Group	Working Class		Middle Class	
Teens	.78	(32)	1.34	(32)
20's	.60	(57)	1.25	(69)
30's	.35	(48)	1.06	(49)
40's	.32	(28)	.96	(26)
50's	.60	(30)	.93	(14)
60+	.10	(10)	.89	(10)

Where shifts in vote occurred, one would expect that participation in the various protest activities would be linked with shifts from the Gaullist coalition to the opposition parties. (1) Active participation exposed individuals to communication from other members of a group that was strongly anti-Gaullist in mood. (2) It provided intense group interaction and a sense of belonging. Perhaps because of this psychological support, participants were markedly less likely to have perceived a danger of civil war than were non-participants.[17] Yet the *impact* of these activities was much greater on participants from middle-class backgrounds than on working-class protesters. Middle-class participants who shifted their vote from 1967 to 1968 moved to the Left by a three-to-one margin. Even when exposed to the influences of protest activity, working-class participants shifted to the Left by only a narrow

[17] Among those answering the question about danger of civil war in our subsample of protest participants, nearly half (47 percent) denied that there had been a danger of civil war (N = 366), while only 27 percent of non-participants gave the same answer (N = 1,263). Relatively intense interaction developed within some of the groups taking direct action against the government. This evidently provided a sense of comradeship and security that counteracted fears the disorder may have produced. It is noteworthy that fully half the protesters nevertheless *did* perceive a danger of civil war.

margin. The psychological rewards of taking part in protest activities apparently were less important to them, and the negative aspects of the May Revolt carried a correspondingly greater weight.

A similar pattern applied to the effect of participation on the different age cohorts. The younger participants (those under forty years of age) shifted to the *Gaullist* side, even though they had taken part in protest activities at some point.

Thus, not only did motivations for participation in the May Revolt vary according to age and class, but the outcome of such participation shows a revealing contrast. When events seemed to run beyond the goals that originally brought older and working-class groups to support the movement, they tended to react against it; on the other hand, younger middle-class elements maintained their support throughout the crisis and still supported it at the time of the elections.

To the extent that it was based on different underlying values, the alliance between student activists and striking workers was doomed—the more so because the student leaders tended to confuse rhetoric with reality. "The consumer society deserves to die a violent death," said Daniel Cohn-Bendit; "we refuse a world where the certainty of not dying of hunger is gained at the risk of dying of boredom."[18] But to the striking workers, especially the older ones, it was not so certain that the risk of hunger had been forever eliminated. The consumer society was a world they had just entered, and it seemed very attractive indeed.

In the early stages of the May Revolt, public opinion was predominately favorable to the student protesters.[19] This situation deteriorated rapidly after the night of May 10, when protesters barricaded the Latin Quarter, causing extensive property damage and burning large numbers of automobiles. To the student activists, burning the Renaults and Citroëns was a dramatic gesture, which consumed nothing of real value. But something like half of France's workers had acquired an automobile for the first time during the preceding decade; for them, this was a shocking and

[18] Quoted in *Le Monde*, May 14, 1968.

[19] After several weeks of increasing conflict between police and students, an IFOP survey of May 8, 1968, showed that 61 percent of a sample of the Paris population felt that "the present student demonstrations express justifiable grievances"; only 16 percent were then opposed to the demonstrations. Subsequent IFOP surveys show that opposition had jumped to 37 percent in Paris (and 44 percent in France as a whole) by May 14. Disapproval of the student demonstrations continued to mount thereafter.

wanton act. By the time of the elections, our survey indicates, a clear majority of the French public disapproved of the student demonstrations, although a plurality remained favorable to the relatively orderly union demonstrators.[20]

The protest movement apparently started out with the sympathy of most of French society, but was vulnerable to splits along generational and class lines. The younger members of the modern middle class were relatively strongly attracted by the ideology of "participation," while the workers were more interested in traditional economic gains. When events seemed to threaten recent economic gains, the workers withdrew their support, and many of them, especially the older ones, contributed to a pro-Gaullist reaction.

Yet even as they were sending a huge majority of Gaullists to the new National Assembly, only a minority of the French electorate were actually satisfied with De Gaulle's policies. Our sample was asked, "Are you satisfied or dissatisfied with the policies of General De Gaulle over the course of the last few years?" Only 45 percent gave a positive response to this question; yet fully 65 percent of the same respondents had at the same time endorsed the statement, "France will always need a strong leader like De Gaulle to avoid disorder." A crucial middle group, which would not express approval of his policies (even immediately after he had surmounted the great crisis), nevertheless felt he was needed against civil violence. It seems that De Gaulle was rescued in 1968 by the excesses of the more extreme protesters. The familiar pendulum of French politics had swung again: from discontent, to revolt, to revolutionary enthusiasm, to fear, and, in reaction, back to authoritarian rule. This time the events had been compressed into a period of two months.

By comparison with De Gaulle (who sometimes seemed to be losing his grip), Pompidou had performed rather coolly during the crisis, emerging with a prestige within the government that rivaled De Gaulle's and a popularity (as reflected in public opinion polls) considerably higher than De Gaulle's. From the General's point of view the solution was clear: Pompidou had to go. He was dismissed shortly after the electoral victory he had helped achieve.

[20] Among our respondents, 54 percent were unfavorable and only 31 percent were still favorable to the student demonstrations. At the same time, a 46 percent plurality of the same respondents were favorable to the union demonstrations with only 33 percent opposed.

During the previous two years, De Gaulle had taken a number of actions that ran counter to the prevailing preferences of French public opinion. His position in the Arab-Israeli conflict, his expenditures on the *force de frappe*, his withdrawal from NATO, his policy on social security, his veto of British entry to the Common Market, and his call for *Quebec Libre* were all viewed with resentment or chagrin by the bulk of the French public. Nevertheless, his overall level of support remained high as long as he held a seeming monopoly on the ability to provide something that was valued even more than any of the foregoing: political and economic stability. The events of May, 1968, revealed that even *he* could not necessarily provide them and (on the other hand) that other leaders might be equally effective.

De Gaulle had lost his monopoly as France's indispensable man. By April, 1969, when De Gaulle called a national referendum, the atmosphere of fear largely had abated. This time it no longer seemed to be a choice between De Gaulle and revolution, but between De Gaulle and some moderate successor. A small but crucial part of the electorate changed sides and the era of De Gaulle was over.[21]

V. Conclusions

France's 1968 crisis has given rise to an immense and rich literature. To convey some idea of its variety, let us simply note that one inventory categorizes the various interpretations under eight headings.[22] Thus, the May Revolt can be seen as: (1) an abortive takeover attempt by the French Communist Party; or by

[21] The age and class trends shown in 1968 continued to operate in the downfall of De Gaulle. A further loss of support from the modern middle class helped defeat the 1969 referendum. Rejected by 53 percent of the voters, among families headed by executives or professionals it was opposed by an overwhelming 70 percent. Manual workers and farmers split almost evenly on the referendum, with the retired and widowed (and the older cohorts in general) giving heavy support. See Alain Lancelot and Pierre Weill, "L'evolution politique des Electeurs Français de fevrier à juin 1969," *Revue Française de Science Politique*, 20, 2 (April, 1970), 249–281.

Interestingly enough, it was only after De Gaulle had made it clear that he would retire from office if the referendum were defeated that a negative majority appeared in the polls.

[22] See Phillippe Béneton and Jean Touchard, "Les interprétations de la crise de mai-juin 1968," *Revue Française de Science Politique*, 20, 3 (June, 1970), 503–544. This provides an excellent review of the early literature (though it emphasizes publications in French).

Left-wing splinter groups; or one instigated by the CIA as an anti-Gaullist maneuver; (2) a university crisis due to the overcrowding and rigidity of the system of higher education; or to the marginal position of students in society; or due to their declining prospects for economic success in a shrinking job market; (3) an eruption of youthful rebellion—perhaps motivated by the desire to murder the father; or a large psychodrama; (4) a crisis of civilization; a revolt against a particular type of society; (5) a new type of class conflict between the "professionals" and the "technocrats"; (6) a traditional class conflict; (7) a political crisis due to the institutions of the Fifth Republic; or to the absence of any real alternative on the Left; and (8) a more or less accidental chain reaction.

Subsequent publications have provided additional explanations, many of which seem useful.[23] We will not attempt to review this vast body of analysis here, for our purpose is not to provide the definitive interpretation of the crisis. Instead, we wish to focus on one component of these events which may have broad relevance.

The politics of the late 1960's in the United States, Germany, and France had certain features in common: (1) the advocacy of social change tended to have a middle-class rather than a working-class base; (2) age cleavages became virtually as important as social class cleavages; and (3) non-economic issues achieved a high degree of salience.

These features were related. After a prolonged period of almost uninterrupted economic growth, the principal axis of political cleavage began to shift from economic issues to life-style issues, entailing a shift in the constituency most interested in obtaining change. Following a law of diminishing returns, economic gains became relatively less important, particularly to those segments of

[23] Some of the key recent publications include Adrien Dansette, *Mai 1968* (Paris: Plon, 1971); André Fontaine, *La Guerre Civile Froide* (Paris: Fayard, 1969); Daniel Singer, *Prelude to Revolution* (New York: Hill and Wang, 1970); Bernard E. Brown, "The French Experience of Modernization," in Roy Macridis and Bernard Brown (eds.), *Comparative Politics: Notes and Readings*, 4th ed. (Homewood, Ill.: Dorsey, 1972), 442–460; Philip E. Converse and Roy Pierce, "Die Mai-Unruhen in Frankreich—Ausmass und Konsequenzen," in Klaus R. Allerbeck and Leopold Rosenmayr (eds.), *Aufstand der Jugend? Neue Aspekte der Jugendsoziologie* (Munich: Juventa, 1971), 108–137; A. Belden Fields, "The Revolution Betrayed: The French Student Revolt of May-June, 1968," in Seymour M. Lipset and Phillip G. Altbach (eds.), *Students in Revolt* (Boston: Houghton-Mifflin, 1969), 127–166; and Melvin Seeman, "The Signals of '68: Alienation in Pre-Crisis France," *American Sociological Review*, 37, 4 (August, 1972), 385–402.

society that had never experienced severe economic deprivation.[24] This shift can be explained in a variety of ways. Deutsch, for example, has spoken of man as a goal-seeking organism, but one that progressively shifts its attention to pursuit of new types of goals, once it has attained satisfaction on a given plane.[25] For a significant portion of society (though still a minority) economic gains no longer seemed most urgent.

The resulting shift toward emphasis on new political goals might be called the Post-Materialist phenomenon. For younger, economically secure groups, new items were at the top of the agenda. Efforts to fight the dehumanizing tendencies inherent in Industrial society book high priority; it was a fight against hierarchical relationships on both the domestic scene and in international politics.

This is not to say that overcrowded, outmoded, and rigidly structured universities were not a factor—or that the quality of life of the working class, racial injustice or the brutality of the war in Vietnam were unimportant. On the contrary, these were genuine ills against which protest was directed. Our analysis focuses on another level of causation however: it suggests that long-term forces had made certain groups exceptionally *sensitive* to such problems.

In each of the three countries discussed here (and in a number of others as well) the Post-Materialist phenomenon eventually gave rise to a Materialist reaction that overwhelmed the call for radical social change and left the Post-Materialists feeling defeated and demoralized. For the time being, at least, the Materialist outlook is still by far the more widespread.

Lipset has pointed out that declining elements of the middle class often provide the basis for reactionary movements. He cites evidence that much of the early strength of the Nazi party in Weimar Germany was recruited from among small businessmen; Poujadism in France and McCarthyism in the United States of

---

[24] The idea that the student revolt reflected declining career opportunities may be a rationalization rather than a root cause. For the more gifted students with the most promising careers tended to be most radical. Moreover, in the United States student radicalism reached its peak in a golden age of high demand for university graduates and dwindled in a sharply contracting job market.

[25] See Deutsch, *The Nerves of Government* (New York: Free Press, 1963).

the 1950's are also depicted as drawing largely on these bases of support.[26]

But (as Lipset emphasizes) it is important to distinguish between the *traditional* middle class (self-employed craftsmen and small businessmen) and the *modern* middle class (those having non-manual occupations in large enterprises, and professionals servicing the modern sector of society). At an earlier stage of development, artisans and shopkeepers made up the great bulk of the middle class. But today the other groups constitute a heavy majority of the middle class in modernized economies. They tend to have not only higher levels of education, income, and social status than the traditional middle class but also a distinctive pattern of political behavior. The traditional middle class seems relatively likely to retain a "bourgeois" pre-occupation with preserving property rights and order. It has a particularly personal and vulnerable stake in the preservation of order. If a General Motors plant is damaged, the GM executive is unlikely to suffer directly; if a small shop is wrecked, it may never open again. On the other hand, the abstract and bureaucratic nature of the GM executive's role makes him prey to dissatisfactions which may be less important in the concrete, face-to-face world of the traditional middle class.

While the traditional middle class may still be potentially reactionary, its numbers have dwindled to the point where any sizeable movement in defense of the established order must draw heavily on the working class. At the same time, sufficiently large numbers of people in manual occupations have acquired a stake in the established order and a "bourgeois" mentality that such a basis is

[26] See Lipset, "Fascism—Left, Right and Center," in *Political Man* (New York: Doubleday, 1969). Cf. Karl D. Bracher, *Die Auflosüng Der Weimarer Republik* (Stuttgart and Dusseldorf: Ring Verlag, 1954). More recently Karl O'Lessker had disputed this interpretation. He concludes that the first great surge of Nazi strength (in the 1930 elections) came chiefly from previous non-voters, with former voters for the conservative nationalist DNVP second and members of the (non-Catholic) middle class third in importance. In the 1932 elections, he agrees, the greatest gains were made among the non-Catholic middle class. O'Lessker's argument is interesting although the type of data available to him (aggregate voting statistics) makes it difficult to arrive at a definitive judgment. See O'Lessker, "Who Voted for Hitler? A New Look at the Class Basis of Nazism," *The American Journal of Sociology*, 74, 1 (July, 1968), 62–69. Cf. Philips Shively, "Voting Stability and the Nature of Party Attachments in the Weimar Republic, *American Political Science Review*, 66, 4 (December, 1972), 1203–1225.

possible. The modern middle class, on the other hand, shows signs of becoming less concerned with the defense of property and order. In the future, it seems likely that middle-class radicalism will manifest itself in such phenomena as the McCarthyism of the late 1960's rather than the McCarthyism of the early 1950's.

In the late 1960's, the Old and the New Politics were interlarded in confused fashion. The Post-Materialists saw themselves as the Left, but it was a New Left which did not always harmonize with the Old. In France, the pattern of events contained some striking differences from what took place in Germany or the United States. The crisis was concentrated into a briefer but more intense outburst, and one reason for its greater intensity was the fact that in France, the workers *joined* the students in the initial stages of the crisis.

Four factors help account for the distinctive French pattern. First, the heritage of the French Revolution (and numerous revolutions which succeeded it) have given revolutionary symbols a degree of legitimacy and a set of positive connotations that they lack in most other Western countries. Second, a large and strongly organized Communist Party, helped keep the myth of revolution alive and meaningful to a large part of the working class. A third factor is the extreme centralization of French society and politics. Television, the press, and other forms of communications are heavily concentrated in Paris in close proximity to the political organs of a unitary state and within easy reach of a large proportion of France's students. By comparison, the United States is immensely fragmented. Events at Berkeley or Ann Arbor or Cambridge have an impact on other campuses, but their impact on New York or Washington tends to be delayed and scattered. The fourth factor is related to the third. General De Gaulle, given his unique position of authority and an exceptional concentration of power, was able, for a long time, to repress or ignore most forms of protest. But when public discontent finally found an outlet, the result was explosive.

In France, as in other countries, the underlying priorities of the workers and older citizens proved to be different from those of the young radicals. The latter were not just seeking a more equitable distribution of economic gains, but a society in which fraternity and individual self-expression would be emphasized even at the expense of economic gains. Furthermore, their rejection of hierarchical social relations was difficult to reconcile with the organizational needs of the established leaders of the Left whose power was based on tightly disciplined parties and labor unions. As the crisis moved to its peak, the disparity of priorities became evident and the revolutionary coalition broke apart.

The evidence we have just reviewed suggests that a process of value change may be taking place. Let us review some of the long-term contributing factors.

Throughout most of civilized history, the predominant concern of most human beings has been the problem of subsistence. Hence, a rough but meaningful dichotomy can be made between two types of political motivations: economic and non-economic. On this basis, it seems possible to postulate a general relationship between the level of economic development in a society, and its style of domestic politics. Because man has little power to control them in a purely agrarian society, economic factors tend to be taken for granted—they are the result of fate or the will of God. In industrializing societies, there is an increasing awareness of human potential to solve economic problems, and increasing emphasis on attainment of economic goals. Political conflict shifts toward an economic axis. The ideal-type of "economic man" probably comes closest to being realized in the Captain of Industry of transitional industrialization.[27] In an "affluent" society, economic subsistence may again come to be taken for granted, but for the opposite reason from that of agrarian society: economic factors may appear to be under control.

In Industrial society more and more people become organized in hierarchically structured and routinized factories or offices with their relationships governed by impersonal bureaucratic rules. This type of organization makes large-scale enterprises possible, may lead to increased productivity, and, as long as economic considerations are paramount, a majority may be willing to accept the

[27] This is of course an oversimplified scheme of the dominant value systems in given societies. Factors other than economic development enter the picture, and the pace of economic development is itself probably influenced by prevailing values, in a feedback relationship. David McClelland, for example, has related a nation's need for achievement, as expressed by references to achievement in its literature, to its economic performance at various stages of history. If we view popular literature as an indicator of influences shaping the socialization of a given generation, the relationship found by McClelland fits our explanatory scheme rather well: the fluctuations of the expressed drive for achievement predict, about a generation in advance, the rise and fall of economic production. See McClelland, *The Achieving Society* (Princeton: Princeton University Press, 1961).

accompanying depersonalization and anonymity. But if, as our data suggest, current youth cohorts contain a large element that takes economic security for granted, we would expect to find among them a greater emphasis on the need for belonging. Participation in some form of protest activity can fill this need, especially if the activists are united in conflict with their immediate environment.[28]

We have already noted the important role of active participation in the May Revolt. Despite the widespread fear that the Revolt evoked, it became a highly positive experience for those to whom it gave a sense of social solidarity. The emphasis on "participation" among contemporary protest themes similarly may reflect the growing importance of this need as a political motivation. To the extent that it is caused by the need to belong, activism would not necessarily disappear when a given grievance is resolved or becomes less salient: it may shift to other issues that provide a focus for group unity and a sense of purpose that economic achievement no longer furnishes. The American student protest movement, for example, began with an emphasis on civil rights, shifted later to the war in Vietnam, and more recently to a crusade against pollution, overpopulation, and despoiling of nature.

The Post-Materialists may have a perspective that makes them relatively sensitive to the political issues of the future. In this sense, one might view them as a prophetic minority. But this interpretation is valid only to the extent that one can take increasing economic security for granted. If our interpretation is correct, the destruction or debilitation of Industrial society would probably be followed by the emergence of a Philistine generation.

Conversely, with continued economic expansion one would expect the base of recruitment for Post-Materialist radicalism to expand. Insofar as the radicals are reacting against problems inherent in production-oriented bureaucratic society, conflict is not likely to be resolved by marginal concessions. The spread of the Post-Materialist outlook implies basic social reorganization.

[28] This need, of course, is not necessarily expressed in politically relevant ways. It can also be filled by participation in other-worldly cults, for example—a tendency that seems to be growing.

PART IV

Cognitive Mobilization

CHAPTER 11

Cognitive Mobilization and Political Participation
Among Western Publics

Two basic changes are taking place among Western publics. One
is cognitive, the other evaluative, and they seem equally significant.
We have discussed the nature and consequences of changing value
priorities in some detail. Now let us turn our attention to another
process that we will call Cognitive Mobilization.

Western publics are developing an increasing potential for political participation. This change does not imply that mass publics
will simply show higher rates of participation in traditional activities such as voting but that they may intervene in the political
process on a qualitatively different level. Increasingly, they are
likely to demand participation in *making* major decisions, not just
a voice in selecting the decision-makers. The two processes tend
to reinforce each other: change is occurring not only in the goals
of Western publics but also in the way they pursue them. These
changes have important implications for established political parties, labor unions, and professional organizations, for mass politics
are increasingly apt to be elite-challenging rather than elite-
directed. The source of these changes is a shift in the balance of
political skills between elites and mass.

Educational statistics probably furnish the clearest indicator
of these changes, although education is merely one aspect of a
broader underlying process. Among the Americans who turned
seventeen years old in 1920, only 17 percent graduated from high
school. Among the comparable group in 1930, the figure was 29
percent; in 1960 it was 65 percent, and in 1970, nearly 80 percent.
As these figures show, there has been an enormous increase in the
proportion getting a secondary education, but the expansion of
higher education has been even more impressive. From 1920 to
1970 the American population almost doubled, but more than sixteen times as many college degrees were awarded in 1970 as in
1920. This pattern has prevailed throughout advanced Western
countries. In all nine countries of the European Community, the

proportion of the population from the ages of twenty to twenty-four that was receiving higher education at least doubled from 1950 to 1965. European Community estimates indicate that by 1980 the proportion receiving higher education will be at least three times as high as in 1950 with some countries showing a four-fold or fivefold increase. Recently the increase in the proportion getting higher education has leveled off in the United States (which already had a rate nearly three times as high as any of the European Community countries). This could be an indication that the United States has reached a saturation level, or it could be a temporary condition. But even if we assume it to be permanent, the mean educational level of the American electorate will continue to rise substantially for several decades, as older and less educated age groups die off and are replaced by more highly educated younger ones. The group born in 1900 contained about 54,000 holders of higher degrees; the group born in 1950 contains almost a million.

The effects of rising educational levels are probably reinforced by the permeation of electronic media, which bring political information even to those without much formal education. Radio and (even more so) television make distant political events seem near and vital. Although television penetrated throughout the United States in the 1950's, it became a part of the typical European household only in the 1960's. In the brief span from 1963 to 1969, the proportion of French households having a television set rose from 27 percent to 69 percent.[1] During this period, the figures for Italy are almost identical: television ownership rose from 29 percent to 69 percent; in West Germany, from 41 percent to 82 percent; and in Britain (which started earlier) from 82 percent to 92 percent. Today television is almost universal in Western nations. Together with other factors, it gives these societies unprecedented capabilities for rapid dissemination of information across large distances.

A sharp decline in farm populations is reducing the number of people who are physically isolated, and is thereby helping make education and information about national politics more readily accessible. In the 1960's, the share of the French population that was working on the land fell by nearly one-half. In France, Italy, Germany, and the Benelux nations, the number of farmers is ex-

[1] The figures for all four countries are from Reader's Digest Association, *A Survey of Europe Today* (London: Reader's Digest, 1970), 104.

pected to drop from about ten million in 1970 to about five million in 1980.

We are interested in these changes insofar as they contribute to the process of Cognitive Mobilization. The essence of this process is the development of the skills needed to manipulate political abstractions and thereby to coordinate activities that are remote in space or time. Without such skills, one is more or less doomed to remain outside the political life of a modern nation-state. Consequently, historical changes in the distribution of these skills have been a major factor in defining the politically relevant public. Let us review some key phases of this process.

I. THE SHIFTING BALANCE OF POLITICAL SKILLS

In the earliest political communities—the tribe or city state—virtually everyone possessed the skills necessary for political participation. Political communication was by word of mouth, and it referred to people or things one knew first hand. Such communities could be (and sometimes actually were) relatively democratic: decision-making could take place through councils in which every adult male (and sometimes adult women) had a voice.

The development of specialized administrative skills helped make it possible to establish extensive political communities—states that governed millions rather than thousands of people, extending over relatively vast areas.

Administrative skills were only one factor, of course. Improved agricultural techniques were also important, for they provided the economic surplus needed to support specialized military and administrative elites. The new scale of politics required special skills among which the ability to read and write was a crucial element. Word of mouth communications were no longer adequate—messages had to be sent and received across great distances; human memory was no longer capable of retaining such details as the tax base of a given district or the military manpower it could raise—written records were needed; and personal chains of loyalties were inadequate to hold together large empires—legitimating myths based on abstract symbols had to be elaborated and propagated.[2]

The extensive political community could draw on an enlarged population and resource base, and in the long run it drove smaller

[2] See Gerhard Lenski, *Power and Privilege: A Theory of Social Stratification* (New York: McGraw-Hill, 1966).

competitors out of existence. But a price was paid for its enlarged capacities. The national level of politics was moved beyond the ken of the ordinary citizen. Elites with specialized skills—priests or mandarins or members of the King's household—became differentiated from the general population, in order to perform the various coordinating functions. These elites were not numerous. An economy based largely on subsistence agriculture can provide only a small minority with the leisure required to develop literacy, administrative skills, and (often) fluency in a cosmopolitan language distinct from the vernaculars spoken by the common people. Thus, the early phases of political development tended to open a wide gap between the population as a whole, which did not receive the specialized training needed to cope with politics at a distance, and a small ruling class. The masses became irrelevant, as far as national politics were concerned.

With further economic development and especially industrialization, it became possible to narrow the gap between elites and masses by redressing the balance of political skills. Lerner has provided a fascinating account of the transformation of "parochials" into "cosmopolitans."[3] Using survey data from several Middle Eastern countries, he traces the psychological changes that take place as an individual becomes urbanized, literate, and exposed to mass media, and consequently, able to relate to an extensive political community rather than the parochial world of his village or tribe. Deutsch gives further insight into this transformation with his analysis of "social mobilization."[4] This process begins when people are uprooted from physical and intellectual isolation, and from old traditions, occupations, and places of residence. Gradually they become integrated into modern organizations and extensive communications networks—expanding their horizons beyond the scope of word-of-mouth communication and bringing them increasingly in touch with national politics.

Social mobilization is a broad process. Western countries have long since completed many of its most important stages, such as urbanization, basic industrialization, widespread literacy, mass military service, and universal suffrage. Nevertheless, an essential

[3] See Daniel Lerner, *The Passing of Traditional Society* (New York: Free Press, 1958).
[4] See Karl W. Deutsch, "Social Mobilization and Political Development," *American Political Science Review*, 55, 3 (September, 1961), 493–514; cf. Karl W. Deutsch, *Nationalism and Social Communication* (Cambridge, Mass.: M.I.T. Press, 1966).

aspect continues—the very core of the process: the increasingly wide dissemination of the skills necessary to cope with an extensive political community. We use the term "Cognitive Mobilization" to refer to this central aspect of the broader process.

II. POLITICAL PARTICIPATION IN INDUSTRIAL SOCIETIES

In a study which has become one of the fountainheads of modern political science, Almond and Verba developed the concept of "subjective political competence" and argued that it may be a prerequisite to democratic politics. Only insofar as the citizen feels that he is capable of influencing political decision-makers, is he apt to play a participant role (rather than that of an obedient "subject" or a politically irrelevant "parochial").[5] The authors demonstrate that the more educated a person is, the more likely he is to have a sense of "subjective political competence" and therefore be a political participant. Numerous other studies in various countries have demonstrated that citizens of higher socio-economic status are most apt to participate in politics.[6]

But is this relationship due to social status itself or to the process of Cognitive Mobilization? Are the better educated more likely to have a say in politics because they know how to press their demands more effectively; or because they have better social connections, more money with which to induce officials to bend the rules on their behalf, and because officials give deferential treatment to the upper classes?

It would be naïve to think that wealth and personal connections are irrelevant. But if we are interested in long-term changes, cognitive variables are particularly interesting. By definition, there will always be an upper third, a middle third and a lower third in socio-economic status. But pronounced changes have occurred in *absolute* levels of education and information and they may be changing the political process. We believe that there has been a shift in the balance of political skills between elites and mass; as a result, even lower status groups may be increasing their ability to make significant political inputs.

Other observers emphasize other factors. In a particularly ele-

[5] See Gabriel A. Almond and Sidney Verba, *The Civic Culture: Political Attitudes and Democracy in Five Nations* (Princeton: Princeton University Press, 1963).

[6] See Lester W. Milbrath, *Political Participation* (Chicago: Rand McNally, 1965), 114–128, for a summary of these findings.

gant analysis, Nie, Powell, and Prewitt argue that economic development leads to higher rates of political participation, but it does so chiefly because of its impact on a society's class structure and organizational infrastructure.[7] Economic development increases the size of the middle class, which in turn leads to higher rates of membership in formal organizations. The middle class also tends to have attitudes which (like "subjective political competence") encourage participation.

Verba and Nie conclude that those with higher socio-economic status are relatively likely to participate in politics—partly because they tend to have a particular set of "civic orientations."[8] These orientations include a relatively strong sense of efficacy and of contribution to the community, attentiveness to politics, and high levels of political information. The impact of social status *in itself* is modest. Taking both into account, "civic orientations" explain eight times as much of the variance in overall political activity as does social status.

From our present perspective, this cluster of "civic orientations" seems to combine a mixture of attitudes *and* skills. While political efficacy or "subjective political competence" are subjective attitudes, political information and attentiveness to politics are relatively objective characteristics. They all tend to go together, as the authors demonstrate, but they are not the same thing.

Similarly, education undoubtedly *is* an indicator of one's social status, but it is also an indicator of certain skills. The distinction is important, for in multi-variate analysis, education and political information turn out to be more powerful indicators of political participation than such relatively pure social-class variables as income or occupation.

Verba and Nie, like many others including Nie, Powell, and Prewitt, find that organizational membership is strongly associated with political participation.[9] From this, the authors conclude, rather optimistically, that the masses can become participants by

[7] See Norman H. Nie, G. Bingham Powell and Kenneth Prewitt, "Social Structure and Political Participation: Developmental Relationships," *American Political Science Review*, 63, 2 and 3 (June and September, 1969), 361–378 and 808–832.

[8] See Sidney Verba and Norman H. Nie, *Participation in America: Political Democracy and Social Equality* (New York: Harper & Row, 1972).

[9] See Milbrath, *Political Participation*, 134–135, for citations of additional evidence on this score.

joining organizations, even without changes in basic attitudes (or skills). This is true in a sense, but it depends on what *kind* of participation one is interested in. Organizational membership, for the most part, seems to encourage *elite-directed* rather than *elite-challenging* forms of participation. It may not reflect the translation of public preferences into elite decisions, so much as the successful marshaling of the public by elites. Nie, Powell, and Prewitt's causal analysis suggests that political participation may result from two quite distinct processes, one springing from things inside the individual and the other linked with organizational involvement. "Social status" and organizational membership are at the origins of the two respective causal chains. The great bulk of the relationship between "social status" and political participation can be explained by intervening attitudinal variables, particularly political information and attentiveness to politics. On the other hand, the relationship between organizational involvement and participation is largely unrelated to the individual's attitudes or skills. Nie, Powell, and Prewitt find that, in each of five countries analyzed, about 60 percent of the linkage between organizational involvement and participation is via a direct link that does not pass through any other variable in their model. In other words, organizational membership's main impact is not due to the fact that it raises skill levels or inculcates participatory attitudes in any generalized fashion. Furthermore, Verba and Nie demonstrate that organizational membership does not *in itself* lead to increased political participation—it is only the *active* members of organizations who are relatively active. Above all, the active members of organizations engaged in explicitly *political* activities. Organizational membership helps us identify *who* participates in politics; it does not tell us much about *why* they participate.

We suggest that participation springs from two fundamentally different processes, one underlying an older mode of political participation, the other a newer. The institutions that mobilized mass political participation in the late nineteenth and early twentieth century—labor union, church, and mass political party—were typically hierarchical organizations in which a small number of leaders or bosses led a mass of disciplined troops. They were effective in bringing large numbers of newly enfranchised citizens to the polls in an era when universal compulsory education had just taken root and the average citizen had a low level of political skills.

But while these organizations could mobilize large numbers, they usually produced only a relatively low qualitative level of participation, generally the simple act of voting.[10]

The newer mode of participation is capable of expressing the individual's preferences with far greater precision than the old. It is a more issue-oriented participation, based less on established bureaucratic organizations than on *ad hoc* groups; it aims at effecting specific policy changes rather than simply supporting "our" leaders. This mode of participation requires relatively high levels of skills.

If we re-examine the data that Almond and Verba gathered, it suggests there are various *thresholds* of political participation (a point on which Verba and Nie agree). These thresholds range from voting in a national election—apparently the easiest and most widespread form of participation; upward through following what is going on in politics; to the more active behavior of *talking* about politics; and on up to the most demanding threshold: having actually attempted to *do* something about a specific aspect of national politics. Only 5 percent of the publics of Almond and Verba's five-nation sample report having engaged in this type of activity.

These respective levels of participation seem to be linked with given skill levels. Thus, if we take one's formal education as an indicator of political skills, we find that sheer literacy seems sufficient to lead to voting in the Western context. The bulk of Western citizens reached this threshold generations ago. The Almond and Verba data indicate that only a minority of the wholly uneducated had voted in the most recent national election. But fully 76 percent of those with a primary school education said they had voted, and the figure does not rise much with further education: it remains at 76 percent among those with a secondary school education, rising to 82 percent among those with a higher education. But voting is a relatively poor indicator of active political participation. As Giuseppe Di Palma points out, Italy has the highest rate of voting turnout among the five nations studied but by far the

<hr/>

[10] See Walter Dean Burnham, *Critical Elections and the Mainspring of American Politics* (New York: Norton, 1970); Richard F. Jensen, *The Winning of the Midwest: Social and Political Conflict, 1888–1896* (Chicago: University of Chicago Press, 1971); and Philip E. Converse, "Change in the American Electorate," in Angus E. Campbell and Philip E. Converse (eds.), *The Human Meaning of Social Change* (New York: Russell Sage, 1972), 263–337.

lowest rate of *overall* participation, because very few Italians participate in higher-level activities.[11]

The skill threshold is far higher when we move to the opposite end of the participation scale. Literally *none* of the 322 respondents with no formal education reported having tried to influence a decision at the national level. The figures remain very low among those with a primary or secondary school education—respectively, 2 percent and 7 percent reported having undertaken some form of activity at the national level. But the figure jumps to a relatively substantial 23 percent among those with a higher education. Literacy alone may be sufficient to produce a high rate of voting, but taking the initiative at the national level seems to require at least a secondary education, and probably a university education.

This finding is not surprising. For modernization "discourages participation by creating a complex organizational network based on high specialization and division of political labor that requires participants to possess unprecedented expertise."[12] Today most national officials have a university-level education. The citizen with a bare primary school education is hardly on a footing of equality with them not only in terms of social graces but also in regard to essential bureaucratic techniques and even in figuring out whom he should contact in order to articulate a specific grievance. As a result, he is likely to depend on some kind of broker who purports to serve his interests *in general.*

The "new" mode of political participation tends to be far more issue-specific and more likely to function at the higher thresholds of participation. It is new in the sense that only recently has a large percentage of the population possessed the skills required for this form of participation. And it is new in that it relies less heavily on a permanent and relatively rigid organizational infrastructure.

Nie, Powell, and Prewitt argue that economic development encourages increased political participation because it leads to more widespread organizational membership. But they find that in the United States, by far the most developed of their five countries, the explanatory power of organizational membership is *lower* than in the other countries. We suggest that at high levels of development, traditional kinds of organizational involvement may become

[11] See Giuseppe Di Palma, *Apathy and Participation: Mass Politics in Western Societies* (New York: Free Press, 1970). The five nations dealt with are Italy, Germany, Mexico, United States and Great Britain.
[12] Cited from Di Palma, *Apathy and Participation,* 12.

progressively less effective. Rising levels of education apparently tend to move people *out* of such established organizational networks as labor union and church. Both union membership rates and church attendance have been falling in most Western countries. Similarly, traditional political party ties seem to be weakening. In the United States, the proportion identifying themselves as Independents rather than as Democrats or Republicans has risen slowly but steadily during the last decade. Non-identifiers constituted less than one-fourth of the electorate in 1964; by 1972 they made up more than one-third of the eligible voters. Party voting has declined sharply: in 1950 about 80 percent of the voters cast straight party ballots, while in 1970 only about 50 percent did.

Recently, labor unions have begun to assume a role of unprecedented importance in British and Italian politics; but they simply may be filling a void left by the once-powerful political parties, which seem increasingly unable to govern. If so, this reflects a transfer of power from one set of old-line institutions to another rather than a growing ability of such institutions to mobilize the masses. As the process of Cognitive Mobilization progresses, the relative importance of these organizations is likely to decline, giving way to less hierarchical, more issue-oriented *ad hoc* organizations in which the individual has a greater opportunity to articulate his or her preferences on given decisions.

Political participation remained relatively dependent on permanently established organizations as long as most of the people with bureaucratic skills held positions within these institutions. Today *ad hoc* organizations can be brought into being more or less at will because the public has an unprecedentedly large leavening of non-elites possessing high levels of political skills. A balance between elites and mass that was upset centuries ago has been partially redressed.

Here, as throughout this book, we must acknowledge the importance of structural factors. Strong organizational networks can help less advantaged groups attain higher participation rates than groups having skill levels. For example, Rokkan has shown that under special circumstances, working-class groups may be politically more active than the middle class.[13] In the United States, the most spectacular increase in political participation during the past two decades has taken place among blacks. This increase has far

[13] See Stein Rokkan, *Citizens, Elections, Parties* (Oslo: Universitets Forlaget, 1970), Chapter 12.

outstripped the pace of rising educational levels—most of it must be attributable to greatly enhanced organizational effectiveness together with legal changes and a new sense of black identity. Somewhat similarly, Nie has argued that increasing political awareness among the American public in recent years can be attributed to the impact of specific political events, more than to changes at the individual level.[14] We would not dispute the importance of such situational factors; during a given period, they can swamp the effects of more gradual, underlying changes. But in a long time perspective, changes at the individual level may be at least equally significant. Exciting periods seems to alternate with dull periods of politics. In the short run, the period effects predominate; in the long run, they may cancel each other out. But the long-term effects of individual-level change are apt to be *cumulative*. They set new limits to the rise and fall of activism in response to immediate events. Cognitive Mobilization may be gradually raising the baseline of potential political participation, especially of an elite-challenging type.

III. ACTUAL AND POTENTIAL POLITICAL PARTICIPATION

We believe that the social processes currently at work tend to raise the public to new thresholds of participation and that this implies a long-term increase in elite-challenging forms of political participation. Yet one can readily find indications that political participation is *not* increasing. For example, voting turnout rates have been stagnant in most Western countries for many years. In the United States in the 1972 Presidential election, turnout dropped to a mere 55 percent of those eligible to vote. In part the low turnout in 1972 can be attributed to extension of the franchise to those between eighteen and twenty years of age. The number of newly eligible voters was far larger than normal, and voting seems to be partly a matter of habit. The old are more apt to do it, because they have had more practice. Nevertheless, the unusually low turnout of 1972 underscores the fact that we *cannot* expect an automatic increase in voting rates simply because the educational level of the electorate is rising. As was noted above, the skill threshold for voting is very low, and the vast majority of Western

---

[14] See Norman Nie with Kristi Andersen, "Mass Belief Systems Revisited: Political Change and Attitude Structure," *Journal of Politics*, 36, 3 (August, 1974), 540–591.

populations have already passed it; any further fluctuations in turnout will largely reflect habituation and macro-political events. The fact that voting turnout remains stagnant, therefore, does not contradict our hypothesis about rising thresholds of participant potential; but another piece of evidence does seem to do so.

A sense of "political efficacy," like its analogue, "subjective political competence," seems to be a prerequisite to the more active and demanding forms of political participation. But it has *not* risen in recent years—at least not in the United States (the only country for which we have reasonably adequate time-series data). Table 11–1 shows responses to the four classic "political efficacy" items during a twenty-two-year period.[15] Although responses to these

TABLE 11–1. Changing Levels of Political Efficacy, 1952–1974[a]
(Percent giving "efficacious" response)

	1952	1956	1960	1964	1966	1968	1970	1972	1974	Change 1964– 1974
Public officials care what people like me think	63%	70%	71%	61%	59%	56%	50%	49%	46%	−15%
People like me have some say in what government does	68	71	71	69	61	59	64	59	41	−28
Politics and government not too complicated to understand	29	36	40	31	27	29	26	26	27	− 4
Voting not only way to influence government	17	25	25	26	27	42	39	37	38	+12

[a] Inter-University Consortium for Political Research codebooks for Survey Research Center and Center for Political Studies election surveys, 1952–1974.

four items tend to be closely inter-correlated, three of them show a decline in "efficacious" responses in recent years, while the fourth shows an increase. The anomalous behavior of the fourth item is significant and will be discussed below. But on the whole, it seems that prevailing levels of political efficacy among the American public have fallen significantly during the past decade.

[15] The concept of "political efficacy" is described and operationalized in Angus Campbell *et al.*, *The American Voter* (New York: Wiley, 1960).

At first glance, this might seem contrary to all logical expectations. Political efficacy shows a clear and consistent positive correlation with education; and education levels have uncontestably been rising. Doesn't it follow, then, that we should have observed rising levels of political efficacy?

The answer, of course, is "No." The correlation between efficacy and education suggests that there is an underlying *tendency* for efficacy levels to rise, but this does not produce an automatic increase any more than the process of value change produces an automatic increase in the percentage of votes for the Left. Social processes are rarely that simple. As usual, we must deal with system-level phenomena, as well as individual-level phenomena.

One's sense of political efficacy reflects a relationship between the individual and the system. It involves one's sense of personal competence *and* one's perceptions of system responsiveness. The public's objective political competence has been rising, but perceived system-responsiveness has been falling at an even faster rate. Converse notes that from 1952 through 1960, political efficacy did rise, and it rose at almost exactly the rate that would be generated by the replacement of older, less educated age cohorts with younger, more highly educated groups. He concludes that changes were "education-driven" during this earlier period.[16] But from 1964, the process became system-driven: the gradual increase which might be expected as a consequence of rising educational levels was overwhelmed by the impact of traumatic events at the system level; the net result was a decline in the prevailing sense of political efficacy and of faith in the system. Reasons for this decline are not hard to find. The most obvious ones include: the civil rights struggles of the 1960's during which the government seemed unresponsive to some because it moved too swiftly in bringing about racial integration and lost the confidence of others because it moved too slowly; the deceptions and disillusionment of the Vietnam era almost certainly added to this process, when again the government frustrated some because it failed to win, and others because it failed to withdraw; and finally the scandals that brought the resignations of Vice President Agnew and then of President Nixon.

Faith in the system *did* decline, and it is all too evident. Table 11–2 shows responses to two indicators of trust in government at various time points since 1958. The change shown here is far

[16] See Converse, "Change in the American Electorate."

TABLE 11–2. Levels of Trust in Government Among
American Public, 1958–1974[a]
(Percentage indicating distrust)

1. "How much of the time do you think you can *trust* the government in Washington to do what is right—just about always, most of the time, or only some of the time?"

	1958	1964	1966	1968	1970	1972	1974	Rise in distrust, 1964– 1974
only some of the time	23%	22%	31%	37%	44%	45%	63%	+40%

2. "Would you say the government is pretty much run by a *few big interests* looking out for themselves or that it is run for the benefit of all the people?"

	1958	1964	1966	1968	1970	1972	1974	Rise in distrust, 1964– 1974
few big interests	(N.A.)	29%	34%	39%	50%	48%	73%	+44%

[a] ICPR Codebooks for given years.

more dramatic than the decline in political efficacy: for the three efficacy items that show a decline in Table 11–1, the mean change amounts to 16 percentage points; the trust indicators show well over twice as much change (with a mean difference of 42 points between 1964 and 1974).

As we would expect, one's sense of political efficacy is correlated with trust in government: no matter how great one's political skills may be, they can have little impact if the political system is fundamentally unresponsive. Hence, a decline in perceived system-responsiveness would almost inevitably tend to drag down political efficacy and discourage those forms of participation which are based on the premise that established elites will respond to conventionally expressed grievances. But the combination of rising political skills and a declining sense of system-responsiveness would not discourage *all* form of participation; if anything, we might expect it to encourage elite-challenging activities outside of conventional channels. The two opposite trends revealed in Table 11–1 seem quite understandable when examined from this viewpoint. They reflect, on the one hand, a declining sense that the government cares about, or is comprehensible to, or responsive to the average citizen, but, on the other hand, an increased awareness that "voting is *not* the only way" by which one can influence governmental decisions and probably a growing readiness to use unconventional techniques of political participation.[17]

It is doubtful that this pattern of change applies only to the United States. Certain specific problems such as the civil rights struggle and the war in Vietnam may be more or less unique to this country. But, in a broader sense, the emergence of these issues seems to reflect a shift in public expectations of government and an inadequate effort of governments to adjust to new demands. The rise of the Materialist/Post-Materialist dimension as a basis of political polarization has greatly complicated the task of governing elites. Insofar as this is true, declining trust in government is probably a widespread phenomenon.

How profound is this loss of confidence? Available evidence indicates that, at present, it applies mainly to the authorities rather than to the regime or political community.[18] There has been a substantial decline in esteem for the Presidency and for both leading political parties since 1964; but other key establishment institutions remain relatively untouched. The American public's affect for the military, the police, clergymen, big business, and labor unions has declined very little during the past decade. Yet all of these attitudes are empirically related. Distrust for the current political powerholders *does* tend to be generalized into distrust for other institutions and other levels of the political system. By 1974, more than half of the American public no longer trusted their government. If these levels of distrust persisted for long, it probably *would* undermine support for the present form of government, or even the political community itself. Fortunately, however, we can probably assume that 1974 represented a low point: it would be difficult to imagine another combination of circumstances under which so many things could be going wrong simultaneously.

It has often been argued that a high rate of party identification furnishes an element of predictability and stability to a nation's

[17] See Alan Marsh, "Explorations in Unorthodox Political Behavior: A Scale to Measure 'Protest Potential,'" *European Journal of Political Research*, 2 (1974), 107–129.

[18] See David Easton, *A Systems Analysis of Political Life* (New York: Wiley, 1966) for an analysis of the distinction between "authorities," "regime" and "political community."

politics. The sudden rise of the Nazi Party in Weimar Germany or the Poujadists and other "flash" parties in France under the Fourth Republic have been attributed to the presence of a relatively large mass of uncommitted or "available" voters.[19] If this is true, recent changes in American politics are increasing the potential for sudden, unpredictable shifts by the electorate, for traditional party loyalties have shown a gradual but steady decline during the past decade. As Table 11–3 indicates, the distribution of party identification in the United States was remarkably stable throughout the 1950's and early 1960's. From 1952 to 1962 the

TABLE 11–3. Changes in Party Identification in the
United States, 1952–1976

"Generally speaking, do you usually think of yourself as a Republican,
a Democrat, an Independent or what?"

	Democrat	Independent	Republican	Apolitical, Don't know	N
1952	47%	22%	27%	4%	(1,614)
1954	47	20	27	4	(1,139)
1956	44	24	29	3	(1,772)
1958	47	19	29	5	(1,269)
1960	46	23	27	4	(3,021)
1962	46	22	28	4	(1,289)
1964	51	23	24	2	(1,571)
1966	45	28	25	2	(1,291)
1968	45	30	24	1	(1,553)
1970	43	31	25	1	(1,802)
1972	40	34	23	1	(2,705)
1974	38	40	22	—	(2,513)
1976	42	37	21	—	(1,491)

[a] Source: ICPR codebooks for SRC/CPS election surveys, 1952–1974; NORC General Social Survey for 1976.

proportion of Republican, Democrats, and Independents scarcely changed at all; in almost every case, the fluctuations from one year to the next were small enough to be attributed to sampling error. Until 1966 non-identifiers or "Independents" constituted the smallest of the three main categories. Independents became more

[19] See Philip E. Converse and Georges Dupeux, "Politicization of the Electorate in France and the United States," *Public Opinion Quarterly*, 26, 1 (Spring, 1962); and Philip E. Converse, "Of Time and Partisan Stability," *Comparative Political Studies*, 2, 2 (July, 1969), 139–171.

numerous than Republicans in 1966 and have remained stronger ever since; by 1974 they had become almost twice as numerous as the Republicans and had moved ahead of the Democrats.

There are quite substantial age-cohort differences in rates of party identification. In 1972 less than a fifth of those over sixty-four were non-identifiers, but a *majority* of those under twenty-five considered themselves neither Republicans nor Democrats. Cohort analysis indicates that life-cycle effects contribute to this phenomenon, but an even larger part of it reflects generational differences.[20] At present, both long-term and short-term forces are working to reduce the rate of party identification; the proportion of uncommitted voters may rise still higher in the immediate future.

The reasons for the decline in party identification seem similar to those underlying diminishing trust in government: new issues and new bases of political polarization have become salient in recent years, and they cut squarely across the traditional Republican-Democrat party identification dimension, which related mainly to social welfare issues.[21] Insofar as voters polarize along the new issue dimension, they tend to be drawn away from traditional party loyalties.[22]

An interesting bit of irony is involved here: the decline in party identification probably tends to *reduce* the rate of voter turnout; but this decline in party loyalty seems partly due to *rising* levels of mass political consciousness.

For there is rather strong evidence that the American public has become increasingly issue-conscious in recent years, more likely to have a coherent "ideological" view of politics, and increasingly apt to vote on the basis of issues rather than out of sheer party loyalty.[23] Klingemann and Wright recently replicated Con-

---

[20] See Glenn and Ted Hefner, "Further Evidence on Aging and Party Identification," *Public Opinion Quarterly*, 36, 1 (Spring, 1972), 31–47. Cf. Ronald Inglehart and Avram Hochstein, "Alignment and Dealignment of the Electorate in France and the United States," *Comparative Political Studies*, 5, 3 (October, 1972), 343–372; and Paul R. Abramson, *Generational Change in American Politics* (Lexington, Mass.: D.C. Heath, 1975).

[21] See Herbert F. Weisberg and Jerrold G. Rusk, "Dimensions of Candidate Evaluation," *American Political Science Review*, 64, 4 (December, 1970), 1167–1185.

[22] See Inglehart and Hochstein, "Alignment and Dealignment."

[23] See Gerald M. Pomper, "From Confusion to Clarity: Issues and American Votes, 1956–1968," *American Political Science Review*, 66, 2 (June, 1972), 415–428; and Arthur H. Miller *et al.*, "A Majority Party in Disarray: Policy Polarization in the 1972 Election," *American Political Science Review*, 70, 3 (September, 1976), 753–758.

verse's well-known analysis of levels of conceptualization among mass publics, using data from the 1968 election survey as well as the 1956 data used in the earlier study.[24] They find that the percentage classified as "ideologues" or "near-ideologues" rose from 11.5 percent among the 1956 sample, to 23.0 percent among the 1968 sample. In the 1972 Presidential election, issues seem to have outweighed party loyalty as an influence on how one voted for the first time since survey research began to measure these variables.[25]

Despite diminishing confidence in political institutions, the objective political competence of the American public seems to have increased. But a heightened ideological sensitivity among the electorate may have *reduced* the public's amenability to elite-directed political mobilization and consequently the probability of high voter turnout.

If our analysis is correct, rising levels of political skills—and consequently a potential for higher levels of political participation—should be found in Europe, as well as the United States. The available European data do not permit a conclusive test of whether participant potential has been rising. For example, relatively little time-series data are available. However, the surveys carried out in 1973 do contain three questions that should provide a reasonably good indication of how likely an individual is to play an active role in his or her country's political life. Let us see whether the pattern of response to these items seems consistent with the hypothesis of a rising potential for political participation. The first of these items was intended to capture general feelings of subjective political competence or political efficacy. Our respondents were asked: "Do you think that if things are not going well in (Britain, France, etc.) people like yourselves can help to bring about a change for the better or not?"

Responses to this item were closely correlated with responses to two other questions which ask about actual *behavior*. The first was: "When you, yourself, hold a strong opinion, do you ever persuade your friends, relations or fellow workers to adopt this opinion?" (If Yes): "Does this happen often, from time to time or rarely?" This item taps one's tendency to be socially passive

[24] See Hans D. Klingemann and Eugene Wright, "Levels of Conceptualization in the American and German Mass Publics," paper presented at Workshop on Political Cognition, University of Georgia, Athens, Georgia, May 24–25, 1974.
[25] See Miller *et al.*, "Majority Party in Disarray" (forthcoming).

or to play an active part in convincing others. This tendency undoubtedly reflects one's relative self-confidence in part, but it also probably reflects how *skillful* one is in persuading others. The following item was intended to tap the same characteristics, but puts them in a specifically political context:

> When you get together with your friends, would you say that you discuss political matters frequently, occasionally or never? . . . (If "frequently" or "occasionally"): And which of the statements on this card (SHOW CARD) best describes the part you, yourself, take in these discussions?
>
> —Even though I have my own opinions, I usually just listen
> —Mostly I listen, but once in a while I express my opinions
> —I take an equal share in the conversation
> —I do more than just hold up my end in the conversation; I usually try to convince others that I am right.

The pattern of response to these items is quite consistent cross-nationally. In all nine of the European Community countries, "efficacious" responses to each of the three items are positively correlated with education. The more educated are more likely to feel that they can help change things in their nation, more likely to persuade friends, relatives, etc., to adopt their opinions, and more apt to take an active role in political discussions. The differences are substantial. For example, in the nine-nation sample as a whole, only 12 percent of those with a primary school education "often" persuade friends, relatives, or co-workers to adopt an opinion, as compared with 22 percent of the university-educated. Similarly, 42 percent of the primary school educated feel that they can change things in their nation, as compared with 65 percent of the university-educated. Thus, on the basis of the cross-sectional pattern, one would expect rising levels of education to lead to higher levels of political participation in the long run.

There is nothing surprising about these findings; they merely corroborate the results of previous studies. But another finding is much less obvious.

On the one hand, we might expect the younger age-cohorts to have higher levels of participant potential than older cohorts, since they have received much more formal education. But this expectation appears to contradict clear-cut findings from numerous studies in numerous countries to the effect that the young consistently show lower rates of political participation than the old. Voting turnout in particular has been shown to be lowest among those under thirty, rising to a peak in middle age, and tapering off somewhat in old age.[26] Adjusting for the different educational levels of the respective age groups, the declining rates among the elderly disappear, but the young show even *lower* rates.[27] This phenomenon seems related to three causes: (1) political activity is partly a habit, which is developed through repetition; (2) the young are not yet fully integrated into their communities; and (3) the young are less effectively mobilized by established organizations. There seems to be little doubt that life-cycle factors play a prominent part here.

Yet *underlying* these life-cycle effects, the younger cohorts possess a cluster of attributes suggesting that in the long run they will show *higher* rates of political participation than the older cohorts. The young rank higher on all three indicators of Participant Potential just described, and again the pattern is consistent cross-nationally; in each of the nine European countries, responses to each of the three items show the young to be more efficacious or more active than the old. The correlation is weak in some countries and strong in others, but its direction is the same in all nine countries. Results from the combined nine-nation sample are shown in Table 11–4.

Note the contrast between the correlations with age for the second and the third items. These two questions are very similar, except that the former asks how often one persuades others to adopt one's opinions *in general*, while the latter asks about specifically *potlitical* discussions. There is a 35-point percentage spread between the youngest and oldest groups in response to the former question and only a 12-point difference in regard to specifically *political* persuasion. One interpretation would be that the younger group's basic attitudes and skills provide them with a higher potential for participation, but that they are not yet fully integrated into *political* activities. Table 11–4 also shows the relationship between age and an indicator of political knowledge. This indicator is based on how many of the European Community countries the respondent was able to name; this proved to be a very discriminat-

---

[26] See Milbrath, *Political Participation*, 134–135, for a summary of relevant findings.

[27] See Verba and Nie, *Participation in America*; and Norman Nie *et al.*, "Political Participation and the Life Cycle," *Comparative Politics*, 6, 3 (April, 1974), 319–340.

TABLE 11-4. Political Efficacy, Activity in Discussions, and
Political Information by Age Group[a]

Ages	Feel they can help change things at national level		Persuade friends, relations or fellow workers to adopt an opinion "often" or "from time to time"	
15–24	59%	(2,305)	64%	(2,504)
25–34	54	(2,258)	58	(2,451)
35–44	49	(2,179)	53	(2,372)
45–54	50	(1,944)	50	(2,094)
55–64	46	(1,586)	48	(1,702)
65+	32	(1,644)	29	(1,759)

Ages	Talk about politics and usually try to convince others or take an equal part in conversation		Able to name correctly seven or more members of European Community	
15–24	37%	(2,590)	44%	(2,591)
25–34	40	(2,541)	44	(2,541)
35–44	35	(2,457)	41	(2,457)
45–54	33	(2,196)	41	(2,196)
55–64	31	(1,801)	36	(1,801)
65+	25	(1,895)	29	(1,895)

[a] Based on combined nine-nation European samples in 1973.

ing measure; the vast majority (91 percent) of our respondents were able to name at least one member, but only one person in eight was able to name all nine members. This item shows a pattern similar to that found with political discussion. The young score higher than the old, but the differences are relatively modest and they disappear when we control for education. Political knowledge tends to be acquired with age. The old are actually *better* informed than their educational level would predict. But this suggests that as they age the younger cohorts will tend to show *higher* political information scores, rather than declining to the level of the older groups, for the young start from a much higher educational base.

In short, feelings of efficacy and a general social activism are significantly higher among the young than the old in all nine nations. The young are only slightly more active in specifically political discussions. But all of these findings point in precisely the opposite directions from the well-established fact that the young show the *lowest* rates of voter turnout.

This apparent contradiction may be partially resolved when we recall that voting is the easiest and least discriminating form of political activism among those dealt with here. By the same token, it is an activity which established organizations are particularly well-equipped to stimulate. The young have relatively weak ties with political party machines, labor unions, and the church. Hence, they are less readily mobilized via conventional organizational channels.

But the young seem more likely than the old to engage in elite-challenging forms of political participation. Marsh has developed a scale to measure Protest Potential. He finds that for the British population protest activities can be located along a single dimension ranging from acts that are almost universally acceptable to those that are almost universally unacceptable.[28] At the former end of the scale are petitions and peaceful demonstrations; at the latter end are violence against people and the use of guns and explosives. In between are a variety of activities that certain groups regard as acceptable ways to influence political decisions, but other groups reject. Marsh drew equal proportions of his sample from four target groups: young workers, older workers, students, and an older middle-class group.

His four groups drew the line at different points on the protest continuum with older workers most conservative in their definition of what was acceptable. A majority of them accepted petitions and peaceful demonstrations, but drew the line at boycotts. Older middle-class respondents accepted all of the foregoing activities, but were against rent strikes; young workers accepted all of the foregoing, but opposed obstructing traffic; students accepted all of the foregoing plus the occupation of buildings, but drew the line at damaging property.

Though Marsh finds striking differences according to both social class and age group, age seems to be the dominant variable. In the absence of longitudinal data, it is impossible to be certain, but Marsh tentatively concludes that the pattern reflects inter-generational change toward broader definitions of acceptable techniques of political activism.

[28] See Alan Marsh, "Explorations in Unorthodox Political Behavior: A Scale to Measure 'Protest Potential,'" *European Journal of Political Research*, 2 (1974), 107–129.

IV. The Social Context of Participant Potential

The three items dealing with one's sense of efficacy and whether one plays an active or passive role in discussions with others should give a fairly good indication of one's potential for self-initiated rather than externally mobilized political participation. We hypothesize that they reflect the presence of relatively high levels of political *skills* and that these skills facilitate political activism even in the absence of organizational ties. Active and efficacious responses to these items, we would argue, tap one's degree of "Cognitive Mobilization," a dimension based on one's ability to deal with politics at a distance. Insofar as participant potential does reflect such a dimension, it should be linked with indicators of *objective* political competence and a tendency to see politics from a relatively cosmopolitan rather than parochial perspective.

On the other hand, it might be argued that participant potential mainly grows out of socializing experiences provided by formal organizations in which it should be more closely linked with organizational membership than with individual-level skills. Finally, it could be argued that participant potential reflects social status more than skills in which it would be linked with higher income and non-manual occupations, but with education only insofar as it taps status rather than skills.

Let us examine the empirical relationships between participant potential and these other variables in each of the nine countries. Our first step is to construct an index of Participant Potential, based on the items dealing with efficacy and activism in discussions.[29] Responses to these three items were closely correlated in each national sample; in the nine-nation sample as a whole, among those who "never" persuade their friends or relations to adopt an opinion, only 39 percent feel that they can help to change things for the better in their country; among those who "often" persuade their friends, 63 percent think that they can change things. Simi-

---

[29] This index was constructed by summing one's scores as follows: (1) An individual was scored +1 if he felt that he could change things at the national level and zero if he didn't; (2) one was scored +2 if he persuaded friends, relatives, etc. "often"; he received +1 if he did so "from time to time" or "rarely"; and zero if he did so "never"; (3) one was scored +2 if he "usually tried to convince others that he was right"; +1 if he merely "took an equal part in the conversation" or expressed opinions "once in a while"; and zero if he just listened or never discussed politics.

larly, only 34 percent of those who never discuss politics feel that they can help change things, as compared with 67 percent among the group who "usually try to convince others that they are right." Finally, among those who "never" persuade their friends, 60 percent never discuss politics, a figure that drops to 20 percent among those who "often" persuade friends or relations to adopt an opinion.

Our Participant Potential index was subjected to various forms of multi-variate analysis on a country-by-country basis. Some of the most interesting results emerge from a series of factor analyses of Participant Potential scores plus the following variables:

1. *Social Class Indicators*: family income; occupation; head of family; labor union membership; and respondent's education.

2. *Political Skills Indicators*: political information index; respondent's education.

3. *Cosmopolitan/Parochial Focus Indicators*: Parochial/Cosmopolitan identity (based on response to the items in Table 3–6); European integration index (based on support for three key measures of European integration); openness to new things.

4. *Organizational Affiliation Indicators*: frequency of church attendance; labor union membership.

It will be noted that some of the above items (education and union membership) appear in more than one category, because their significance is ambiguous. Education, for example, could quite reasonably be used as an indicator of cognitive development *or* as an indicator of social class. Dimensional analysis can help us distinguish one component from another on the basis of empirical relationships.

Because of their possible connection with social class, political party preference and self-placement on the Left-Right scale were also included in the factor analyses run for each country. Finally, we thought it important to examine the relationship between Cognitive Mobilization and value type. If a broad Cognitive Mobilization dimension exists, reflecting a cluster of skills that help equip one to deal with politics at a distance, we would expect it to be correlated with value type, for, as was argued in Chapter 2, the Post-Materialist type consists of individuals who take satisfaction of immediate personal needs for granted and who are able to place greater emphasis on relatively remote concerns. Thus, through two quite distinct processes, Cognitive Mobilization and Post-Materialist values should both contribute to a relatively cosmopolitan political focus. Table 11–5 summarizes the overall configuration of these variables in our nine European nations as a whole.

TABLE 11–5. Cognitive Mobilization, Value Type, and Political Preference in Western Europe, 1973
(Loadings over .300 in factor analysis of nine-nation sample—Varimax rotation)

I Cognitive mobilization (16%)		II Left-Right political preference (12%)	
Political information index	.601	Left-Right voting intention	.750
Participant Potential index	.600	Left-Right ideological self-	
Education	.571	placement	.732
European integration index	.510	Church attendance	.441
Attracted by new things	.393	Post-Materialist values	
Cosmopolitan political identity	.377	index	−.301[b]
Post-Materialist values index	.372		
Age	−.323[a]		

[a] Negative sign indicates that the older groups are *lower* on information, participant potential, etc.

[b] Negative sign indicates that Post-Materialists are less likely to vote for the *Right*, attend church, etc.

The first factor that emerges corresponds to the hypothesized Cognitive Mobilization dimension. Its three highest-loading items are our Participant Potential index plus two skill-level indicators, political information and formal education. Subjective political competence seems to go together with *objective* political competence. Those who feel that they can do something about national affairs and play an active role in persuading their friends tend to be those who *know* most about politics and probably (insofar as they are more educated) about society in general. Precisely, as we hypothesized, the indicators of political activism and skills are linked with a broadly outward-looking political orientation. Support for European integration, openness to new things, and a cosmopolitan sense of identity form part of the Cognitive Mobilization factor. If the essence of Cognitive Mobilization is the ability to cope with politics at a distance, this process may affect not only the *types* of political participation in which one engages but also the scope of the political community in which one acts. It may orient one toward larger political units. We will explore this topic in greater detail in the following chapter.

The Cognitive Mobilization dimension is equally notable for what it does *not* include. The unambiguous social class indicators, income and occupation, do not have significant loadings on this factor (their loadings reach the .20 level at best). Country-by-country analyses tend to confirm the pattern shown in Table 11–5; in Germany and France, income has loadings slightly above the .30 level, but Political Information, Participant Potential, and Education have much higher loadings than this in each of the nine countries. The pattern suggests that the *cognitive* component of education, rather than its class-linked component, is what accounts for its strong correlation with this dimension. Skills seem more crucial than social status. Similarly, neither union membership nor church attendance have significant loadings on this dimension; membership in organizations *per se* does not seem strongly related to Cognitive Mobilization, although we would certainly expect that those who play an active or leading role in organizations would have a high level of Cognitive Mobilization.

Table 11–5 indicates that the processes of value change and Cognitive Mobilization tend to go together empirically. As we saw in Chapter 3, the fact that one is integrated into elite (or cosmopolitan) communications networks makes it more likely that one will adopt the values prevailing in that milieu. Currently, the upper strata in Western countries tend to be relatively Post-Materialist. Our present data show a .372 correlation between Post-Materialist values and the Cognitive Mobilization dimension.

But Cognitive Mobilization and value change are analytically distinct. It is by no means certain that elite circles have *always* had a Post-Materialist outlook. In fact, there is evidence that they have attained this view only recently. Thus it is conceivable that at an earlier phase of development Cognitive Mobilization did not encourage the assimilation of Post-Materialist values, but may have had the opposite effect.

There is also an empirical distinction between Cognitive Mobilization and value type. Cognitive Mobilization affects the *vertical* axis of one's political outlook; that is, those who have high levels of political skills are apt to have a cosmopolitan rather than a parochial focus. But this dimension has little to do with the Left-Right axis of one's political preferences. Those who have a high level of political skills may use them on behalf of either the Left or the Right. But one's value type *does* tend to orient one toward a specific side of the political spectrum: Post-Materialists are likely to support the parties of the Left and place themselves on the Left side of the ideological scale.

The Left-Right dimension is a second and independent basis of polarization. Its attributes are striking, but they merely serve to corroborate findings reported in the three previous chapters. On the one hand, Church Attendance is closely related to both Left-Right voting and Left-Right Ideological Self-Placement, and value type has a significant loading on this factor, *despite* its linkage with the completely unrelated first factor.

On the other hand, our various social class indicators do not have significant linkages either with the Left-Right factor *or* with Cognitive Mobilization. In given countries (notably, Great Britain) social class has relatively strong linkages with the Left-Right dimension; for Europe as a whole, the correlation is quite modest.

The first factor in Table 11–5 reflects the fact that Participant Potential is closely interwoven with cosmopolitan skills and attitudes. The wealthy may be relatively apt to possess these characteristics, but wealth *per se* seems peripheral. Similarly, organizations unquestionably are a major factor shaping political participation. Here, as throughout this book, we emphasize our conviction that structure, values and skills must all be taken into account in any analysis of political phenomena. Our data suggest that individual-level skills are *also* a crucial influence on the type and intensity of political participation that emerges in a given society.

Finally, Table 11–5 indicates that the younger cohorts rank higher than older ones on the whole Cognitive Mobilization cluster, as well as on Participant Potential. This suggests that the dimension may reflect an ongoing process, not just a static relationship. We can not, of course, be certain until we have more adequate time-series data. But the overall configuration is consistent with the notion that a process of Cognitive Mobilization is slowly transforming Western publics.

V. THE NEW ACTIVISM IN 1972

Relatively high levels of political skills give the younger cohorts an unusually great potential to participate in the more demanding forms of political activity, and while the 1972 American Presidential elections demonstrated once again their relatively low rate of voting, the campaign that preceded it was marked by an unprecedented penetration of young activists into the higher levels of political decision-making. The delegates to the Democratic Party's 1972 national convention were a strikingly new set of people. Only 11 percent had been at the party's 1968 convention.[30] Much of this newness can be traced to changes in the rules governing delegate selection, but these rules did not emerge in a vacuum. They reflected the rising political effectiveness of certain segments of the electorate.

Among the more than three thousand delegates, 38 percent were women and 15 percent were black—impressive increases over any previous convention. On the other hand, less than one-tenth of the delegates were members of labor unions, and two-thirds had held no previous office of any kind. In 1968 probably no more than 3 percent of the delegates were less than thirty years of age; in 1972 nearly 27 percent were under thirty. One statistic is particularly remarkable: this may have been the most highly educated convention in modern history. Among the American population as a whole, only about 4 percent have done post-graduate studies; 45 percent of the delegates had post-graduate education.

In the past, convention delegates have been regarded as the creatures of a handful of king-makers, and their social backgrounds may not matter very much. But to a great extent, this was a group that had arrived by their own initiative, having seized the right to take part in the nomination against the wishes of established leaders in many cases. The candidate they nominated lost badly in 1972 and we can probably assume that established organizations will regain some of their lost ground in future nominations; but it seems very doubtful that things will return to the former *status quo*. For the McGovern nomination represented the breakthrough of a new and probably growing style of political participation.

Here we encounter one last paradox. We have emphasized the importance of bureaucratic skills throughout this chapter. But the movement that captured the nomination for George McGovern had a remarkably non-bureaucratic appearance. Four key characteristics of classic bureaucracy are hierarchy, permanence, impersonality, and central control. In its successful struggle to win delegates in primary elections, the McGovern movement emphasized

[30] This and the following figures are from an analysis of the convention delegations published in the *New York Times*, July 10, 1972, 1.

the opposite of each of these characteristics. Decentralization was the watchword; new organizations were put together from scratch, with a minimum of hierarchical coordination, but with enthusiastic local initiative; and the campaigns emphasized personal contact with as many voters as possible.

Once again, the paradox is only apparent. The classic bureaucratic model was designed for a society in which highly trained people were very scarce. By reducing information processing to a set of highly standardized, centrally directed routines, it enables a small number of highly skilled decision-makers to control a larger body of moderately skilled clerks, who administer vast numbers of uneducated masses. The McGovern campaigns were run by relatively large numbers of people who were highly skilled in communication and organization. They were therefore able to relax much of the standardization and hierarchy of classic bureaucracy and still maintain reasonably coordinated efforts.

VI. Conclusion

Special skills are prerequisite to playing an effective role in the politics of an extensive political community. Consequently, rising levels of political skills should enable Western publics to participate in politics at a higher level. These publics may be approaching a threshhold at which they can again take part in actual decision-making processes rather than entrust it to relatively skilled minorities.

CHAPTER 12

Parochialism, Nationalism, and Supra-nationalism

I. INTRODUCTION

As we saw in the preceding chapter, the process of Cognitive Mobilization and the shift to Post-Materialist values both seem to be linked with the development of a cosmopolitan rather than parochial sense of identity. This changing sense of identity may have profoundly important consequences for Western politics, for it increases the potential support for a supra-national European Community that in time may bring an end to the nation-state as we know it in Western Europe.

This process is complex and by no means sure to succeed. Between the underlying changes in values and skill levels, and the monumental transformation of political institutions that may eventually occur, there is much room for slippage. We can only say that long-term trends seem to favor the disappearance of nationalism among European publics (even while it is growing in less developed nations). But do these trends have any real importance? The conventional wisdom depicts public opinion as a marginal factor in European integration. Do mass attitudes actually play a significant role? Today the answer is a demonstrable "yes." But it was not always so. Initially, the European integration movement got its impetus from a small number of highly motivated individuals.

II. EUROPE FROM ELITE CONSPIRACY TO PUBLIC CONCERN

The European Community was launched in hopes that it would rule out the possibility of war between the nations of Western Europe by abolishing the independent nation-state.[1] This goal was

---

[1] For a brief but well-balanced introduction to this subject, see Roy Pryce, *The Politics of the European Community Today* (London: Butterworths, 1973). Another good general treatment, rich in factual details, is Roger Broad and R. J. Jarrett, *Community Europe Today* (London: Wolff, 1972). Basic theoretical analyses include: Ernst Haas, *The Uniting of Eu-*

adopted in the wake of a series of escalating tragedies, with the realization that still another round of war between Germany and her neighbors might literally destroy these societies and their peoples.

The Franco-Prussian War of 1870–1871 killed many thousands, caused widespread suffering, and left an aftermath of bitterness that made another war between France and Germany almost inevitable. The resulting bloodshed, when it came, exceeded everyone's wildest expectations. Using new and deadlier technology, World War I brought almost seven million battle deaths and millions of disabled and mutilated men. Most of the nations of Europe were drawn into the conflict. Again, the peace left a sense of bitterness and hatred that prepared the way for yet another war.

World War II was the most massive tragedy in human history. This time fifteen million men were killed in battle. But the slaughter of civilians was even more staggering. Half the world's Jews were murdered and entire nations vanished in a butchery that consumed thirty to forty million civilians.

The state was set for an aftermath of even deeper hatreds than those that followed World War I. But history took a different turn this time. Leading figures from the nations defeated in 1940 and those defeated in 1945 resolved to institutionalize a set of arrangements that would make it impossible for their countries to fight each other again. In 1952, the European Coal and Steel Community came into being, integrating the steel industries of Germany, France, Italy, Belgium, The Netherlands, and Luxembourg. Far more limited in scope than the League of Nations or the United Nations, it nevertheless went far beyond them in one crucial respect: it gave genuine authority to supra-national institutions. In a circumscribed but important domain, a European authority could overrule the national governments. It was a modest start toward European unity. And it prepared the way for the birth of the European Common Market and Euratom in 1958, greatly broad-

rope: Political, Social and Economic Forces, 1950–1957 (Stanford: Stanford University Press, 1958); Karl W. Deutsch et al., Political Community and the North Atlantic Area (Princeton: Princeton University Press, 1968); Amitai Etzioni, Political Unification: A Comparative Study of Leaders and Forces (New York: Holt, Rinehart, and Winston, 1965); Leon Lindberg and Stuart Scheingold, Europe's Would-Be Polity (Englewood Cliffs, N.J.: Prentice-Hall, 1970); and several of the chapters in Lindberg and Scheingold (eds.), Regional Integration: Theory and Research (Cambridge, Mass.: Harvard University Press, 1971).

ening the scope of integration among the six nations of the Coal and Steel Community. These three organizations were later merged into a European Community that has continued to increase its functions and expand geographically.

The European Coal and Steel Community was launched by a small technocratic elite, acting almost conspiratorially. Throughout their first several years, European publics remained only dimly aware of, and faintly concerned with, the emerging European institutions. Writing of this early period, Haas has argued that in order to understand the process of European integration, "It suffices to single out the political elites in the participating countries, to study their reactions to integration, and to assess changes in attitude on their part."[2] Haas' claim is correct concerning the first decade or so of institutionalized European integration. But by 1962 the European Community institutions had scored a remarkable round of successes. European publics were becoming increasingly aware of these institutions and tended to associate them with the peace and prosperity they were enjoying.[3]

This development was not visible at the level of macro-events, however. On the contrary, nationalism appeared to be staging a spectacular comeback in the Europe of the mid-1960's. In Germany the electoral successes of the National Democrats were raising widespread fears that a particularly vicious form of nationalism might be resurgent. While not openly neo-Nazi (which would have been illegal) the National Democrats manifested a Brownshirt mentality on an alarmingly broad range of issues. Their growing strength made the outlook seem dim for any normalization of Germany's relations with her Eastern neighbors.

In France a Gaullist drive for national prestige was at its zenith, with emphasis on *gloire*, the *force de frappe*, and *défense à tous azimuts*. The British, overcoming an earlier reluctance to share their fate with the Continental nations, were seeking to join the Common Market. But in 1963 and again in 1967, General De Gaulle unilaterally vetoed British applications for membership. And a far-reaching set of proposals to strengthen the institutions of the European Community and give them independent financial resources was stalemated by a French boycott that lasted six months, threatening to paralyze the European institutions. Pro-

[2] Haas, *The Uniting of Europe*, 17.
[3] See "L'Opinion Publique et l'Europe des Six," *Sondages*, 1 (1963) entire issue.

European elites were demoralized and pessimistic. There was a widespread feeling that European integration might have come to an end.

Yet underlying these events there was evidence of broad public support for European integration among the French public as well as elsewhere within the Common Market.[4] The French government's opposition to supra-national integration did not seem to reflect an ineradicable nationalism on the part of the French people so much as the preferences of a relatively small elite and, above all, those of one exceptionally powerful individual, General De Gaulle.

In 1967 it seemed improbable that De Gaulle would remain in power for many more years (he was almost eighty). His battle with the European Community had already weakened his prestige among the French public. In the 1965 Presidential elections, a substantial share of the electorate he could normally count on had deserted him, largely due to his boycott of the Common Market. Any likely successor would need to conciliate the relatively pro-European Center. Analysis of elite and mass opinion data suggested that with his departure, important changes would occur in French foreign policy. Consequently, we conjectured that when De Gaulle left office France's veto of British entry to the Common Market would be lifted, her opposition to supra-national European integration would diminish, and her relations with America would shift from confrontation toward cooperation.[5]

General De Gaulle left office in April, 1969. In December of that year, his successor called a European summit conference at The Hague. There and in subsequent negotiations the leaders of the six European Community countries agreed to reopen negotiations on British entry; to form a European economic and monetary union; and to provide the European institutions with their own

[4] In 1957 (just before the formation of the Common Market) 55 percent of the French public said that they were in favor of "efforts to unify Europe." In 1962, this figure stood at 72 percent and remained roughly constant in 1970 (at 70 percent). The 1957 figure is from Richard L. Merritt and Donald C. Puchala, *West European Perspectives on International Affairs: Public Opinion Studies and Evaluations* (New York: Praeger, 1968), 283; that for 1963 appears in *Journal of Common Market Studies*, 2, 2 (November, 1963), 102; and that for 1970 in Commission of the European Communities, *Les Européens et l'Unification de l'Europe* (Brussels, 1972), 72.

[5] See Ronald Inglehart, "Trends and Non-Trends in the Western Alliance: A Review," *Journal of Conflict Resolution*, 12, 1 (March, 1968), 128. Cf. Ronald Inglehart, "An End to European Integration?" *American Political Science Review*, 61, 1 (March, 1967), 91–105.

326 — Cognitive Mobilization

financial resources, independent of contributions from national governments. European integration had been relaunched.

By 1972 the impact of public opinion on European integration was manifest. In connection with the negotiations to admit new members to the European Community, national referenda were held in five different countries.

In one case, it could be argued that the referendum was somewhat spurious. The French electorate was invited to simultaneously express their support for: (1) the policy of expanding the European Community and (2) the government of Georges Pompidou. The two did not necessarily go together and many Frenchmen viewed it as a loaded question; it was approved by 68 percent of those voting, but with an embarrassingly high rate of abstention. Still, Pompidou had reversed one of De Gaulle's most controversial policies. The referendum's wording may have been something less than a model of clarity; but the fact that the French government sought a vote of confidence in connection with its new policy at least reflects a certain sensitivity to public opinion concerning European integration.

The four other referenda of 1972 were relatively straightforward. In each case, the public of a given nation was asked to decide whether their country should join the European Community or not (except in Switzerland, where the vote concerned association, rather than full membership). A large majority of the Irish voted "yes," and Ireland went in. The Norwegians voted "no," and Norway stayed out. The Danes voted "yes," and Denmark went in. Finally, the Swiss voted in favor of association, and their government acted accordingly. There was a 1.00 correlation between public vote and government decision.

But perhaps the most interesting case of all was that of Great Britain, where no referendum took place. The Conservative and Liberal parties officially backed membership and Labour opposed it, but in fact, both larger parties were badly split on the issue. Since the referendum was contrary to British political practices, entry was decided upon by vote of the House of Commons. It was assumed that the supposedly deferential British public would follow their leaders. But the issue refused to die. Surveys showed that, while opinion was volatile, a plurality of the public remained opposed to membership even after Britain joined in January, 1973; opposition continued to prevail during most of 1973 and 1974.

In 1974 a Labour government took office; later that year it

TABLE 12-1. Support and Opposition to Membership in the Common Market Prior to the British Referendum[a]

	Sept. 1973	May, 1974	Nov. 1974	Feb. 1975[a]	March 5-10 1975	March 20-24 1975	April 1-6 1975[a]	April 4-7 1975	April 15-20 1975[a]	April 17-21 1975	April 23-28 1975	May 1-5 1975	May 7-12 1975	May 21-27 1975	June 5, 1975 Actual Result
Favorable to membership	31%	33%	36%	48%	52%	59%	60%	57%	56%	57%	58%	57%	60%	59%	67%
Unfavorable to membership	34	39	35	34	36	30	28	31	28	28	30	33	29	31	33

[a] Results for 1973 and 1974 are based on responses to the question: "Generally speaking, do you think that membership in the Common Market is a good thing for Britain, a bad thing, or neither good nor bad?" These surveys were sponsored by the European Community, with fieldwork by Gallup Poll, Ltd. The 1975 results are based on responses to the question: "Do you think the United Kingdom should stay inside the European Community (the Common Market)?" The two ways of formulating the question give equivalent results, and were excellent predictors of the actual vote, as is demonstrated on page 354. (Results do not add up to 100 percent since the indifferent and undecided figures are not shown.)

decided to hold a referendum on whether Britain should remain in the European Community. But opinion was shifting in favor of membership. By late 1974, a narrow plurality of the British public was favorable; by February, 1975, support for membership heavily outweighed opposition. In mid-March, the Labour government reversed its position, on the grounds that it had won substantially more favorable financial terms for British membership than those agreed on originally. In the subsequent referendum campaign, a majority of the Labour Cabinet argued in favor of continued membership, although about one-third of the Labour ministers campaigned against it.

Survey data from 1962 to 1975 make it clear that when a given party took a position either for or against joining the Community portions of that party's electorate would rally to their leaders' position. But it is equally apparent that certain major shifts in British public opinion *preceded* rather than followed shifts by party leadership. This was the case both times that the Labour Party reversed its stand.

The Labour Party had actively sought membership in the Community when it was in office from 1964 to 1970. It reversed itself after the Conservatives came to power and when, in the wake of De Gaulle's two discouraging vetoes, public opinion had soured on membership. Labour's second reversal could be attributed to the fact that the party unquestionably *had* secured better terms for British membership. But it would be naïve to ignore the fact that this reversal took place only after a shift in public opinion had made it a politically viable strategy in the referendum campaign. Elites influence the public *and* vice versa in this domain. As Easton has argued, publics and decision-makers are linked in a feedback relationship.[6]

Of the four nations that applied for membership in the European Community, only three actually joined. In each case—and ultimately, even in Britain—public opinion was a decisive factor. It is no longer a question of *whether* public opinion plays an important role in European integration, but *when*.

Under what conditions do mass attitudes have the greatest impact on European policy-making? It depends on the interplay of the three types of variables stressed throughout this book: structure, values and skills.

[6] See David Easton, *A Systems Analysis of Political Life* (New York: Wiley, 1966) for a discussion of some basic concepts underlying this view.

1. *Skills.* Skills have an obvious importance. In the short run, the question is, "How well-informed and aroused is the public about this particular issue?" But in the long run, the crucial question is, "What proportion of the public consists of inert parochials, and how many are skilled participants?" As we suggested in the preceding chapter, the process of Cognitive Mobilization increases the public's relevance to foreign policy decisions.

2. *Values.* It is also a question of values. Insofar as a given issue taps only shallow preferences, elites can lead the public rather easily; but when relatively deep-rooted values are evoked, elites can change public opinion only slowly and with difficulty. They are constrained by public opinion to a relatively great extent.

3. *Structure.* But, of course, neither the values nor the skills of individuals exist in a vacuum. One must take account of the macro-political setting. One important aspect is the structure of national decision-making institutions. Do they tend toward the pluralistic or monolithic end of the spectrum? Insofar as there *is* institutionalized competition between alternative groups of decision-makers, they are likely to bid against each other for public support. Conversely, as long as no genuine alternative is offered to the public, its influence will probably be minor.

Thus, as long as De Gaulle seemed the sole person capable of governing France, the French public had no alternative but to accept his brand of foreign policy. Similarly, as long as all of Britain's leading political parties remained committed to membership in the European Community, none of them risked paying a political price for this stand. It was only when the Labour Party broke ranks that the public's preferences became crucial. On the other hand, it is doubtful whether the Labour leadership would have reversed their stand if they had not seen an opportunity to gain support due to the distribution of public opinion at the time.

The national decision structure is important, but we must also take account of the supra-national structure. The publics of the original Six members have lived under European institutions for many years; the publics of the three new members have had this experience only since 1973, and (as we will see below) there is a striking contrast between the attitudes of the original Six publics and those of the three new members. Within France, Germany, Italy, and the Benelux countries, we find a broad, deep-rooted, and stable pro-European consensus; public attitudes seem relatively resistant to external influences. By comparison, in Britain, Ireland,

and Denmark, support for European integration is less wide-spread; these attitudes are less firmly integrated with one's general outlook; and opinion is relatively volatile, more readily influenced by the socio-political environment and elite cues.

This contrast between the publics of the Six and the Three does *not* seem to reflect the political cultures of the respective nations. Despite their important cultural differences and despite sizeable initial differences in their degree of pro-Europeanness, the publics of all six original members have converged to a remarkably homogeneous consensus in support of European integration; the publics of the three new members remain manifestly different from those of the Six and from each other.

It is interesting to find that those who have been in the Community for a long time tend to support further integration. But the effect of membership goes beyond this. It seems to change one's basic sense of political identity.

III. The Emergence of a Cosmopolitan Political Identity Within the European Community

In order to analyze long-term trends in public attitudes, we must probe somewhat deeper than one usually does in asking opinions about current issues. Our 1973 surveys included a question designed to tap one's basic sense of geo-political identity. The item was:

Which one of the following geographical units would you say you belong to first of all? . . . and the next?

—The locality or town where you live
—The region or province where you live
—(Great Britain, Germany, etc.) as a whole
—Europe
—The world as a whole.

As one would probably expect, the respondent's nation was the most popular choice: a majority gave it as first or second choice in each of ten countries surveyed with the lowest figure (53 percent) being obtained in Belgium—a country undergoing a national identity crisis. But the nation was by no means a universal focus of primary loyalty. A sense of identification with one's home town was surprisingly widespread, actually ranking ahead of the nation in Belgium, Denmark, and Germany. A feeling of belonging to a given province or region was also fairly widespread, especially in Belgium and Denmark.

Relatively few respondents felt any allegiance to Europe or the world as a whole, which is hardly surprising. Yet supra-national loyalties *do* exist. They are most prevalent in Germany, Italy, and The Netherlands. In each of these countries more than one-third of the public felt they belonged to a supra-national unit as either first or second choice. Supra-national loyalties are least widespread among the three new members of the European Community—Denmark, Ireland, and Britain, where the figures range from 16 percent (in Denmark) to 28 percent (in Britain). The American public also falls in this range, with 20 percent identifying with "the Western world" or "the world as a whole."

Much higher percentages of the population in the nine European countries favor various specific proposals for European integration, sometimes by overwhelming majorities. Yet such questions do not tap one's basic sense of identity. In the ten nations surveyed in 1973, only a minority have a sense of supra-national political identity. But they seem to represent the hard-core support for supra-national political integration, the group that would support European integration even under the most trying circumstances.

Feelings of belonging to some unit greater than the nation-state are most widespread among the publics of the original Six. The pattern leaves little room for doubt that membership in Europe has contributed to the emergence of a supranational identity. *All six* of the original member-nations rank above *all four* of the other nations in the percentage having a supra-national sense of identity. The publics of the original Six are far more likely to feel that they belong to *Europe*, but this attitude also spills over into a sense of identification with the world as a whole. Those who belong to Europe first are the more likely to make "the world as a whole" their second choice; and the publics of the Six have high rates of identification with the world as a whole (though the British and American publics also rank fairly high in this respect).

Long-term membership in Europe seems to have given rise to a relatively strong sense of supra-national identity. This can probably be attributed to the fact that the publics of the Six perceived membership in the Community as beneficial in a number of ways, during the years they have lived within it. Consequently, the Community had generated a reservoir of "diffuse support" (to use Easton's term). But isn't it possible that the Six formed the Coal and Steel Community in 1952 and then the Common Market in 1958 because these nations have *always* had a relatively supra-national outlook? We can answer this question with a pretty definite "no." First, survey data from the 1950's indicate that the French were then *less* supra-national in their outlook than the British. Furthermore, the 1973 surveys suggest that the publics of the Six now have relatively high levels of supra-national identity because they have been undergoing *change*. Figure 12–1 illustrates this point. In all ten nations, the young are more likely to have supra-national loyalties than the old. But evidence of change is far stronger within the Six than elsewhere. *All six* of the original members' publics show age-related differences that are larger than those in *any* of the other four nations. Britons over fifty-five years of age are *more* likely to have a supra-national outlook than Frenchmen or Belgians of comparable age; it is only among the youngest cohort that Britain falls behind. While the American sample shows a fairly strong increase in supra-national identity as we move from older to younger cohorts, the trend in Ireland and Denmark is weak.

In the original six European Community countries, on the other hand, the change across age groups is uniformly strong. Only 16 to 27 percent of the oldest group feels any sense of supra-national identity. Among the youngest group the figures range from roughly 40 to 50 percent. The apparent change is impressive. Among those who have grown up under European institutions, a sense of supra-national identity is found among nearly half the population. This relatively cosmopolitan outlook does not seem to be an inherent part of being young. Among the four countries that had not experienced long-term membership in the European Community, such an outlook is found among only 16 to 34 percent of the same age group. The publics of the Six seem to have made considerable progress in developing a supra-national sense of belonging. Perhaps the publics of Britain, Ireland, and Denmark will also move in this direction.

But the presence of a supra-national identity cannot be *entirely* due to the effects of membership in the European Community. For a sizeable fraction of the public possesses it in each of the other four countries—three of which had just joined and one of which was not even a prospective member. Insofar as the Six are *more* supra-national than the other countries, the difference might be

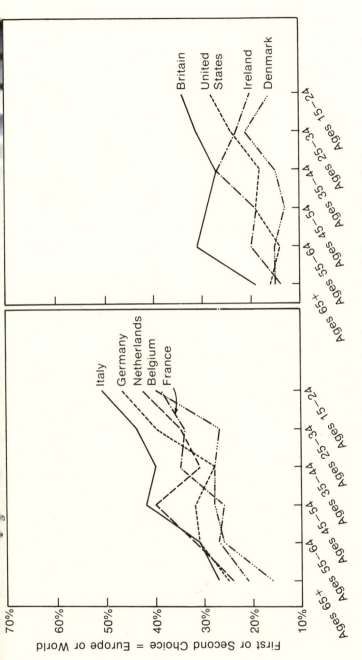

FIGURE 12–1. Proportion Having Supra-national Sense of Identity by Age Group.

Percent naming "Europe" or "the world as a whole" as either first or second choice for "the geographical unit I belong to first of all," 1973. For the American public, the supra-national alternatives were "the Western world" and "the world as a whole."

attributed to the long-term effects of membership; but the remaining feelings of supra-national identity must be due to other causes. Two processes working within individuals seem to be important. One is cognitive and the other evaluative.

We argued in Chapter 2 that as long as an individual is preoccupied with the sustenance and safety needs, he or she will have little energy left to invest in more distant concerns. Thus, the process of value change facilitates the emergence of a cosmopolitan political identity. It does not make it inevitable, however. There are numerous other ways in which a Post-Materialist might conceivably engage the energy liberated from Materialist concerns. The *raison d'être* of the nation-state had been to maintain order and defend its people and property against outsiders. Such considerations weigh less heavily among the priorities of Post-Materialists than of other types. Hence, Post-Materialists are relatively open to a supra-national orientation, but it is possible that their attention may turn inward toward smaller, more cohesive centers of loyalty. In the case of the Flemish nationalists, as we have seen, the Post-Materialists move in *both* directions, simultaneously emphasizing greater autonomy for their ethnic group *and* supporting European integration.

By and large, Post-Materialists have a broader sense of belonging than that of the Materialists. As Figure 12–2 shows, this tendency prevails in each of the ten nations for which we have data. And for Europe as a whole, only 23 percent of the most Materialist group identify with "Europe" or "the world." At the Post-Materialist end of the spectrum, fully 65 percent of the respondents identify with one of the supra-national units. One's value priorities certainly seem relevant to whether one has a cosmopolitan or parochial outlook. But another individual-level process is equally important. In the preceding chapter we explored the impact of Cognitive Mobilization on political participation. Now let us examine its linkage with the development of supra-national loyalties.

IV. THE COGNITIVE MOBILIZATION PROCESS

Since World War II, Western Europe had experienced a sharp rise in mean levels of formal education and a sharp decline in rural population. Ownership of television sets and automobiles has spread widely, providing the potential for broader communication.

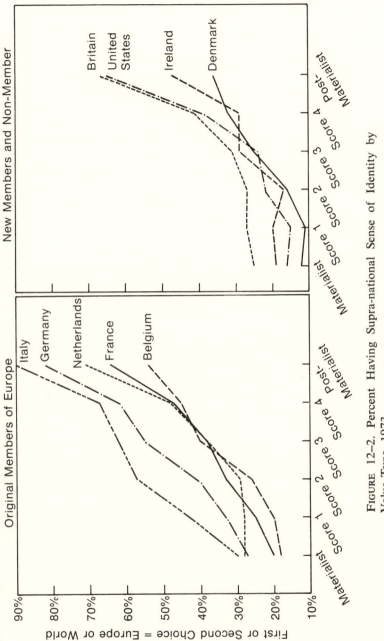

FIGURE 12–2. Percent Having Supra-national Sense of Identity by Value Type, 1973.

The percent naming "Europe" or "the world as a whole" as either first or second choice for "the geographical unit I belong to first of all."

What does this portend for the development of supra-national loyalties?

Deutsch has brilliantly analyzed the process of "social mobilization."[7] Though they have taken on new aspects, the basic factors that brought about social mobilization in Deutsch's case studies of nineteenth- and early twentieth-century Europe—and in the contemporary new nations—are still operating in Western Europe. Indeed, they are now moving European publics across new thresholds. The question is, "Will these events have integrative or disintegrative consequences?"

In the past, the process of social mobilization has been fraught with difficulties. Especially when a political community is multiethnic in character, mobilization of parochial populations may lead to fragmentation along linguistic, religious, or tribal lines. Deutsch has shown how the mobilization of disparate ethnic groups encouraged the growth of separatist movements, tending to tear apart such polities as the Austro-Hungarian Empire; one might add a number of recent examples to the list, such as India, Nigeria, and Pakistan. Generally, these movements were led by the better-educated members of the given ethnic groups.

When social mobilization has avoided such disintegrative tendencies, it has often led instead to intense and aggressive forms of nationalism that can themselves be dangerous. An excess of national spirit among the newly mobilized population may encourage (or even force) the national decision-makers to follow jingoistic policies—as happened in France, Germany and Japan in the late nineteenth- and early twentieth-centuries, and sometimes happens in the Third World today. Current social dynamics may be integrating increasing numbers of Europeans into cosmopolitan com-

---

[7] See Karl W. Deutsch, "Social Mobilization and Political Development," *American Political Science Review*, 55, 2 (June, 1961), 497–502; and *Nationalism and Social Communication* (Cambridge, Mass.: M.I.T. Press, 1966). One might view social mobilization as a vertical dimension of political integration: the incorporation of formerly submerged strata into the political community. This can greatly increase the resources of the polity, giving it a more profound reservoir of support. It can also multiply the demands on the political system to an extent which exceeds its responsive capacity, under given conditions threatening horizontal (or geographic) disintegration. Deutsch's book presents an analysis of cases in which the existing system was either swamped or split, as a result of the mobilization of formerly passive populations who were linguistically heterogeneous, in relation to the dominant political culture. The new politically-relevant majority, being unable to articulate effectively its interests in the cosmopolitan language, eventually forced a shift into one (or more) of the vernaculars.

munications networks. But into what sort of network are they being integrated, a national or a supra-national one?

Let us note that both formal education and the radio-television networks of Western Europe are, for the most part, controlled by the respective national governments either directly or indirectly. Education and electronic communications could, quite conceivably, be used to develop an intense and exclusive nationalism. But despite control by the national governments, and despite the heavy predominance of mass communications which originate within the same nation as the recipient, it appears that in the contemporary West European setting, rising levels of exposure to formal education and mass communications tend to favor integration at the European, as well as the national level.[8]

It is not primarily a question of having a national versus a supra-national outlook, but one of being relatively parochial or cosmopolitan. In our 1973 surveys, those who say that they belong to the nation first of all are markedly *more* likely to identify with Europe or the world at large than those who feel closest to their town, province, or region. In contemporary Europe, those who see things from a national perspective (rather than a more parochial one) have an increased potential for identifying with supra-national units. The two levels tend to function as one cosmopolitan communications network rather than as separate competing networks. In short, a key aspect of social mobilization is still going on in Western Europe, and it tends to encourage the development of support for a European polity.

If one of the key consequences of Cognitive Mobilization is an increasing ability to relate to remote roles and situations, then the expansion of higher education may have important implications for European integration. Given the fact that European institutions are even more remote and (for the present, at least) have an even more indirect relationship to the average citizen than does his national government, it seems likely that the mobilization of public support for European institutions would tend to require a relatively high level of Cognitive Mobilization.

Cognitive Mobilization increases the individual's capacity to receive and interpret messages relating to a remote political community. As such, the process is a necessary but not sufficient condition for the development of support for a European community:

[8] See my article "Cognitive Mobilization and European Identity," *Comparative Politics*, 3, 1 (October, 1970), 45–70.

one must become aware of it before one can develop a sense of commitment. Furthermore, Cognitive Mobilization should encourage support for European institutions insofar as it helps make them more familiar, less threatening.

Awareness does not necessarily lead to favorable feelings. The *content* of the messages one receives is vitally important. But for those with high levels of political awareness and skills in political communication, there is at least a good *chance* that one will come to identify with a supra-national political community; for those who lack them, the probability seems low.

It is not easy to test the foregoing hypotheses. For cognitive mobilization refers to rising levels of *skills*, and one cannot readily measure skills in public opinion surveys. But our 1973 surveys include several items that seem promising indicators of political skills, as was suggested in the preceding chapter. One item was: "When you, yourself, hold a strong opinion, do you ever persuade your friend, relations or fellow workers to adopt this opinion?" (If Yes): "Does this happen often, from time to time or rarely?" In all nine countries, responses to this item were strongly correlated with responses to another item:

> When you get together with your friends, would you say that you discuss political matters frequently, occasionally or never? . . . (If Frequently or Occasionally): And which of the statements on this card (SHOW CARD) best describes the part you, yourself, take in these discussions?
>
> —Even though I have my own opinions, I usually just listen
> —Mostly I listen, but once in a while I express my opinions
> —I take an equal share in the conversation
> —I do more than just hold up my end in the conversation; I usually try to convince others that I am right.

These items undoubtedly tap political interest, in part. But it seems more than likely that one's propensity to persuade others about political matters would also reflect one's skill in doing so. According to the two-step flow of communications hypothesis,[9] those who play a more active part in political discussions are likely to be oriented toward nationwide communications networks, and should be apt to have a relatively cosmopolitan sense of identity.

[9] See Elihu Katz and Paul F. Lazarsfeld, *Personal Influence* (New York: Free Press, 1955); cf. Bernard Berelson *et al., Voting* (Chicago: University of Chicago Press).

Our data indicate quite clearly that this is the case with each of the nine European publics. Table 12–2 illustrates this relationship in our combined nine-nation sample. Among those who never discuss politics, only 21 percent feel that they belong to a supra-national unit. The proportion rises regularly with increasing degrees of activity in political discussion. Among those who usually try to convince others that their position is right, 45 percent feel a supra-national identity.

TABLE 12–2. Supra-national Sense of Identity by Activity in
Political Discussions
(Percent identifying with "Europe" or "World as Whole" in
combined nine-nation sample, 1973)

Never discuss politics	21%	(4,813)
Usually just listen	28	(747)
Mostly listen, sometimes express opinion	30	(3,145)
Take equal share in discussion	38	(3,395)
Usually try to convince others	45	(1,122)

Responses to the two items just cited consistently have rather strong positive correlations with one's level of information and formal education—two variables that should be good indicators of political skills. These two variables, in turn, are also rather powerful predictors of the presence of a supra-national identity. Among those with no more than a primary school education, 22 percent are supra-nationally oriented; among those who have attended a university, the figure is 46 percent. Similarly, among those who cannot name any of the countries in the Common Market, 19 percent fall into our supra-national category; among those who can name all nine members, 43 percent are supra-nationals.

We constructed a Cognitive Mobilization Index, based on three of the variables just discussed.[10] This new variable "explains"

[10] This index was constructed by summing one's scores on the following three items:

1. An individual was scored +2 if he persuaded friends, relatives, etc. "often"; he received +1 if he did so "from time to time" or "rarely"; and zero if he did so "never."

2. One was scored +2 if he "usually tried to convince others that he was right"; +1 if he merely "took an equal part in the conversation" or expressed opinions "once in a while"; and zero if he just listened or never discussed politics.

3. One was scored +2 if he could correctly name seven to nine members

parochial versus supra-national identity more powerfully than any of its constituent elements. But it does not replace value type as an explanatory variable. Cognitive and evaluative processes *both* contribute to the presence of a supra-national identity. As Table 12–3 demonstrates, the combined effects of our Cognitive Mobilization Index and our Value Priorities Index account for a large amount of variance in one's sense of identity. Those who rank

TABLE 12–3. Supra-National Sense of Identity by Cognitive
Mobilization and Value Type
(Percent identifying with "Europe" or "World as Whole"
in nine-nation sample)

	Value Type		
Score on Cognitive Mobilization Index:	Materialists (score = 0)	Intermediates (score = 1–2)	Post-Materialists (score = 4–5)
Low: 0	12% (695)	14% (341)	25% (28)
1	18 (1,202)	21 (622)	44 (99)
2	22 (1,317)	27 (840)	40 (174)
3	24 (1,396)	29 (862)	53 (354)
4	33 (1,351)	36 (883)	61 (481)
High: 5–6	37 (498)	45 (377)	69 (287)

lowest on Cognitive Mobilization (that is, those who never persuade friends to adopt their opinion, never discuss politics and are unable to name any members of the Common Market) are unlikely to be supra-nationally oriented. But the likelihood partly depends on one's value type. The Post-Materialists among this group show a 25 percent supra-nationalist rate; the Materialists have only 12 percent. Among those with a high level of Cognitive Mobilization, even the Materialists have a rather high rate of supranationalist orientation—37 percent. But fully 69 percent of the Post-Materialists are supra-nationally oriented.

Multi-variate analysis including these and a variety of standard social background variables indicates that nationality, value type,

---

of the European Common Market; +1 if he could name four to six of the members; and zero if he could name three or less.

The respondent's education was not included in this index because of its relatively strong correlations with income and occupational status: we wished to focus on skills, keeping the new variable distinct from social class insofar as possible.

and Cognitive Mobilization (in that order) are the three most powerful predictors of parochial versus supra-national identity. While each of these three variables makes an important independent contribution to one's focus of belonging, other variables are relatively unimportant. The more educated, the wealthier, the younger, and the residents of larger cities are relatively apt to have supra-national loyalties, but these characteristics are not particularly significant in themselves: their effects tend to disappear when we control for the three leading predictors.

Membership in the European Community seems to have encouraged the emergence of a sense of supra-national loyalty, although this may have been partly due to the fact that the European institutions were born in an era of exceptional prosperity. The entry of the three new members coincided with the onset of adverse economic conditions, and the European institutions may take some of the blame. Yet it is conceivable that membership in a supra-national community fosters a more cosmopolitan outlook in and of itself. To some extent, a polity may attain legitimacy as time goes by simply because it becomes familiar, part of the normal order of things. In either case, if the processes of Cognitive Mobilization and Post-Materialist value change continue, the proportion of supra-nationally oriented Europeans should increase over time.

V. The Evolution of Support for European Integration

We have been focusing our attention on a general and probably basic attitude: one's sense of belonging to a relatively parochial or cosmopolitan political unit. Now let us turn to something more specific, with direct political relevance: support for various forms of European integration.

As we would expect, those who identify with some geographical unit larger than the nation are more likely to support European integration than those with a parochial outlook. But the translation of a general attitude into a position on specific issues is not automatic; it varies considerably from nation to nation.

The most striking feature of mass attitudes toward European integration is, once again, the contrast between the publics of the six original member nations and those of the three new members. The publics of the original Six have lived under supra-national institutions for many years. At the time of our 1973 survey, sixteen years had elapsed since the founding of the Common Market and

Euratom and twenty-one years since the founding of the European Coal and Steel Community. A sense of supra-national identity had become relatively widespread, and orientations toward European integration had been assimilated into one's attitude structure. But the three *new* publics had entered the Community only in 1973, in a time of economic crisis and controversy.

The former are markedly more favorable to concrete proposals for European integration, just as they were more apt to have a supra-national sense of identity. And there is evidence that in the Six, attitudes toward European integration are more closely integrated with one's basic values and sense of identity than they are in the Three. Accordingly, in the Six, support for European integration seems relatively deep-rooted and stable; in the Three, opinion remains more volatile and malleable.

Table 12–4 illustrates one aspect of this pattern: the fact that support or opposition to European integration is more strongly

TABLE 12–4. Correlation Between Support for European
Integration and Geographic Sense of Identity
(Product moment correlations)

Publics of original members		Publics of new members	
Belgium	.31	Britain	.26
Germany	.29	Ireland	.15
Netherlands	.26	Denmark	.13
Italy	.26		
France	.26		
Mean	.28	Mean	.18

correlated with one's basic sense of belonging in the Six than in the Three. These correlations are based on the geographic identity item discussed in the preceding section, plus a broad-gauge index of support or opposition to European integration.[11] Support

[11] Our European Integration Support Index was constructed by summing responses to three of the highest-loading items on a European integration support factor. Factor analysis of responses to a series of thirty questions concerning European integration demonstrated that these items were particularly sensitive indicators of overall support or opposition to European integration in each of our nine nations. (To minimize the effects of response set, we did not use any two items which were adjacent to each other in the interview schedule.) The items used were:

1. "If you were to be told tomorrow that the Common Market had been abandoned, would you be very sorry about it, indifferent or relieved?

2. "Would you, or would you not, be willing to make some personal

for integration has a fairly strong correlation with one's sense of belonging, throughout the six original members of the Community. Of the three new publics, only the British show a relationship of comparable strength—perhaps because the question of member-ship in the Community has been a salient part of British politics for a relatively long time. For the three newly admitted publics as a whole, one's stand on European integration seems less a reflection of an underlying parochial cosmopolitan identity and more a result of current conditions and cues from political elites.

We could illustrate this pattern at considerable length. It applies to cognitive factors as well. The correlation between support for integration and *knowledge* of the European Community (as in-dicated by one's ability to name some or all of its members) is much stronger among the Six than in the Three. This relationship is stronger in every one of the Six than it is in any of the Three, individually; and overall, the correlation is about twice as strong in the Six as it is in the Three.

Table 12–5 provides more evidence of the same broad phe-nomena. Throughout the Six (except perhaps for Italy) support

TABLE 12–5. Correlation Between Support for European Integration and Value Priorities
(Product moment correlations between scores on pro-European index and twelve-item values index)

Publics of original members		Publics of new members	
Belgium	.26	Denmark	−.10[a]
Netherlands	.23	Ireland	.11
Germany	.22	Britain	.08
France	.20		
Italy	.12		
Mean	.21	Mean	.03

[a] Negative sign indicates that Post-Materialists are *less* pro-European than Materialists. Luxembourg omitted due to sample size (r = .18).

for European integration is rather strongly related to one's value priorities. Among the publics of the Three this relationship is con-

---

sacrifice—for example, pay a little more in taxes—to help bring about the unification of Europe?

3. "All things considered, are you in favor of the unification of Europe, against it, or are you indifferent? (If 'In favor' or 'Against'): 'Very much or only somewhat?' "

sistently weaker, and in one case, Denmark, the usual relationship is reversed. This finding seems surprising given the fact that in all nine countries (even in Denmark) the Post-Materialists are more likely to have a supra-national sense of identity. Accordingly, in each of these countries, except Denmark, Post-Materialists are more supportive of European integration than are Materialists. But in Denmark the relationship reverses itself. Post-Materialists are *less* pro-European. And the negative correlation, though modest, is too strong to be a statistical accident. It seems to reflect a genuine and significant relationship. In short, the linkage between Post-Materialist values and pro-European policy preferences is not the result of some universal law, it is only a probabilistic tendency. Denmark's reversal of the general pattern reflects the fact that, while Post-Materialists tend to be supra-nationally oriented, they have an even *stronger* tendency to support the Left. And at the time of our survey, much of the Danish Left was bitterly hostile to membership in the European Community.[12] Was this an isolated quirk on the part of the Danish Left? No. It is part of a broader picture that shows a number of parallel cases when examined in historical perspective. Let us look at the evolution of support for European integration since 1952.

As always, good time-series data are hard to find. The best available indicator is a question that was asked in a series of USIA surveys in the 1950's and 1960's, and was then repeated in the European Community surveys of the 1970's in modified form. The original wording was: "Are you, in general, for or against efforts toward uniting Western Europe?" The European Community version was: "Would you say that you are very favorable, rather favorable, indifferent, unfavorable or very unfavorable to European unification?"[13] Despite the changes in wording, both

[12] For an interesting and far more detailed analysis of the interplay between values, partisan cues and attitudes toward European integration in Denmark, see Nikolaj Petersen, "Federalist and anti-Integrationist Attitudes in the Danish Common Market Referendum," paper presented to the European Consortium for Political Research, London, April 7–12, 1975.

[13] For detailed information on the United States Information Agency surveys, see Merritt and Puchala, *Western European Perspectives on International Affairs.* For the period 1952–1962, Figure 12–2 is based on data in Merritt and Puchala, 283–284. For a detailed report on the European Community findings, see Jacques-René Rabier, "L'Europe vue par les Européens" (Brussels: European Community, 1974, mimeo) and succeeding reports by Rabier on the bi-annual European Community surveys. Figures for 1964 were calculated from USIA data; and the 1970 figure for Britain is estimated from responses to related items (this precise question not having

versions are designed to tap one's general feelings of support or opposition to European unification. This is virtually the only relevant item that has been asked repeatedly over a period of many years, and as such, it is precious. But clearly, it cannot be viewed as an absolute measure of support levels. Even more important than the change in wording is the fact that it has a floating referent: the "efforts toward uniting Europe." In 1952, this phrase may have evoked the comparatively modest Coal and Steel Community; in 1957, one probably would have thought of the Common Market. In the mid-1970's, far more ambitious plans were being discussed, including such goals as a directly elected European Parliament and a greatly strengthened president of the European Commission. In short, we must interpret the responses to this item with caution. It *does* give a good idea of relative support levels in given nations, and of given groups within each nation at any one point in time since the question was uniform in any given year. But we should bear in mind that the events to which this item refers were gradually escalating, so that in absolute terms it was a more demanding question in 1975 than in 1952. This is all the more true because of the fact that in the European Community surveys, "indifferent" was explicitly suggested as a possible alternative; prior to 1970 it was a residual category. Suggesting the "indifferent" option tends to increase such responses. Since the analyses that follow are based on the *favorable* responses only, "indifferent" becomes, in effect, a negative response (as does non-response).

With this in mind, let us turn to Figure 12–3, which charts the rise and fall of responses to this question over a twenty-three year period.[14] The pattern reveals several important points. First let us note that in the period prior to 1958—the year the Common Market began to function—response in all four countries fluctuated *together*, apparently in reaction to current events. We cannot demonstrate the causal linkages, of course, but it seems plausible to suppose that the Korean War, together with the founding of the Coal and Steel Community in 1952, gave an early impetus to support for European integration. North Korea's invasion of the South gave rise to fears that Western Europe might be next on

---

been asked in 1970). In the analysis that follows, the two positive options from the European Community surveys have been *combined*, for comparison with the single positive option from the USIA surveys.

[14] Results from the four larger nations only are shown: the USIA did not, as a rule, carry out surveys in the smaller countries.

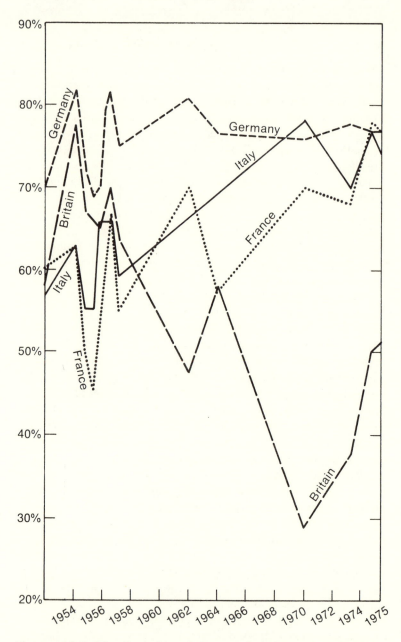

FIGURE 12–3. The Evolution of Support for European Unification, 1952–1975.

Based on percent "for" "efforts to unify Europe." Missing data are included in percentage base; thus, in 1952, 70 percent of the German public was "for," 10 percent "against" and 20 percent "undecided" or "no opinion."

the agenda; while the achievement of integration in the steel industry may have encouraged the feeling that further integration was feasible. Conversely, the failure of the European Defense Community in 1954 probably lowered morale and led to a withdrawal of support; while renewed fears of war, in connection with the Soviet invasion of Hungary and the Suez crisis late in 1956, may have rekindled a sense of urgency for European unification.

In any case, we find a series of pronounced upward and downward movements in the 1950's in which all four countries move together. But starting from about 1958 the pattern changes. The British public, which had ranked below only the Germans, moves completely out of phase with the other three publics. Within the three Common Market countries, fluctuations taper off and support levels gradually converge upward toward the German level; by 1975 the Italians and the French are virtually indistinguishable from the Germans. The British level, by contrast, drops drastically, falling slightly below the 50 percent mark at the time of the first veto, and far below it after the second veto. Only in 1975 do the British again rise above the 50 percent line, but there is still a large gap between the British and the three original European Community publics. This does not mean that the British were *less* European in 1975 than in 1952; on the contrary, in 1952 they were unwilling to join even the Coal and Steel Community, while in 1975 they supported full membership in the European Community by a better than two-to-one margin. What the pattern *does* suggest is that a large relative gap has opened up between the British, on one hand, and the publics of the original Common Market countries on the other. Until 1973, the British (and, of course, the Irish and Danes) remained outside the European Community framework, while the publics of the Six developed an increasingly European outlook.

Aside from the divergence between the British and the other three publics, Figure 12-3 has another almost equally striking aspect. It is the degree to which the French and Italian publics, who originally were far less European than the Germans, have progressively narrowed the gap, to the point where it has virtually disappeared in 1975. This reflects the development of a pro-European consensus among the French and Italian publics; and the most important element in the process was winning over the large Communist electorates in these countries.

For the French and Italian Communists initially perceived the

European integration movement as an alliance directed against the
Soviet Union. And, indeed, in the Cold War era, when the threat
of Soviet invasion sometimes seemed imminent, the idea of uniting
for the common defense contributed to the movement's appeal.
But with the defeat of the European Defense Community in 1954,
it became clear that defense against the Soviet Union would play
little part among the Community's functions. As its benefits to
Europe's workers became evident, the Communist electorates of
the Six were gradually won over from suspicion to overwhelming
support. In October, 1950, a representative sample of the French
public was asked, "Are you for or against the efforts being made
to unify Europe?" Among the French public as a whole, 65 percent
were favorable; among supporters of the Communist Party, the
figure was 19 percent.[15]

A heavy majority of the French public at large favored integration, but a heavy majority of the Communists among them opposed
it. This tremendous gap between Communists and non-Communists persisted through the early years of European integration; in
May, 1957, 53 percent of the general public favored unification
compared with only 13 percent of the Communists. The birth of
the Common Market in 1958 seems to have led to a transformation of this pattern. Its early years were a period of rapidly growing trade and other exchanges among the Six as well as remarkable
prosperity. By 1962, the Communist voters among the French
public were predominately favorable to European integration and
almost as supportive as the public at large: 72 percent of the total
electorate favored unification and so did 60 percent of the Communists. This newer pattern has remained fairly stable in subsequent years. In May, 1975, the figures were 78 percent and 64
percent, respectively. The rest of the electorate is somewhat more
supportive of integration than the Communists, but even among
the Communists support is vastly more widespread than opposition. Only 15 percent of the Communists said that they were "unfavorable" in 1975, and the rest stated that they were "indifferent"
or gave no response.

A similar process of conversion took place in Italy, but con-
vergence has gone even farther there than in France. In 1973, 70
percent of the total Italian public were favorable to integration as

[15] Figures for 1950–1967 are from IFOP surveys cited in *Sondages*, 1
and 2 (1972), 16; figures for subsequent years are from the European
Community surveys.

were 65 percent of the Italian Communists. In May, 1975, the gap had virtually disappeared altogether: 77 percent of the general public favored integration along with 75 percent of the Communists. In response to some questions (for example a proposal for political union of the European Community countries) the Communists were actually a trifle *more* European than the electorate as a whole.

This remarkable change of heart among the Communist electorates of France and Italy was accompanied by a parallel movement at the elite level. By the mid-1960's it had become politically costly to oppose membership in the Common Market in these countries. Partly for this reason, the leadership of the Communist Party in both countries abandoned overt opposition. But there were important differences between the positions of the French and Italian party elites, which reflected their diverging relationships with the Soviet Union. On the one hand, the Italian Communist Party began to display a large measure of independence from Soviet guidance, developing a flexible and distinctively Italian approach to European politics. The occasional pro-European statements of Italian Communist leaders seem relatively genuine. Since the early 1970's, Italian Communist deputies have participated in the parliament of the European Community, where they have played a highly constructive role. The French Communist Party, on the other hand, remained one of the most Moscow-oriented parties in the West. Acutely sensitive to cues from the Soviet Union, it tends to reflect Soviet hostility to the European Community, but does so in muted tones. To advocate French withdrawal seems out of the question, and it would be overwhelmingly unpopular with both the Communist and non-Communist public. But the party leadership remains decidedly cool to any proposal that might strengthen the European Community.

By contrast with the surprising degree of consensus found among the publics of the Six, sharp political cleavages exist among the British and Danish publics. In Britain, as of late 1975, only 40 percent of the Labour electorate favored "efforts to unify Europe," as compared with 51 percent of the entire British public. In Denmark the Left-wing Socialist People's Party vehemently opposed membership in the European Community; the other major parties (including the Social Democrats) supported it. In the 1972 referendum campaign, Danish membership became a matter of ideological controversy with opposition being presented as the position of the Left.[16] Denmark should strengthen her ties with the other Nordic countries, it was argued, rather than move closer to the allegedly more conservative European Community countries. This rift remains visible among the respective electorates. In our 1973 survey, 45 percent of the Danish electorate supported European unification, as compared with only 24 percent of those who supported the Socialist People's Party—a gap of 21 points, far larger than the Communist/non-Communist cleavages in France or Italy. This gap had narrowed somewhat (to 13 points) in 1975, still a relatively large figure. Thus, astonishing though it may seem, in the mid-1970's there was far more difference between Conservative and Labour voters in Britain concerning European integration, than between Communists and Christian Democrats in Italy. The cleavages among the Danish public were larger still.

Table 12–6 shows the overall relationship between political party preference (grouped into a Left-Right dichotomy, as was done in Chapter 8) and our index of Support for European Integration. Overall, the relationship with political party preference is considerably weaker in the Six than in the Three. Here, using our broader Index, we find the same pattern that appeared in response to the question about "European unification": partisan cleavages are far stronger in Denmark and Britain than they are in France and Italy. This might seem highly counter-intuitive, given the fact that France and Italy have powerful Communist parties, while Britain and Denmark have very weak ones. Yet this pattern makes sense, in the context of other findings reviewed in this chapter. In the Six, attitudes toward European institutions have had more time to become assimilated and internalized; in the Three they are still relatively volatile and subject to external cues, such as those given by political parties.

As Table 12–6 indicates, support for European integration tends

[16] See Nikolaj Petersen and Jorgen Eklit, "Denmark Enters the European Communities," *Scandinavian Political Studies*, 8, 1 (1973), Annual, 157–177. This article traces fluctuations among the Danish public, from 1970 through 1972. Also see Peter Hansen *et al.*, "The Structure of the Debate in the Danish European Community Campaign, April to October, 1972," paper presented to the European Consortium for Political Research annual meeting, Strasbourg, March 28–April 2, 1974. For an excellent account of the conversion of first the Italian Communist electorate and later the Italian Communist elite from an anti-European stand to a pro-European one, see Robert Putnam, "Italian Foreign Policy: The Emergent Consensus" (Washington, D.C.: American Enterprise Institute, forthcoming).

TABLE 12–6. Correlation Between Support for European
Integration and Left-Right Voting Intention
(Product moment correlations)

Publics of original members		Publics of new members	
Germany	.17	Britain	−.32[a]
France	−.14[a]	Denmark	−.27[a]
Netherlands	.07	Ireland	.03
Italy	.02		
Belgium	−.01[a]		
Mean	.02	Mean	−.19

[a] Negative sign indicates that electorate of the Left is *less* pro-European than that of the Right.

to be stronger on the *Right* half of the political spectrum in the Three. In the original Six, the overall relationship is negligible, but there is a faint tendency for the electorates of the *Left* to be more pro-European.

Is European integration really a policy of the Left or the Right? It seems probable that the existence of the European Community has gradually raised the standard of living of the working class in these countries—which is one reason why the Community is generally popular with labor in the original Six. On the other hand, it can be argued that the Community is a Europe of the capitalists. There is considerable evidence that large corporations *are* too powerful within the Community—but we must ask: Do they exercise great power *because* of the Community or despite it? Big business was organized on a supra-national basis before the Community existed, and would probably remain so even if the Community were abolished: one compelling piece of evidence is the fact that many of the strongest supra-nationals are American-based, but operate both inside and outside the Community with little difficulty. Their supra-national scale can give the great corporations important advantages in dealing with labor, which remains compartmentalized along national lines, for the most part. Thus, if a multi-national corporation faces a major strike in one country, it can sometimes shift production to another country, where the striking union doesn't exist. Similarly, if social contributions or taxes are high in one country, a multi-national can sometimes realize their profits in another country or shift production elsewhere. The question is *not* whether or not big business will become supra-national: it already is. The question is whether labor is going to organize on a commensurate scale; and whether government will operate on a level that permits it to exert countervailing power, in order to be able to carry out policies supported by the majority.

Is European integration a policy of the Left or the Right? Ultimately, the answer depends on one's perspective. For obvious historical reasons, the Soviet Union has consistently shown a strong preference for having weak, divided neighbors to her West. For equally obvious reasons, since the Sino-Soviet split the Chinese have shown a strong desire for the Soviet Union to have a strong, united Europe to her West. Viewing Europe as a potential counterweight to Soviet "Social Imperialism," the Chinese Communist leaders in recent years have outdone all but the most dedicated Europeans in their advocacy of European unification, stressing the fundamentally progressive nature of the European Community. With a nice sense of timing, Peking announced an agreement to exchange ambassadors with the European Community just before the British referendum on membership. In bestowing this seal of approval, the Chinese became the first Communist country (other than Yugoslavia) to officially recognize the Community and were bitterly rebuked by the Secretary General of the French Communist Party.

Insofar as there is a lingering tendency for the European Left to look to Moscow for cues concerning what is authentically Marxist, Europe tends to be seen as an anti-Communist conspiracy. Insofar as one looks to Peking for an alternate model—or, like the Italians or Yugoslavs, develops one's own model—European integration may be viewed as enhancing the unity of the working class.

VI. MULTIPLE THRESHOLDS OF SUPPORT FOR EUROPEAN INTEGRATION

The preceding section of this chapter dealt mainly with one general indicator of support for European integration. But public attitudes are not monolithic. We cannot assume that because 77 percent of the Italian public are favorable to the general idea of European unification, they would support any and all specific proposals for unification under any and all circumstances. If one asks a variety of questions ranging from "easy" to "hard" ones, they reveal a number of different thresholds at which some people support the underlying idea, while others do not. This final section offers a more detailed picture of exactly what the various European publics would and would not accept in the way of integration.

Let us begin with the *status quo*: To what extent are European publics pleased or displeased that their country is a member of the European Community? We would expect this to be a relatively "easy" question. It demands nothing new, merely the continuation of existing arrangements. Still, it is by no means something we can take for granted. It is precisely this question, whether or not to remain in the Community, that the British were debating so heatedly from January, 1973, to June, 1975.

In each of the European Community surveys from 1973 to 1975, the publics were asked: "Generally speaking, do you think that (British, French, etc.) membership is a good thing, a bad thing, or neither good nor bad?" Table 12–7 gives the results for May, 1975. The responses reveal a now familiar pattern. Among

TABLE 12–7. Attitudes Toward Membership in the Common Market Among Nine European Publics[a]

"Generally speaking, do you think that (your country's) membership in the Common Market is a good thing, a bad thing, or neither good nor bad?"

	A good thing	A bad thing
Italy	71%	3%
Netherlands	64	3
Belgium	57	3
France	64	4
Luxembourg	65	7
Germany	56	8
Ireland	50	20
Britain	47	21
Denmark	36	25

[a] Results from the May, 1975, European Community survey.

the publics of the Six an overwhelming consensus supports membership, whereas among the publics of the Three opinion remains relatively divided. In the *least* favorable nation (Germany) those who consider membership good, outnumber those who consider it bad by better than seven to one! In the *most* favorable country (Italy) the preponderance of favorable over unfavorable opinion is extreme: 71 percent feel that membership is good and only 3 percent consider it bad—a ratio of nearly 24 to one. There is substantial opposition in the three new member nations, although support outweighs opposition in each of them. In the case of Britain, we can calibrate the responses to our question against the results of an actual referendum, held only a few weeks after field-work was completed for the May, 1975, survey. Among our British respondents, 47 percent say that membership is "a good thing," while 21 percent say it is "a bad thing." Let us assume that these two groups represent those who voted respectively "for" and "against" British membership in the actual referendum (while the undecided were apt to abstain). When we exclude the "undecided" and non-response categories from our percentage base, our figures of 47 percent and 21 percent become 69 percent "for" and 31 percent "against"—in almost perfect anticipation of the actual referendum result (in which 67.3 percent voted "for" membership and 32.7 voted "against."

Calculated on this same basis, 59 percent of the Danish electorate would have voted in favor of membership if another referendum had been held at the same time. But these responses show considerable volatility over time in the Three, and our data suggest that membership would have been *rejected* in both Denmark and Great Britain, if referenda had been called at given moments during the first two years of membership (see Figure 12–4). The dramatic upward and downward swings of opinion in the Three may well reflect the effects of the Recession and oil embargo that made themselves felt during this period. But despite these events, opinion remained remarkably stable and supportive among the publics of the Six.

Support for the *status quo* outweighed opposition in all nine European Community countries by 1975, generally by very wide margins, and even in rather difficult times. Does this mean that the Community is populated largely by unconditional Europeans, who would make any sacrifice and pay any price for European unification? Certainly not. The preceding question was worded in neutral terms. Now let us shift to a question in which European unification is depicted as having a negative economic impact on the person interviewed. Our respondents were asked: "Would you be willing to make certain personal sacrifices, for example to pay slightly higher taxes, for the sake of European integration?" In the troubled economic climate of 1975, the thought of paying higher taxes proved decidedly unpopular. Responses were predominantly

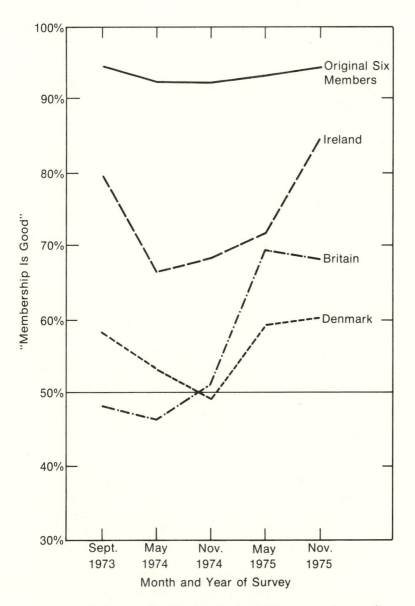

FIGURE 12–4. Support for Membership in the European Community, Sept., 1973–Nov., 1975.

Percent saying that their country's membership in the Common Market is "a good thing" among those expressing an opinion ("neither good nor bad" and non-response were excluded).

negative in all nine countries in May, 1975 (although there had been favorable pluralities in Germany and Italy in 1973). In the nine nations as a whole, 67 percent of those interviewed said that they would *not* be willing to pay higher taxes for the sake of European unification, while only 26 percent said they would. This is a sobering thought. Does it mean that the professions of support for European integration made elsewhere in the interviews are insincere or meaningless? Certainly not. Such professions can provide a very good indication of actual behavior—for example, the British vote in the referendum. But people's commitments extend to various depths. Cast in a neutral context, one can evoke a large measure of support for questions about European integration. Placed in a negative context, as here, one evokes far less support. And if the context were made still more negative, one would undoubtedly evoke even less support: presumably, very few people would be willing to die for the sake of European unity—though they may be perfectly sincere supporters under less extreme circumstances.

What is the *real* measure of support for European integration —the generally favorable attitude under neutral conditions or continued support even at personal sacrifice? Both are real. The question about personal sacrifices is a sensitive indicator of pro-European sentiment, and it suggests that if it were generally felt that the Community had fundamentally negative economic effects, the Community would become generally unpopular. But *is* this the reality? Probably not. By and large, the European Community seems to have had *positive* economic effects on most of its people. If this is true (or is believed to be true), people will act on the basis of their generally favorable attitudes toward the Community rather than on the basis of hypothetical negative effects.

We have looked at responses to one relatively "easy" question, and one relatively "hard" one. Now let us turn to a question that goes well beyond the *status quo*, though without explicitly suggesting any negative consequences (other than those inherent in the loss of national sovereignty). In the 1975 survey, the nine European publics were asked: "Are you, yourself, for or against the Common Market developing into a European political union?" This goal was endorsed by the leaders of the nine nations at a 1972 summit meeting, but it goes far beyond any existing arrangements. It implies the creation of a genuine European Federation. Table 12–8 shows the distribution of support among the respective publics. Given the far-reaching nature of this proposal and the ex-

TABLE 12–8. Support and Opposition to a
European Political Union[a]

"Are you, yourself, for or against the Common Market
developing into a European political union?"

	For	Against
Italy	71%	11%
Luxembourg	71	11
Germany	70	13
Belgium	51	9
France	66	17
Netherlands	54	15
Ireland	37	38
Britain	36	46
Denmark	21	54

[a] Results from May, 1975, European Community survey.

treme caution with which the national elites have handled it, the
degree of public support is quite astonishing. Within the original
member nations all six publics support the idea and not by narrow
margins, but overwhelmingly. In the Six the favorable outnumber
the opposed by at least three to one and generally more. In the
Three opinion is predominately opposed, but even there, the situation is not hopeless. The Irish are evenly divided. In Britain opposition is clearly preponderant, but support has been growing. In
1973 only 24 percent were for, while 54 percent were against; by
1975 the figures had shifted to 36 percent and 46 percent respectively. Opposition seems overwhelming only in Denmark, where it
prevails by better than two to one.

Political union is an ambitious goal. A surprisingly strong consensus in favor of it has been reached already among the publics
of the Six. Nevertheless, the goal will probably be unattainable
until a broader base of support can be developed among the publics of the countries that entered the European Community in
1973.

Yet there are a number of important but less ambitious tasks
which the European Community might undertake at once and
do so with the support of the publics of *all nine countries*. In 1973
our respondents were asked, "For each of the problems I am going
to mention, would you say whether they would be better dealt with
by a European government or by the (British, French, etc.) government?" The problems were:

Pollution of the environment
Military defense
Scientific research
Investments by foreign firms in (Britain, France, etc.)
Drug addiction
Economic growth
Major political negotiations with the Americans,
    the Russians, etc.
Poverty and unemployment
Aid to underdeveloped countries
Rising prices

Responses to these items were rather closely related to one's overall support or opposition to European integration.[17] Table 12–9 summarizes the distribution of support for a European solution to each of the ten problems. Once again, we see the contrast between attitudes in the Six and those in the Three. The publics of the Six felt that a European government would be better equipped than their national government to handle seven of the ten problems. Indeed, except in Belgium, a European solution was preferred for *nine* of the ten problems. The publics of the new member-countries were comparatively hesitant about the transfer of additional authority to a European government. Nevertheless, there was a consensus among all nine publics that certain functions *would* be handled better by a European government than by the respective national governments, and these functions are far from insignificant. They include scientific research, aid to underdeveloped nations, and political negotiations with the super-powers.

More striking still was the degree to which the European publics favor solidarity in the face of economic problems. In 1973 respondents in all nine countries were asked, "If one of the countries of the European Community finds itself in major economic difficulties, do you feel that the other countries including (your country) should help it or not?" As Table 12–10 indicates, mutual economic assistance was supported by overwhelming majorities in all nine countries. Among the publics of the Six, partisans of eco-

[17] These items were included in the factor analyses mentioned above. Across the nine samples, their mean loadings on the European integration support factor were above .400 in every case but one: the item concerning foreign investment showed insignificant factor loadings in most countries. This item apparently fails to tap any broad attitudinal dimension—possibly because it was poorly worded or because this particular topic is not salient to the general public.

TABLE 12–9. Problems Better Handled by a European Government Than by the National Government

Problem	Original Six Members						Three New Members		
	Italy	Nether-lands	Luxem-bourg	Germany	France	Belgium	Denmark	Britain	Ireland
Scientific research	X[a]	X	X	X	X	X	X	X	X
Aid to underdeveloped countries	X	X	X	X	X	X	X	X	X
Negotiations with the United States, Soviet Union	X	X	X	X	X	X		X	X
Pollution	X	X	X	X	X	X	X		
Drug addiction	X	X	X	X	X	X	X		
Military defense	X	X	X	X	X	X	X		
Economic growth	X	X	(X)[b]	X	X	X			
Rising prices	X	X	X	X	X				
Poverty, unemployment	X	X	X	X	(X)				
Foreign investments in respondent's country	X								

[a] X = European solution favored by an absolute majority.
[b] (X) = European solution favored by a majority of those expressing an opinion.

TABLE 12–10. Support and Opposition to
Intra-European Economic Assistance

"If one of the countries of the European Community finds
itself in major economic difficulties, do you feel that the
other countries, including (Britain, France, etc.)
should help it or not?"

	Yes, should help	No, should not
Italy	88%	2
Luxembourg	87	8
Germany	77	7
Netherlands	79	9
France	78	9
Belgium	78	9
Ireland	80	10
Denmark	62	25
Britain	59	28

nomic assistance outnumbered their opponents by better than nine
to one. But the publics of the Three *also* gave a strong vote of
confidence to this policy: the British supported it by better than
two to one; the Danes and Irish were even more favorable.

It is a supreme irony that a few weeks after these surveys were
carried out, the governments of the nine countries adopted precisely the opposite policy in reaction to the Arab oil embargo. Oil
shipments to Europe were reduced generally, but The Netherlands
was singled out for special pressure because of Dutch support for
Israel. *All* shipment of Arab oil to The Netherlands was banned,
threatening the Dutch with economic disaster. It was a genuine
challenge to European economic solidarity. The response of the
respective national governments was a frantic scramble to make
the best possible deal on the basis of every man for himself.[18] By a
further irony, the embargo against Holland was partly circum-
vented not by the national governments or by the European Community, but by the multi-national petroleum companies that di-
verted shipments of non-Arab oil to Rotterdam. They were, of

[18] Interestingly enough, the respective *publics* (or at least one of them)
seem to have remained steadfast in face of the oil embargo. The survey
described above was executed just before the embargo. But another survey
carried out by SOFRES in November (when the crisis was acute) asked the
French public if they were willing, for the sake of European solidarity, to
share the consequences of the petroleum shortage: 70 percent said that
they *were* willing. See *L'Express*, November 7–8, 1973, 44.

course, simply serving their own interests in doing so, but they (like the Arabs) at least *had* a sense of supra-national interest.

In the ensuing period of financial and economic difficulties, there was a series of further rebuffs to European solidarity—unilateral actions by individual nations that threatened to undo the European Community. Worst of all, the actions were basically self-defeating. For such problems as the energy crisis, inflation, trade balances, pollution, and food shortages can no longer be solved by individual nation-states. Nor can the nation-states handle the danger of nuclear war—a danger that today is all but ignored, but that remains a possibility at any time. In a long-term perspective, its implications for international security remain one of the strongest arguments for the European idea. The Father of Europe, Jean Monnet, originally conceived of European integration as a step toward Atlantic Community and eventually toward an East-West security community. There are formidable obstacles in the way of these developments. Monnet's approach was to reduce a large, long-term effort to problems of relatively manageable size. In the construction of Europe, limited but real powers have been turned over to supra-national authorities, stimulating the growth of public support for political integration.

During the palmy days of Gaullist nationalism there was a growing tendency on both sides of the Atlantic to dismiss grand designs like Monnet's as illusory, and to view Gaullist ethno-centrism as hard-headed realism. It was a short-term realism, comparable to the realism that triumphantly points out "We needn't fix the roof —it isn't raining." In the short term there is no need to make arrangements for collective control of major weapons systems: we have *detente*. But not long ago, the superpowers were at the brink of war. If nothing is done to institutionalize control of major violence, at least among the major powers, they will be there again sooner or later. As the time perspective lengthens, the likelihood of super-disaster rises toward certainty.

Euratom came into being in 1958, based on the idea that at some future time Europe was likely to run short of petroleum, and that efforts to develop alternative energy sources could only be carried out effectively on a supra-national basis. Euratom's growth was stunted by short-term calculations of national interest and "realistic" illusions of national glory. For fifteen years it went nowhere, starved for funds, and restricted to minor projects. In 1973 the Arabs quadrupled the price of oil and restricted its flow. Suddenly it became apparent that the basic idea behind Euratom had been correct, but nearly sixteen years had been wasted.

A rainy day had come—but it's difficult to fix the roof in a thunderstorm. The leaders of the Arab nations acted in a unified and decisive manner. From their viewpoint, it has worked out very well; they have become fantastically rich. One must admire their unity of purpose, and hope that the leaders of more backward countries in Europe and North America will someday show an equal measure of imagination and determination.

In a recent study, West European political leaders and government officials were asked a series of questions about European integration. One of the reasons most frequently cited to explain why European integration had not progressed more rapidly was the claim that the public was not ready for it.[19] In a sense, the very opposite seems to be true. In a number of respects, European publics are quite ready to go beyond the present scope of European integration. They show a growing sense of supra-national identity and a widespread willingness to entrust broader responsibilities to supra-national institutions. In the turmoil following 1973, their leaders were not only failing to move toward the goals they had set themselves, but threatened to undo progress already attained.

[19] See Ronald Inglehart and Robert Putnam, "European Elites, European Publics and European Integration" (forthcoming).

CHAPTER 13

World Views and Global Change

BENEATH the frenzied activism of the 1960's and the seeming quiescence of the 1970's, a Silent Revolution has been occurring that is gradually but fundamentally changing political life throughout the Western world. This book has described two major aspects of this revolution: a shift from overwhelming emphasis on material consumption and security toward greater concern with the quality of life; and an increase in the political skills of Western publics that enables them to play a more active role in making important political decisions.

The first of these changes can be traced to the fact that people have a variety of needs and give top priority to those that are in short supply. The needs most directly related to physical survival take top priority when they are not adequately met. A person lacking adequate food or shelter is likely to devote virtually full attention to obtaining them. But when at least minimal economic and physical security are present, needs for love, belonging, and esteem become increasingly salient; and when all of these are met, intellectual and aesthetic satisfaction take on central importance.

We have seen evidence that some groups in advanced Industrial society have attained a sense of economic and physical security that enables them to give top priority to the belonging and intellectual-aesthetic needs. These Post-Materialists, as we term them, are a relatively small minority, comprising only 12 percent of the public in the United States, for example. But they occupy a strategic position for they are concentrated among the best educated and politically most active. They are heavily over-represented among the young. While they make up as little as 2 or 3 percent of the oldest age groups, among those born after World War II they are almost as numerous as the Materialist type in some countries.

This heavy skew according to age suggests that a process of inter-generational value change is taking place. For the values acquired in childhood and youth tend to remain with one throughout adult life. For the most part, the Post-Materialists have grown up during times of economic and physical security; consequently they tend to take material security for granted and place more emphasis on other goals. Their parents and grandparents, on the other hand, grew up during the Great Depression or during one of the World Wars, when scarcity and physical danger was pervasive in many countries. Their value priorities today still reflect these formative experiences.

The cross-national differences in the way values are distributed across the respective age groups reinforces the impression that they result from a process of generational change. For if generational change is taking place, we would expect these differences to reflect a given nation's recent history. Germany, for example, has undergone particularly extreme changes in the conditions prevailing during the formative years of her respective age cohorts: the older Germans experienced famine and slaughter during World War I, followed by severe inflation, the Great Depression and devastation, invasion and massive loss of life during World War II. Her youngest cohorts have been brought up in relatively peaceful conditions in what is now one of the richest countries in the world. If value types reflect one's formative experiences, we would expect to find relatively large differences between the older and younger German age cohorts.

Great Britain represents the opposite extreme from Germany: the wealthiest country in Europe prior to World War II, she escaped invasion during the war, but has had a relatively stagnant economy ever since. For the last twenty-five years, her European neighbors have had economic growth rates about twice as large as Britain's. We would expect to find relatively small differences between the youngest and oldest British respondents.

The data certainly verify these expectations. The age-related differences are larger in Germany than in any other country—almost *twice* as large as they are in Britain, where the smallest amount of value change seems to have taken place. The nine other Western countries for which we have data fall between these two extremes, and on the whole there is a very good fit between the economic history of a given country and the amount of apparent value change across that country's age groups.

Multi-variate analyses indicate that formal education, one's current social milieu and life-cycle effects all seem to help shape one's value priorities. But the impact of a given generation unit's formative experiences seems to be at least as important as any other factor and is probably the key explanatory variable.

Moreover, we can safely conclude that inter-generational value change is taking place quite *apart* from other changes in formative experiences. For education has a significant linkage with value type. And varying educational levels are a structural feature of the respective age cohorts. The younger generations are much more highly educated than the older ones and this relationship will not change over time. Thus, differences in cohort experiences and differences in educational level should *both* encourage an inter-generational shift in basic value priorities.

The process of value change has interesting and rather para-doxical implications concerning the Subjective Quality of Life. Despite their relatively favored economic situation, Post-Material-ists do not show relatively high levels of subjective satisfaction with their lives as a whole or even with the material aspects of life. For this group has distinctive value priorities. It places less em-phasis on material welfare and more on qualitative aspects of society. On the whole, Western nations have been successful in achieving economic growth during the past couple of decades, but they have given relatively little attention to the attainment of Post-Materialist goals. The class conflicts of Industrial society have had considerable time in which to move toward peaceful co-existence. But the conventions and institutions of Western countries are based on Materialist assumptions. To have a Post-Materialist world-view means that one is apt to be out of harmony with the type of society in which one lives. Consequently, we might expect Materialists to be relatively supportive of the established order, and Post-Materialists to be relatively change-oriented.

Under the circumstances prevailing in the 1970's, Post-Mate-rialists did tend to show lower levels of political satisfaction and more support for radical change than Materialists. The implica-tions of this fact are far-reaching. In earlier periods of Industrial society, political dissatisfaction usually may have had its origins in material conditions and been concentrated among low income groups. But our findings indicate that the relatively prosperous Post-Materialists now comprise the most likely source of political dissatisfaction and protest.

The linkage between Post-Materialist values and political dis-satisfaction also suggests that we may be witnessing a change in the social bases of the political parties of the Left. For the Post-

Materialists come overwhelmingly from middle-class backgrounds. Yet they tend to support the policies of the Left. Conversely, the most materialistic individuals tend to be concentrated among low income groups—but support key aspects of the established social order. One consequence, apparently, has been a gradual weakening of traditional patterns of social class voting, as younger segments of the middle class break away from family traditions and support the Left; while some working-class elements shift to the Right.

There can be acute strains between an older Left that emphasizes economic gains for the working class, and a newer Left that is more concerned with life-style changes, with qualitative rather than quantitative gains. But both factions share a common concern with social change in an egalitarian direction, and precisely because the goal of equality appeals to different groups for different reasons, it may serve as a bond that holds the Left together.

At the start of the 1970's, the politics of most Western countries seemed to be moving in a rather similar direction. For one thing, the advocacy of social change tended to have a middle class rather than a working class base. For another, non-economic issues achieved a high degree of salience.

The two features were related. After a prolonged period of economic growth, the principal axis of political cleavage began to shift from economic issues to life-style issues, entailing a shift in the constituency most interested in obtaining change. Following a law of diminishing returns, economic gains became relatively less important, particularly to those segments of society that had never experienced severe economic deprivation. For a significant portion of society, economic gains no longer seemed most urgent; new items were at the top of the agenda.

Efforts to fight the dehumanizing tendencies inherent in Industrial society took high priority. For in a sense, the key institutions of Industrial society are the mass-production assembly line and the mass-production bureaucracy. As this form of society developed, more and more people became organized in hierarchically structured and routinized factories or offices with their relationships governed by impersonal bureaucratic rules. This type of organization makes large-scale enterprises possible, may lead to increased productivity, and, as long as economic considerations are paramount, a majority may be willing to accept the accompanying depersonalization and anonymity. But with the emergence of a widespread Post-Materialist outlook, the twin hierarchies of Industrial society increasingly have been called in question.

Long-term prosperity seems to favor the emergence of publics that will place less emphasis on material consumption and security, and more on humanistic and aesthetic goals. There is even some evidence that national priorities are being re-ordered in a direction consistent with these values. From 1967 to 1972, human resource spending in the United States grew from 28 percent to 40 percent of the total federal budget, while defense spending declined in an almost symmetrical fashion from 44 percent to 33 percent of the budget. The government's proposed budget for 1977 allocated 26 percent for defense and 48 percent for human resources.[1]

The other major trend dealt with in this book is a shift in the distribution of political skills. Western publics are developing an increasing potential for political participation. This change does not imply that mass publics will simply show higher rates of participation in traditional activities such as voting, but that they may intervene in the political process on a qualitatively different level. Increasingly, they are likely to demand participation in *making* major decisions, not just a voice in selecting the decision makers. These changes have important implications for established political parties, labor unions and professional organizations; for mass politics are increasingly apt to be elite-challenging, rather than elite-directed. The source of these changes is a shift in the balance of political skills between elites and mass.

We argued that participation springs from two fundamentally different processes, one underlying an older mode of political participation, the other a newer. The institutions that mobilized mass political participation in the late nineteenth and early twentieth century—labor union, church and mass political party—were typically hierarchical organizations in which a small number of leaders led a mass of disciplined troops. They were effective in bringing large numbers of voters to the polls in an era when the average citizen had a low level of political skills. But while these organizations could mobilize large numbers, they usually produced only a relatively low level of participation—generally the simple act of voting.

[1] Figures reported in *Time*, February 2, 1976, p. 10. "Human resources" includes spending for social security, unemployment insurance, public assistance, health, education and social services. It should be noted that though the *proportion* allocated to defense declined, the dollars spent increased by 46 percent from 1967 to 1977.

The newer mode of participation is capable of expressing the individual's preferences with far greater precision than the old. It is more issue-oriented, it aims at effecting specific policy-changes rather than simply supporting a given set of leaders. But a heightened ideological sensitivity among the electorate may be reducing the public's amenability to elite-directed political mobilization. There is evidence from a number of countries that the influence of the political machine, labor union and church may be eroding gradually.

Special skills are a prerequisite for playing an effective role in the politics of an extensive political community embracing millions of citizens. Consequently, rising levels of political skills should enable Western publics to play a more meaningful role in the decision-making process. These publics may be approaching a threshold at which they can take part in actual decision making rather than entrust it to relatively skilled minorities. Moreover, these publics seem to be gradually taking on a sense of supranational identity, which may help make it possible to establish some kind of effective world order before the ultimate political miscalculation takes place.

By and large, the preceding chapters have painted a bright picture of political change among Western publics. But various other writers have emphasized the dark side of these changes. It would be unwise to ignore their warnings. Thus Huntington argues that rising levels of political skills may lead to political breakdown, as participation increases more rapidly than a society's capacity to institutionalize it. According to Huntington, "The core participant institution, the political party, appears to be verging on a state of institutional and political decay. Throughout much of the country, party machines have collapsed completely or become pale shadows of their former selves: weak in finances, personnel, resources and organization. . . . Effective governmental action could be more, rather than less, difficult in a society with a more highly educated and participant population. American cities with more highly educated populations, for instance, tend to have fewer innovations than cities with less educated populations. One reason suggested for this seemingly anomalous situation is that widespread education tends to produce too much interest and participation which in turn leads to political stalemate. Innovation is easiest when substantial proportions of the population are indifferent."[2]

[2] Samuel Huntington, "Postindustrial Politics: How Benign Will It Be?" *Comparative Politics*, 6, 2 (January, 1974), 174–177. Cf. Samuel Hunt-

Sartori, too, sees dangerous possibilities, both in the shift away from centralized, elite-directed organizations, and in the emergence of new values.[3] The shift from the industrial sector to the service sector, and the development of a complex, automated economy renders Post-Industrial society extremely vulnerable, he argues. Huge cities easily can be turned into death traps, and a computer-regulated society can collapse as swiftly as a computer can be wrecked. The effects of a strike in the Industrial sector may not be felt for months, but if vital services are stopped, the impact is immediate. When electricity is cut off, the elevators, lights, air conditioning, and much of the transportation of a huge city are halted instantly. Within a matter of days or even hours survival may be at stake.

According to Sartori, a loss of centralized authority in labor unions now enables small, intransigent minorities to seize control of key centers in the service economy by which they can exert vast blackmail pressures upon society. Against this, "the only reliable self-restraints are the restraints that are internalized via the socialization processes and agencies. Here is the rub; and here the symptoms are ominous. A post-hardship culture looms low—whatever its other merits—in any realistic perspective and prudence, let alone the calculus of consequences."[4]

Sartori's warning may contain an element of truth, but it seems to encompass only part of the truth. For the Post-Materialist or "post-hardship" mentality remains rational. It emphasizes a different *aspect* of rationality from what has been most prominent in Industrial society.

Half a century ago, Weber argued that there is a basic social tension between "substantive rationality," involving judgments about ultimate values, and "functional rationality," dealing with the means to attain a given goal.[5] Both forms of rationality are essential. As Lipset points out, societies "require ultimate values which are believed in, independently of prospects for actual achievement. But they also require people to be instrumentally rational, that is, to choose effective means for attaining given ends.

ington, *Political Order in Changing Societies* (New Haven: Yale University Press, 1968).
[3] See Giovanni Sartori, "The Power of Labor in the Post-Pacified Society: A Surmise," paper presented at the World Congress of the International Political Science Association, Montreal, Quebec, August, 1973.
[4] *Ibid.*, 26.
[5] See Max Weber, *Economy and Society* (New York: Bedminster Press, 1968).

The tension between the two sorts of rationality is built into the whole structure of social action. A society cannot maintain its pursuit of rational means-ends relationships except in the context of a set of absolute values which anchor and direct the search for means."[6]

The value types we have described tend to be oriented toward different forms of rationality. Materialists stress economic and physical security—leading them to emphasize functional rationality. Post-Materialists are less pre-occupied with the means to physical subsistence and more concerned with ultimate ends. As we noted in Chapter 8, conflicts based on individual value priorities are relatively difficult to bargain over, for they do not have the incremental nature of economic issues; like religious conflicts, they tend to take on a moralistic tone. Insofar as Post-Materialists perceive politics as a conflict over ultimate values, compromise may become impossible. Weber stated the problem forcefully: "In the world of realities . . . we encounter the ever-renewed experience that the adherent of an ethic of ultimate ends suddenly turns into a chiliastic prophet. Those, for example, who have preached 'love against violence' now call for the use of force for the *last* violent deed, which would lead to a state of affairs in which *all* violence is annihilated."[7]

Contemporary writers have applied this analysis to the New Left. Thus, Brzezinski argues that "The strong totalitarian tendencies of the New Left are evident from its conduct and prescriptions . . . the sharp edge of the New Left's intellectual—and sometimes even physical—attacks has been aimed at those American institutions whose normal operation relies most on reason and nonviolence. . . . Leading New Left spokesmen have been contemptuous of free speech, democratic procedures, and majority rule. They have left little room for doubt as to how they would handle their critics if the New Left were ever to gain power."[8]

To what extent can this charge be applied to Post-Materialists

[6] Seymour M. Lipset, "Social Structure and Social Change," in Peter Blau (ed.), *Approaches to the Study of Social Structure* (New York: Free Press, 1975), 121–156.

[7] Max Weber, *From Max Weber: Essays in Sociology*, ed. H. H. Gerth and C. Wright Mills (New York: Oxford University Press, 1946), 122.

[8] Zbigniew Brzezinski, *Between Two Ages: America's Role in the Technetronic Era* (New York: Viking, 1970), 235. Brzezinski cites Robert Wolff *et al., A Critique of Pure Tolerance* (Boston: Beacon, 1965) as a glaring example of advocacy of the repression of views divergent from those approved by the New Left.

in general? As we have seen, New Left movements have a disproportionate appeal for Post-Materialists. But they attract only a
minority among this group, and the totalitarian tendencies to which
Brzezinski refers seem to have characterized only a transient phase
of New Left history, and not Post-Materialists as a group. Indeed, one of the core elements of the Post-Materialist syndrome
is a relative emphasis on freedom of expression. It is sobering to
remember that Free Speech movements have been known to deny
that liberty to their opponents, when their opponents could be
defined as fundamentally evil. But, such instances seem exceptional, not the norm.

With the development of advanced Industrial society, the rate
of change and the impact of man on his environment have increased to the point where a greater emphasis on long-term planning for long-range goals seems mandatory. The Post-Materialist
perspective gives greater attention to relatively remote goals. The
bourgeois mentality was shaped in bargaining across the market,
with emphasis on short-term material gains. Buyer and seller may
have opposite interests, but unless both sides can agree on a trans-
action, there is no profit for either of them. Compromise therefore seems normal and, as Moore argues, the victory of this
bourgeois mentality was a prerequisite for the emergence of
democracy.[9]

The Post-Materialist outlook is more attuned to ultimate ends,
which may produce not only a heightened moral sensitivity but
also a more intense need to *find* ultimate values or to believe they
have been found. If this is true, it could diminish one's willingness
to bargain, for in a confrontation between Good and Evil, any
compromise is scandalous.

We have spoken of a certain curvilinearity in the ongoing processes of change. The Post-Materialist phenomenon is genuinely
new in several major respects. Yet it also represents a turning back
to an earlier political style.

A new culture is emerging within Western societies, and a classic
reaction to culture shock is a re-emphasis of traditional ways.
Materialists and Post-Materialists alike show signs of doing so,
though they emphasize different aspects of Western tradition. The
recent wave of nostalgia seems to be one manifestation of retreat
into the past for the population at large. In the Post-Materialist

---

[9] See Barrington Moore, Jr., *Social Origins of Dictatorship and Democracy* (Boston: Beacon Press, 1966).

milieu one can identify several different forms of intellectual response to the need for direction and meaning. None of them represents traditionalism pure and simple, but each combines a tentative dose of innovation with a heavy reliance on elements from the past. For the Marx of the late twentieth century has not yet appeared: no one has yet proposed a truly coherent and broadly acceptable ideology for Post-Industrial society.

The first and most widespread form of Post-Materialist response has been a revival of Marxism itself. It seems ironic that this should occur in the West during a period when the younger and more creative elements of the Soviet Union and Eastern Europe seem to be abandoning Marxism.[10] To be sure, the leading figures of Post-Materialist protest have shown a keen awareness of the inadequacies of the Soviet model of Marxism. Daniel Cohn-Bendit reserved his sharpest barbs for the Stalinist hacks of the Communist Party. But Marxism has been a mainstay of social criticism in the West, and despite their divergences with the old Left, the New Left clings to its rhetoric as to their native language.

It is only a verbal paradox that Dialectical Materialism should have a strong appeal for Western Post-Materialists. For Marxism provides an umbrella of prophetic condemnation, a basic mood rather than substantive guidance. In Eastern Europe, where the name connotes orthodoxy rather than protest, it appeals to a very different constituency. The danger is that their fidelity to traditional categories of thought may put blinders on Western protesters in their search for solutions.

Marx provided a brilliant and productive critique of nineteenth-century industrialization, and insofar as the problems we face remain the same as in his era, his analysis remains relevant. But the problems are *not* altogether the same, and many of the most anguishing ones seem to be inherent to Industrial society, whether

[10] Quantitative data on this subject are scarce, for obvious reasons. For the Soviet Union, one can only point to brief but repeated instances of protest on the part of artists, scientists, and intellectuals, together with much more extensive material from emigrant intellectuals such as Solzhenitsyn. For Poland, a more broadly based illustration is provided by a 1961 poll of university students in Warsaw. In answer to the question "Do you consider yourself a Marxist?" only 18 percent gave an affirmative reply; 59 percent gave negative replies, and 23 percent gave no response. Survey cited in Brzezinski, *Between Two Ages*, 79. As Brzezinski points out, support for Socialist welfare programs is almost universal; the Marxist world view is rejected.

Marxist or not. Marx was an insightful and creative thinker rather than a propounder of orthodoxy. If he were alive today, he would almost certainly be a Revisionist himself.

A set of new challenges has arisen in the late twentieth century, and they have no pre-fabricated answer. Nationalized factories consume and pollute just as much as privately owned ones. A change in ownership does not seem to make those directing things less rigid or repressive; if anything, Soviet bureaucracy seems more so than Western ones. Nor does it seem to make the routine of the assembly line less tedious or dehumanizing. More experimentation seems to be going on in the West than in the Soviet Union aimed at giving workers a more creative, self-directed role in their work. The military-industrial complex is as powerful in the Soviet Union as in the United States, and the former devotes a much larger share of its Gross National Product to defense than the latter. Nor does the abolition of private property put an end to imperialism and war. In terms of the number of nationalities ruled more or less against their will, the Russian empire is probably the world's largest; and among the great powers the two that recently have seemed most likely to start shooting at each other were the Soviet Union and China.

Again, we must acknowledge that Marxist thinkers are concerned with these problems and endeavoring to achieve a new synthesis retaining the economic egalitarianism at the core of Marxism, while avoiding the hierarchical centralization of power which has been a feature of Marxist states. Some of these thinkers find a promise of "socialism with a human face" in the Chinese or Yugoslav examples. Some seek the solution in the young Marx rather than the materialistic old Marx or in Hegel. A close reading of Marx and Hegel is well worth the effort. Only it seems clear that study of the venerated texts will have to be supplemented with imagination, innovation, and attention to current reality. There is no pre-fabricated answer in the citadel of institutionalized Marxism.

A second route chosen by Post-Materialist thinkers is that of mysticism. For some, this means a whole-hearted acceptance of traditional religion, often with a heightened social consciousness and often with a preference for faiths imported from distant countries. For others God is dead; therefore it is necessary to invent one.

Man's growing capability to control the environment has led to a world where all things are possible, including genocide, plague, and holocaust. We could turn on Doomsday tomorrow. A world where everything is permitted is one of intolerable normlessness. For the secular-minded, Nature sometimes becomes a God. Nature was here long before man and will be here after him. In a sense, it is the oldest god of all; it is unquestionable, absolute. It has its inexorable norms—the grass grows in the spring, the leaves fall in the autumn, and water freezes when it gets cold, independently of any human volition. In the search for something sacred, Nature provides a comprehensive set of rules, even its own dietary laws: eat natural foods, the others will poison you. In this theology, there is a clearly defined source of evil: Technology, the enemy of Nature.

One of the most interesting and articulate spokesmen of Post-Industrial mysticism is Roszak, who argues that, "To a mournfully great extent, the progress of expertise, especially as it seeks to mechanize culture, is a waging of open warfare upon joy. It is a bewilderingly perverse effort to demonstrate that nothing, *absolutely nothing*, is particularly special, unique, or marvelous, but can be lowered to the status of mechanized routine. More and more the spirit of "nothing but" hovers over advanced scientific research: the effort to degrade, disenchant, level down."[11]

Roszak's critique of contemporary society is fundamentally more radical than the Marxist one, for he rejects the science, technology, and industry that Marxist and capitalist alike accept as the basis of progress. Unfortunately, Roszak's study of science apparently ended with William Blake, although he does summon some anecdotes about nerve gas and mercury poisoning to show what contemporary advanced scientific research is all about. He seems wholly ignorant of the fact that natural science has long since grown beyond its mechanistic phase or that its basic drift now seems to be in precisely the opposite direction from that which he proclaims. Mechanistic concepts do indeed still influence society all too heavily, particularly through the mass production assembly line and the mass production bureaucracy. But Roszak seems unaware that the science which inspired them is not the science of

[11] Theodore Roszak, *The Making of a Counter Culture* (Garden City: Anchor-Doubleday, 1969); cf. Roszak, *Where the Wasteland Ends* (Garden City: Doubleday, 1973).

today.[12] For him science is just plain evil, in a fundamental and quite uncomplicated way; mankind can find fulfillment and health only by rejecting cold, rational science and embracing Nature.

This world view is attractive in many ways, but ultimately it seems untenable. The law of Nature is not that of the fond Mother Earth which some contemporaries imagine, but the law that population increases to reach a territory's carrying capacity and then is held down by starvation, disease, and mutual extermination. It is a world where the technological basis of women's liberation is absent. There is no pill and one's life expectancy is approximately thirty years. A woman spends most of her adult life in pregnancy and child-bearing, burying most of her offspring before they have grown out of childhood.

Humanism can be read into Nature, but it originates in civilization. In successive portions of the Bible one can trace an evolution from a God of genocide and human sacrifice to a merciful and loving God precisely as pastoral man *left* nature and became civilized. Nature endowed humanity with reason and the drive to realize one's potential.

In the industrialized world, technological developments have led to the evolution of new life-styles. More and more women seek fulfillment in careers, as well as (or instead of) through motherhood. Changing life-styles, combined with the technology of birth control, have led to a decline in births. Already fertility rates in virtually all advanced Industrial societies have dropped to or even below the replacement level.

In contrast with this, we need not speak of some bygone state of Nature. It is all too easy to find contemporary examples, for most of the world is still largely Pre-Industrial. Do the peoples of these regions spend their days rejoicing at the absence of ugly factories, the purity of their rivers and their happy communion with Nature? Heartbreakingly far from it. Millions of them are in danger of starvation. One picture of a gaunt, despairing mother holding her dying child is unbearable, but it is only a symbol of many—and the future could be worse. Population may be leveling off in Industrial society, but it is sky-rocketing in the rest of the world. Tens of millions may be starving tomorrow.

---

[12] For an equally sharp critique of technological society, but one which is informed by a sense of history, see William I. Thompson, *At the Edge of History* (New York: Harper and Row, 1972).

The course of wisdom is difficult. It requires both a warm heart and cold reason. Perhaps the whales are sacred and the trees are sacred and the land is sacred. But mankind is sacred too and unique in that he seeks salvation and uses tools. If he abandons *either*, he abandons humanity.

One sometimes encounters an anti-technological outlook which assumes that millions are starving in South Asia, Africa and Latin America *because* the West is industrialized: the use of technology has violated ageless ecological laws, and the world's hunger is somehow a consequence.

The belief is largely baseless. Existence at the edge of starvation has been the prevailing human condition since the dawn of history. From a Post-Materialist viewpoint, this is difficult to believe; one tends to assume that what one has always known is the way it has always been. But it was only recently that technology liberated part of mankind from bare subsistence.

In the last few decades, hunger in the less-developed world has been alleviated by the shipment of millions of tons of grain from the Industrial world. The United States alone normally exports enough food to feed three hundred million people—a food surplus made possible by mechanization, insecticides, and fertilizer which it may be fashionable to despise in the West, but which the Third World is seeking desperately. Hope for the future lies largely in agricultural and birth control technology developed in the West.

In one sense, part of the Third World's misery *could* be blamed on technology, if we follow ecological logic to its grim conclusion. A substantial part of the Non-Industrial world's population has been kept alive by food and medicine from the industrialized West. But this was treating the symptoms, not the causes. These people have survived to have children and their children have had children. If the food shipments had not been made, population growth would have been less steep either through the direct effects of starvation or because political leaders would have felt compelled to make serious efforts at birth control; and the number starving today would be far smaller.

In short, the sum of human misery has been vastly increased by a well-intended intervention that refused to face its own consequences. But clearly, the problem is one of too little technology, not too much. Going back to Nature is simply not a real option. It implies death by starvation, disease, or war for most of the world's population. By pre-technological standards we have long since exceeded the world's carrying capacity.

Such reasoning about what might have been is grim, but current reality is worse. Food reserves in the West have dwindled. Yet if current trends continue, in a few decades the population of the Third World may be more than double its present size.

What actually happens in Non-Industrialized countries ultimately will be decided there. The developed world can aid them. It cannot force them to arrest the soaring population growth at the root of the tragedy. Not even the total dismantling of Industrial society and its partition into evenly distributed agricultural plots would provide more than a few decades' respite from population pressure after which starvation would continue, only on a larger scale and with no further aid from outside. And the one real hope would then be gone—the sources of technology that seem to provide the only way out of the cycle.

For population growth *can* be halted by means which become simpler and more effective year by year. How much longer will leaders who purport to serve their people continue to reject birth control programs altogether, or give them an absurdly low priority? It is difficult to say. But the need for such programs is growing.

The outlook is not totally hopeless. Japan and other non-Western countries have broken out of the vicious circle in which population increases more rapidly than economic development. Here, as in the West, the result seems to be a new equilibrium. The evolution of life-styles may cause population growth to subside and may bring a shift from emphasis on material consumption.

There is hope even for countries that remain overwhelmingly agricultural. One of the impressive achievements of the Chinese Communist regime seems to be that it has lowered the birth rate significantly in a country with a very low level of economic development. Here the process apparently depends on the presence of an extremely strong government, capable of generating powerful social pressures and reshaping human values. There may be serious costs. So little is known about what takes place inside China that it is difficult to assess them. But it is possible that Western political leaders will some day find themselves welcoming the implantation of regimes modeled on Peking as vigorously as they once opposed them.

The deification of Nature takes many forms. Sometimes it uses pseudo-scientific reasoning to prove that science and technology are evil. Over-enthusiastic nature buffs point to the energy crisis as proof that Industrial society is inherently unhealthy and on the point of collapse.

The world's petroleum is indeed being used up. But (one may reply) nuclear fusion can theoretically produce enough energy for millions of years. There are all sorts of responses to this.

"It will turn out deadly radioactive by-products!"

Nuclear fission does; but nuclear fusion produces very little except inert helium and clean energy.

"But it will still produce thermal pollution, which may be even worse!"

Heat is a valuable form of energy. It can be misused or it can be channeled productively.

"The energy companies are extremely influential; they won't permit the government to undertake any really effective development of nuclear fusion until it's too late."

Unfortunately, this could be true. But if it is, we are no longer talking about inexorable natural limits to Industrial society, but about political problems within man's capacity to solve.

But sometimes it is pointless to even explore such possibilities because we are dealing with matters of faith. Technology *must* be evil because otherwise there would be nothing sacred. Consequently the ultimate, crushing refutation is: "That's the kind of technocratic thinking that got us into the mess we're in!"

Some people have seized on the analysis of *The Limits to Growth*[13] as a rationale for an anti-technological position, although the book strongly emphasizes that only through a major effort in scientific research and development can we hope to avert disaster.

This study, sponsored by The Club of Rome, may be one of the most significant books of the 1970's.[14] It presents the first formal

[13] See Donella Meadows *et al.*, *The Limits to Growth* (Washington, D.C.: Potomac Associates, 1972). This book has been translated into twenty-nine languages and has inspired a number of other books which have been influential in their own right—for example, one by the editors of *The Ecologist, A Blueprint for Survival* (Harmondsworth, England: Penguin, 1972); the latter relies on the former for key elements in its analysis. The modelling technique is based on principles developed in Jay W. Forrester, *World Dynamics* (Cambridge, Mass.: Wright-Allen, 1971). Also see Dennis Meadows and Donella Meadows (eds.), *Toward Global Equilibrium: Collected Papers* (Cambridge, Mass.: Wright-Allen, 1973); and Norman MacRae's critique of *Limits* in *The Economist* (March 11, 1972); and H.S.D. Cole *et al.* (eds.), *Models of Doom* (New York: Universe, 1973). Replies to a number of criticisms appear in A. Petitjean (ed.), *Quelles Limites? Le Club de Rome Répond* (Paris: Seuil, 1974).

[14] It may be an indication of the sluggishness of established institutions that this project was launched by The Club of Rome—an informal group of physical and social scientists, government officials and industrialists, founded in 1968.

model of long-term trends in population, food production, pollution and resource consumption that treats these variables as a dynamic system and views them on a global scale, and has stimulated widespread and serious consideration of their human implications. This work argues that the present pattern of economic growth will lead to the collapse of Industrial society within the lifetime of children now being born, through consumption of non-replenishable resources, the expansion of population beyond the available food supply and the build-up of pollution beyond the planet's capacity to absorb it. The book prescribes adoption of zero population growth and zero capital investment policies on a global scale as the only way to avoid collapse. While zero growth would prevail on a global basis, there would be shifts in the economic level of its various regions. The already developed world would be called upon to accept lower levels of investment and consumption, making it possible to bring the less developed nations up toward a global mean.

Like many pioneering efforts, this book has been widely criticized, and we agree with the critics on some points. But its authors are talking about the most basic problem facing the modern world.

It has been pointed out that the study's projections are based on the assumption that consumption, population, and pollution will increase at exponential rates, while the compensating effects of technology and policy will not—an assumption which is completely contrary to past experience. Similar projections based on data from 1870 could have been used to "prove" that by 1970 the cities of the Industrial world would be asphyxiated beneath mountains of horse manure; in 1850 one could have demonstrated that the cities would soon be dark by night due to the exhaustion of whale oil. But in fact technological developments and societal counter-measures did take place. Even crude legislation like Britain's Clean Air Act of 1956 had reduced the smoke content of London's air by 75 percent within fifteen years. At the same time, British rivers have also become cleaner, as a result of anti-pollution measures. One consequence is that in 1974 a salmon was caught in the Thames near London for the first time in well over a century.[15]

This study prescribes policies of zero population growth and

[15] Associated Press dispatch, November 14, 1974. On the American scene, the deterioration of Lake Erie apparently has been brought to a halt; its recovery is expected to take many years, however.

zero capital investment—that is, capital investment which just equals the rate of depreciation. The need to halt population growth seems incontrovertable. The wisdom of zero capital investment seems extremely dubious. It is a crude way to deal with the real problems. The effects of investment in the steel industry, for example, are very different from those of investment in education or scientific research. The former tends to increase pollution and consumption of non-renewable resources greatly; the latter consume and pollute relatively little and sometimes lead to long-term *reductions* in both of them.

Economic growth is not an evil in itself. The problems it raises are pollution, which can be minimized through applied technology, and depletion of non-renewable resources. The definitions of "non-renewable" and of "resources" have been changing regularly with the results of new research and development. There are limits to how far this can go, but we do not really know what they are.

Meadows *et al.* argue that capital, by its very nature, tends to increase exponentially. They then equate capital investment with increased pollution and resource depletion, and conclude that these too have an inherent tendency to increase exponentially. While they may do so at the early stages of industrialization, there is no evidence of an inseparable link. In fact there is evidence to the contrary.

As Bell and others have pointed out, one of the most basic patterns in the evolution of advanced Industrial society is a shift in emphasis from production of material goods to the service sector and "knowledge industry." Consumption of physical resources becomes a progressively less important component of economic growth. For example, according to Meadows *et al.*, the consumption of steel in the United States has been roughly level since 1950. Although economic growth continued to rise sharply, the production and consumption of this basic industrial product stopped growing at an exponential rate. It remains at a high absolute level. This level could be reduced greatly through computerization, miniaturization, recycling, and more efficient design, but this would require *additional* investment. The early computers were enormous, room-sized things; a small portable computer of the current generation can perform the same functions faster, using far less material and far less power. The need is to halt the growth of pollution and non-renewable resource consumption, not capital investment *per se*. There is rather widespread agreement among both critics and defenders of *The Limits* that zero economic growth is neither necessary nor desirable; the question is what *kind* of growth should be encouraged.

In addition to the other criticisms, Boyle has detected an error in the computer program on which *The Limits*' projections were based.[16] As a consequence of this error, the model greatly over-estimates the difficulty of handling pollution problems at higher levels of industrialization. Since each of the key variables affects the others, reducing the projected impact of pollution makes it easier to cope with other problems as well. A revised model produces substantially different (and less alarming) results. The error detected by Boyle has been seized upon as justification to dismiss *The Limits* as sheer alarmism. It is not, as Boyle would almost certainly agree.

In a reply to Boyle, Meadows and Meadows acknowledged that the error did exist but argued that it does not alter their conclusions in any way.[17] This seems a slight over-statement, but the authors are correct in a broad sense: like the original models, Boyle's modified model points to eventual collapse, but it would come a good deal later than anticipated (as a result of resource depletion).

A technological solution to population growth is at hand; whether or not it will be applied depends on socio-political factors. Action is urgent. Unless birth control techniques are made universally available and their use encouraged, world population will roughly double by the year 2000; even if births fall to the replacement level at that point, population would continue to grow for several decades. It would be an open question whether such masses could *ever* attain a decent standard of living. On the other hand, if population growth is controlled soon enough, food consumption should become manageable. Here again, the problems would be socio-political rather than matters of inexorable trends. Pollution does not appear to be nearly as intractable a problem as had been anticipated. It will require concerted effort, but seems capable of mastery if the appropriate technology is brought to bear.

The one apparently insurmountable limit lies in the depletion of non-renewable resources. This problem may be divided into two areas: energy; and other resources, chiefly metals. The former

[16] See Thomas J. Boyle, "Hope for the Technological Solution," *Nature*, 245, 1 (September 21, 1973), 127–128. This error had already been eliminated in subsequent work by Meadows *et al.*, *Limits to Growth*.

[17] Dennis Meadows and Donella Meadows, "Typographical Errors and Technological Solutions," *Nature*, 247, 5436 (January 11, 1974), 91–98.

is immediately urgent. The crucial question for the next several decades will be whether such techniques as nuclear fusion and solar energy can be put into widespread use before fossil fuels become so scarce that there is general Industrial collapse. If mankind wins this race, sufficient energy would be available for the indefinite future.

On the other hand, metal shortages are not immediately urgent, but there is no foreseeable long-term remedy to their depletion. Significant amounts become non-recoverable each year and there is a finite supply on this planet. It seems likely that mankind will eventually be able to make use of metals from the Moon and other planets, but the relevant research has only begun.[18] Extra-terrestrial resources are, quite understandably, excluded from present estimates. Consequently, *any* current projection of the future of Industrial society eventually points to collapse, and it will come much sooner than one would expect on the basis of past experience.

The Limits may be inaccurate on various points, but it emphasizes crucial facts. One of them is that a society's response to environmental changes entails considerable delay. Policy changes tend to come only when a problem's symptoms have become grossly manifest, and the *effects* of changes in such things as population policy or measures against resource depletion do not begin to reverse the trend until considerable time has passed. In the former case, the lag is apt to be one of several decades. This time lag can be extremely costly. The costs can be avoided by planning far enough ahead so that policy changes are made *before* the symptoms become urgent. Both Western and non-Western governments show a dismaying tendency to do the very opposite. One response of the Nixon Administration to economic difficulty was to *curtail* the funding of basic research. Similarly, in the face of food shortages, the government of India *reduced* the budget for

---

[18] Gerard O'Neill, a physicist at Princeton University, concludes that with technology now available, it would be possible to construct permanently inhabited colonies in space, utilizing materials mined from the moon for the most part. Designed as a manufacturing facility, such a colony would also operate a huge solar power plant that would transmit large amounts of power to earth in the form of microwaves. According to O'Neill, it would be a profitable investment, and could be completed within the next fifteen to twenty-five years. For an interesting account of this project, written for the layman, see O'Neill, "Colonies in Orbit," *New York Times Magazine,* January 18, 1976, 10–11.

birth control programs in the mid-1970's. Such short-term savings can have staggering long-term costs.

The Limits' critics have demonstrated that some of its assumptions are questionable, they have corrected it on important details, and have subjected it to some rather clever ridicule. But they have not demonstrated that its basic premises are false. It is a question of when, not whether, physical growth must come to a halt.

That this planet's resources are finite is undeniable. That we will eventually use up the non-renewable ones is equally axiomatic. That we will use them up much sooner than one expects, if their use continues to rise on an exponential curve, is perhaps the most important point the study makes. For the process is counter-intuitive: past experience is *not* a reliable guide to future conditions on an exponential curve. Its numerous illustrations of this fact, by themselves, make the book valuable: the principle is simple, but its implications run counter to deeply established habits of thought.

We must be prepared to consider a variety of contingencies, including the very bleak. Let us assume, for the moment, that it were necessary to adopt something similar to the "Sustainable State" which Meadows urges. What are its social implications?

If a value shift of the type described in this book is indeed going on, it should ease the transition to the kind of society Meadows envisions. Only among the young do the Post-Materialists come close to equalling the Materialists in numbers. But by the end of this century, Post-Materialists might constitute a large share of the population of Western nations, and they would be concentrated among the most active and influential sectors of society. They would probably be much less numerous in the developing nations, but value change in already developed societies will be more crucial in some respects. The primary requirement for the developing nations will be that they halt population growth—something they will need to do in any case in almost any conceivable future. At the same time, they will experience a rise in material welfare. The people of the already developed societies, on the other hand, will be called upon not only to renounce further material gains but also to accept a *downward* shift in material consumption. Findings cited in Chapter 5 suggest that subjective life satisfaction depends on the *changes* one experiences, at least as much as on any given absolute level of material welfare. During transition, the peoples of industrialized nations will experience the greater subjective deprivation, even though their objective standard of living may still be higher than that of other peoples. Our findings imply that this is a "short-term" situation, one which will last only a matter of decades. For the long run, it appears that human beings can be about equally happy with a modest or a lavish standard of material consumption.

But the transitional decades would be crucial. Will the peoples of economically developed nations tolerate the sacrifices that would be demanded? Insofar as they are Post-Materialists, they might. For material consumption is not the only thing valued by human beings, and for the Post-Materialists, it takes a lower priority than certain other values. The Post-Materialists might find compensation for diminished material consumption in a greater sense of social solidarity and the feeling that they were doing something worthwhile and meaningful. But can the Post-Materialist mentality itself survive a downward shift in material standards? For the short run, the answer appears to be "yes." The distribution of value types was remarkably stable from early 1970 to late 1976 despite the most severe recession since the 1930's. As we saw in Chapter 4, the recession eroded Post-Materialism among the very young but this effect was offset by population replacement among older groups.

We need not assume that the numbers of Post-Materialists would necessarily dwindle in response to a moderate decline in material consumption. The evolution of this value type is probably linked with the presence of economic and physical *security* during formative years rather than with a given economic *level*. A sense of security is more likely if the level is high, but things could conceivably be so arranged that a sense of security would be maintained even in the face of a declining level. It would not, by any means, be easy. Comprehensive social welfare programs would help, but there also would have to be strong feelings of assurance that the downward movement would halt within tolerable limits. To maintain such assurance appears difficult, but not theoretically impossible.

During this transition, Materialists and Mixed types would still be numerous in the most developed nations, and they would be called upon to accept sacrifices in a top priority domain. A sense of humanitarian solidarity would probably not be perceived as adequate compensation. To berate them for their narrow, selfish attitudes would probably only intensify hostility to the plan; from their perspective, they woud be giving up much and getting little in return. One alternative would be repression of the Materialists through physical or social coercion. This could become extremely costly and therefore counter-productive. Another alternative would be an appeal to the Materialist emphasis on physical security needs, arguing that the poorer nations may attack the rich unless the plan is adopted. This too seems apt to backfire. A predictable response would be increased emphasis on military capabilities among nations that already have horrendously powerful means of destruction. Still another alternative would be the relaxation of one policy implied in Meadows' program. Instead of aiming at an even distribution of consumption, one might allow material standards to remain somewhat higher in the already developed regions than in those that are now relatively poor. This introduces an undesirable complexity. The simplicity and elegance of quantitative equality would be sacrificed, opening the door to debate over precisely *how much* difference should be allowed. But if the subjective costs of moving down are greater than those of moving up, this fact should be recognized in our planning.

The process of value change discussed here does not provide any easy solution to the social problems implicit in Meadows' recommendations. But it would facilitate their acceptance. An important and articulate minority among Western publics would probably support such a plan today if the need were demonstrated; and that minority may be growing.

There are some bleaker implications of the Meadows' analysis that need to be stated bluntly.

The Anti-Industrial mysticism of Theodore Roszak might look like a polar opposite to the sober calculations of Meadows *et al.*, but one must see things from the former perspective in order to fully understand the social impact of the Meadows study. There seem to be many who believe that Meadows will build a New Jerusalem, an equilibrium with Nature in which mankind can live as it was in the beginning and (after appropriate changes) will and ever shall be. They have not read the fine print. Meadows' Utopia leads to collapse.

Adopting Meadows' Stabilized World Model might stave off disaster, possibly for as much as a couple of centuries, but it too leads to certain doom if we take his assumptions at face value. Meadows *et al.* do not conceal this fact, but they pass over it rather lightly with the assumption that most people's concerns extend as far in time as the lifetime of their own children and probably no farther. There is an implicit but quite incongruous callousness about the fate of our great-great-grandchildren. We *do* care about what happens to humanity remote in time, as well as those remote in space. The awareness that all our careful policies and sacrifices would only lead to precisely that disaster they were designed to avert would surely have a negative effect on the morale of those living in the Sustainable State, undermining the cooperative efforts that would be needed.

The Sustainable State implies a number of more immediate problems. They will be stated briefly, because they are part of a familiar pattern. The basic principle might be put as follows: the strong tend to get more of any desired commodity than the weak; and the scarcer it is the more they tend to monopolize it. Thus, the rich may drink no more water than the poor, but they consume a great deal more French wine. Income tends to be very unevenly distributed in poor countries. With few exceptions, they have a few very rich people and many very poor ones with relatively few in between. Income distribution remains unequal in rich countries, but they tend to have a much larger middle class.

The analogy might be transposed to the international scene. Historically, the usual pattern has been to plunder one's defeated enemies. Only recently and only on the part of relatively prosperous countries, has the victor begun to give economic aid to the defeated. Today nearly all of the more developed countries provide at least small amounts of foreign aid to poorer countries. The amount is far from generous, but it represents an historical change. The Meadows program calls upon the more developed nations to make really large transfers of capital while reducing their material standard of living. The latter would probably undermine the former.

Furthermore, while this program might maximize the welfare of humanity as a *whole*, it offers the developed nations little concrete return. Industrializing the less developed countries would tend to produce more pollution and resource consumption, not less, and in the short run, might even accelerate population growth by relieving starvation. It is far from evident that the developed nations would participate voluntarily.

Very well, let us think the unthinkable. One solution would be to *force* them to participate. But here we face a dilemma which goes beyond the fact that the rich nations are better armed. It is difficult to imagine anything more prodigiously wasteful of non-renewable resources and destructive of the environment—not to mention humanity—than thermonuclear war. After it were over, it is questionable whether the developed world would still have the capital for development which the war was fought about. Unless one does not care whether the cure is worse than the disease, the solution would have to come non-coercively.

In short, while the program resolutely and rigidly rejects any form of technological optimism, it is founded on an immense social optimism.

This optimism is not necessarily groundless. Very little is beyond the reach of human ingenuity and faith. Most people are neither swine nor mad dogs; they have minds and consciences and if one appeals to them reasonably, unflaggingly, and in a spirit of love, they may well respond. But the program seems to reflect a Post-Materialist mentality which takes it for granted that all will be equally ready to give economic gains a low priority. Evidence in the preceding chapter suggests that there *is* a trend toward a broader, less parochial sense of identity in the West. There may be enough people in the world who are willing to work toward global cooperation that it could become a reality. We have seen enough unbelievably horrible things throughout history to know that we have no guarantee.

The grounds for optimism become much more solid if one is willing to abandon the principle of zero capital investment. This assumption provides a handy way to tie the model together, but it is the main source of the zero-sum tendencies we have just discussed. Unless one views economic growth as an evil in itself, there seems to be no compelling reason why Western economies could not continue to expand for some time—perhaps until the process of value change brought them to a spontaneous halt. Such expansion would need to take place within a framework of rational policies, which is the goal Meadows *et al.* are really seeking. But there is no reason to believe that even the most hardened Materialist would be unwilling to heat his home with solar energy rather than natural gas if the price structure made it attractive; nor does the public view a fifty-pound tape recorder as inherently more desirable than a five-ounce instrument—versions of the latter have been developed that perform better and command a higher price than the former.

The authors of *The Limits to Growth* have made an important contribution to the analysis of crucial problems facing mankind. Their model is the basis for a guess about the future, but a guess that makes its assumptions precise and explicit and therefore available for criticism and improvement. Because they did this, Boyle was able to detect an error in their projections that might have gone undetected or merely been the basis for polemics in less rigorous modes of analysis. The authors have constructed a computer model of world trends over the next century and more. The effort deserves and has attained widespread recognition. But we must bear in mind what *kind* of projections this model provides.

They are based on a bet that there will be no more major breakthroughs. The authors assume that negative trends will continue full-throttle unless their prescription is adopted but that major positive innovations have come to an end.

The computer runs that they depict as highly optimistic allow some fairly large, positive one-shot increments, but they are always one-shot increments, never continuing trends. The only positive changes allowed for are ones that are already foreseeable. Nothing in the way of unexpected savings or continuing gains is built in. By leaving them out, the authors have made a major assumption.

In a sense, this strategy is reasonable. In any case, it is dictated by the method used. It would be virtually impossible to build into their model the effects of unforeseen technology. The authors acknowledge that they have included no such factor because they can see no hard evidence for it, and obviously neither can we. If it were demonstrable and foreseeable, it would not be an innovative breakthrough. Nevertheless, we would be willing to bet heavily that creative scientists, engineers, planners, and policy-makers will come up with a great many useful things which cannot be foreseen at the moment. This is only a guess. Meadows *et al.* would dismiss it as blind technological optimism, and they have a right to do so. Their position is, "We favor taking lesser risks in the conduct of human affairs. We cannot bring ourselves to stake the future of our society on technology which has not yet been invented, and of which we cannot evaluate the secondary effects."[19] In keeping with this outlook, the authors' conclusions err on the side of conservatism—or prudence. A more recent Club of Rome study has a distinctly more optimistic tone.[20]

[19] Meadows and Meadows in *Quelles Limites?*, 54 (author's translation).
[20] See Mihajlo Mesarovic and Eduard Pestel, *Mankind at the Turning Point* (New York: Dutton, 1974).

A responsible person *must* consider the possibility that, in the physical world, all of the great discoveries already have been made. The consequences of being caught unprepared are too grave to ignore, and *The Limits to Growth* helps us prepare for such a contingency. On the other hand, it is important to remember that it is not (and does not pretend to be) a forecast of the future based on privileged knowledge. It is an educated guess based on a bet against human ingenuity. Its value lies not in any specific projection, but in its demonstration that present patterns of behavior could have disastrous consequences; that these consequences tend to be systematically underestimated; and that humanity must take corrective measures in advance or pay staggering costs. *The Limits* is not a prophecy except in the sense of one that is intended to be self-denying. It projects a set of pessimistic but conceivable outcomes that *could* occur if policy continues to be made with its present disregard for the future.

Western politicians tend to be pragmatic men. By a process of selection and socialization, they learn to focus on immediate problems. For them the very long run may mean anything beyond the next election. A strategy of muddling through may have worked fairly well as long as mankind's impact on the planet was narrowly limited in space and time, but these conditions no longer prevail. The ratio between natural processes and human processes has shifted to a point where we can no longer depend on the invisible hand of Nature to take care of our mistakes, and the rate of change has accelerated to a point where we must look much farther ahead than ever before.

The year before the Arab oil embargo, President Nixon strongly opposed a major program of basic energy research: it seemed to offer only a long-range payoff. With the short-sighted "realism" for which he became famous, Nixon helped cross it off the national agenda. A little later, when the energy crisis became acute, he suddenly began urging the need for "Project Independence," a program to make America self-sufficient in its energy needs by 1980. It, of course, included accelerated basic energy research.

But conservatives do not have a monopoly on this kind of thinking. Manned space research has become a liberal *bête noire*. Following the shock of Sputnik, President Kennedy made it a high national priority to reach the moon before the 1970's. It was partly foolish nationalism; and partly because Kennedy wanted to get this country "moving again" and knew that to do so you have to capture people's imaginations; and perhaps partly because Kennedy was a person who needed to aim high. But the follow-through to Project Apollo has withered in the face of slogans such as: "We can put a man on the moon but our cities are uninhabitable." The slogan is based on a false syllogism. The Apollo program took roughly one-third of 1 percent of our Gross National Product; clearly, it was not an either/or choice. But quite apart from this fact, it was never a choice between pure research and social needs.

The benefits from Apollo have only begun to be realized, but it already seems to be giving a better social return than many programs expressly designed to promote social welfare. The manned space program has led to major developments in the fields of medicine, food preservation, non-flammable fabrics, cheaper, more efficient home building, improved computers and pollution control. Such technological spin-offs probably have paid for the program already, and the returns will continue for many years. But even without them, the Apollo program might have justified itself through the fact that it has probably saved thousands of lives by contributing to more effective hurricane tracking. In the long run, not only our cities but also our planet are likely to become uninhabitable if we fail to carry out long-range planning, research and development. And manned space research tends to develop precisely the kind of technology we will need to live on Spaceship Earth. It requires an intense focus on living in a finite self-contained environment. It puts an immense premium on recycling of materials, miniaturization of equipment, and the development of self-replenishing energy sources such as solar power. It also gives a concrete focus to the kind of long-range research effort that needs to be carried on in a steady and rational fashion—not something to be abandoned now and relaunched as a desperate crash program when it seems too late.

Given wise policies and continuing technological progress, this planet probably has adequate resources to enable Industrial civilization to flourish for many centuries.[21] But eventually, the survival

---

[21] The prerequisites seem to be: zero-growth population policies, development of nuclear fusion and solar energy sources, and the adoption of strong policies to minimize pollution, soil erosion, and depletion of other resources. We suggested above that the last item may provide the most intractable long-term constraint. Certain metals such as copper may become scarce in the near future; on the other hand, with a plentiful energy supply, aluminum should be available for a very long time; it can be made from clay.

of civilized humanity may depend on our ability to reach some of the billions of other planets in the universe. Inter-stellar travel is an undertaking that utterly dwarfs the moon voyages, but in the very long run it will be a matter of survival.

But there is another quite different reason for space research. Along with the survival needs, humanity has always needed great projects. The thirst for knowledge and beauty, the need to outdo oneself, are inherent in man's makeup. To be healthy, mankind must fulfill *both* types of needs. Apollo was one of the rare events in history that was a source of pride to humanity as a whole. When Neil Armstrong set foot on the moon in 1969, it was a "giant step for mankind," but at the same time, it gave us all a new perspective on our common home. Armstrong recalls, "It suddenly struck me that that tiny pea, pretty and blue, was the earth. I put up my thumb and shut one eye, and my thumb blotted out the planet Earth. I didn't feel like a giant. I felt very, very small." Another astronaut put it: "You don't look down at the world as an American but as a human being."[22] Thompson wrote of the lift-off of Apollo 17, "You threw away anxiety and lept up with the sheer joy of knowing that men were turning the tables on the heavens and riding that comet out of the earth. . . . One could write on the rocket as the anonymous stonemasons did on Medieval cathedrals: Adam made me."[23] Thompson was describing the final Apollo flight, which took place in December, 1972. Nothing more is scheduled and the infra-structure it established is disintegrating. The exploration of the universe is obviously not the only great project for humanity as a whole, but it seems to be a logical and essential part of the human adventure. In the long run, the knowledge that civilized humanity was not simply doomed but would survive somewhere might have a crucial effect on the outlook of mankind.

For thousands of years man has looked up at the stars in wonder and awe, making myths about them and discoveries as wonderful as the myths. It seems inconceivable that humanity will ultimately settle back like an aging bourgeoisie, content to spend their days calculating how they can eke out the capital inherited from the past. Long before the Sputnik, man resolved to reach the stars through difficulties.

[22] Cited in *Newsweek*, December 11, 1972, 68.
[23] Cited in *Time*, January 1, 1973, 50–51.

The changing values and skills of Western publics present alarming aspects. We seem to be witnessing a weakening of institutional restraints, a diminishing reliance on functional rationality and its chief tool, technology—to some extent, even a rejection of them. These trends are alarming because in excess they would be disastrous.

But it seems to me that the process represents a redressment of the balance rather than the breakdown of society. The Industrial era was a time for the development of great means. Post-Industrial society may provide a time for the application of these means to great ends.

I have set thee at the world's center, to observe whatever is in the world. I have made thee neither of heaven nor of earth, neither mortal nor immortal, so that thou mayest with greater freedom of choice and with more honor, as though the maker and moulder of thyself, fashion thyself in whatever shape thou shalt prefer. Thou shalt have the power to degenerate into the lower forms of life, which are animal; thou shalt have the power, out of thy soul's judgement, to be reborn into the higher forms of life, which are divine.—God at the Creation of Man; Pico della Mirandola, *Oratio de Hominis Dignatae*, 1486.

Appendices

APPENDIX A[1]

European Community Survey, 1973

T HE following questionnaire was administered to representative national samples of the publics of the nine nations of the newly-expanded European Community in September/October, 1973. The questionnaire was designed by Jacques-René Rabier in collaboration with Helène Riffault, Robert Gijs and the author. Variable number 1 is nationality, coded as follows:

1 France
2 Belgium
3 Netherlands
4 West Germany
5 Italy
6 Luxembourg
7 Denmark
8 Ireland
9 Great Britain

Variable 2 is interview number. Variable 3 is country-specific, indicating study number or interviewer districts. The interview was started with the question: "What problems are preoccupying you most at the present time?" Responses to this item were not coded. The next question was: "More precisely, I would like to ask you how you regard certain aspects of your present situation. I will *read out* a number of aspects and for each of them I would like you to say whether you are very satisfied, fairly satisfied, not very satisfied, or not at all satisfied.

V4 The house, flat or place you live in:
    1 Very satisfied
    2 Fairly satisfied

---

[1] Nearly all of the survey data used in this book are available from the Inter-University Consortium for Political Research, P.O. Box 1248, Ann Arbor, Michigan, 48106 or from the Belgian Archive for the Social Sciences, Leuven, Belgium. Questionnaires for the two surveys which we have used most heavily are reproduced here. For the convenience of potential users, the variable number from the ICPR codebook appears at the left of each question. A SETUPS teaching unit by Charles Taylor, based on the 1973 data, is available from the American Political Science Association.

    3 Not very satisfied
    4 Not at all satisfied
    0 Not ascertained

V5 Your income:
    1 Very satisfied
    2 Fairly satisfied
    3 Not very satisfied
    4 Not at all satisfied
    0 Not ascertained

V6 Your work as a housewife or on the job:
    1 Very satisfied
    2 Fairly satisfied
    3 Not very satisfied
    4 Not at all satisfied
    0 Not ascertained

V7 Education for children:
    1 Very satisfied
    2 Fairly satisfied
    3 Not very satisfied
    4 Not at all satisfied
    0 Not ascertained

V8 Your leisure (spare time):
    1 Very satisfied
    2 Fairly satisfied
    3 Not very satisfied
    4 Not at all satisfied
    0 Not ascertained

V9 The social welfare benefits you would receive if you became ill or unable to work:
    1 Very satisfied
    2 Fairly satisfied
    3 Not very satisfied
    4 Not at all satisfied
    0 Not ascertained

V10 In general terms, your relations with others:
    1 Very satisfied
    2 Fairly satisfied
    3 Not very satisfied
    4 Not at all satisfied
    0 Not ascertained

A few more areas of interest. Are you very satisfied, fairly satisfied, not very satisfied, not at all satisfied with: (Read out)

V11 The kind of society in which we live in (R's country) today:
   1 Very satisfied
   2 Fairly satisfied
   3 Not very satisfied
   4 Not at all satisfied
   0 Not ascertained

V12 Relations between the generations:
   1 Very satisfied
   2 Fairly satisfied
   3 Not very satisfied
   4 Not at all satisfied
   0 Not ascertained

V13 The way democracy is functioning in (R's country):
   1 Very satisfied
   2 Fairly satisfied
   3 Not very satisfied
   4 Not at all satisfied
   0 Not ascertained

V14 On the whole, are you very satisfied, fairly satisfied, not very satisfied, or not at all satisfied with the life you lead?
   1 Very satisfied
   2 Fairly satisfied
   3 Not very satisfied
   4 Not at all satisfied
   0 Not ascertained

V15 If you think back to your life 5 years ago, would you say that you are:
   1 More satisfied now than you were 5 years ago
   2 Less satisfied
   3 No change
   0 Don't know/no reply
   9 (Great Britain: additional missing data code)

V16 Do you think that your everyday conditions will improve over the next five years or not? *If yes*: Can you say whether they will improve a lot or a little?
   1 Yes, a lot
   2 Yes, a little

3 No, will not

0 Don't know/no reply

9 (Great Britain, France: additional missing data code)

V17 Do you think, generally speaking, that people give you the respect which you deserve, or not?

1 Yes

2 No

0 Don't know/no reply

9 (France, Great Britain: additional missing data code)

3 Wild code—Denmark

4 Wild code—Denmark

Now I would like to ask you something about the things which seem to you personally most important if you are looking for a job.

V18 *Show CARD A*: Here are some of the things people usually take into account in relation to their work. Which one would you personally place first?

1 A good salary so that you do not have any worries about money

2 A safe job with no risk of closing down or unemployment

3 Working with people you like

4 Doing an important job which gives you a feeling of accomplishment

0 Not ascertained

V19 And which next?

1 A good salary so that you do not have any worries about money

2 A safe job with no risk of closing down or unemployment

3 Working with people you like

4 Doing an important job which gives you a feeling of accomplishment

0 Not ascertained

V20 At the present time they are discussing in the press, on radio and TV about the future of our society—and especially about the protection of the environment. Have you read or heard anything about this?

1 Yes

2 No

0 Don't know

9 (Ireland, Great Britain: additional missing data code)

V21 *If Yes*: From your own personal point of view, does this debate seem to you:
  1 Very important
  2 Important
  3 Not very important
  4 Not important at all
  0 Don't know/no reply
  9 Inap., coded 2, 0 in V20
V22 Do you think that if things are not going well in (R's country) people like yourself can help to bring about a change for the better, or not?
  1 Yes, can
  2 No, cannot
  0 Don't know/no reply
  9 (France, Great Britain: additional missing data code)

There is a lot of talk these days about what the aims of this country should be for the next 10 years.

V23 *Show CARD B*: On this card are listed some of the goals which different people would give top priority. Would you please say which of these you, yourself, consider the most important?
  1 Maintaining a high level of economic growth
  2 Making sure that this country has strong defense forces
  3 Seeing that people have more to say about how things are done at their jobs and in their communities
  4 Trying to make our cities and countryside more beautiful
  0 Not ascertained
  9 Undoc. code—Belgium
V24 And which would be the next most important?
  1 Maintaining a high level of economic growth
  2 Making sure that this country has strong defense forces
  3 Seeing that people have more to say about how things are done at their jobs and in their communities
  4 Trying to make our cities and countryside more beautiful
  0 Not ascertained
V25 *Show CARD C*: If you had to choose, which one of the things on this card would you say is most desirable?
  1 Maintaining order in the nation
  2 Give the people more say in important governmental decisions

3 Fighting rising prices
4 Protecting freedom of speech
0 Not ascertained

V26 And what would be your second choice?
1 Maintaining order in the nation
2 Give the people more say in important governmental decisions
3 Fighting rising prices
4 Protecting freedom of speech
0 Not ascertained

V27 Here is another list (Show CARD D). In your opinion, which one of these is most important?
1 A stable economy
2 Progress toward a less impersonal and more humane society
3 Progress toward a society in which ideas count more than money
4 The fight against crime
0 Not ascertained

V28 And what would be your second choice?
1 A stable economy
2 Progress toward a less impersonal and more humane society
3 Progress toward a society in which ideas count more than money
4 The fight against crime
0 Not ascertained

V29 Now would you look again at all of the goals listed on these three cards together (show CARDS B, C, D) and tell me which one you think is the *most* desirable of all? Just read off the letter of the one you choose.
00 Economic growth
01 Strong defense
02 Seeing that people have more to say
03 More beautiful cities and countryside
04 Maintaining order
05 More say in government
06 Fighting rising prices
07 Freedom of speech
08 Stable economy
09 Fighting crime

10 Humane society
11 Ideas count
99 Don't know/not ascertained

V30 And which is the next most desirable?
00 Economic growth
01 Strong defense
02 See that people have more to say
03 More beautiful cities and countryside
04 Maintaining order
05 More to say in government
06 Fighting rising prices
07 Freedom of speech
08 Stable economy
09 Fight crime
10 Humane society
11 Ideas count
99 Don't know

V31 And which one of all the aims on these cards is *least important* from your point of view? Just read off the letter of the one you choose.
00 Economic growth
01 Strong defense
02 See that people have more to say
03 More beautiful cities and countryside
04 Maintaining order
05 More say in government
06 Fighting rising prices
07 Freedom of speech
08 Stable economy
09 Fight crime
10 Humane society
11 Ideas count
99 Don't know

V32 To which one of the following geographical groups would you say you belong to first of all?
1 The locality or town where you live
2 The region or county where you live
3 (R's country) as a whole
4 Europe
5 The world as a whole
0 Don't know/no reply

9 (Denmark, Ireland, France, Britain: additional missing data code)

V33 And the next? (Show CARD E indicating the groups)
1 The locality or town where you live
2 The region or province where you live
3 (R's country) as a whole
4 Europe
5 The world as a whole
0 Don't know/no reply
9 (Denmark, Ireland, France, Britain: additional missing data code)

V34 Have you been abroad in the past 5 years?
1 Yes
2 No
0 No reply
9 (France, Britain: additional missing data code)

V35 *If Yes*: How long did you stay on your last visit?
1 Less than a week
2 1–4 weeks
3 More than 4 weeks
0 No reply
9 Inap., coded 0, 2 in V34

V36 Are you personally very interested, a little interested, or not at all interested in the problems of the European Community —that is, the Common Market?
1 Very interested
2 A little interested
3 Not at all interested
0 Don't know/no reply
9 (France, Britain: additional missing data code)

V37 Do you think that you are sufficiently well informed, or not sufficiently well informed, about the problems of the European Community—that is, the Common Market?
1 Sufficiently well informed
2 Not sufficiently well informed
0 Don't know/no reply
9 (France, Britain: additional missing data code)

V38 There is not always time to read everything of interest. When you see in your newspaper, or in any other publication, an article about the European Community, do you read it almost always, from time to time, or never?

1 Almost always
2 From time to time
3 Never
0 Don't know/no reply
9 (France, Britain: additional missing data code)
V39 And on television, when there is a programme about the European Community, do you watch it almost always, from time to time, or never?
1 Almost always
2 From time to time
3 Never
0 Don't know/no reply
9 (Ireland, France, Britain: additional missing data code)
V40 With regard to the information about the European Community issued by the press, radio and television, how would you rate the information that is given? (Show CARD F).
1 Too little
2 Too much
0 Not ascertained
V41 Information rating with regard to the information about the European Community issued by the press, radio and television, how would you rate the information that is given?
1 Simple
2 Complicated
0 Not ascertained
V42 Information rating with regard to the information about the European Community issued by the press, radio and television, how would you rate the information that is given?
1 Not interesting
2 Interesting
0 Not ascertained
V43 Information rating with regard to the information about the European Community issued by the press, radio and television, how would you rate the information that is given?
1 Useful
2 Not useful
0 Not ascertained
V44 Information rating with regard to the information about the European Community issued by the press, radio and television, how would you rate the information that is given?
1 Mainly good news

    2 Mainly bad news
    0 Not ascertained

V45 Information rating with regard to the information about the
     European Community issued by the press, radio and tele-
     vision, how would you rate the information that is given?
     1 Biased
     2 Not biased
     0 Not ascertained
     9 (Denmark: additional missing data code)

V46 In a general way, would you rather have more short news
     topics about European affairs, or would you rather have
     more in depth reports and articles on European affairs?
     1 More short news topics
     2 More in depth reports or articles
     0 Don't know/no reply
     9 (Ireland, France, Britain: additional missing data code)

V47 As you know, several countries have recently joined the
     Common Market, i.e., the European Community. Can you
     tell me which countries they are? Any others? (Give contact
     time to think. Do NOT prompt—mark a code for each
     country.)
     Great Britain/UK/England mentions
     1 Named
     2 Not named
     0 Not ascertained

V48 Ireland mentions (question above)
     1 Named
     2 Not named
     0 Not ascertained

V49 Denmark mentions (question above)
     1 Named
     2 Not named
     0 Not ascertained

V50 Other countries mentioned (question above)
     1 Named
     2 Not named
     0 Not ascertained
     9 Undoc. code—Ireland, Denmark

V51 And can you name some of the countries which were already
     members of the Common Market before these new countries
     joined? (Give contact time to think. Do Not prompt—mark
     a code for each country.)

Germany mentions
1 Named
2 Not named
0 Not ascertained
V52 Belgium mentions (question above)
1 Named
2 Not named
0 Not ascertained
V53 France mentions
1 Named
2 Not named
0 Not ascertained
V54 Italy mentions
1 Named
2 Not named
0 Not ascertained
V55 Luxembourg mentions
1 Named
2 Not named
0 Not ascertained
V56 Holland/Netherlands mentions
1 Named
2 Not named
0 Not ascertained
V57 Other countries mentions
1 Named
2 Not named
4 Wild code—Netherlands
0 Not ascertained
V58 Generally speaking, do you think that (R's country) membership in the Common Market is a good thing, a bad thing, or neither good nor bad?
1 Good thing
2 Bad thing
3 Neither good nor bad
0 Don't know/no reply
9 (Ireland, France, Britain: additional missing data code)
V59 *And for you personally*, do you think that (R's country) membership is a good thing, a bad thing, or is neither good nor bad?
1 Good thing
2 Bad thing

3 Neither good nor bad

0 Don't know/no reply

9 (Ireland, France, Britain: additional missing data code)

V60 If you were to be told tomorrow that the Common Market had been scrapped, would you be very sorry about it, indifferent, or relieved?

1 Very sorry

2 Indifferent

3 Relieved

0 Don't know/no reply

9 (France, Britain: additional missing data code)

V61 Are you, yourself, for or against the Common Market developing into a political European union? If for or against: How strongly do you feel about it?

1 Completely favor

2 Favor on the whole

3 Disagree in general

4 Disagree completely

0 Don't know/no reply

9 (France, Britain: additional missing data code)

V62 Are you for or against the election of a European parliament by a popular vote of all the citizens in the member states of the European Community?

1 Completely favor

2 Favor on the whole

3 Disagree in general

4 Disagree completely

0 Don't know/no reply

9 (France, Britain: additional missing data code)

V63 Some people say that, in a united Europe, the various nations might lose their culture and their individuality. Do you agree or disagree with this view? A lot or a little?

1 Yes, agree a lot

2 Yes, agree a little

3 No, disagree a little

4 No, disagree a lot

0 Don't know/no reply

9 (France, Britain: additional missing data code)

V64 *Show CARD G*: Here are a few problems that are much debated at the present time. Could you tell me what are the *three problems* from this list you, yourself, consider the most important? (Mark one only in each column)

FIRST PROBLEM MENTIONED

01 Pollution of the environment
02 Military defense
03 Scientific research
04 Investments by foreign firms in (R's country)
05 Drug addiction
06 Economic growth
07 Major political negotiations with the Americans, the Russians, etc.
08 Poverty and unemployment
09 Aid to underdeveloped countries
00 Rising prices
99 Not ascertained

V65 SECOND PROBLEM MENTIONED (question as above)

01 Pollution of the environment
02 Military defense
03 Scientific research
04 Investments by foreign firms in (R's country)
05 Drug addiction
06 Economic growth
07 Major political negotiations with the Americans, the Russians, etc.
08 Poverty and unemployment
09 Aid to underdeveloped countries
00 Rising prices
99 Not ascertained

V66 THIRD PROBLEM MENTIONED

Same list as for V64, V65

V67 For each of the problems I am going to mention, would you say they would be better dealt with by a European Government or by an (R's country) government? (read out—mark a code for each item)

Pollution of the environment

1 R's government
2 European government
0 Not ascertained
9 (France: additional missing data code)

V68 Military defense

1 R's government
2 European government
0 Not ascertained
9 (France: additional missing data code)

V69 Scientific research
   1 R's government
   2 European government
   0 Not ascertained
   9 (France: additional missing data code)

V70 Investments by foreign firms in (R's country)
   1 R's government
   2 European government
   0 Not ascertained
   9 (France: additional missing data code)

V71 Drug addiction
   1 R's government
   2 European government
   0 Not ascertained
   9 (France: additional missing data code)

V72 Economic growth
   1 R's government
   2 European government
   0 Not ascertained
   9 (France: additional missing data code)

V73 Major political negotiations with the Americans, the Russians, etc.
   1 R's government
   2 European government
   0 Not ascertained

V74 Poverty and unemployment
   1 R's government
   2 European government
   0 Not ascertained

V75 Aid to underdeveloped countries
   1 R's government
   2 European government
   0 Not ascertained

V76 Rising prices
   1 R's government
   2 European government
   0 Not ascertained
   9 (Denmark: additional missing data code)
   3 Wild code—Denmark

V77 If one of the countries of the European Community finds itself in major economic difficulties, do you feel that the other countries, including (R's country) should help it or not?

1 Yes, should help
2 No, should not
0 Don't know/no reply
9 (France, Britain: additional missing data code)

V78 Would you, or would you not, be willing to make some personal sacrifices—for example, pay a little more taxes to help bring about the unification of Europe?
1 Very willing
2 Fairly willing
3 Not very willing
4 Not at all willing
0 Don't know/no reply
9 (France, Belgium, Britain: additional missing data code)

V79 *Show CARD H*: Here is a list of problems that the European Community is concerned with at present. For each item on this list, can you say whether in your view it is very important, fairly important, not very important, or not at all important?
Replacement of all member countries' currencies including the (R's country's currency) with a single European currency
1 Very important
2 Fairly important
3 Not very important
4 Not at all important
0 Not ascertained
9 (Belgium, France: additional missing data code)

V80 Reduction of the differences between developed regions and less developed regions of the member countries
1 Very important
2 Fairly important
3 Not very important
4 Not at all important
0 Not ascertained
9 (Belgium, France: additional missing data code)

V81 Co-ordination of the social policies of the member countries in the field of employment and job training
1 Very important
2 Fairly important
3 Not very important
4 Not at all important
0 Not ascertained
9 (France, Belgium: additional missing data code)

V82 Implementation of a common policy on energy supplies
1 Very important
2 Fairly important
3 Not very important
4 Not at all important
0 Not ascertained
9 (France, Belgium: additional missing data code)

V83 Modernization of European agriculture by encouraging the most productive farms and providing retraining for people who leave agriculture
1 Very important
2 Fairly important
3 Not very important
4 Not at all important
0 Not ascertained
9 (France, Belgium, Denmark: additional missing data code)

V84 Introduction of a common policy on aid to underdeveloped countries
1 Very important
2 Fairly important
3 Not very important
4 Not at all important
0 Not ascertained
9 (France, Belgium: additional missing data code)

V85 Achieving a common foreign policy
1 Very important
2 Fairly important
3 Not very important
4 Not at all important
0 Not ascertained
9 (France, Belgium, Denmark: additional missing data code)

V86 All things considered, are you in favor of the unification of Europe, against it, or are you indifferent? *If in favor or against*: Very much, or only somewhat?
1 Very much in favor
2 Somewhat in favor
3 Don't mind/indifferent
4 Somewhat against
5 Very much against
0 Don't know/no reply
9 (Ireland, France, Belgium, Britain: additional missing data code)

V87 From your own personal point of view, does this problem of European unification seem to you very important, important, not very important, or not at all important?
1 Very important
2 Important
3 Not very important
4 Not at all important
0 Don't know/no reply
9 (Ireland, France, Belgium, Britain: additional missing data code)

V88 As for the future, do you think the movement towards the unification of Europe should be speeded up, slowed down or continued as it is at present?
1 Speeded up
2 Continued as it is at present
3 Slowed down
0 Don't know/no reply
9 (Ireland, France, Britain: additional missing data code)

V89 In the future, for the unification of Europe, which of the following formulas are you more in favor of? (Show CARD I).
1 Create some sort of European Government to which each national government delegates a large part of its powers
2 Establish closer ties between the member states of the European Union but without a European Government
3 Maintain the degree of national independence
0 Don't know/no reply
9 (Ireland, France, Britain: additional missing data code)

V90 When you, yourself, hold a strong opinion, do you ever persuade your friends, relations, or fellow workers to adopt this opinion? *If Yes*: Does this happen often, from time to time, or rarely?
1 Often
2 From time to time
3 Rarely
4 Never
0 Don't know/no reply
9 (Ireland, France, Britain: additional missing data code)

V91 Some people are attracted to new things and new ideas, while others are more cautious about such things. What is your own attitude to what is new? (Read out)

1 Very much attracted
2 Attracted on the whole
3 It depends; varies
4 Cautious on the whole
5 Very cautious
0 Don't know/no reply
9 (Ireland, France, Britain: additional missing data code)

V92 When you get together with your friends, would you say that you discuss political matters frequently, occasionally, or never?
1 Frequently
2 Occasionally
3 Never
0 Not ascertained

V93 *If frequently or occasionally*: And which of the statements on this card (show CARD J) best describes the part you, yourself, take in these discussions?
1 Even though I have my own opinions, I usually just listen
2 Mostly I listen, but once in a while I express my opinions
3 I take an equal share in the conversation
4 I do more than just hold up my end in the conversation; I usually try to convince others that I am right
0 Not ascertained

V94 Have you ever discussed the Common Market or the unification of Europe with anyone else in (R's country) or abroad?
1 Yes
2 No
0 Don't know/no reply
9 (Ireland, France, Britain: additional missing data code)

V95 On the whole, do you feel that in forming a political opinion you can rely most on: the views of those who are close to you, such as family or friends; information from the press, radio and television; or statements by politicians? (Mark one only)
1 Views of those close to you
2 The press, radio and television
3 Statements by politicians
4 It depends
0 Don't know/no reply
9 (Ireland, France, Britain: additional missing data code)

V96 In political matters people talk of "the left" and "the right."

How would you place your views on this scale? (Show SCALE 1—do NOT prompt)
(The 10 boxes are not numbered. If the contact hesitates, mark on form and ask him to try again. Mark all refusals. For alternative contacts say "the right" first and then "the left.")

Left   Right

(If contact points to a line, then code him as choosing the nearest box to the right)
01 Left
02
03
04
05
06
07
08
09
10 Right
00 (Belgium, Luxembourg: additional missing data code)
99 Not ascertained
V97 R's response to V96
1 Replies without hesitation
2 Hesitates but replies
3 Refuses to reply
0 Not ascertained
V98 Generally speaking, do you feel closer to one of the (R's country) political parties than the others? *If Yes*: Which one?
IRELAND
01 No, not close to any party
02 Yes, Fainna Fail
03 Yes, Fine Gael
04 Yes, Labour
05 Yes (National, The Coalition)
06 Other party (state & code)
00 No answer/refused/DK
FRANCE
01 None
02 Communist
03 Socialist

V98 Political party (*cont.*)
  04 PSU
  05 Left Radicals
  06 Reform Movement
  07 Gaullists
  08 Other
  00 DK, NA
  99 Not ascertained
  BRITAIN
  01 None
  02 Conservative
  03 Labour
  04 Liberal
  05 Nationalist
  06 Other
  00 NA
  99 Not ascertained
  BELGIUM
  01 None
  02 Socialist
  03 Soc. Christian
  04 Liberal
  05 Volksunie
  06 Communist
  07 Other
  08 FDF/RW
  00 NA
  LUXEMBOURG
  01 None
  02 Socialist
  03 Chr. Social
  04 Dem. (Liberal)
  05 Soc. Democrats
  06 Communist
  07 Other
  00 NA
  GERMANY
  01 None
  02 Christian Dems.
  03 Social Democrats

04 Free Democrats
06 Undocumented code
00 NA
DENMARK
01 None
02 Social Dem.
03 Radical Lib.
04 Conservative
05 Liberal Dem.
06 Other
07 Socialist People's
08 Progress Party
00 NA
NETHERLANDS
01 Catholic
02 Labor
03 Liberal
04 AR
05 CHU
06 D'66
07 DS'70
08 PSP
09 PPR
10 Other
11 Communist
00 NA
99 DK
ITALY
01 Communist (L)
02 Socialist (L)
03 Social Democrat (L)
04 Republicans
05 Christian Democrat (R)
06 Liberal (R)
07 Neo-Fascist (R)
08 Other
00 DK, refused
V99 If there were a General Election tomorrow, which party would you give your first preference vote to? (Show CARD K)

V99 Political Party (*cont.*)
IRELAND
01 Fainna Fail
02 Fine Gael
03 Labour
04 Coalition (FG/Lab.)
05 Other party (state & code)
06 Cannot vote; too young
98 Don't know
00 Refuse to reply
99 Additional missing data code
FRANCE
01 Communist
02 Socialist
03 PSU
04 Left Radicals
05 Reform Movement
06 Gaullist
07 Other
08 Too young
98 DK
00 Refused
99 Additional missing data code
BRITAIN
01 Conservative
02 Labour
03 Liberal
04 Nationalist
05 Other
06 Too young
98 DK
00 Refused
99 Additional missing data code
BELGIUM
01 Soc. Christian
02 Liberal
03 Volksunie
04 Communist
05 Other
06 Too young

08 FDF/RW
10 Socialist
98 DK
00 Refused
LUXEMBOURG
01 Chr. Social
02 Dem. Liberal
03 Soc. Democrats
04 Communist
05 Other
06 Too young
10 Socialist
98 DK
00 Not ascertained
GERMANY
01 CDU
02 SPD
03 FDP
05 Other
06 Too young
98 DK
00 Not ascertained
DENMARK
01 Social Dem.
02 Radical Lib.
03 Conservative
04 Liberal Dem.
05 Other
06 Too young
08 Socialist People's
09 Fremskridts (Progress)
98 Don't know
00 Refused
NETHERLANDS
01 Catholics
02 Labor
03 Liberals
04 AR
05 Chr. Historical
06 D'66, PPR
07 DS'70

V99 Political Party (*cont.*)
   08 PSP
   09 Communist
   10 Other
   11 BP, NMP
   00 NA
   99 Additional missing data code
   ITALY
   01 Communist
   02 Socialist
   03 Social Democrat
   04 Republican
   05 Christian Dem.
   06 Liberal
   07 Neo-Fascist
   08 Other
   98 DK, refused
   00 Too young
V100 Do you belong to some religious denomination?
   IRELAND
   1 None
   2 Roman Catholic
   3 Other
   9 Not ascertained
   FRANCE; BELGIUM; LUXEMBOURG
   1 None
   2 Catholic
   3 Protestant
   4 Other
   0 NA
   9 France: additional missing data code
   NETHERLANDS
   1 No church persuasion
   2 Roman Catholic
   3 Dutch Reformed
   4 Reformed (Calvinist sect)
   5 Jewish
   6 Other religion
   0 NA, refused

DENMARK
1 None
2 (Den danske Folkekirke)
5 Roman Catholic
6 Other

GREAT BRITAIN
1 None
2 Church of England
3 Church of Scotland
4 Free Church; Non-Conformist
5 Roman Catholic
6 Other
9 Not ascertained

WEST GERMANY
1 None
2 Protestant
4 Free Church
5 Roman Catholic
6 Other

ITALY
1 Catholic
2 Protestant
3 Other
4 None
9 Not ascertained

V101 (Ask those stating a religion:) Do you go to religious services several times a week, once a week, sometimes during the year, or never at all?
1 Several times weekly
2 Once a week
3 Sometimes during the year
4 Never
0 Not ascertained
9 Did not state religion in V100

V102 Respondent has:
1 Full-time occupation (30 hours or more a week)
2 Part-time occupation (8–29 hours a week)
3 No paid occupation
0 Not ascertained

V103 Respondent is:
1 Head of household
2 Not head of household
0 Not ascertained

V104 Sex:
1 Male
2 Female
9 (Ireland, Britain: not ascertained)

V105 How old are you? (Write in exact age and code)
Exact age coded
99 Not ascertained

V106 Age—Bracketed
1 15–19
2 20–24
3 25–34
4 35–44
5 45–54
6 55–64
7 65 +
9 Not ascertained
NOTE: Sums of frequencies of exact age variable do not total frequencies of distribution of this variable.

V107 In which year were you born?
Last two digits of year of birth coded
99 Not ascertained

V108 Marital status:
1 Married
2 Single
3 Other (widowed, divorced, separated)
0 Not ascertained

V109 How many people are there in your household, including yourself and any children?
01 One person
02 Two people
etc.
10 10 people or not ascertained
00 Not ascertained

V110 How many of these are children under 18 years of age?
00 None
01 One

02 Two

etc.

10 Britain: 10 or not ascertained

99 Not ascertained

V111 Is the head of this household self-employed or does (s)he receive a salary?

1 Self-employed

2 Salaried

0 Not ascertained

9 Not ascertained

V112 *If salaried*: Is (s)he a member of a trade union?

1 Yes

2 No

0 Not ascertained

9 Inap., coded 1 in V111

V113 Occupation of respondent (or husband if housewife/widow not working)

01 Farmer/trawler owner, etc. (own account only)

02 Farm worker

03 Businessman; top manager

04 Executive; professional

05 Skilled tradesman, artisan, craftsman

06 Salaried, white collar, junior executive

07 Worker (unskilled, manual)

08 Student

09 Housekeeper

00 Unemployed; retired (pensioners)

10 (Luxembourg, Belgium, Italy: retired or not ascertained)

99 Not ascertained

V114 Occupation of the head of household:

01 Farmer/trawler owner, etc. (own account only)

02 Farm worker

03 Businessman; top manager

04 Executive; professional

05 Skilled tradesman, artisan, craftsman

06 Salaried, white collar, junior executive

07 Worker (unskilled, manual)

08 Student

09 Housekeeper

00 Unemployed; retired (pensioners)
10 Retired (Italy); (Lux., Bel., retired or not ascertained)
99 Not ascertained
V115 Usual language of household: (Ireland, Belgium, Luxembourg only)
IRELAND
1 English
2 Irish
0 Not ascertained
BELGIUM; LUXEMBOURG
1 French
2 Dutch
3 Other
4 Both
NETHERLANDS
Number of times a case appears in the data set. Values range from 1–5.
NOTE: All other countries coded zero.
V116 What was the last educational establishment you attended or you are now attending?
IRELAND
0 None
1 Primary school
2 Secondary school
3 Technical school/college
4 University
5 Others (write in)
DENMARK; ENGLAND; FRANCE
0 None
1 Primary school
2 Upper primary/middle school
3 School for technical/professional training
4 Secondary school
5 High school; university
6 Other
BELGIUM; LUXEMBOURG; NETHERLANDS
1 Primary
2 Lower middle school
3 Upper middle school
4 Secondary (not university)

5 University
0 None
GERMANY
1 Primary
2 Middle school
3 Technical or professional
4 High school (Gymnasium)
5 University
6 Other
ITALY
1 None
2 Primary—third year
3 Primary—beyond third year
4 Middle
5 Secondary—vocational
6 Secondary—other
7 University
V117 At what age did you leave school or university?
    1 14 or less
    2 15
    3 16
    4 17
    5 18
    6 19
    7 20
    8 21
    9 22–23
    10 Over 23
    11 Not yet completed
    00 Not ascertained
V118 Living in:
    1 Rural village (less than 10,000)
    2 10,000–20,000
    3 20,000–100,000
    4 100,000–500,000
    5 500,000–1,000,000
    6 Over 1,000,000
    0 (Ireland, Belgium: not ascertained)
    9 (Ireland, France, Britain: not ascertained)

V119 Commune (size):
BELGIUM; LUXEMBOURG
0 Under 2,000 popula.
1 2,000–5,000
2 5,000–10,000
3 10,000–25,000
4 Over 25,000
5 Large Cities (Over 1,000,000)
8 wild code—Belgium
IRELAND
1 County Boroughs
2 Other Urban areas
3 Rural
ITALY
0 Up to 2,000
1 2,000–3,000
2 3,000–5,000
3 5,000–10,000
4 10,000–20,000
5 20,000–30,000
6 30,000–50,000
7 50,000–100,000
8 100,000–250,000
9 Over 250,000
BRITAIN; DENMARK; NETHERLANDS
Variable not coded for these countries; all respondents coded 0
GERMANY (note reversed order)
1 Central city of 500,000 and over
2 Central city of 100,000–500,000
3 Central city of under 100,000
4 Suburban
5 Town of 20,000–50,000
6 Town of 10,000–20,000
7 2,000–10,000
8 Under 2,000
V120 Province; Land; Region; etc.
BELGIUM
00 Antwerp
01 Brabant
02 Hainaut

03 Limburg
04 Namur
05 E. Flanders
06 W. Flanders
07 Liege
08 Luxembourg
LUXEMBOURG
01 Luxembourg city
02 Luxembourg district
03 Diekirchen
04 Grevenmacher
IRELAND
01 Dublin
02 Leinster—urban
03 Leinster—rural
04 Munster—borough
05 Munster—other urban
06 Munster—rural
07 Connaught—Ulster, urb.
08 Connaught—Ulster, rural
FRANCE: Province
1 Northwest (Lower Normandy, Brittany, Loire, Poiton-
Charentes, Limousin)
2 Southwest (Aquitaine, Auvergne, Midi-Pyrenees, Lan-
guedoc)
3 North (Nord, Pas de Calais)
4 Paris Region
5 Paris Basin (Upper Normandy, Picardy, Champagne,
Burgundy, Center)
6 East (Alsace, Lorraine)
7 Southeast (Franche Comte, Rhone-Alps, Provence-Côte
d'Azur, Corsica)
BRITAIN
00 Wales
01 North
02 Yorks & Humberside
03 Northwest
04 East Midlands
05 West Midlands
06 East Anglia
07 Outer Metropolitan

V120 Province; Land; Region; etc. (*cont.*)
08 Outer South East
09 Southwest
10 London
11 Scotland
NETHERLANDS
00 Groningen, Friesland
01 Drenthe
02 Overijssel
03 Gelderland
04 Utrecht
05 North Holland
06 South Holland
07 Zealand
08 North Brabant
09 Limburg
GERMANY
00 Saar
01 Schleswig-Holstein
02 Hamburg
03 Lower Saxony
04 Bremen
05 N. Rhine-Westphalia
06 Hesse
07 Rhine-Palatinate
08 Baden-Wurttemberg
09 Bavaria
10 W. Berlin
DENMARK
00 Sealand
01 Bornholm
02 Lolland-Fal.
03 Funen
04 E. Jutland
05 N. Jutland
06 W. Jutland
07 S. Jutland
ITALY
North-West
11 Piedmont

12 Liguria
13 Lombardy
14 Milan
North-East
24 Trentino/Alto Adige
25 Veneto
26 Friuli/Venezia Giulia
27 Emilia
Center
31 Tuscany
32 Marche
33 Umbria
34 Lazio
South
41 Abbruzzi
42 Campania
43 Puglie
44 Basilicata
45 Calabria
Islands
51 Sicily
52 Sardinia
FRANCE (Department code)

01 Ain	19 Correze
02 Aisne	20 Corse
03 Allier	21 Cote-D'Or
04 Alpes (Basses-)	22 Cotes-Du-Nord
05 Alpes (Hautes-)	23 Creuse
06 Alpes-Maritimes	24 Dordogne
07 Ardeche	25 Doubs
08 Ardennes	26 Drome
09 Ariege	27 Eure
10 Aube	28 Eure et Loir
11 Aude	29 Finistere
12 Aveyron	30 Gard
13 Bouches-du-Rhone	31 Garonne (Haute-)
14 Calvados	32 Gers
15 Cantal	33 Gironde
16 Charente	34 Herault
17 Charente-Inferieure	35 Ille-et-Vilaine
18 Cher	36 Indre

V120 Province; Land; Region; etc. (*cont.*)

37 Indre-et-Loire	67 Rhin (Bas-)
38 Isere	68 Rhin (Haute-)
39 Jura	69 Rhone
40 Landes	70 Saone (Haute-)
41 Loir-et-Cher	71 Saone-et-Loire
42 Loire	72 Sarthe
43 Loire (Haute)	73 Savoie
44 Loire-Inferieure	74 Savoie (Haute-)
45 Loiret	75 Seine
46 Lot	76 Seine-Maritime
47 Lot-et-Garonne	77 Seine-et-Marne
48 Lozere	78 Yvelines
49 Maine-et-Loire	79 Sevres (Deux-)
50 Manche	80 Somme
51 Marne	81 Tarn
52 Marne (Haute-)	82 Tarn-et-Garonne
53 Mayenne	83 Var
54 Meurthe-et-Moselle	84 Vaucluse
55 Meuse	85 Vendee
56 Morbihan	86 Vienne
57 Moselle	87 Vienne (Haute-)
58 Nievre	88 Vosges
59 Nord	89 Yonne
60 Oise	90 Territoire de Belfort
61 Orne	91 Essonne
62 Pas-de-Calais	92 Hauts de Seine
63 Puy-de-Dome	93 Seine-St. Denis
64 Pyrenees (Basses-)	94 Val de Marne
65 Pyrenees (Hautes-)	95 Val d'Oise
66 Pyrenees-Orientales	

V121 We would like to analyze the results of this survey according to the income of the people interviewed. Show CARD L: Here is a scale of monthly incomes and we would like to know in what group your family is located, counting all salaries, pensions and other income that comes in per month. All these figures are before deductions.

Just give me the letter of the group your family falls into.

01 A Less than $200 per month
02 B $200–$399

03 C $400–$599
04 D $600–$799
05 E $800–$999
06 F $1,000 and over
07 (Denmark: $1,100–$1,999)
08 (Denmark: $1,200 and over)
00 No reply
99 (Ireland, France, Belgium, Britain: not ascertained)
NOTE: CARD L should show above categories in terms of national money, rounded off to nearest round figure.

V122 If "Good thing": In what way is the Common Market a good thing for you?
00 DK, NA
01 Give higher standard of living/keep cost of living down, cheaper goods
02 Give more employment opportunities
03 Help (British) industries/agriculture benefit/expand
04 Help underdeveloped countries
05 Closer *political* links with European countries
06 Less travel restrictions in EEC countries
07 Better wages/working conditions
08 Social/medical/educational services will improve
09 Allow freer trade arrangements/align prices
10 COUNTRY SPECIFIC: (see below)
11 Other advantages
99 Inap., coded 2, 3, 0 in V59
40 Data originally multiply punched
COUNTRY SPECIFIC CODES (10)
Ireland—can't exist outside/depend on Britain
Denmark—advantage to the nation as a whole
Belgium—in the long run good for Belgium, Belgium is too small to play a part
Luxembourg—in the long run good for Luxembourg, Luxembourg is too small to play a part
Germany—wild code
Italy—undocumented
Netherlands—undocumented

V123 If "Bad thing": In what way is the Common Market a bad thing for you?
00 DK, NA
01 Cost of living will go up/prices will rise

02 Cut in wages/working conditions
03 Unemployment/labor imported from Europe
04 (British) industries will suffer
05 (British) agriculture will suffer
06 Increased competition for (British) industry
07 Social/medical/educational services will suffer
08 Loss of political identity/sovereignty
09 Too close *political* links with European countries
10 COUNTRY SPECIFIC: (see below)
11 Other disadvantages
99 Inap., coded 1, 3, 0 in V59
40 Data originally multiply punched
COUNTRY SPECIFIC CODES (10)
Denmark—afraid of the influence of big countries
Ireland—would be better off on our own
Belgium—Belgian interests would be harmed
Britain—Commonwealth will suffer
Netherlands—wild code

APPENDIX B

European Community Survey, 1970

THE following questionnaire was administered to representative national samples of the publics of the six Common Market countries in February/March, 1970. The numbers appearing beside each question are the variable numbers in the ICPR data set. Variable number 1 is the interview number. Variables 2–10 are sex, age, occupation, education, size of community and province. Variable 11 is nationality, coded as follows:

1 Germany
2 Belgium
3 Netherlands
4 Luxembourg
5 France
6 Italy

May I ask you now how your household is made up according to age and sex? Would you begin with the *oldest*, down to the youngest, without omitting *yourself*.

V2 Sex:	1 Male
	2 Female
V3 Age, in years:	*Codes*:
	0 16–20
	1 21–24
	2 25–29
	3 30–34
	4 35–39
	5 40–44
	6 45–49
	7 50–54
	8 55–64
	9 65+
V4 Head of House:	1 Respondent is head of household

V5 Profession of Respondent:

2 Respondent is not head of household

0 Farmer, salaried farm worker
1 Head of business, high-level executive, engineer
2 High-level civil servant, professional
3 Shopkeeper, artisan
4 Clerk, middle-level executive, low or middle-level civil servant
5 Worker
6 Student
7 Housewife
8 Retired, person of independent means, no profession
9 Not ascertained

V6 Profession of head of household:
0 Farmer, salaried farm worker
1 Head of business, high-level executive, engineer
2 High-level civil servant, professional
3 Shopkeeper, artisan
4 Clerk, middle-level executive, low or middle-level civil servant
5 Worker
6 Student
7 Housewife
8 Retired, person of independent means, no profession
9 Not ascertained

V7 Language usually spoken by the head of the household:
(for Belgium and Luxembourg only)
1 Flemish
2 French
7 German
9 NA

V8 What is the last institution of learning that you atended, or the institution that you attend now? (Codes vary from country to country.)

V9 Size of community in which respondent lives (Codes vary from country to country).

V10 Province, Land or department in which respondent lives (Codes vary from country to country).

V11–19 Do you know the names of the countries which belong to the Common Market, or the European Economic Community to use the official name? (INT. DON'T SUGGEST ANYTHING. ALLOW THE RESPONDENT TIME TO THINK. NOTE ALL THE COUNTRIES NAMED).

Suppose there were a referendum today in the countries of the Common Market to decide on the following questions, how would you vote?

V20 Are you for or against the evolution of the Common Market toward the formation of a United States of Europe?
1 For
2 Against
3 Don't know/no answer (for France, code 9 is used).

V21 Are you for or against the entrance of Great Britain into the Common Market?
1 For
2 Against
3 D.k./no ans.

V22 Are you for or against the election of a European parliament by direct universal suffrage—that is, a parliament elected by all the citizens of the member countries?
1 For
2 Against
3 D.k./no ans.

V23 Would you accept it if there were, over the (Belgian) government, a European government responsible for a common policy in the areas of foreign affairs, defense and the economy?
1 For (would accept)
2 Against (would not accept)
3 D.k./no ans.

V24 If a president of the United States of Europe were being elected by universal suffrage, would you vote for a candidate who wasn't (Belgian) if his personality and program corresponded better to your ideas than those of the (Belgian) candidates?
1 Would vote for a non-(Belgian) candidate

2 Would not vote for non-(Belgian)

3 D.k./no ans.

V25 Would you say that you are favorable, somewhat favorable, indifferent, somewhat unfavorable, or very unfavorable to European unification?

1 Very favorable

2 Somewhat favorable

3 Indifferent

4 Somewhat unfavorable

5 Very unfavorable

6 D.k./no ans.

Would you be favorable, opposed or indifferent to . . .

	Favor-able	Opposed	Indif-ferent	D.k./no ans.
V26 The (Belgian) currency being replaced by a European currency	1	2	3	4
V27 The (Belgian) team in the next Olympic games being merged into a European team	1	2	3	4
V28 The (Belgian) flag being replaced by a European flag in large ceremonies	1	2	3	4

Among the following countries, which do not belong to the Common Market, are there any which you would like to see enter? Which ones? (INTERVIEWER: HAND OVER CARD A.)

	For admission	Not for admission
V29 Denmark	1	9
V30 Spain	2	9
V31 East Germany	3	9
V32 Poland	4	9
V33 U.S.S.R.	5	9
V34 Switzerland	6	9

V35 Concerning the realization of European unification, which of the following three formulas would you prefer? (INTERVIEWER: READ THE 3 FORMULAS.)

1 "There is no government on the European level, but the governments of each country meet regularly to decide on a common policy"

2 "There is a European government which takes care of the

most important questions, but each country keeps a government which takes care of its particular problems"

3 "There is a European government which takes care of all questions and the member countries no longer have a national government"

4 None of these formulas

9 D.K./no ans.

V36 If you were told tomorrow that the Common Market had been abandoned, would you feel very sorry, a little sorry, indifferent, or relieved?

1 Very sorry

2 A little sorry

3 Indifferent

4 Relieved

9 D.k./no ans.

V37 Would you be willing to make certain personal sacrifices, for example, on the financial level, to accomplish European unification? Would you be completely willing, fairly willing, slightly willing, not at all willing?

1 Completely willing

2 Fairly willing

3 Slightly willing

4 Not at all willing

5 D.k./no ans.—Bel., Lux., Holland

9 D.k./no ans.—France, Italy

V38 Do you think that the Common Market has had a favorable effect, very favorable, somewhat favorable, somewhat unfavorable, or very unfavorable?

1 Very favorable

2 Somewhat favorable

3 Somewhat unfavorable

4 Very unfavorable

9 D.k./no ans.

V39 Are you satisfied with your standard of living right now?

1 Yes

2 No

3 D.k./no ans.

V40 Do you think that your standard of living will improve noticeably in the course of the next five years?

1 Yes

2 No

3 D.k./no ans.

We hear a lot of things about the United States of Europe. I am going to read you a certain number of opinions, and I would like you to tell me (for each one of them) whether you agree completely, agree somewhat, disagree somewhat, or disagree completely.

		Agree completely	Agree somewhat	Disagree somewhat	Disagree completely	D.k./ no ans.
V41	I am proud to be a (Belgian).	1	2	3	4	5
V42	The United States of Europe should become a third force equal to that of the U.S.A. or the U.S.S.R.	1	2	3	4	5
V43	In the existing state of things everything is working out pretty well for us: so why change?	1	2	3	4	5
V44	The United States of Europe would be a first step toward a world government which would do away with war.	1	2	3	4	5
V45	European unification is impossible since we speak different languages.	1	2	3	4	5
V46	In the United States of Europe life would be more expensive and there would be a greater risk of unemployment.	1	2	3	4	5

	Agree com- pletely	Agree some- what	Disagree some- what	Disagree com- pletely	D.k./ no ans.
V47 You can't change anything about the fact that the strong always dominate the weak.	1	2	3	4	5
V48 In the framework of the United States of Europe, European scientists could catch up with the Americans.	1	2	3	4	5
V49 In general I have nothing against foreign workers but there really are too many of them in our country.	1	2	3	4	5
V50 In a United States of Europe different peoples risk losing their culture and their distinctiveness.	1	2	3	4	5
V51 In a United States of Europe the most disadvantaged groups of the population would have a better chance of improving their lot.	1	2	3	4	5
V52 In a United States of Europe the standard of living would probably be better.	1	2	3	4	5

I am going to list a certain number of things which might be desirable to you. Will you tell me (for each one of these) whether you actively wish for it to come about, whether you are indifferent, or whether you are mostly opposed. (INT. HAND OVER CARD B.)

	Actively wish for	Indif- ferent	Mostly opposed	D.k./ no ans.
V53 For (Belgium) to have a strong army	1	2	3	4
V54 To have no more world wars	1	2	3	4
V55 To live in a free country where everybody can say freely what he thinks	1	2	3	4
V56 To be able to go freely to all countries without passports	1	2	3	4
V57 For (Belgium) to play an important role in world politics	1	2	3	4
V58 Not to have any financial difficulties—in buying a car or a house for example	1	2	3	4
V59 For (Belgium) to make great scientific discoveries	1	2	3	4

V60 Recently there have been large student demonstrations in numerous countries. In a general way, do you feel very favorable, somewhat favorable, somewhat unfavorable, or very unfavorable to students who have demonstrated?
1 Very favorable
2 Somewhat favorable
3 Somewhat unfavorable
4 Very unfavorable
5 D.k./no ans.

V61 (INT. HAND OVER CARD C.) On this card are three fundamental attitudes toward the society in which we live. Will you choose the attitude which corresponds best to your personal ideas?

1 We must radically change the entire organization of our society by revolutionary action
2 We must improve our society little by little through intelligent reform
3 We must courageously defend our present society against all subversive forces
4 D.k./no ans.

V62–63 I will now propose a certain number of concrete objectives. (INT. HAND OVER CARD D.) Among the following things which are the *two* which seem to you most desirable? (V62 = first choice; V63 = second choice.)
1 Guarantee the greatest job security
2 Make our society more humane
3 Raise salaries
4 Guarantee the participation of the workers in the management of business enterprises
5 D.k./no ans.—France, Italy
9 D.k./no ans.—Bel., Lux.

V64–65 (INT. HAND OVER CARD E.) And among the following things which are the *two* which seem to you the most desirable? (V64 = first choice; V65 = second choice.
1 Maintain order in the country
2 Improve the participation of citizens in the political decisions of the government
3 Fight rising prices
4 Guarantee freedom of expression so that everyone can say freely what he thinks
5 D.k./no ans.—France, Italy
9 D.k./no ans.—Bel., Lux.

I would like to ask you now some questions about the trust you have in different peoples in the world. I will give you the names of different peoples; will you tell me if you have a lot of trust in them, some trust, not so much trust, no trust at all. You can answer with the help of this card. (INT. HAND OVER CARD F.)

	A lot of trust	Some trust	Not so much trust	No trust	D.k./ no ans.
V66 The Americans	1	2	3	4	5
V67 The Russians	1	2	3	4	5
V68 The Italians	1	2	3	4	5

		A lot of trust	Some trust	Not so much trust	No trust	D.k./ no ans.
V69	The Germans	1	2	3	4	5
V70	The French	1	2	3	4	5
V71	The Chinese	1	2	3	4	5
V72	The British	1	2	3	4	5
V73	The Swiss	1	2	3	4	5

I will propose again a certain number of concrete political objectives. (INT. HAND OVER CARD J.) I would like to ask you to tell me for each objective if you consider it as an objective which should have absolute priority, an important objective, a secondary objective, or not important at all?

		Absolute priority	Important objective	Secondary objective	Not important at all	D.k./ no ans.
V74	Guarantee greater job security	1	2	3	4	5
V75	Make our society more humane	1	2	3	4	5
V76	Guarantee the participation of the workers in management of business	1	2	3	4	5
V77	Help under-developed countries	1	2	3	4	5
V78	Raise salaries	1	2	3	4	5
V79	Stop making atomic bombs	1	2	3	4	5
V80	Do away with capitalism	1	2	3	4	5
V81	Reform education	1	2	3	4	5
V82	Fight communism	1	2	3	4	5
V83	Guarantee freedom of speech	1	2	3	4	5
V84	Maintain order in the country	1	2	3	4	5
V85	Encourage private initiative in the economic sphere	1	2	3	4	5

		Absolute priority	Important objective	Secondary objective	Not important at all	D.k./ no ans.
V86	Guarantee work to young people	1	2	3	4	5
V87	Guarantee a suitable pension to all the aged	1	2	3	4	5

V88 Do you participate personally in political activities or do you follow politics with interest without actively participating, or does politics not interest you more than other things or not at all?

1 Participate personally
2 Interest without participation
3 Only slightly interested
4 No interest at all
5 D.k./no ans.

V89 Can you tell me who is presently the Prime Minister of (Belgium)?

1 Correct name
2 Wrong name
3 Aldo Moro (for Italy only)
4 Governmental crisis (for Italy only)
9 D.k./no ans.

V90 Can you tell me who is presently the (Belgian) Minister of Foreign Affairs?

1 Correct name
2 Wrong name
3 Governmental crisis (for Italy only)
9 D.k./no ans.

V91 Do you watch news broadcasts on television . . .

1 Every day
2 Several times a week
3 One or two times a week
4 Less often
5 Never
6 D.k./no ans.

V92 Do you read in the daily newspaper news of current politics . . .

1 Every day
2 Several times a week

3 One or two times a week

4 Less often

5 Never

6 D.k./no ans.

V93 Do you listen to news broadcasts on radio . . .

1 Every day

2 Several times a week

3 One or two times a week

4 Less often

5 Never

6 D.k./no ans.

V94 Have you been abroad? (IF YES) In which countries have you spent at least one day? (INT. INSIST AND NOTE.)

0 No country

1 1 country

2 2 countries

3 3 countries

4 4 countries

5 5 countries

6 6 countries

7 7 countries

8 8 countries

9 9 countries or more

V95 As for yourself, is there any political party which you feel closer to among the present parties?

1 Yes

2 No (interviewer: skip to variable 97)

3 D.k./no ans. (interviewer: skip to variable 97)

V96 (If "yes" to variable 95) Do you feel deeply attached to this party or only a little?

1 Deeply

2 Only a little

3 D.k./no ans.

V97 (HAND OVER CARD H.) If elections took place tomorrow to elect deputies, for which party among the following ones would you be most likely to vote? (OR: . . . For which of these parties would you vote if you were already eligible to vote? INT. THE LAST SENTENCE ONLY APPLIES TO YOUNG PEOPLE BELOW VOTING AGE.)

Code	FRANCE	GERMANY	ITALY
0	D.k./no ans.		D.k./no ans./none
1	Center	Christian Democrat	Communist
2	Communist	Social Democrat	Prole. Socialist Unity
3	Radical	Free Dmocrat	Socialist
4	Gaullist	A.U.D.[1]	Social Democrat
5	Socialist	A.D.F.[1]	Republican
6	Indep. Republican	National Democrat	Christian Democrat
7	Unified Socialist	F.S.U.[1]	Liberal
8	Other	Other	Monarchist
9	None	D.k./no ans.	Neo-Fascist

Code	NETHERLANDS	BELGIUM	LUXEMBOURG
0	Minor parties	D.k./no ans.	(Not included
1	Catholic Party	Socialist	in ICPR data set)
2	Socialist	Christian Social	
3	Liberals	Liberal	
4	Anti-Revolutionary	Communist	
5	Christian Historical	Walloon	
6	Democrats, 1966	Francophone Front	
7	Pacific Socialist	Flemish	
8	Communist	Other	
9	None	None	

V98 Do you know if your parents had a preference for any particular political party?
 1 Yes
 2 No (interviewer: skip to variable 100).
 3 D.k./no ans. (int: skip to variable 100).

V99 Was it of the same persuasion as the political party for which you would vote now or another persuasion?
 1 Same persuasion
 2 Another persuasion
 3 D.k./no ans.

---

[1] These initials indicate three splinter parties that appeared on the German scene in 1970 and earlier. The letters stand for, respectively: Aktionsgemeinschaft Unabhangiger Deutscher; Aktion Demokratischer Fortschrift; and Freisoziale Union.

V100 What was the political persuasion of your parents?

Code	FRANCE	GERMANY	ITALY
0	D.k./Other		
1	"The Right," Ext. Rt.	Christian Democrat	Left, Ext. Left, Comm., PSIUP
2	Indep. Republican	Social Democrat	Left Socialist, PSI, PSU
3	UNR, UDR	Free Democrat	Democratic Center, DC, PRI
4	Gaullist, RPF	A.U.D.	Liberal, Liberal Right
5	M.R.P.	A.D.F.	Right, Ext. Right, MSI, PDIUM
6	Center	National Democrat	Local Parties
7	Radical, Rad. Social.	F.S.U.	D.k.
8	SFIO, Socialist	Other	
9	"The Left," Ext. Left, Communist	D.k./no ans.	Other

Code	NETHERLANDS	BELGIUM
0	Splinter Parties	
1	Catholic Party	Socialist
2	Socialist	Catholic; Christian; Christian Social
3	Liberal	Liberal
4	Anti-Revolutionary	Flemish
5	Christian Historical	Flemish Nationalist; Rexist
6	Democrats, 1966	
7	Pacificist Socialist	
8	Communist	Other
9	D.k./no ans.	D.k./no ans.

V101 Do you know if the leaders of the party are in favor or not of European unification? Select your answer from among the following possibilities:
1 Very favorable
2 Somewhat favorable
3 Somewhat unfavorable
4 Very unfavorable
5 D.k./no ans.

V102 If this party took a position in regard to European unification contrary to your ideas do you think you would vote for
another party?
1 Definitely
2 Probably
3 Probably not
4 Definitely not
5 D.k./no ans.

V103 Do you belong to a union?
1 Yes (Int. skip to V105)
2 No

V104 Without being a member, are you nonetheless sympathetic
to a union?
1 Yes
2 No (Int. to V107)

V105 Which union?

	ITALY	FRANCE	NETHERLANDS
1	C.S.L.	C.G.T.	N.V.V.
2	C.I.S.L.	C.F.D.T.	C.N.V.
3	U.I.L.	C.F.T.C.	N.K.V.
4	C.I.S.N.A.L.	C.G.T.-F.O.	Others
5	Agricultural syndicate	C.G.C.	
6	Leaders syndicate	Others	
7	Others	D.k./no ans.	
9	D.k./no ans.	Undoc. code	D.k./no ans.

	GERMANY	BELGIUM
1	D.C.T.B.	C.S.C./C.C.S.P./C.N.E.
2	D.A.G.	F.G.T.D./C.G.S.P./S.E.T.C.A.
3		
4		C.G.S.L.B.
5		F.G.T.I.
6		A.A.B.
7		F.E.N.I.B.
8	Others	Others
9	D.k./no ans.	D.k./no ans.

V106 Do you feel very attached to this union or only a little or
not at all?
1 Very attached

2 Only a little
3 Not at all
4 D.k./no ans.

V107 Do you know if the heads of this union are very favorable, somewhat favorable, somewhat unfavorable, or very unfavorable to European unification?
1 Very favorable
2 Somewhat favorable
3 Somewhat unfavorable
4 Very unfavorable
5 D.k./no ans.

V108 (INT. IF RESPONDENT IS NOT HEAD OF HOUSEHOLD.) In your home, does the head of the household belong to a union?
1 Yes
2 No (Int. to V110)

V109 Which union?
CODES SAME AS FOR VARIABLE 105.

V110 Do you belong to a religion?
1 Yes
2 No (Int. to V112)

V111 Which one?
1 Catholic
2 Protestant
3 Other, France
4 Other, Netherlands
8 Other, Belgium
9 D.k./no ans.

V112 Do you go to religious services several times a week, one time a week, a few times a year, or do you never go?
1 Several times a week
2 One time a week
3 A few times a year
4 Never

V113 Would you like to tell me about what level your family is in regard to financial means? You can answer by giving me a number from 1–7. (INT. HAND OVER CARD I.) The number 1 means poor family, number 3 family of somewhat reduced financial means, number 5 family well-off, number 7 a rich family. The other numbers allow you to choose the cases in between.

1	2	3	4	5	6	7
poor		somewhat reduced means		well-off		rich

BIBLIOGRAPHY

Abelson, Robert P. "Are Attitudes Necessary?" in Bert T. King and Elliott McGinnies (eds.), *Attitudes, Conflict and Social Change* (New York: Academic Press, 1972), 19–32.

Aberbach, Joel D. "Alienation and Political Behavior," *American Political Science Review*, 63, 1 (March, 1969), 86–99.

———— and Jack L. Walker. "Political Trust and Racial Ideology," *American Political Science Review*, 64, 4 (December, 1970), 1199–1219.

Abrams, Mark. "Subjective Social Indicators," in Muriel Nissel (ed.), *Social Trends*, No. 4 (London: Her Majesty's Stationery Office, 1973), 1–39.

Abramson, Paul R. *Generational Change in American Politics* (Lexington, Mass.: Lexington Books, 1975).

————. "Social Class and Political Change in Western Europe: A Cross-National Longitudinal Analysis," *Comparative Political Studies*, 4, 2 (July, 1971), 131–155.

————. "Intergenerational Social Mobility and Electoral Choice," *American Political Science Review*, 66, 4 (December, 1972), 1291–1294.

————. "Generational Change in American Electoral Behavior," *American Political Science Review*, 68, 1 (March, 1974), 93–105.

Adam, Gérard *et al. L'Ouvrier Français en 1970* (Paris: Armand Colin, 1970).

Adelson, Joseph and Robert P. O'Neil. "The Growth of Political Ideas in Adolescence: The Sense of Community," *Journal of Personality and Social Psychology*, 4, 3 (September, 1966), 295–306.

Adorno, T. W. *et al. The Authoritarian Personality* (New York: Harper & Row, 1950).

Alford, Robert R. *Party and Society: The Anglo-American Democracies* (Chicago: Rand McNally, 1963).

Allardt, Erik. *About Dimensions of Welfare: An Exploratory Analysis of a Comparative Scandinavian Survey* (Helsinki: Research Group for Comparative Sociology, 1973).

Allardt, Erik and Yrjo Littunen (eds.), *Cleavages, Ideologies, and Party Systems* (Helsinki: Academic Bookstore, 1964).

Allerbeck, Klaus R. "Some Structural Conditions for Youth and Student Movements," *International Social Science Journal*, 24, 2 (1972), 257–270.

Allerbeck, Klaus R. and Leopold Rosenmayer (eds.). *Aufstand der Jugend? Neue Aspekte der Jugendsoziologie* (Munich: Juventa, 1971).

Almond, Gabriel. "Comparative Political Systems," *Journal of Politics*, 18, 3 (August, 1956), 391–409.

Almond, Gabriel A. and Sidney Verba. *The Civic Culture: Political Attitudes and Democracy in Five Nations* (Princeton: Princeton University Press, 1963).

Altbach, Philip G. and Robert S. Laufer (eds.). *The New Pilgrims: Youth Protest in Transition* (New York: McKay, 1972).

Ambler, John S. "Trust in Political and Non-Political Authorities in France," *Comparative Politics*, 8, 1 (October, 1975), 31–58.

Andrews, Frank and Stephen Withey. "Developing Measures of Perceived Life Quality: Results from Several National Surveys," *Social Indicators Research*, I, 1 (1974), 1–26.

————. *Social Indicators of Well-Being in America* (New York: Plenum, 1976).

Apter, David. *Choice and the Politics of Allocation* (New Haven: Yale University Press, 1971).

Ardagh, John. *The New French Revolution: Social and Economic Study of France, 1945–1968* (New York: Harper, 1969).

Aristotle. *The Basic Works of Aristotle* (New York: Random House, 1941).

Axelrod, Robert. "Communication," *American Political Science Review*, 68, 2 (June, 1974), 717–720.

————. "The Structure of Public Opinion on Policy Issues," *Public Opinion Quarterly*, 31, 1 (Spring, 1967), 51–60.

Baier, Kurt and Nicholas Rescher. *Values and the Future: The Impact of Technological Change on American Values* (New York: Free Press, 1969).

Baker, Kendall *et al.* "Political Affiliations: Transition in the Bases of German Partisanship," paper presented at the sessions of the European Consortium for Political Research, London, April 7–12, 1975.

————. "The Residue of History: Politicization in Post War Germany," paper presented at the Western Social Science Convention in Denver, May 1–3, 1975.

————. *Transition in German Politics* (forthcoming).

Bales, Robert F. and Arthur S. Couch. "The Value Profile: A Factor Analytic Study of Value Statements," *Sociological Inquiry* (Winter, 1968).

Bandura, Albert. "Social-Learning Theory of Identificatory Processes," in David Goslin (ed.), *Handbook of Socialization Theory and Research* (Chicago: Rand McNally, 1969).

Banfield, Edward C. *The Moral Basis of a Backward Society* (Chicago: Free Press, 1958).

Barnes, Samuel H. "Italy: Oppositions on Left, Right, and Center," in

Robert Dahl (ed.), *Political Oppositions in Western Democracies* (New Haven: Yale University Press, 1966), 303–331.

———. "Leadership Style and Political Competence," in Lewis Edinger (ed.), *Political Leadership in Industrialized Societies* (New York: Wiley, 1967), 59–83.

———. "The Legacy of Fascism: Generational Differences in Italian Political Attitudes and Behavior," *Comparative Political Studies*, 5 (1972), 41–57.

———. "Left, Right, and the Italian Voter," *Comparative Political Studies*, 4, 2 (July, 1971), 157-175.

———. *Party Democracy: Politics in an Italian Socialist Federation* (New Haven: Yale University Press, 1967).

———. "Religion and Class in Italian Electoral Behavior," in Richard Rose (ed.), *Electoral Behavior: A Comparative Handbook* (New York: Free Press, 1974), 171–225.

——— and Roy Pierce. "Public Opinion and Political Preferences in France and Italy," *Midwest Journal of Political Science*, 15, 4 (November, 1971), 643–660.

Barnett, Richard J. and Ronald E. Muller. *Global Reach* (New York: Simon and Schuster, 1975).

Bauer, Raymond A. (ed.). *Social Indicators* (Cambridge: M.I.T. Press, 1966).

Bell, Daniel. *The Coming of Post-Industrial Society* (New York: Basic Books, 1973).

———. *The Cultural Contradictions of Capitalism* (New York: Basic Books, 1976).

———. *The End of Ideology* (New York: Free Press, 1960).

———. "The Measurement of Knowledge and Technology," in Eleanor Bernert Sheldon and Wilbert E. Moore (eds.), *Indicators of Social Change: Concepts and Measurements* (New York: Russell Sage, 1968), 145–246.

———. "The Idea of a Social Report," *The Public Interest*, 15 (Spring, 1969), pp. 72–84.

——— (ed.). *The Radical Right* (Garden City: Doubleday, 1964).

Bendix, Reinhard. *Nation-Building and Citizenship: Studies of Our Changing Social Order* (Berkeley: University of California Press, 1964).

Benello, C. George and Dimitrios Roussopoulos (eds.). *The Case for Participatory Democracy* (New York: Viking, 1971).

Béneton, Phillippe and Jean Touchard. "Les interprétations de la crise de mai-juin 1968," *Revue Française de Science Politique*, 20, 3 (June, 1970), 503–544.

Berelson, Bernard *et al. Voting: A Study of Opinion Formation in a Presidential Campaign* (Chicago: University of Chicago Press, 1954).

Black, C. E. *The Dynamics of Modernization* (New York: Harper & Row, 1967).

Blau, Peter and Otis Dudley Duncan. *The American Occupational Structure* (New York: Wiley, 1967).

Bloom, Benjamin S. *Stability and Change in Human Characteristics* (New York: John Wiley, 1964).

Blumenthal, Monica *et al. Justifying Violence* (Ann Arbor, Michigan: Institute for Social Research, 1972).

Bon, Frédéric and Michel-Antoine Burnier. *Les Nouveaux Intellectuels* (Paris: Cujas, 1966).

———. *Classe Ouvriere et Révolution* (Paris: Seuil, 1971).

Boudon, Raymond. "Sources of Student Protest in France," in Philip G. Altbach and Robert S. Laufer (eds.), *The New Pilgrims: Youth Protest in Transition* (New York: McKay, 1972), 297–310. 297–310.

Boulding, Kenneth E. "The Learning Process in the Dynamics of Total Societies," in Samuel Z. Klausner (ed.), *The Study of Total Societies* (Garden City: Anchor, 1967), 98–113.

Bowen, Don R. *et al.* "Deprivation, Mobility and Orientation Toward Protest of the Urban Poor," in Louis H. Masotti and Don R. Bowen (eds.), *Riots and Rebellion: Civil Violence in the Urban Community* (Beverly Hills: Sage, 1968), 187–200.

Boyle, Thomas J. "Hope for the Technological Solution," *Nature*, 245, 1 (September 21, 1973), 127–128.

Bracher, Karl D. *Die Auflösing der Weimarer Republik* (Stuttgart and Dusseldorf: Ring Verlag, 1954).

Bradburn, Norman. *The Structure of Psychological Well-Being* (Chicago: Aldine, 1969).

——— and David Capolvitz. *Reports on Happiness: A Pilot Study of Behavior Related to Mental Health* (Chicago: Aldine, 1965).

Brim, Orville G., Jr. and Stanton Wheeler. *Socialization After Childhood* (New York: Wiley, 1966).

——— *et al. American Beliefs and Attitudes About Intelligence* (New York: Russell Sage, 1969).

Broad, Roger and R. J. Jarrett. *Community Europe Today* (London: Wolff, 1972).

Bronfenbrenner, Urie. "Socialization and Social Class Through Time and Space," in Harold Proshansky and Bernard Seidenberg (eds.), *Basic Studies in Social Psychology* (New York: Holt, Rinehart and Winston, 1965), 349–365.

Brown, Bernard E. "The French Experience of Modernization," in Roy Macridis and Bernard Brown (eds.), *Comparative Politics: Notes and Readings*, 4th ed. (Homewood: Dorsey, 1972), 442–460.

Brzezinski, Zbigniew. *Between Two Ages: America's Role in the Technetronic Era* (New York: Viking, 1970).

Buchanan, William and Hadley Cantril. *How Nations See Each Other: A Study in Public Opinion* (Urbana: University of Illinois Press, 1953).

Burnham, Walter Dean. *Critical Elections and the Mainspring of American Politics* (New York: Norton, 1970).

Butler, David and Donald Stokes. *Political Change in Britain*, 1st, 2nd eds. (New York: St. Martin's, 1969, 1974).

Cameron, David R. "Stability and Change in Patterns of French Partisanship: A Cohort Analysis," *Public Opinion Quarterly*, 31, 1 (Spring, 1972), 19–30.

————. "Consociation, Cleavage and Realignment: Post-Industrialization and Partisan Change in Eight European Nations," paper presented to the American Political Science Association, Chicago, September, 1974.

Cameron, Paul, "Social Stereotypes: Three Faces of Happiness," *Psychology Today*, 8, 3 (August, 1974), 62–64.

Campbell, Angus. *White Attitudes Toward Black People* (Ann Arbor, Michigan: Institute for Social Research, The University of Michigan, 1971).

———— and Stein Rokkan. "Citizen Participation in Political Life: Norway and the United States," *International Social Science Journal*, 12, 1 (1960), 69–99.

———— and Philip Converse (eds.). *The Human Meaning of Social Change* (New York: Russell Sage, 1972).

———— et al. *The Quality of Life: Perceptions, Evaluation and Satisfaction* (New York: Russell Sage, 1976).

———— et al. *The American Voter* (New York: Wiley, 1960).

———— et al. *Elections and the Political Order* (New York: Wiley, 1966).

———— and Henry Valen. "Party Identification in Norway and the United States," *Public Opinion Quarterly*, 25, 4 (Winter, 1961), 505–525.

Cantril, Hadley, ed. *Public Opinion, 1935–1946* (Princeton: Princeton University Press, 1951).

Cantril, Hadley. *The Politics of Despair* (New York: Collier, 1958).

————. *The Pattern of Human Concerns* (New Brunswick: Rutgers University Press, 1968).

———— and Charles W. Roll, Jr. *Hopes and Fears of the American People* (New York: Universe, 1971).

Charlot, Jean. *Le Phénomène Gaulliste* (Paris: Fayard, 1970).

Christie, Richard. "Authoritarianism Revisited," in Christie and Marie Jahoda (eds.), *Studies in the Scope and Method of "The Authoritarian Personality"* (Glencoe: Free Press, 1954), 123–196.

———— and Marie Jahoda (eds.). *Studies in the Scope and Method of "The Authoritarian Personality"* (Glencoe: Free Press, 1954).

Citrin, Jack. "Comment: The Political Relevance of Trust in Government," *American Political Science Review*, 68, 3 (September, 1974), 973–988.

Cohn-Bendit, Daniel *et al. The French Student Revolt: The Leaders Speak* (New York: Hill and Wang, 1968).

———— and Gabriel Cohn-Bendit. *Obsolete Communism: The Left-Wing Alternative* (New York: McGraw-Hill, 1968).

Cole, H.S.D. *et al.* (eds.). *Models of Doom* (New York: Universe, 1973).

Coleman, James S. (ed.). *Education and Political Development* (Princeton: Princeton University Press, 1965).

————. *The Adolescent Society* (New York: Free Press, 1961).

Connell, R. W. "Political Socialization in the American Family: The Evidence Re-examined," *Public Opinion Quarterly*, 36, 3 (Fall, 1972), 323–333.

Converse, Philip. "The Problem of Party Distances in Models of Voting Change," in M. Kent Jennings and L. Harmon Ziegler, *The Electoral Process* (Englewood Cliffs: Prentice-Hall, 1966), 175–207.

Converse, Philip E. "The Nature of Belief Systems in Mass Publics," in David E. Apter (ed.), *Ideology and Discontent* (New York: Free Press, 1964), 202–261.

————. "Of Time and Partisan Stability," *Comparative Political Studies*, 2, 2 (July, 1969), 139–171.

————. "Attitudes and Non-Attitudes: Continuation of a Dialogue," in Edward R. Tufte (ed.), *The Quantitative Analysis of Social Problems* (Reading, Mass.: Addison-Wesley, 1970), 168–190.

————. "Change in the American Electorate," in Angus E. Campbell and Philip Converse (eds.), *The Human Meaning of Social Change* (New York: Russell Sage, 1972), 263–337.

————. "Comment: The Status of Nonattitudes," *American Political Science Review*, 68, 2 (June, 1974), 650–660.

———— and Georges Dupeux. "Politicization of the Electorate in France and the United States," *Public Opinion Quarterly*, 26, 1 (Spring, 1962), 1–23.

———— and Roy Pierce. "Basic Cleavages in French Politics and the Disorders of May and June 1968." Paper presented at the Seventh World Congress of Sociology, Varna, Bulgaria, 1970.

————. "Die Mai-Unruhen in Frankreich—Ausmass und Konsequenzen," in Klaus R. Allerbeck and Leopold Rosenmayr (eds.), *Aufstand der Jugend? Neue Aspekte der Jugendsoziologie* (Munich: Juventa, 1971), 108–137.

Cox, Robert W. (ed.). *Future Industrial Relations and Implications for the ILO: An Interim Report* (Geneva: International Institute for Labour Studies).

The CPS 1974 American National Election Study (Ann Arbor: ICPR, 1975).

Crittenden, John. "Aging and Party Affiliation: A Cohort Analysis," *Public Opinion Quarterly*, 26, 4 (Winter, 1962), 648–657.

Cutler, Neal. "Generation, Maturation and Party Affiliation," *Public Opinion Quarterly*, 33, 4 (Winter, 1969–70), 583–588.

Dahl, Robert A. and Edward R. Tufte. *Size and Democracy* (Stanford: Stanford University Press, 1974).

Dahl, Robert A. (ed.). *Political Oppositions in Western Democracies* (New Haven: Yale University Press, 1966).

Dahrendorf, Ralf. *Class and Class Conflict in Industrial Society* (Stanford: Stanford University Press, 1959).

——. *Society and Democracy in Germany* (Garden City: Doubleday, 1967).

Dalton, Russell. "Was There a Revolution? A Note on Generational versus Life Cycle Explanations of Value Differences," *Comparative Political Studies*, 9, 4 (January, 1977).

Dansette, Adrien. *Mai 1968* (Paris: Plon, 1971).

Davies, James C. *Human Nature and Politics* (New York: Wiley, 1963).

——. "The Priority of Human Needs and the Stages of Political Development," unpublished paper.

Davis, James A. *Great Aspirations: The Graduate School Plans of America's College Seniors* (Chicago: Aldine, 1964).

——. *Education for Positive Mental Health: A Review of Existing Research and Recommendations for Future Studies* (Chicago: Aldine, 1965).

——. *Undergraduate Career Decisions: Correlates of Occupational Choice* (Chicago: Aldine, 1965).

De Grazia, Sebastian. *Of Time, Work and Leisure* (New York: Twentieth Century Fund, 1962).

Deledicq, A. *Un mois de mai orageux: 113 étudiants parisiens expliquent les raisons* (Paris: Privat, 1968).

Delors, Jacques. *Les Indicateurs Sociaux* (Paris: Futuribles, 1971).

Demerath, N. J., III. "Trends and Anti-Trends in Religious Change," in Eleanor Bernert Sheldon and Wilbert E. Moore (eds.), *Indicators of Social Change* (New York: Russell Sage, 1968), 349–445.

Deutsch, Emeric *et al. Les Familles Politiques aujourd'hui en France* (Paris: Editions de Minuit, 1966).

Deutsch, Karl W. "Social Mobilization and Political Development," *American Political Science Review*, 55, 2 (September, 1961), 493–514.

——. *The Nerves of Government* (New York: Free Press, 1963).

——. *Nationalism and Social Communication* (Cambridge, Mass.: M.I.T. Press, 1966).

Deutsch, Karl W. "Integration and Arms Control in the European Political Environment," *American Political Science Review*, 60, 2 (June, 1966), 354–365.

―――. *Arms Control and the Atlantic Alliance* (New York: Wiley, 1967).

――― and Lewis J. Edinger. *Germany Rejoins the Powers: Mass Opinion, Interest Groups and Elites in Contemporary German Foreign Policy* (Stanford: Stanford University Press, 1959).

――― and William J. Foltz. *Nation-Building* (New York: Atherton Press, 1963).

――― *et al. France, Germany and the Western Alliance: A Study of Elite Attitudes on European Integration and World Politics* (New York: Scribners, 1967).

――― *et al. Political Community and the North Atlantic Area* (Princeton: Princeton University Press, 1968).

DiPalma, Giuseppe. *Apathy and Participation: Mass Politics in Western Societies* (New York: Free Press, 1970).

Dogan, Mattei. "Le Vote ouvrier en France: Analyse écologique des élections de 1962," *Revue française de Sociologie*, 6, 4 (October–December, 1965), 435–471.

―――. "Political Cleavage and Social Stratification in France and Italy," in Seymour M. Lipset, *Party Systems and Voter Alignments* (New York: Free Press, 1967), 129–195.

Donahue, Wilma and Clark Tibbitts (eds.). *Politics of Age* (Ann Arbor: Division of Gerontology, The University of Michigan, 1962).

Duquesne, Jacques. *Les 16–24 Ans* (Paris: Centurion, 1963).

Dutschke, Rudi. *Écrits politiques* (Paris: Bourgeois, 1968).

Easterlin, Richard A. "Does Economic Growth Improve the Human Lot: Some Empirical Evidence," in Paul A. David and Melvin W. Reder (eds.), *Nations and Households in Economic Growth* (New York: Academic Press, 1974), 89–126.

Easton, David. *A Systems Analysis of Political Life* (New York: Wiley, 1966).

――― and Jack Dennis. *Children in the Political System* (New York: McGraw-Hill, 1969).

Eisenstadt, S. N. *From Generation to Generation* (New York: Free Press, 1956).

―――. *Modernization: Protest and Change* (Englewood Cliffs, N.J.: Prentice Hall, 1966).

Erikson, Erik H. "Identity and the Life Cycle," *Psychological Issues*, Monograph 1 (1959).

―――. *Childhood and Society* (New York: Norton, 1963).

―――. *Insight and Responsibility* (New York: Norton, 1964).

Etzioni, Amitai. *The Active Society* (New York: Free Press, 1968).

―――. *Political Unification: A Comparative Study of Leaders and Forces* (New York: Holt, Rinehart and Winston, 1965).

European Communities, *Les Européens et l'Unification de l'Europe* (Brussels, 1972).

Feirabend, Ivo K. and Rosalind L. Feirabend. "Aggressive Behaviors Within Polities, 1948–1962: A Cross-National Study," *Journal of Conflict Resolution*, 10, 3 (September, 1966), 249–271.

Feldman, Kenneth A. and Theodore M. Newcomb. *The Impact of College on Students*, vols. I and II (San Francisco: Jossey-Bass, 1969).

Feuer, Lewis S. *The Conflict of Generations* (New York: Basic Books, 1969).

Fields, A. Belden. "The Revolution Betrayed: The French Student Revolt of May-June, 1968," in Seymour M. Lipset and Phillip G. Altbach (eds.), *Students in Revolt* (Boston: Houghton Mifflin, 1969), 127–166.

Finifter, Ada (ed.). *Alienation and the Social System* (New York: Wiley, 1972).

Foner, Anne. "The Polity," in Matilda W. Riley *et al.*, *Aging and Society* (New York: Russell Sage, 1972), 115–159.

Fontaine, André. *La Guerre Civile Froide* (Paris: Fayard, 1969).

Forrester, Jay W. *World Dynamics* (Cambridge, Mass.: Wright-Allen, 1971).

Friedman, Lucy N. *et al.* "Dissecting the Generation Gap: Intergenerational and Intrafamilial Similarities and Differences," *Public Opinion Quarterly*, 36, 3 (Fall, 1972), 334–346.

Frognier, A. P. "Distances entre partis et clivages en Belgique," *Res Publica*, 2 (1973), 291–312.

Frohner, Rolf. *Wie Stark sind die Halbstarken?* (Bielefeld: von Stackelberg, 1956).

Galli, Giorgio and Alfonso Prandi. *Patterns of Political Participation in Italy* (New Haven: Yale University Press, 1970).

Gamson, William A. *Power and Discontent* (Homewood, Ill.: Dorsey, 1968).

Girod, Rober. *Mobilité Sociale: Faits établis et problèmes ouverts* (Geneva and Paris: Droz, 1971).

Glenn, Norval D. "Class and Party Support in the United States: Recent and Emerging Trends," *Public Opinion Quarterly*, 37, 1 (Spring, 1973), 1–20.

———. "Aging, Disengagement and Opinionation," *Public Opinion Quarterly*, 33, 1 (Spring, 1969), 17–33.

———. "Aging and Conservatism," *Annals of the American Academy of Political and Social Science*, 4, 5 (September, 1974), 176–186.

——— and Ted Hefner. "Further Evidence on Aging and Party Identification," *Public Opinion Quarterly*, 36, 1 (Spring, 1972), 31–47.

Goguel, François. "Les élections legislatives des 23 et 30 juin, 1968," *Revue Française de Science Politique*, 18, 5 (October, 1968), 837–853.

Goode, William J. "The Theory and Measurement of Family Change," in Eleanor Bernert Sheldon and Wilbert E. Moore (eds.), *Indicators of Social Change: Concepts and Measurements* (New York: Russell Sage, 1968), 295–348.

Graham, Hugh D. and Ted R. Gurr (eds.). *The History of Violence in America* (New York: Bantam, 1969).

Greenstein, Fred I. "The Impact of Personality on Politics: An Attempt to Clear Away Underbrush," *American Political Science Review*, 61, 3 (September, 1967), 629–641.

————. *Personality and Politics* (Chicago: Markham, 1969), 94–119.

Grofman, Bernard N. and Edward N. Muller. "The Strange Case of Relative Gratification and Protest Potential: The V-Curve Hypothesis," *American Political Science Review*, 67, 2 (June, 1973), 514–539.

Gross, Bertram M. (ed.). *Social Intelligence for America's Future* (Boston: Allyn and Bacon, 1969).

————. "The State of the Nation: Social Systems Accounting," in Raymond A. Bauer (ed.), *Social Indicators* (Cambridge: M.I.T. Press, 1966), 154–271.

———— (ed.). "Social Goals and Indicators for American Society," *The Annals: American Academy of Political and Social Science* (1967), 371 and 372.

————. "The City of Man: A Social Systems Accounting," in William R. Ewald, Jr. (ed.), *Environment for Man* (Bloomington: Indiana University Press, 1967).

Gurin, Gerald *et al. Americans View Their Mental Health* (New York: Basic Books, 1960).

Gurr, Ted. *Why Men Rebel* (Princeton: Princeton University Press, 1970).

————. "A Causal Model of Civil Strife: A Comparative Analysis Using New Indices," *American Political Science Review*, 62, 4 (December, 1968), 1104–1124.

Gussner, Robert. "Youth Deauthorization and the New Individualism," *Youth and Society*, 4, 1 (September, 1972), 103–125.

Haas, Ernst. *The Uniting of Europe: Political, Social and Economic Forces, 1950–1957* (Stanford: Stanford University Press, 1958).

Habermas, Jurgen *et al. Student und Politik* (Neuwied: Luchterhand, 1961).

Hagen, Everett. *On the Theory of Social Change* (Homewood, Ill.: Dorsey Press, 1962).

Hamilton, Richard F. *Affluence and the French Worker in The Fourth Republic* (Princeton: Princeton University Press, 1967).

————. *Class and Politics in the United States* (New York: Wiley, 1972).

Hansen, Peter *et al.* "The Structure of the Debate in the Danish European Community Campaign, April to October, 1972," paper presented to the European Consortium for Political Research annual meeting, Strasbourg, March 28–April 2, 1974.

Haranne, Markku and Erik Allardt. *Attitudes Toward Modernity and Modernization: An Appraisal of an Empirical Study* (Helsinki: University of Helsinki, 1974).

Louis Harris Associates. *Confidence and Concern: Citizens View American Government* (Washington: Government Printing Office, 1973).

Harris, Louis. *The Anguish of Change* (New York: Norton, 1973).

Hefner, Glenn and Ted. "Further Evidence on Aging and Party Identification," *Public Opinion Quarterly*, 36, 1 (Spring, 1972), 31–47.

Heidenheimer, Arnold J. *The Governments of Germany*, 3rd ed. (New York: Crowell, 1971).

Heilbroner, Robert L. *An Inquiry Into the Human Prospect* (New York: Norton, 1974).

Heisler, Martin O. "Institutionalizing Societal Cleavages in a Cooptive Polity," in Heisler (ed.), *Politics in Europe: Structures and Processes in Some Postindustrial Democracies* (New York: McKay, 1974), 178–220.

Hilgard, E. and G. Bower. *Theories of Learning* (New York: Appleton-Century-Crofts, 1966).

Huntington, Samuel P. *Political Order in Changing Societies* (New Haven: Yale University Press, 1968).

———. "Postindustrial Politics: How Benign Will It Be?" *Comparative Politics*, 6, 2 (January, 1974), 174–177.

Hyman, Herbert H. *Political Socialization* (New York: Free Press, 1959).

———. *Secondary Analysis of Sample Surveys: Principles, Procedures and Potentialities* (New York: Wiley, 1972).

———. "Dimensions of Social-Psychological Change in the Negro Population," in Angus Campbell and Philip Converse (eds.), *The Human Meaning of Social Change* (New York: Russell Sage, 1972), 339–390.

——— and Paul B. Sheatsley. " 'The Authoritarian Personality': A Methodological Critique," in Christie and Jahoda (eds.), *Studies in the Scope and Method of "The Authoritarian Personality"* (Glencoe: Free Press, 1954), 50–122.

Ike, Nobutaka. "Economic Growth and Intergenerational Change in Japan," *American Political Science Review*, 67, 4 (December, 1973), 1194–1203.

Inglehart, Ronald. "An End to European Integration?" *American Political Science Review*, 61, 1 (March, 1967), 91–105.

———. "Trends and Non-Trends in the Western Alliance: A Review," *Journal of Conflict Resolution*, 12, 1 (March, 1968), 120–128.

Inglehart, Ronald. "Cognitive Mobilization and European Identity," *Comparative Politics*, 3, 1 (October, 1970), 45–70.

———. "The New Europeans: Inward or Outward Looking?" *International Organization*, 24, 1 (Winter, 1970), 129–139.

———. "Public Opinion and Regional Integration," in Leon Lindberg and Stuart Scheingold (eds.), *Regional Integration: Theory and Research* (Cambridge: Harvard University Press, 1971), 160–191.

———. "Revolutionnarisme Post-Bourgeois en France, en Allemagne et aux États-Unis," *Il Politico*, 36, 2 (June, 1971), 209–236.

———. "Changing Value Priorities and European Integration," *Journal of Common Market Studies*, 10, 1 (September, 1971), 1–36.

———. "The Silent Revolution in Europe: Intergenerational Change in Post-Industrial Societies," *The American Political Science Review*, 65, 4 (December, 1971), 991–1017.

———. "The Nature of Value Change in Post-Industrial Societies," in Leon Lindberg (ed.), *Politics and the Future of Industrial Society* (New York: McKay, 1976), 57–99.

———. "Value Priorities, Objective Need Satisfaction and Subjective Satisfaction Among Western Publics," *Comparative Political Studies*, 9, 4 (January, 1977), 429–458.

——— and Paul Abramson. "The Development of Systemic Support in Four Western Democracies," *Comparative Political Studies*, 2, 4 (January, 1970), 419–442.

——— and Samuel H. Barnes. "Affluence, Individual Values and Social Change," in Burkhard Strumpel (ed.), *Subjective Elements of Well-Being* (Paris: OECD, 1974), 153–184.

——— and Avram Hochstein. "Alignment and Dealignment of the Electorate in France and the United States," *Comparative Political Studies*, 5, 3 (October, 1972), 343–372.

——— and Hans D. Klingemann, "Party Identification, Ideological Preference and the Left-Right Dimension Among Western Publics," in Ian Budge *et al.* (eds.), *Party Identification and Beyond* (New York: Wiley, 1976), 243–273.

——— and Dusan Sidjanski. "The Left, the Right, the Establishment and the Swiss Electorate," in Ian Budge *et al.* (eds.), *Party Identification and Beyond* (New York: Wiley, 1976), 225–242.

——— and Margaret Woodward. "Language Conflicts and Political Community," *Comparative Studies in Society and History*, 10, 1 (October, 1967), 27–45.

International Studies of Values in Politics. *Values and the Active Community* (New York: Free Press, 1971).

Jacob, Philip E. *Changing Values in College* (New York: Harper & Row, 1957).

Jaide, Walter, *Das Verhaltnis der Jugend zur Politik* (Neuwied and Berlin: Luchterhand, 1964).

————. *Jugend und Demokratie* (Munich: Juventa, 1971).

Janda, Kenneth. *A Conceptual Framework for the Comparative Analysis of Political Parties* (Beverly Hills: Sage Professional Papers in Comparative Politics, 1970).

————. "Measuring Issue Orientations of Parties Across Nations" (Evanston: International Comparative Political Parties Project, 1970 [mimeo]).

Janowitz, Morris and David R. Segal. "Social Cleavage and Party Affiliation: Germany, Great Britain and the United States," *American Journal of Sociology*, 72, 6 (May, 1967), 601–618.

Jaros, Dean, Herbert Hirsch and Frederic J. Fleron, Jr. "The Malevolent Leader," *American Political Science Review*, 62, 2 (June, 1968), 564–575.

Jennings, M. Kent. "Pre-Adult Orientations to Multiple Systems of Government," *Midwest Journal of Political Science*, 2, 3 (August, 1967), 291–317.

———— and Paul Beck. "Lowering the Voting Age: The Case of the Reluctant Electorate," *Public Opinion Quarterly*, 33, 3 (Fall, 1969), 370–379.

———— and Richard G. Niemi. "Party Identification at Multiple Levels of Government," *American Journal of Sociology*, 72 (1966), 86–101.

————. "The Transmission of Political Values from Parent to Child," *American Political Science Review*, 62, 1 (March, 1968), 169–184.

————. "The Division of Political Labor Between Mothers and Fathers," *American Political Science Review*, 65, 1 (March, 1971), 69–82.

————. *The Political Character of Adolescence: The Influence of Families and Schools* (Princeton: Princeton University Press, 1974).

————. "Continuity and Change in Political Orientations," *American Political Science Review*, 69, 4 (December, 1975), 1316–1335.

Jensen, Richard F. *The Winning of the Midwest: Social and Political Conflict, 1888–1896* (Chicago: University of Chicago Press, 1971).

Kaase, Max. "Demokratische Einstellungen in der Bundesrepublik Deutschland," in Rudolf Wildenmann (ed.), *Sozialwissenschaftliches Jahrbuch für Politik* (Munich and Vienna: Guenter-Olzog, 1971), 119–326.

————. "Determinants of Political Mobilization for Students and Non-academic Youth." Paper read at the 7th World Congress of Sociology, Varna, September, 1970. German version: "Die Politische Mobilisierung von Studenten in Der BRD," Klaus R. Allerbeck and Leopold Rosenmayr (eds.), *Aufstand der Jugend? Neue Perspectiven der Jugendsoziologie* (Munich: Juventa, 1971), 155–177.

Kahn, Robert L. "The Meaning of Work: Interpretation and Proposals for Measurement," in Angus Campbell and Philip E. Converse (eds.), *The Human Meaning of Social Change* (New York: Russell Sage, 1972), 159–203.

Katona, George. "Consumer Behavior: Theory and Findings on Expectations and Aspirations," *American Economic Review*, 58, 2 (May, 1968), 19–30.

——— *et al. Aspirations and Affluence* (New York: McGraw-Hill, 1971).

Katz, Elihu and Paul F. Lazarsfeld. *Personal Influence* (New York: Free Press, 1955).

Kenniston, Kenneth. *Young Radicals: Notes on Uncommitted Youth* (New York: Harcourt, Brace, and World, 1968).

King, Bert T. and Elliott McGinnies (eds.). *Attitudes, Conflict and Social Change* (New York: Academic Press, 1972).

———. "Overview—Social Contexts and Issues for Contemporary Attitude Change Research," in Bert T. King and Elliott McGinnies (eds.), *Attitudes, Conflict, and Social Change* (New York: Academic Press, 1972), 1–14.

Klingemann, Hans D. "Politische und soziale Bedingungen der Wahlerbewegungen zur NPD," in Rudolf Wildemann (ed.), *Sozialwissenschaftliches Jahrbuch für Politik* (Munich and Vienna, 1971), 563–601.

———. "Testing the Left-Right Continuum on a Sample of German Voters," *Comparative Political Studies*, 5, 1 (April, 1972), 93–106.

——— and Erwin K. Scheuch. "Materialien zum Phanomen des Rechtsradikalismus in der Bundersrepublik" (Köln: Institut für vergleichende Sozialforschung der Universität zu Köln, 1967 [mimeo, Cologne: University of Cologne]).

——— and Thomas A. Herz. "Die NPD in den Landtagswahlen 1966–1968" (Köln: Institut für vergleichende Sozialforschung, Zentralarchiv für empirische Sozialforschung, Universität zu Köln, 1969 [mimeo, Cologne: University of Cologne]).

——— and Eugene Wright. "Levels of Conceptualization in the American and German Mass Publics." Paper presented at the Workshop on Political Cognition, University of Georgia, Athens, Georgia (May 24–25, 1974).

Kluckhohn, Florence R. and F. L. Strodtbeck. *Variations in Value Orientations* (New York: Row Peterson, 1961).

Knutson, Jeanne N. *The Human Basis of the Polity: A Psychological Study of Political Men* (Chicago: Aldine-Atherton, 1972).

Kohlberg, Lawrence. *Stages in the Development of Moral Thought and Action* (Holt, Rinehart and Winston, 1970).

Lambert, T. Allen. "Generations and Change: Toward a Theory of Generations as a Force in Historical Process," *Youth and Society*, 4, 1 (September, 1972), 21–46.

Lancelot, Alain and Pierre Weill. "L'evolution politique des Électeurs Français de février à juin 1969," *Revue Française de Science Politique*, 20, 2 (April, 1970), 249–281.

Land, Kenneth. "Some Exhaustible Poisson Process Models of Divorce by Marriage Cohort," *Journal of Mathematical Sociology*, 1, 2 (July, 1971), 213–232.

Lane, Robert. *Political Life* (New York: Free Press, 1959).

————. *Political Ideology* (New York: Free Press, 1962).

————. *Political Thinking and Consciousness* (Chicago: Markham, 1969).

————. "Patterns of Political Belief," in Jeanne M. Knutson (ed.), *Handbook of Political Psychology* (San Francisco: Jossey-Bass, 1973), 83–116.

————. "The Politics of Consensus in an Age of Affluence," *American Political Science Review*, 59, 4 (December, 1965), 874–895.

Langton, Kenneth P. "Peer Group and School and the Political Socialization Process," *American Political Science Review*, 61, 3 (September, 1967), 751–758.

———— and M. Kent Jennings. "Political Socialization and the High School Civics Curriculum in the United States," *American Political Science Review*, 62, 3 (September, 1968), 852–867.

LaPalombara, Joseph D. (ed.). *Bureaucracy and Political Development* (Princeton: Princeton University Press, 1963).

————. "Decline of Ideology: A Dissent and an Interpretation," *American Political Science Review*, 60, 1 (March, 1966), 5–16.

———— and Myron Weiner (eds.). *Political Parties and Political Development* (Princeton: Princeton University Press, 1966).

Lasswell, Harold D. *Power and Personality* (New York: Viking, 1948).

————. *Psychopathology and Politics* (New York: Viking, 1960).

Lazarsfeld, Paul F. *et al.* *The People's Choice: How the Voter Makes Up His Mind in a Presidential Campaign* (New York: Columbia University Press, 1944).

Lenski, Gerhard. *Power and Privilege: A Theory of Social Stratification* (New York: McGraw-Hill, 1966).

————. *The Religious Factor* (Garden City: Doubleday, 1963).

Lerner, Daniel and Morton Gordon. *Euratlantica: The Changing Perspectives of the European Elites* (Cambridge: M.I.T. Press, 1969).

Lerner, Daniel. *The Passing of Traditional Society* (New York: Free Press, 1958).

Levin, M. L. "Social Climates and Political Socialization," *Public Opinion Quarterly*, 25, 4 (Winter, 1961), 596–606.

Liepelt, Klaus. "The Infra-Structure of Party Support in Germany and Austria." In Mattei Dogan and Richard Rose (eds.), *European Politics: A Reader* (Boston: Little, Brown, 1971), 183–201.

464 — Bibliography

Liepelt, Klaus and Alexander Mitscherlich. *Thesen zur Wählerfluktuation* (Frankfurt am Main: Europaische Verlaganstalt, 1968).

Lijphart, Arend. *The Politics of Accommodation: Pluralism and Democracy in The Netherlands* (Berkeley: University of California Press, 1968).

———. *Class Voting and Religious Voting in the European Democracies: A Preliminary Report* (Glasgow: University of Strathclyde, 1971).

Lindberg, Leon and Stuart Scheingold. *Europe's Would-Be Polity* (Englewood Cliffs: Prentice-Hall, 1970).

——— (eds.). *Regional Integration: Theory and Research* (Cambridge, Mass.: Harvard University Press, 1971).

"L'Opinion Publique et L'Europe des Six," *Sondages: Revue Française de l'Opinion Publique*, 25, 1 (Trimester, 1963), 1–108.

Lipset, Seymour M. "The Changing Class Structure and Contemporary European Politics," *Daedalus*, 93, 1 (Winter, 1964), 271–303.

———. *Political Man: The Social Bases of Politics* (Garden City: Doubleday, 1960).

———. "The Activists: A Profile," *The Public Interest*, 13 (Fall, 1968), 39–52.

———. *Revolution and Counter-Revolution: Change and Persistence in Social Structures* (New York: Basic Books, 1968).

———. "Ideology and No End: The Controversy Till Now," *Encounter*, 39, 6 (December, 1972), 17–24.

———. "Social Structure and Social Change," in Peter Blau (ed.), *Approaches to the Study of Social Structure* (New York: Free Press, 1975).

——— and Richard B. Dobson. "The Intellectual as Critic and Rebel," *Daedalus*, 101, 3 (Summer, 1972), 137–198.

——— and Everett C. Ladd. "College Generations—From the 1930's to the 1970's," *The Public Interest*, 25 (Fall, 1971), 99–113.

———. "The Political Future of Activist Generations," in Philip G. Altbach and Robert S. Laufer (eds.), *The New Pilgrims: Youth Protest in Transition* (New York: McKay, 1972), 63–84.

——— and Stein Rokkan. "Cleavage Structures, Party Systems and Voter Alignments," in Lipset and Rokkan (eds.), *Party Systems and Voter Alignments* (New York: Free Press, 1967), 1–64.

——— and Sheldon S. Wolin. *The Berkeley Student Revolt* (Garden City, New York: Doubleday Anchor, 1965).

Lipsky, Michael. "Protest as a Political Resource," *American Political Science Review*, 62, 4 (December, 1968), 1144–1158.

Litt, Edgar. "Civic Education, Community Norms and Political Indoctrination," in Roberta S. Sigel (ed.), *Learning About Politics* (New York: Random House, 1970), 328–336.

Loewenberg, Peter. "The Psychohistorical Origins of the Nazi Youth

Cohort," *The American Historical Review*, 77, 1 (December, 1971), 1456–1503.

Lofland, John. "The Youth Ghetto," in Edward O. Laumann, Paul M. Siegel and Robert W. Hodge (eds.), *The Logic of Social Hierarchies* (Chicago: Markham, 1970), 756–778.

Maccoby, Eleanor E. *et al.* "Youth and Political Change," *Public Opinion Quarterly*, 18, 1 (Spring, 1954), 23–39.

MacRae, Duncan, Jr. *Parliament, Parties and Society in France, 1946–1958* (New York: St. Martin's, 1967).

MacRae, Norman. "Limits to Misconception," *The Economist*, 242, 6707 (March 11, 1972), 20, 22.

————. "America's Third Century: Recessional for the Second Great Empire?" *The Economist*, 257, 6896 (October 25, 1975), 65–73.

Mallet, Serge. *La Nouvelle Classe Ouvrière* (Paris: Seuil, 1969).

Mankoff, Milton and Richard Flacks. "The Changing Social Base of the American Student Movement," in Philip G. Altbach and Robert S. Laufer (eds.), *The New Pilgrims: Youth Protest in Transition* (New York: McKay, 1972), 46–62.

Mannheim, Karl. *Ideology and Utopia* (New York: Harcourt, Brace, 1949).

————. "The Problem of Generations," in Philip G. Altbach and Robert S. Laufer (eds.), *The New Pilgrims: Youth Protest in Transition* (New York: McKay, 1972), 25–72.

Marsh, Alan. "Explorations in Unorthodox Political Behavior: A Scale to Measure 'Protest Potential,' " *European Journal of Political Research*, 2 (1974), 107–129.

————. "The 'Silent Revolution,' Value Priorities and the Quality of Life in Britain," *American Political Science Review*, 69, 1 (March, 1975), 21–30.

Maslow, Abraham H. *Toward a Psychology of Being* (Englewood Cliffs, N.J.: D. Van Nostrand, 1962).

————. *Religions, Values, and Peak-Experiences* (Columbus: Ohio State University Press, 1964).

————. *Motivation and Personality*, 2d ed. (New York: Harper & Row, 1970).

McClelland, David. *The Achieving Society* (Princeton: Van Nostrand, 1961).

McClintock, C. G. and H. A. Turner. "The Impact of College Upon Political Knowledge, Participation, and Values," *Human Relations*, 15, 2 (May, 1962), 163–176.

McCloskey, Herbert. "Conservatism and Personality," *The American Political Science Review*, 52, 1 (March, 1958), 27–45.

Mead, Margaret. *Culture and Commitment* (Garden City: Natural History Press, 1970).

Meadows, Dennis *et al.* *The Limits to Growth* (Washington, D.C.: Potomac Associates, 1972).

———— and Donella Meadows (eds.). *Toward Global Equilibrium* (Cambridge, Mass.: Wright-Allen, 1973).

————. "Typographical Errors and Technological Solutions," *Nature*, 247, 5436 (January 11, 1974), 97–98.

Merelman, Richard. "The Development of Political Ideology: A Framework for the Analysis of Political Socialization," *American Political Science Review*, 63, 3 (September, 1969), 750–767.

Merritt, Richard L. and Donald J. Puchala (eds.). *Western European Perspectives on International Affairs: Public Opinion Studies and Evaluations* (New York: Praeger, 1968).

Mesarovic, Mihajlo and Eduard Pestel. *Mankind at the Turning Point* (New York: Dutton, 1974).

Middleton, Russell and Snell Putney. "Political Expression of Adolescent Rebellion," *American Journal of Sociology*, 68, 5 (March, 1963), 527–535.

Milbrath, Lester. *Political Participation* (Chicago: Rand McNally, 1965).

————. "The Nature of Political Beliefs and the Relationship of the Individual to the Government," *American Behavioral Scientist*, 12, 2 (November–December, 1968), 28–36.

Miller, Arthur H. "Political Issues and Trust in Government: 1964–1970," *American Political Science Review*, 68, 3 (September, 1974), 951–972.

———— *et al.* "A Majority Party in Disarray: Policy Polarization in the 1972 Election," *American Political Science Review*, 70, 3 (September, 1976), 753–778.

Miller, Warren E. "Majority Rule and the Representative System of Government," in E. Allardt and Y. Littunen (eds.), *Cleavages, Ideologies and Party Systems: Contributions to Comparative Political Sociology* (Helsinki: Transactions of the Westermarck Society, 1964), 343–376.

———— *et al.* "Components of Electoral Decision," *American Political Science Review*, 52, 2 (June, 1958), 367–387.

———— *et al.* "Continuity and Change in American Politics: Parties and Issues in the 1968 Election," *American Political Science Review*, 63, 4 (December, 1969), 1083–1105.

———— and Teresa E. Levitin. *Leadership and Change: New Politics and the American Electorate* (Cambridge, Mass.: Winthrop, 1976).

———— and Donald E. Stokes. "Party Government and the Saliency of Congress," *Public Opinion Quarterly*, 26, 4 (Winter, 1962), 531–546.

————. "Constituency Influence in Congress," *American Political Science Review*, 57, 1 (March, 1963), 45–56.

Mitchell, Arnold *et al.* "An Approach to Measuring Quality of Life" (Menlo Park, Ca.: Stanford Research Institute, 1971), mimeo.

Moore, Barrington, Jr. *Social Origins of Dictatorship and Democracy* (Boston: Beacon Press, 1966).

Morgan, James N. "The Achievement Motive and Economic Behavior," in John W. Atkinson (ed.), *A Theory of Achievement Motivation* (New York: Wiley, 1966), 205–230.

Morin, Edgar *et al. Mai 1968: La Brèche* (Paris: Fayard, 1968).

Muller, Edward N. "A Test of a Partial Theory of Potential for Political Violence," *American Political Science Review*, 66, 3 (September, 1972), 928–959.

————. "Relative Deprivation and Aggressive Political Behavior," paper presented for the annual meeting of the American Political Science Association, San Francisco, September, 1975.

Muller, Herbert. *The Children of Frankenstein* (Bloomington, Ind.: Midland, 1973).

Myers, Frank. "Social Class and Political Change in Western Industrial Systems," *Comparative Politics*, 2, 2 (April, 1970), 389–412.

Nasatir, David. "A Note on Contextual Effects and the Political Orientations of College Students," *American Sociological Review*, 33, 2 (April, 1968), 210–219.

Nederlandse Stichting voor Statistiek. *De Toekomst op Zicht: Een Wetenschappelijk onderzoek naar de verwachtingen van de Nederlanders voor de Periode, 1970-1980* (Amsterdam: Bonaventura, 1970).

Newcomb, Theodore M. *Personality and Social Change* (New York: Dryden, 1943).

Nie, Norman *et al.* "Political Participation and the Life Cycle," *Comparative Politics*, 6, 3 (April, 1974), 319–340.

———— and Kristi Andersen. "Mass Belief Systems Revisited: Political Change and Attitude Structure," *Journal of Politics*, 36, 3 (August, 1974), 540–591.

———— *et al.* "Social Structure and Political Participation: Developmental Relationships," *American Political Science Review*, 63, 3 (September, 1969), 808–832.

Nieburg, H. L. *Culture Storm: Politics and the Ritual Order* (New York: St. Martin's, 1973).

Nobile, Philip (ed.). *The Con III Controversy: The Critics Look at The Greening of America* (New York: Pocket Books, 1971).

Nordlinger, Eric A. *The Working Class Tories* (London: MacGibbon and Kee, 1967).

O'Lessker, Karl. "Who voted for Hitler? A New Look at the Class Basis of Nazism," *The American Journal of Sociology*, 74, 1 (July, 1968), 63–69.

Olson Mancur, Jr. "The Purpose and Plan of a Social Report," *The Public Interest*, 15 (Spring, 1969), 85–97.

O'Neill, Gerard K. "Colonies in Orbit," *New York Times Magazine* (January 18, 1976), 10–11.

Organski, A.F.K. *The Stages of Political Development* (New York: Random House, 1965).

Page, Benjamin I. and Richard A. Brody. "Policy Voting and the Electoral Process: The Vietnam War Issue," *American Political Science Review*, 66, 3 (September, 1972), 979–995.

Parsons, Talcott and Gerald M. Platt. "Higher Education and Changing Socialization," in Matilda W. Riley *et al.* (eds.), *Aging and Society*, 3 (New York: Russell Sage, 1972), 236–291.

Patterson, Franklin *et al. The Adolescent Citizen* (New York: Free Press, 1960).

Petersen, Nikolaj. "Federalist and Anti-Integrationist Attitudes in the Danish Common Market Referendum," paper presented to the European Consortium for Political Research, London, April 7–12, 1975.

———— and Jorgen Eklit. "Denmark Enters the European Communities," *Scandinavian Political Studies*, 8 (1973), 157–177.

Petitjean, A. (ed.). *Quelles Limites? Le Club de Rome Répond* (Paris: Seuil, 1974).

Pierce, John C. and Douglas D. Rose. "Nonattitudes and American Public Opinion: The Examination of a Thesis," *American Political Science Review*, 68, 2 (June, 1974), 626–649.

Pinner, Frank A. "Students—A Marginal Elite in Politics," in Philip G. Altbach and Robert S. Laufer (eds.), *The New Pilgrims: Youth Protest in Transition* (New York: McKay, 1972), 281–296.

Pomper, Gerald M. "From Confusion to Clarity: Issues and American Voters, 1956–1968," *American Political Science Review*, 66, 2 (June, 1972), 415–428.

Pryce, Roy. *The Politics of the European Community Today* (London: Butterworths, 1973).

Putnam, Robert. "Studying Elite Political Culture: The Case of 'Ideology,' " *American Political Science Review*, 65, 3 (September, 1971), 651–681.

————. *The Beliefs of Politicians* (New Haven: Yale University Press, 1973).

Pye, Lucian (ed.). *Communications and Political Development* (Princeton: Princeton University Press, 1963).

Pye, Lucian and Sidney Verba (eds.). *Political Culture and Political Development* (Princeton: Princeton University Press, 1965).

Reader's Digest Association. *A Survey of Europe Today* (London: Reader's Digest, 1970).

Reich, Charles A. *The Greening of America* (New York: Random House, 1970).

Rejai, M. (ed.). *Decline of Ideology?* (Chicago: Aldine-Atherton, 1971).

Remers, H. H. (ed.). *Anti-Democratic Attitudes in American Schools* (Evanston: Northwestern University Press, 1963).

Richardson, Bradley M. *The Political Culture of Japan* (Berkeley: University of California Press, 1974).

Riesman, David *et al. The Lonely Crowd* (New Haven: Yale University Press, 1950).

Riley, Matilda W. *et al.* (eds.). *Aging and Society III* (New York: Russell Sage, 1972).

Robinson, John P. *et al. Measures of Political Attitudes* (Ann Arbor: Institute for Social Research, The University of Michigan, 1968).

———— and Phillip R. Shaver. *Measures of Social Psychological Attitudes* (Ann Arbor: Institute for Social Research, The University of Michigan, 1969).

Roig, Charles and Françoise Billon-Grand. *La Socialisation Politique des Enfants* (Paris: Colin, 1968).

Rokeach, Milton. *The Open and Closed Mind: Investigations Into the Nature of Belief Systems and Personality Systems* (New York: Basic Books, 1960).

————. *Beliefs, Attitudes and Values* (San Francisco: Jossey-Bass, 1968).

————. "The Role of Values in Public Opinion Research," *Public Opinion Quarterly*, 32, 4 (Winter, 1968–1969), 547–559.

————. *The Nature of Human Values* (New York: Free Press, 1973).

————. "Change and Stability in American Value Systems, 1968–1971," *Public Opinion Quarterly*, 38, 2 (Summer, 1974), 222–238.

Rokkan, Stein. *Citizens, Elections and Parties* (Oslo: Universitets Forlaget, 1970).

Roper, Elmo and Associates. *American Attitudes Toward Ties with Other Democratic Countries* (Washington, D.C.: The Atlantic Council, 1964).

Rose, Richard. "Class and Party Divisions: Britain as a Test Case," *Sociology*, 2, 2 (May, 1968), 129–162.

————. *Governing without Consensus: An Irish Perspective* (Boston: Beacon, 1971).

———— (ed.). *Comparative Electoral Behavior* (New York: Free Press, 1974).

———— and Derek Urwin. "Social Cohesion, Political Parties and Strains in Regimes," *Comparative Political Studies*, 2, 1 (April, 1969), 7–67.

————. "Persistence and Change in Western Party Systems Since 1945," *Political Studies*, 18, 3 (September, 1970), 287–319.

Rosenmayr, Leopold. "Introduction: New Theoretical Approaches to the Sociological Study of Young People," *International Social Science Journal*, 24, 2 (1972), 215–256.

Rostow, W. W. *The Stages of Economic Development* (Cambridge: Cambridge University Press, 1961).

Roszak, Theodore. *The Making of a Counter Culture* (Garden City: Doubleday, 1969).

———. *Where the Wasteland Ends* (Garden City: Doubleday, 1973).

de Rougemont, Denis. *La Suisse: L'Histoire d'un Peuple Heureux* (Paris: Hachette, 1965).

Ryder, Norman B. "The Cohort as a Concept in the Study of Social Change," *American Sociological Review*, 30, 6 (December, 1965), 843–861.

Sakamoto, S. "A Study of the Japanese National Character—Part V: Fifth-Nation Survey," *Annals of the Institute for Statistical Mathematics* (Tokyo: Institute for Statistical Mathematics, 1975), 121–143.

Sartori, Giovanni. "European Political Parties: The Case of Polarized Pluralism," in Joseph LaPalombara and Myron Weiner (eds.), *Political Parties and Political Development* (Princeton: Princeton University Press, 1966), 137–176.

———. "The Power of Labor in the Post-Pacified Society: A Surmise," paper presented at the World Congress of the International Political Science Association, Montreal, Quebec, August, 1973.

Sauvy, Alfred. *La Révolte des Jeunes* (Paris: Calman-Levy, 1970).

Scammon, Richard M. and Ben J. Wattenberg. *The Real Majority* (New York: Coward McCann, 1970).

Schmidtchen, Gerhard. *Zwischen Kirche und Gesellschaft* (Freiburg: Herder Verlag, 1972).

Searing, Donald D. "The Comparative Study of Elite Socialization," *Comparative Political Studies*, 1, 4 (January, 1969), 471–500.

Sebert, Suzanne *et al.* "The Political Texture of Peer Groups," in M. Kent Jennings and Richard A. Niemi, *The Political Character of Adolescence* (Princeton: Princeton University Press, 1974), 229–248.

Seeman, Melvin. "Alienation and Engagement," in Angus Campbell and Philip Converse (eds.), *The Human Meaning of Social Change* (New York: Russell Sage, 1972), 467–528.

———. "The Signals of '68: Alienation in Pre-Crisis France," *American Sociological Review*, 37, 4 (August, 1972), 385–402.

Segal, David R. *Society and Politics: Uniformity and Diversity in Modern Democracy* (Glenview, Illinois: Scott, Foresman, 1974).

——— and David Knoke. "Political Partisanship: Its Social and Economic Bases in the United States," *American Journal of Economics and Sociology*, 29, 3 (July, 1970), 253–262.

Sheldon, Bernert Eleanor and Wilbert E. Moore (eds.). *Indicators of*

Social Change: Concepts and Measurements (New York: Russell Sage, 1968).

———. "Monitoring Social Change in American Society," in Bernert E. Sheldon and Wilbert E. Moore (eds.), *Indicators of Social Change: Concepts and Measurements* (New York: Russell Sage, 1968), 3–24.

Sheppard, Harold L. and Neil Q. Herrick. *Where Have All the Robots Gone?* (New York: Free Press, 1972).

Sherrill, Kenneth S. "The Attitudes of Modernity," *Comparative Politics*, 1, 2 (January, 1969), 184–210.

Shively, Philips. "A Reinterpretation of the New Deal Realignment," *Public Opinion Quarterly*, 35, 4 (Winter, 1971–72), 621–624.

———. "Voting Stability and the Nature of Party Attachments in the Weimar Republic," *American Political Science Review*, 66, 4 (December, 1972), 1203–1225.

Sigel, Roberta (ed.). *Learning About Politics: Studies in Political Socialization* (New York: Random House, 1968).

Silverman, Bertram and Murray Yanowitch (eds.). *The Worker in "Post-Industrial" Capitalism: Liberal and Radical Responses* (New York: Free Press, 1974).

Singer, Daniel. *Prelude to Revolution: France in May, 1968* (New York: Hill and Wang, 1970).

Skolnick, Jerome H. *The Politics of Protest* (New York: Ballantine, 1969).

Slater, Philip. *The Pursuit of Loneliness: American Culture at the Breaking Point* (Boston: Beacon, 1970).

Sonquist, John A. *Multivariate Model Building: The Validation of a Research Strategy* (Ann Arbor: Institute for Social Research, 1970).

——— and James N. Morgan. *The Detection of Interaction Effects* (Ann Arbor: Institute for Social Research, 1964).

Steiner, Jurg. *Amicable Agreement versus Majority Rule: Conflict Resolution in Switzerland* (Chapel Hill: University of North Carolina Press, 1974).

Stokes, Donald E. "Spatial Models of Party Competition," in Angus E. Campbell *et al., Elections and the Political Order* (New York: Wiley, 1966), 161–179.

———. "Some Dynamic Elements of Contests for the Presidency," *American Political Science Review*, 60, 1 (March, 1966), 19–28.

Stouffer, Samuel *et al. The American Soldier: Adjustment During Army Life* (Princeton, N.J.: Princeton University Press, 1949).

Strumpel, Burkhard. "Economic Life Styles, Values and Subjective Welfare—An Empirical Approach," paper presented at 86th Annual Meeting of American Economic Association, New Orleans, 1971.

——— (ed.). *Subjective Elements of Well-being* (Paris: OECD, 1974).

"Students and Politics," *Daedalus*, 97, 1 (Winter, 1968).

A Survey of Europe Today (London: Reader's Digest Association, 1970).

Suzuki, Tatsuzo. "Changing Japanese Values: An Analysis of National Surveys," paper presented at the 25th Annual Meeting of the Association for Asian Studies, Chicago, 1973.

Tarrow, Sidney. *Peasant Communism in Southern Italy* (New Haven: Yale University Press, 1967).

Thompson, William I. *At the Edge of History* (New York: Harper and Row, 1972).

Tilly, Charles. "Food Supply and Public Order in Modern Europe," in Charles Tilly (ed.), *The Formation of National States in Western Europe* (Princeton: Princeton University Press, 1975), 380–455.

Toffler, Alvin. *Future Shock* (New York: Random House, 1970).

———— (ed.). *The Futurists* (New York: Random House, 1972).

Touraine, Alain. *The Post-industrial Society* (New York: Random House, 1971).

Triandis, Harry. "The Impact of Social Change on Attitudes," in Bert T. King and Elliott McGinnies (eds.), *Attitudes, Conflict and Social Change* (New York: Academic Press, 1972), 127–136.

U. S. Department of Health, Education, and Welfare. *Toward a Social Report* (Washington, D.C.: Government Printing Office, 1969).

Verba, Sidney. "Germany: The Remaking of Political Culture," in Lucian Pye and Sidney Verba (eds.), *Political Culture and Political Development* (Princeton: Princeton University Press, 1965), 131–154.

———— and Norman Nie. *Participation in America: Political Democracy and Social Equality* (New York: Harper and Row, 1972).

———— et al. "Public Opinion and the War in Vietnam," *American Political Science Review*, 62, 2 (June, 1967), 317–334.

Watanuki, Joji. "Japanese Politics: Changes, Continuities and Unknowns" (Tokyo: Sophia University Institute of International Relations, 1973), mimeo.

Waterman, Harvey. *Political Change in Contemporary France* (Columbus, Ohio: Merrill, 1969).

Weber, Max. *From Max Weber: Essays in Sociology*, ed. H. H. Gerth and C. Wright Mills (New York: Oxford University Press, 1946).

————. *Economy and Society* (New York: Bedminster Press, 1968).

Weil, Gordon L. *The Benelux Nations: The Politics of Small-Country Democracies* (New York: Holt, Rinehart and Winston, 1970).

Weisberg, Herbert F. and Jerrold G. Rusk. "Dimensions of Candidate Evaluation," *American Political Science Review*, 64, 4 (December, 1970), 1167–1185.

Weiss, Walter. "Mass Media and Social Change," in Bert T. King and

Elliott McGinnies (eds.), *Attitudes, Conflict, and Social Change* (New York: Academic Press, 1972), 175–224.

Westby, David L. and Rochard G. Braungart. "The Alienation of Generations and Status Politics: Alternative Explanations of Student Political Activism," in Roberta S. Sigel (ed.), *Learning About Politics* (New York: Random House, 1970), 476–490.

Withey, Stephen. *A Degree and What Else?* (New York: McGraw-Hill, 1971).

Wylie, L. *Village in the Vancluse* (Cambridge: Harvard University Press, 1957).

Yankelovich, Daniel. *The Changing Values on Campus* (New York: Washington Square Press, 1973).

————. *Changing Youth Values in the 1970's* (New York: JDR 3rd Fund, 1974).

————. *The New Morality: A Profile of American Youth in the 1970's* (New York: McGraw-Hill, 1974).

INDEX

Library of Congress Cataloging in Publication Data

Inglehart, Ronald.
  The silent revolution.

  Bibliography: p.
  Includes index.
  1. Political participation—European Economic Community countries. 2. Political participation—United States. 3. Social values. I. Title.
JN94.A91I54   301.5′92′091821   76-24294
ISBN 0-691-07585-9
ISBN 0-691-10038-1 pbk.